£10

Oxford Bibliographical Society

Publications

NEW SERIES VOLUME XVII

STATIONERS' COMPANY
APPRENTICES
1641-1700

Edited by

D. F. McKENZIE

OXFORD

THE OXFORD BIBLIOGRAPHICAL SOCIETY

1974

Inquiries about the Society and its publications
should be addressed to the Honorary Secretary,
Oxford Bibliographical Society, c/o Bodleian
Library, Oxford OX1 3BG

International Standard Book No.   0 901420 09 3

Printed and Bound in Great Britain
by
THE SCOLAR PRESS LTD
59/61 East Parade
Ilkley
Yorkshire

CONTENTS

INTRODUCTION

The present list of Stationers' apprentices continues those printed in *Stationers' Company Apprentices 1605–1640*, published in 1961 by the Bibliographical Society of the University of Virginia. It completes the printed record of all apprentices bound to or made free by members of the Company during the seventeenth century.

The information given here has been drawn from the Registers of Apprentices 1605–1666 and 1666–1727 and the Registers of Freemen 1605–1703 and 1703–1751. Other relevant volumes which have been consulted are an index of Apprentices Bound Turned Over Free and Cloathed 1640–1748, two Calendars of Masters and Apprentices for the years 1646–1718, the Apprentices' Register Relief of Orphans Act 1694–1738, and the Court Books.

The original registers list bindings in strict chronological order, but such an arrangement is less useful than one which groups them under masters. Indeed the seventeenth-century calendars were a rough attempt to create something like the present list. Here then all apprentices have been regrouped alphabetically under masters. To save space and increase clarity, the original entries have been rigorously abbreviated but no substantive information has been omitted. The list includes all men bound between January 1641 and December 1700 inclusive and all men made free within that period even if not formally bound. It also includes all men made free within that period but bound before it and incorporates the date of freedom for all men bound within that period but made free after it.

A word of warning may be necessary about the variant forms of names. Where an apprentice's name appears more than once in the registers (for example, when bound to one man and turned over to or made free by another), any difference in spelling here reflects the variant entries. The names of masters, however, have had to be standardized. Short of literal transcription in every case, such an editorial expedient is unavoidable, and for the most part it is a sensible way of resolving irritating ambiguities in the original entries. But some problems remain. Two or more masters with similar names may be listed as one. Conversely, one master may be listed twice if his name appears in two spellings so distinctive that they resist any subsuming of their identities under a single standard form; and sometimes, although family links could be established, persistent example may forbid the adoption of a standard form for successive generations (for example, Robert Dolman's son is regularly Isaiah Dawlman whose son in turn is John Doleman). Different masters who share the same name, like John Clarke, John Darby, John Jones or John Smith, cannot always be accurately separated. Given the time span of the present list, even distinctions such as 'Senior' and 'Junior' do not always help, and although one can date a son's freedom it is often impossible to say when he, rather than his father, bound an apprentice thereafter.

An index number precedes each entry. The entry itself gives, in the following order: 1. the apprentice's full name, transcribed exactly from the registers; 2. his father's christian name, adding (d) if dead; 3. town and county, as given in the register; 4. the father's trade or status; 5. the date of entry in the register; 6. the date from which the term of binding was to run; 7. the date of freedom, if any; 8. the term of binding in years. The names of the apprentice, his father, and his town, village or parish, are given in their original spelling. Superior letters have been brought down but not expanded, and punctuation marking abbreviation has not been reproduced. The other items (county, trade, dates) are normally abbreviated. Feast days have been translated into their appropriate dates and legal dating has been consistently altered to ordinary calendar year dating. The form 'fd by', it should be noted, really means 'fd in the name or names of'; hence the name of a deceased master may well appear in the Book of Freedoms alongside that of an apprentice who once served him. Finally, an entry wholly enclosed within square brackets relates to the master himself.

It remains to thank the Master, Wardens and Assistants of the Worshipful Company of Stationers and Newspaper Makers for their continued generosity in giving permission to consult, transcribe and reproduce the registers concerned.

The editor and the Society are most grateful to them.

KEY TO ABBREVIATIONS

The following abbreviations are used:

(a) for the father's trade or status:

B	Baker	E	Esquire	Mch	Merchant
BSg	Barber-Surgeon	F	Fishmonger	MT	Merchant Taylor
Bl	Blacksmith	G	Gent	Mi	Miller
Bs	Bookseller	Gl	Glover	Pw	Pewterer
Br	Brewer	Go	Goldsmith	S	Sadler
Bu	Butcher	Gr	Grocer	Sc	Scrivener
C	Citizen	Ha	Haberdasher	Sh	Shoemaker
Ca	Carpenter	H	Husbandman	Sk	Skinner
Cl	Clerk	I	Innholder	St	Stationer
Cw	Clothworker	J	Joiner	T	Tailor
Cd	Cordwainer	L	Labourer	Tn	Tanner
Cu	Cutler	M	Maltman	V	Vintner
D	Draper	Mr	Mercer	Y	Yeoman
Dy	Dyer				

(b) for counties:

Ang.	Anglesey	Lincs.	Lincoln
Beds.	Bedford	M'sex	Middlesex
Berks.	Berkshire	Mon.	Monmouth
Brec.	Brecon	Mont.	Montgomery
Bucks.	Buckingham	Norf.	Norfolk
Caerns.	Caernarvon	N'hants.	Northampton
Cambs.	Cambridge	N'land.	Northumberland
Cards.	Cardigan	Notts.	Nottingham
Carms.	Carmarthen	Oxon.	Oxford
Ches.	Cheshire	Pem.	Pembroke
Cumb.	Cumberland	Rad.	Radnor
Den.	Denbigh	Rut.	Rutland
Dev.	Devon	S'hants.	Southampton
Dors.	Dorset	Shrops.	Shropshire or Salop
Dur.	Durham	Som.	Somerset
Glam.	Glamorgan	Staffs.	Stafford
Glos.	Gloucester	Suff.	Suffolk
Hants.	Hampshire	Surr.	Surrey
Herefs.	Hereford	War.	Warwick
Herts.	Hertford	W'land.	Westmorland
Hunts.	Huntington	Wilts.	Wiltshire
I.O.M.	Isle of Man	Worcs.	Worcester
Lancs.	Lancashire	Yorks.	Yorkshire
Leics.	Leicester		

(c) for common terms:
    bd   bound
    fd   freed
    f.n. foot note
    m.n. marginal note

    n.d. no date
    q.v. quod vide
    t.o. turned over

Dates are given in order of day, month, year. It follows that the form given for 10 July 1653 is 10.7.1653 and that for 18 February 1645/6 is 18.2.1646.

ABBINGTON, William
1. Joseph Cocker; Edward; Parrish of St Fosters alius Vedast, London; - ; 7.4.1684; 7.4.1684; - ; 7.
2. John Science; John; Abingdon, Oxon; Y; 3.1.1681; 3.1.1681; 7.5.1688; 7. The master's name is given as 'Abragdon'. Fd by Henry Hills Junior. Fined 2s. 6d. 'for not being turned over at the Hall'.

ACTON, Valentine
3. William Hawkins; Joseph; parish of St Sepulchres, M'sex; Ca; 9.1.1688; 9.1.1688; - ; 7.

ADAMS, Richard
4. George Sherwood. Fd by Adams and Alexander Fifield 16.1.1643. Bd to Adams 14.1.1636.

ADAMS, William
5. [William Adams. Son of Charles Adams; fd by redemption 6.5.1678.]

ADAMSON, James
6. Jasper Chaplin; Jasper (d); Taunton, Som; Ironmonger; 7.2.1687; 7.2.1687; 6.10.1712; 7.
7. John Jones; John; Worcester; Bs; 23.6.1692; 23.6.1692; - ; 7. A John Jones was fd by patrimony 24.4.1697.

ADDAMS, Charles
8. Thomas Holding; Thomas (d); Rugbey, War; Y; 1.8.1653; 1.8.1653; - ; 7.
9. Samuell Lownes; John (d); Martha, Ches; Y; 2.6.1656; 2.6.1656; 30.6.1663; 7.
10. John Peerse; John (d); Kingston vppon Hull, Yorks; G; 5.10.1663; 5.10.1663; - ; 8.

ADDERTON, William
11. John Lea; John; Braisborow, Lincs; Cl; 6.3.1648; 6.3.1648; - ; 7.
12. Edward Lewis; Hugh (d); City of Bristol; E; 6.11.1660; 6.11.1660; - ; 7.
13. Melchezedecke Meddins; George; Clement Danes, M'sex; Cook; 5.5.1656; 5.5.1656; - ; 7.
14. John Sheares; John; London; C & Cw; 8.5.1665; 6.5.1665; 3.6.1672; 7.

ALBYN, Alice, Widow
15. Hugh Albyn; Richard; London; St; 6.10.1651; 29.9.1651; 7.11.1659; 9. Presumably bd to his mother. Fd by Mrs Albyn and Timothy Smart.

ALBYN, Richard
16. Thomas Collins. Fd by Albyn 1.4.1650. Bd to him 20.1.1640.

ALCHORNE, John
17. Edmond Calverly; Edmond; Hellingly, Sussex; Y; 6.2.1693; 6.2.1693; 5.2.1711; 7.
18. John Hammond; John; the Devizes, Wilts; Bs; 7.11.1692; 7.11.1692; - ; 7.
19. John Mathew; Thomas; London; C & Ha; 4.4.1687; 4.4.1687; - ; 7.
20. Benjamin Riddell; John (d); Wapping, M'sex; Cl; 7.12.1696; 7.12.1696; - ; 7.

ALCHORNE, Thomas
21. Lawrence Chatterton; Wm (d); Hasting, Sussex; G; 1.9.1645, 1.9.1645; 7.2.1653; 7.

ALDE, [Elizabeth, Widow]
22. Seth Mason. Fd by Mrs Alde 5.8.1650. Apparently never formally bd.

ALIFFE, John
23. John Heptinstall; John; Clerkenwell, M'sex; Cd; 4.3.1672; 4.3.1672; 5.5.1679; 7.

ALLAM, Matthew
24. William Long; John; Claver Scevernache Forest, Wilts; Y; 3.6.1695; 3.6.1695; - ; 7.
25. John Tayleure; Wm; London; G; 7.4.1690; 7.4.1690; - ; 7.

ALLEN, Benjamin
26. Livewell Chapman; Edward (d); London; Sc; 6.11.1643; 6.11.1643; 13.11.1650; 7. Fd by Mrs Allen.

ALLEN, Hannah, Widow
27. John Allen; John; Matchin, Essex; Cl; 2.11.1645; 2.11.1646; 6.2.1654; 7.
28. John Garfeild; Thomas; Tickhill, Yorks; Cl; 6.12.1647; 6.12.1647; 10.1.1655; 7. Fd by Mrs Allen and Joseph Hunscott.

ALLEN, John
29. John Marhon; Willm; Durley Hucknall, Notts; H; 3.3.1669; 3.3.1669; - ; 7.
30. Richard Watson; Simon; Longhamborough, Oxon; H; 1.6.1657; 25.12.1656; - ; 8.

ALLEN, Nathaniel
31. John Abell; Richard; Knightsbridge, M'sex; Y; 21.10.1650; 21.10.1650; - ; 8.

ALLESTREE, James
32. Marmaduke Forster; Bassill; Wormley, Herts; G; 12.7.1655; 24.6.1655; 30.6.1663; 8. Fd as Foster.
33. Spencer Hickman; William; Barnicle, War; G; 5.10.1663; 29.9.1663; 3.10.1670; 7.

ALLISTON, Edward
34. William Reeue; Edmund (d);

Ipswich, Suff; Ha; 3.2.1651; 25.12.1650; - ; 9.

ALLOTT, Thomas
35. Robert Fletcher; Wm; Citty of Chester; D; 4.10.1641; 4.10.1641; 3.4.1654; 7. Fd by Allott and John Crooke.

ALLOWAY, John
36. [John Alloway. Fd by redemption 1.5.1676.]

ALSOP, Benjamin
37. Joseph Sprey; Joshua; Newark; Mr; 29.3.1680; 29.3.1680; - ; 7.
38. Richard Tirrell; Richard (d); Abington, Berks; Linendraper; 6.6.1681; 6.6.1681; - ; 7.

ALSOP, Bernard
39. George Horton. Fd by Alsop 14.12.1646. Bd to him 4.9.1637.
40. Adam Marsh; Wm (d); Wiggen, Lancs; G; 16.8.1647; 16.8.1647; 1.7.1661; 9.
41. Thomas Spring. Fd by Alsop 11.6.1655. Apparently never formally bd.

ALSOP, Elizabeth, Widow
42. George Eland; Thomas (d); London; C & Gr; 9.2.1657; 9.2.1657; - ; 8.

ALSOP, Nicholas
43. John Marshall. Fd by Alsop 14.4.1645. Bd to him 2.4.1638.

ALSOP, Thomas
44. John Addams; Edward (d); London; C & Gr; 4.9.1654; 4.9.1654; - ; 7. Entry deleted; m.n. 'This Appr. is gone from his master & his mr promiseth not to make him Free.' (n.d.).
45. Samuell Freeman. Fd by Alsop, John Hammersham and Roger Bartlett 7.12.1663. Bd to Bartlett (q.v.) 1.12.1656.
46. Thomas Norman; Walter; Blockley, Worcs; Y; 8.7.1668; 8.7.1668; 4.7.1681; 7.

47. Samuell Sherborne; Roger; London; C & Waxchandler; 5.5.1656; 5.5.1656; 3.8.1663; 7.

AMERY, John
48. Edward Bradhurst; Willm (d); London; C & Cw; 2.5.1670; 2.5.1670; - ; 7.
49. Joseph Sergeant; Tho; Northampton; D; 7.5.1677; 7.5.1677, - ; 7.

ANDERTON, William
50. Humphrey Lee. Fd by Anderton 2.4.1655. Apparently never formally bd.

ANDREWS, Elizabeth, Widow
51. Phillip Brookesby; Phillip; London; C & MT; 5.5.1662; 5.5.1662; 6.6.1670; 7.

ANDREWS, John
52. Walter George; Barton; Bladon, Oxon; H; 31.3.1656; 31.3.1656; - ; 7.
53. John Johnson; John; Holborne, M'sex; T; 4.5.1657; 4.5.1657; - ; 9.

ANDREWS, Richard
54. John Burd; William (d); Stratford, Essex; Bl; 2.12.1672; 2.12.1672; - ; 7.
55. John Butter; George (d); Newent, Glos; Y; 2.4.1666; 2.4.1666; 4.8.1673; 7.
56. Samuell Harris; Walter (d); Oldstreete, parish of Cripplegate, [London]; Gl; 7.9.1663; 7.9.1663; - ; 7.
57. Jonothan Pearson; Samuell; parish of St Buttolph, Bishopgate, [London]; T; 5.4.1669; 5.4.1669; 4.2.1684; 7.
58. Joseph Shotwell; Abraham; London; C & Leatherseller; 5.7.1669; 5.7.1669; 1.8.1692; 7. Fd by Andrews' executor.

ANDREWS, Robert
59. [Robert Andrews, 'Letter Founder'. Fd 4.9.1676. Apparently never formally bd. No master's name is given.]

60. Thomas Arkesden; Thomas (d); Aspley, Beds; G; 3.7.1682; 3.7.1682; 4.8.1701; 7.
61. Thomas James; John; Beaseing Stoak, S'hants; Cl; 3.6.1700; 3.6.1700; 9.2.1708; 7.
62. Ralph Sadleir; William; - , Beds; G; 8.11.1680; 8.11.1680; 5.12. 1687; 7.

ANDREWS, Sarah
63. [Sarah Andrews. Fd by redemption 26.3.1688, paying £5.]

ANDREWS, Thomas
64. John Andrewes. Fd by patrimony 6.2.1654.
65. Michaell Burgesse. Fd by Andrews 4.10.1647. Bd to him 1.10.1638.

ANSELL, John
66. Robte Shelden. Fd by Ansell 5.10.1646. Bd to him as Robert Shelton 25.2.1628.

ANSON, Elizabeth
67. Elizabeth Robins; Thomas; Burmingham, War; Ironmonger; 3.5.1697; 14.2.1697; - 7.

APPLEBY, Marmaduke
68. Thomas Edwards; Nicholas; Oxbridg, M'sex; Cd; 10.6.1661; 10.6.1661, - ; 7.

ARCHER, Francis
69. Edward Cleave. Fd by Archer 13.1.1642. Bd to him 20.12.1633; t.o. to Francis Egglesfield 1.10.1638.

ARCHER, Thomas
70. William Rogers; Robert; Somerton, Oxon; H; 6.11.1671; 6.11.1671; 4.11.1678; 7.

ARGENT, Richard
71. [Richard Argent. Brother of Robert Argent; fd by redemption 3.4. 1665.]

ARNOLD, Jeremy
72. John Coates; Thomas; Blaby, Leics; Grazier; 14.6.1647; 14.6.1647, - ; 7.

73. Samuell Lilley; Wm; Coventry, War; Chandler; 6.5.1644; 24.6.1643, - : 9.

ARNOLD, John

74. Samuell Mearne. Fd by Arnold and Robert Bates 6.7.1646. Bd to Bates 6.11.1637.

ASH, Francis

75. George Beacroft; Thomas; —, Worcs; G; 16.12.1650; 16.12.1650; - ; 7.

76. John Jones. Fd by Ash 26.9.1646. Bd to him 13.11.1637.

77. Francis Rea; Anne; Churchill, Worcs; Widow; 7.12.1646; 29.9.1646; 17.4.1654; 7. 'This Indr was made in ye Countrey & dated ye 6th of January 1644[-5] & allowed of in Cort.'

ASPLEY, William

78. James Chantler. Bd to Aspley 6.11.1637; t.o. to Luke Fawne 6.12. 1641. Fd by Fawne and Aspley 2.12. 1644.

ASTLEY, Elizabeth

79. William Arnold; William; parish of St Martin in the Feilds, M'sex; G; 5.12.1698; 5.12.1698; - ; 7.

ASTLEY, Thomas

80. Joshua Silvester; Mathew; Parish of St Buttalphs Aldersgate, London; G; 1.9.1690; 1.9.1690; 8.11.1697; 7.

81. Josuah Webb; Josuah (d); London; C & Ha; 4.2.1689; 4.2.1689; - ; 7.

ASTWOOD, James

82. James Astwood; James; [London]; [C & St]; 5.8.1689; 5.8.1689; 4.12.1693; 7. Bd to his father. Fd by patrimony.

83. John Astwood. Fd by patrimony 1.10.1688.

84. Tho Bunce; George; London; C & Cu; 3.5.1680; 3.5.1680; 6.6.1687; 7.

85. Richard Newcomb; Richard; London; Gl; 6.9.1680; 6.9.1680; 4.11. 1689; 8.

86. John Slape. Bd to Henry Hills Junior (q.v.) 7.8.1682; t.o. (n.d.) to Astwood and fd by him 3.11.1690, but fined 2s. 6d. 'for not being turned over at the Hall'.

87. William Smith; Ralph (d); London; C & St; 2.10.1693; 2.10.1693; 2.12.1700; 7. Fd by Astwood and John Darby Senior.

ASTWOOD, John

88. Bryan Mills; Nathaniell; parish of St Mary Overyes in the Burrough of Southwark in the Citty of London; BSg; 5.2.1694; 5.2.1694; 7.7.1701; 7.

ATHERTON, William

89. Samuel Ravenshaw; John (d); Walherton, Ches; Cl; 7.12.1674; 7.12.1674; - ; 7.

ATKINSON, Henry

90. Henry Atkinson. Fd by patrimony 5.6.1671.

91. John Read. Fd by Atkinson 27.3.1648. Bd to him 1.4.1639.

ATKINSON, John

92. Robert Gibson; Edmond (d); Dalton in Furnis, Lancs; Y; 7.9.1691; 7.9.1691; - ; 7.

93. Thomas Scaife; R-; parish of Sparsholt, Berks; Cl; 3.2.1696; 3.2. 1696; - ; 7.

ATKINSON, William

94. Mathew Hart. Fd by Atkinson and John Tunman 5.5.1656. Bd to Tunman (q.v.) 6.5.1648.

ATLEY, William

95. Andrew James. Fd by Atley 23.12.1641. Bd to him 1.12.1634.

96. John Lewis; Cadwallad; Plurisputtee, Den; H; 23.12.1641; 23.12. 1641; 2.4.1649; 7.

AUDLEY, John

97. Wm Harby; John; Hiblestow, Lincs; Cl; 9.7.1652; 24.6.1652; 4.6. 1660; 7.

AUSTEN, Robert

98. Edward Baker; Edw; London; C & B; 5.3.1655; 5.3.1655;   -   ; 8.

99. Robert Chapman; Robt; London; C & St; 3.7.1654; 3.7.1654; 5.8.1661; 7. Fd by Austen and John Grismond.

100. Thomas Locke; John; parish of St Dunstans in the West, [London]; Cl; 2.6.1645; 25.3.1645; 26.3.1652; 8.

101. Humphrey Wattlework; Robt; Castletown, Isle of man; Smith; 3.9.1655; 3.9.1655;   -   ; 7.

AWNSHAM, Nicholas

102. [Nicholas Awnsham. Fd by patrimony 2.9.1650.]

AYLMER, Brabazon

103. Brabazon Aylmer; Brabazon; London; C & St; 7.2.1698; 7.2.1698; 4.6.1705; 7. Bd to his father.

104. Samuell Aylmer; Anthoney (d); London; G; 13.6.1670; 13.6.1670;   -   ; 7.

105. John Baker; Hugh; Towne of Dorchester, [Dors]; Mr; 7.2.1687; 7.2.1687; 2.4.1694; 7.

106. Robert Robinson. Fd by Aylmer 6.7.1691. Bd to Thomas Parkhurst (q.v.) 6.2.1682.

107. James Round; John; Stratford upon Avon, War; G; 3.12.1694; 3.12.1694; 2.3.1702; 7.

108. John Tillotson; Israell (d); Soarby, Yorks; G; 6.3.1682; 1.1.1682;   -   ; 8.

109. Wm Wilkins; Richard; Newick, Sussex; Minister; 5.7.1680; 5.7.1680; 7.11.1687; 7. Described in the entry of freedom as 'servant to Robert Cox' and fined 2s. 6d. 'for not being turned over a[t] Hall'.

AYLWEY, Thomas

110. John Brooke; Rich; Debtford, Kent; Bl; 1.3.1680; 1.3.1680; 25.6.1688; 7.

AYRTON, Richard

111. [Richard Ayrton. Fd by patrimony 2.12.1650.]

BACHE, Thomas

112. John Jackson; John; Barrowhead, Lancs.; H; 8.6.1646; 8.6.1646; 1.8.1653; 7.

113. Robert Turner. Fd by Bache 3.9.1649. Bd to him 5.3.1638.

BACK, John

114. Arthur Bettesworth; Arthur; Middlehurst, Sussex; G; 6.10.1690; 6.10.1690; 6.6.1698; 7.

115. Mathew Hatham; Robert; City of Yorke; Tn; 6.9.1697; 6.8.1697;   -   ; 7.

BACON, William

116. Wm Ballard. Fd 17.9.1650. m.n. 'vide the waste Book'.

BADDELEY, Richard

117. Richard Baddeley; Richard; Citty of Durham; E; 29.10.1650; 29.10.1650; 7.12.1657; 7.

118. Adam Felton; Jno; Grinsell, Shrops; G; 11.6.1655; 11.6.1655; 4.8.1662; 7.

119. John Maise; William (d); London; C & Cd; 3.5.1658; 3.5.1658;   -   ; 7.

BADGER, George

120. Theodore Crowley; Theodore; Bedford, Beds; Cl; 4.2.1650; 4.2.1650; 9.2.1657; 7.

121. Theodosius Dalston; Thomas (d); Uldan, Cumb; G; 24.3.1647; 21.12.1646;   -   ; 8.

BADGER, Richard

122. Richard Badger. Fd by patrimony 25.2.1642.

123. George Hawkins. Fd by Badger 14.8.1641. Bd to him 4.8.1634.

124. Wm Hughes. Fd by Mrs Badger, widow, 3.11.1645. Bd to Richard Badger 6.8.1638.

125. William Mountford; Richard; Stratford vpon Avon; War; Wheelwright; 5.12.1642; 1.11.1642; - ; 8.

126. Richard Parker. Fd by Badger 2.8.1647. Bd to him 4.5.1640.

BADGER, Thomas

127. Christop Barker. Fd by Badger 7.2.1653. Apparently never formally bd.

128. Edward Broughton. Bd to Thomas Purfoote, Junior, 5.5.1634; t.o. to Badger 7.5.1638; fd by Purfoote 28.6.1641.

129. Wm Collis; John; London; C & Freemason; 15.1.1646; 15.1.1646; 7.2.1653; 7.

130. Richard Constable. Fd by Badger 3.11.1645. Bd to him 2.7.1638.

131. Mathew Morris. Bd to Badger 2.11.1640; t.o. to Adam Islip 6.7.1646. Fd by Badger 7.5.1649.

BAILEY, Mathias

132. Elias Clark; Thomas (d); Thenshington, Leics.; H; 5.7.1669; 5.7.1669; - ; 8.

133. Peter Fish; Peter; London; Ca; 9.9.1678; 9.9.1678; - ; 8.

134. Robert Hillyard; John; Ware, Herts; M; 12.11.1677; 12.11.1677; - ; 7.

135. Wm King; Saunders (d); Kircebery in Galloway, Scotland; Y; 4.8. 1679; 4.8.1679; 1.3.1688; 7.

BAILEY, Richard

136. Richard Baily. Fd by patrimony 7.4.1679.

137. Robert More; Robert (d); Chipping, Lancs; Y; 5.8.1672; 5.8.1672; - ; 7.

138. Thomas Rider; Richard; Chilton, Wilts; Clothier; 1.8.1659; 1.8.1659; - ; 7. Originally bd to Edward Gawill (q.v.) 12.10.1657.

139. Edward Stephens; Edwd; Parish of St Andrews Holborne, M'sex; Gardener; 4.6.1683; 4.6.1683; - ; 7.

BAILEY, Susannah, Widow

140. John Alexander; Edward; Stony Stratford, Bucks; Woolman; 4.8.1673; 4.8.1673; - ; 8.

BAILEY, Thomas

141. Mathias Baily; Jno; Thrussington, Leics; Sh; 2.10.1654; 29.9.1654; 16.7.1666; 8.

142. John Darley; John; Ivingoe, Bucks; L; 8.6.1668; 8.6.1668; - ; 7.

143. Richard Henfrey; Thomas; Hickling, Notts; Weaver; 5.7.1669; 5.7.1669; 14.1.1679; 7.

144. Thomas Middleton; Thomas (d); Reresby, Leics; Bl; 3.12.1660; 25.12.1660; 3.3.1668; 7.

BAILEY, William

145. Charles Kellam; Wm (d); Asferby, Leics; Y; 16.1.1643; 16.1.1643; 6.5.1650; 7.

BAKER, George

146. Nicholas Lidgold. Fd by Baker 29.3.1641. Bd to him 5.7.1630.

BAKER, John

147. William Clerk; Wm; Citty of York; D; 4.12.1676; 4.12.1676; - ; 8.

148. Clement Elis; Clement; Kirkby, Notts; Cl; 7.4.1684; 7.4.1684; - ; 7.

149. William Fletcher. Bd to George Thomason (q.v.) 2.2.1662; t.o. to Baker 12.6.1666.

150. James Lambert; James; London; C & Ha; 7.2.1670; 7.2.1670; - ; 7.

151. John Legg; Richard; Parish of St Clement Danes, M'Sex; Chandler; 8.11.1697; 8.11.1697; - ; 7.

152. Theophilus Price. Bd to Thomas Newberry (q.v.) 7.12.1657; t.o. to Baker 6.12.1658. Fd by Baker 7.10.1672.

153. John Shaw; Robt (d); London; C & Confectioner; 6.3.1671; 6.3.1671; - ; 7.

154. Thomas Smith; Thomas; Marlborough, Wilts; Carrier; 23.10.1657; 23.10.1657; - ; 7.

BAKER, Thomas
155. Humphrey Baker, alius Bowrey. Fd by patrimony 1.5.1648.

BAKER, William
156. [William Baker. Translated from the Company of Haberdashers 1.2.1686. The entry reads: 'In pursuance of the Kings Letter to the Lord Major and Court of Aldrmen of the Citty of London for reduceing Dealers in Books of other Companies into this Company William Baker a Freeman of the Haberdashers Company and made free of the Citty of London as appeared by his Coppy the First of July 1664 was this day sworne and Admitted into the Freedome of this Company gratis.']
157. William Baker; John (d); Quinton, Glos; Cl; 5.2.1694; 5.2.1694; 3.3.1701; 7.
158. Thomas Bartlett; Thomas (d); Eaton, Berks; Bookbinder; 4.2.1689; 4.2.1689; 2.3.1696; 7.
159. Edne Bourn; Joseph; parish of St Martin in the Feilds, M'sex; T; 3.4.1699; 3.4.1699; - ; 7. An Edward Bourn was fd by Robert Steele 7.10.1706.
160. Isaac Stanton; Nicholas; London; C & MT; 1.2.1686; 1.2.1686; 1.10.1694; 8.

BALDRY, John
161. [John Baldry. Fd 3.3.1684 by order of the Court of Alderman.]

BALDWIN, Richard
162. John Bowen; Thomas; Parish of Longalhin, Carmarthen; Y; 2.8.1680; 2.8.1680; 1.7.1689; 8.
163. Samuel Briscoe; Samuel (d); Barton on the Heath, War; Cl; 2.6.1684; 2.6.1684; - ; 7.
164. Richard Humphrey. Fd by Baldwin 6.10.1690. Originally bd to

Joseph Hutchinson (n.d.); t.o. to Baldwin, but fined 5s. 'For being bound by a Forraine Indr & not being turned over at the hall'.
165. Tho Ogle; Town of Nottingham; Y; 7.10.1689; 7.10.1689; - ; 9.
166. Joseph Preast; Richard; Wickham, Bucks; G; 26.3.1683; 26.3.1683; - ; 8.
167. Joseph Rydale; Robert; Great Hampden, Bucks; Y; 14.7.1676; 14.7.1676; - ; 7.

BALE, George
168. John Faywell; John; Tamworth, Staffs; Y; 7.11.1681; 7.11.1681; 6.7.1696; 8. Fd as Fowell.
169. Samuell Gent; Edward (d); Northampton; T; 5.7.1669; 5.7.1669; 12.2.1677; 8.
170. Robert Ryall; Simon; Sherborn, Dors; Mr; 19.5.1675; 19.5.1675; - ; 7.
171. Charles Seale; Charles; Croydon, Surr; Apothecary; 24.10.1676; 24.10.1676; - ; 7.

BANBURY, Edward
172. John Burdett. Fd by Banbury 1.3.1647. Bd to him 20.6.1639.

BANKS, Allen
173. Samuell Hall; Samuel (d); London; Y; 1.9.1673; 1.9.1673; - ; 8.

BARBER, Daniel
174. Richard Holloway; John (d); Farneham, Surr; Chandler; 3.11.1673; 29.9.1673; - ; 7.

BARBER, Joseph
175. John Evans; Jno; St Clements, M'sex; T; 1.10.1655; 1.10.1655; - ; 7.

BARKER, Mathew
176. [Mathew Barker. Son of Robert Barker, deceased; fd by patrimony 7.10.1651.]

[7]

BARKER, Thomas
177. Thomas Arnold; Richard (d); Mewell, Norf; Y; 1.10.1688; 1.10.1688; - ; 7.

BARKER, William
178. John Aylward; John; Pettworth, Sussex; Chandler; 3.6.1695; 3.6.1695; 1.2.1720; 7.
179. John Buckler; Edward; Parish of St Martins in the Fields, M'sex; Ca; 2.4.1683; 2.4.1683; - ; 7.
180. Robert Williamson; Robert (d); parish of St Leonard Shoreditch, M'sex; Victualler; 6.9.1686; 6.9.1686; 8.4.1695; 7. m.n. 'Turned over to Robt Radford the 7th Septr 1691.' Fd by Barker and Radford.

BARLOW, Francis
181. [Francis Barlow. Son of Timothy Barlow; fd by patrimony 21.6.1658.]
182. Charles Crofts; John; St Clements Danes, M'sex; G; 7.2.1659; 7.2.1659; - ; 8.
183. Thomas Farthing; George; parrish of St Dunstan in the West, London; G; 5.8.1661; 5.8.1661; - ; 7.

BARNES, John
184. Andrew Rogers; Phineas; Uske, Mon; Cl; 7.3.1681; 7.3.1681; - ; 7.

BARNES, Richard
185. John Barnes; Willm; Wickham, Bucks; - ; 6.12.1669; 6.12.1669; - ; 7.
186. John Bishop; John (d); London; C & St; 7.4.1679; 7.4.1679; - ; 7.
187. Stephen Dagnall. Fd by Barnes 7.8.1643. Bd to him 5.10.1635.
188. John Williams; Richard; Cladock, Herefs; H; 5.6.1671; 5.6.1671; 3.5.1680; 7.

BARNES, William
189. John Aburne; John; London; G; 6.8.1683; 6.8.1683; - ; 7.

BARRETT, John
190. William Rysley; John (d); Bedford holton, Beds; H; 6.8.1660; 6.8.1660; - ; 7.

BARTHOLOMEW, George
191. Isaac Humphreys; Jonathan; Earle Stoak, Wilts; Clothweaver; 7.11.1692; 7.11.1692; - ; 7.

BARTLETT, John
192. John Andrewes. Fd by Bartlett 4.5.1641. Bd to him 26.3.1632.
193. John Bartlett. Fd by patrimony 1.3.1653.
194. Samuell Bartlett; John; London; C & St; 22.12.1658; 22.12.1658; - ; 7. Bd to his father.
195. Ellis Beverley. Fd by Bartlett 1.6.1646. Bd to him 6.5.1639.

BARTLETT, Roger
196. Edmond Beresford; John; Bentley, Derby; G; 7.8.1654; 7.8.1654; 7.7.1662; 7. Fd by Bartlett and Edward Powell.
197. Samuell Freeman; Howsley; Howsley Hall, Yorks; G; 1.12.1656; 1.12.1656; 7.12.1663; 7. Fd by Bartlett, Thomas Alsop and John Hammersham.
198. Richard Gilman; Francis; City of Oxon; B; 17.12.1667; 17.12.1667; 3.5.1675; 7.

BARWELL, Richard
199. William Clayton. Bd to Simon Burton (q.v.) 4.5.1674; t.o. on Burton's death to Barwell. Fd 11.4.1681.

BASKERVILLE, Gabriel
200. Daniell Barber; George; London; G; 10.12.1653; 10.12.1653; 6.12.1669; 7.
201. Wm Ceshions; Richard; Burford, Oxon; Bu; 9.3.1647; 9.3.1647; - ; 8.
202. John Chamney; Phillip; London; C & Cw; 9.2.1657; 9.2.1657; 1.3.1664; 7.
203. Henry Evans. Fd by Baskerville 3.12.1646. Bd to him 2.12.1639.

[8]

204. Thomas Kequick; Thomas; Citty of Westmr; G; 25.10.1647; 25.10. 1647; 5.2.1655; 7.

205. Henry Maddison; Humphrey; Wainsted, Essex; Cl; 2.9.1644; 2.9.1644 7.10.1651; 7.

206. Richard Story; Henry; Sturton, Lincs; Weaver; 2.9.1661; 2.9.1661; - ; 7.

207. Affable Strange. Fd by Baskerville and Nicholas Vavasor 2.6.1656. Bd to Vavasor (q.v.) 6.12.1647.

208. Eleazer Walter; John (d); Highgate, M'sex; Sh; 19.1.1663; 19.1.1663; - ; 7.

BASKERVILLE, John
209. John Baskervill. Fd by patrimony 8.11.1669.

BASKETT, John
210. John Sherwood; Alexander; parish of St Martin in the Feilds, M'sex; Barber; 6.6.1692; 6.6.1692; - ; 7.

211. Edward Sibley; George (d); London; C & Cooper; 6.2.1693; 6.2.1693; - ; 7.

212. Henry Symonds; John (d); Dorchester, Dors; G; 2.12.1695; 2.12. 1695; - ; 7.

213. Henry Taylor; John; London; C & V; 3.7.1699; 3.7.1699; - ; 7.

BASSETT, Thomas
214. Thomas Arther; Edward; Cookham, Berks; Cl; 25.6.1662; 25.6.1662; 6.5.1670; 8.

215. Judith Bassett. Fd by patrimony 3.5.1697.

216. Richard Carter; Richard; Cobham, Surr; Cl; 7.12.1674; 7.12.1674; 22.12.1681; 7.

217. John Doleman; Richd; parish of St. Clemt Danes in the Libty of Westmr; Printer; 7.4.1690; 7.4.1690; 3.5.1697; 7.

218. Percival Gilbourne. Originally bd to Joshua Sharpe, Citizen and Leatherseller of London, 2.8.1689 for 7 years; t.o. to Thomas Bassett 25.6. 1691. Fd by Bassett 3.8.1696.

219. Richard Heaviside; Richard; London; C & - ; 6.12.1680; 6.12. 1680; - ; 7.

220. Thomas Horsman; Richard; St Martins in the Fields, M'sex; St; 6.5.1659; 6.5.1659; - ; 7. T.o. to John Jackson 25.6.1662.

221. John Leete. Fd by Thomas Dring 4.7.1670, but described as servant to Bassett. Bd to Dring (q.v.) 20.6.1662.

222. Layton Smith; John; London; C & Cook; 7.10.1678; 7.10.1678; - ; 7.

223. Richard Southby. Fd by Bassett 3.7.1693. Apparently never formally bd.

224. Jacob Tonson; Jacob (d); Holborne, M'sex; BSg; 6.6.1670; 6.6.1670; 7.1.1678; 8.

225. Thomas Webb; Hugh; Bowwood Parke, Wilts; E; 7.12.1685; 7.12.1685; 3.7.1693; 7.

BATCHELOR, Thomas
226. Matthew White; Matthew (d); Walthamstow, Essex; Ca; 6.6.1681; 6.6.1681; - ; 7.

BATEMAN, Christopher
227. James Driver; James; Gisborne, Lancs; G; 6.7.1691; 6.7.1691; - ; 7.

228. John Hartley; Hugh (d); Kirby Steven, W'land; Y; 3.12.1684; 3.12. 1684; 1.8.1692; 7.

229. Thomas Hodgson; Thomas; London; C & Gunsmith; 5.9.1692; 5.9.1692; 3.5.1703; 8.

BATEMAN, Stephen
230. John Atkinson; John; - , W'land; Y; 6.8.1683; 6.8.1683; 1.9. 1690; 8.

231. Christopher Bateman; Robert; Kendall, W'land; Sheereman; 7.8.1676; 7.8.1676; 3.11.1684; 8.

232. Richard Bell; Thomas; Hawkeshead, Lancs; Minister; 7.7.1690; 7.7.1690; - ; 7.

233. Stephen Bowman; John; Kendall, W'land; Y; 3.8.1691, 3.8.1691; - ; 7.

234. Edward Fox; Edward; Wantage, Berks; G; 2.5.1670; 2.5.1670; - ; 7.

235. John Parrett; Thomas (d); London; G; 1.5.1671; 1.5.1671; 2.8.1680; 7.

BATES, Charles
236. Wm Bates; Richd (d); London; C & St; 1.2.1692; 1.2.1692; 2.10.1699; 7.

BATES, Richard
237. Francis Backett; Humphrey; Stafford, Staffs; Sh; 4.9.1671; 4.9.1671; 6.10.1678; 7.

BATES, Robert
238. Samuell Andrewes. Fd by Bates 24.5.1647. Bd to him 7.5.1638.

239. Samuell Mearne. Fd by Bates and John Arnold 6.7.1646. Bd to Bates 6.11.1637.

BATES, Thomas
240. Richard Bates. Fd by patrimony 1.4.1661.

241. George Roberts; Hugh; London; C & Cw; 9.2.1642; 9.2.1642, - ; 7.

242. Phillip Wadleworth; Rich (d); London; C & Leatherseller; 17.4.1648; 25.3.1648; 24.4.1655; 8. Fd as Waddleworth.

BATES, Timothy
243. Samuel Bernard; John; [London]; C & D; 7.3.1692; 7.3.1692; - ; 7.

244. Benjamin Bradley; Richard (d); London; C & Dy; 1.10.1683; 1.10.1683; - ; 7.

BATTERSBY, Robert
245. St John Baker; John (d); Cobham, Surr; Cl; 3.7.1699; 3.7.1699; - ; 7.

246. Nathan Paris; Richard; City of Glauc, [Glos]; Bricklayer; 6.6.1670; 6.6.1670; 30.7.1677; 9. Fd as Pharas.

BATTERSBY, William
247. Robert Battersby; William; London; C & St; 1.9.1684; 1.9.1684; 7.9.1691; 7. Bd to his father; fd by patrimony.

BAUGH, Francis
248. Samuel Brightwell; John; parish of Chasely, Bucks; G; 4.8.1684; 4.8.1684; 8.5.1693; 7. Fd by Thomas Penford.

249. Thomas Penford; Tho; Leicr; Gr; 2.7.1677; 2.7.1677; - ; 7.

BEADLE, Gabriel
250. Jeremiah Sparkes; Raph (d); parish of St Clement Danes, M'sex; T; 3.5.1647; 3.5.1647; - ; 8.

BEAKE, William
251. James Beake; William; Cuddington, Bucks; G; 1.8.1659; 1.8.1659; - ; 7.

BEALE, John
252. Robert Beale; Barth; parish of St Andrews in Holborne; G; 7.8.1643; 7.8.1643; - ; 7.

253. Thomas Harding. Fd by Beale 1.2.1647. Bd to him 3.12.1638.

254. Thomas Roycroft. Fd by Beale and John Parker 23.6.1647. Bd to Beale 4.12.1637.

255. Thomas Stacey; Wm (d); Fosell, War; G; 3.10.1642; 3.10.1642; - ; 8.

BEARDWELL, Benjamin
256. James Edwards; George; Marrybone, M'sex; Engraver; 5.2.1700; 5.2.1700; - ; 7.

257. Joseph Hodges; John; parish of St Giles Cripplegate, M'sex; Bu; 5.2.1694; 5.2.1694; 3.3.1701; 7.

BEAVER, Thomas
258. Thomas Smith; John; parish of St Andrew Holbourne, M'sex; Clothdrawer; 4.10.1697; 4.10.1697; - ; 7.

BEDDINGFIELD, John

259. Henry Beaumont; John; Barrow, Derby; E; 6.9.1675; 6.9.1675; - ; 7.

260. Cheadle Bradshaw; George (d); Scale, Lancs; MT; 1.6.1663; 1.6.1663; - ; 7.

261. Henry Bruning; Edmond; Hambleton, S'hants; E; 11.4.1673; 11.4.1673; - ; 7. The master's name is incorrectly given as Benningfeild.

262. Willm Fairfax; Willm; City of York; G; 5.7.1669; 5.7.1669; - ; 7.

263. Roger Fenwick; Willm; Boywell, N'land; G; 4.7.1670; 4.7.1670; - ; 7.

264. Charles Gifford; Walter; Chillington, Staffs; E; 3.3.1662; 3.3.1662; - ; 7.

265. Robert Willoughby; George; Nottingham; E; 5.7.1675; 5.7.1675; - ; 7.

BEDDOE, John

266. Robert Brisenden; Isaac; Ashford, Kent; Netmaker; 7.10.1689; 7.10.1689; - ; 7.

267. Paul Griffin; Paul; - , Bucks; Minister; 11.10.1680; 11.10.1680; 2.4.1688; 7. Fd by John Thomas, and fined 2s. 6d. 'for not being turned over at the Hall'.

BEDFORD, Helkiah

268. Robert Jole; Christopher (d); Stratton Margretts, Wilts; Cl; 2.6.1656; 1.6.1656; 6.6.1664; 8.

269. William Yorke; William; Redriff, Kent; V; 6.10.1662; 6.10.1662; 8.10.1669; 7.

BEE, Cornelius

270. William Edwin. Servant to Bee and Nathaniel Hooke. Fd 6.10.1673 by redemption from the Haberdashers' Company by order of the Lord Mayor and Court of Aldermen. m.n. 'Free from ye Haberdashers Company'.

271. Nathaniell Hooke. 'In pursuance of the Kings Letter to the Lord Major and Cort of Aldermen of the Citty of London, for reduceing Booksellers of other Companyes, into this Company; Nathaniell Hooke, Servant to Cornelius Bee of the Company of Haberdashers, was this Day [2.10.1671] Sworne and Admitted a Freeman of this Company.' m.n. 'Free from the Haberdashers Company'.

BELL, Andrew

272. Hugh Mountgomery; Wm; Citty of Edinburgh, Scotland; Mch; 1.7.1695; 1.7.1695; 4.7.1702; 7.

BELL, Henry

273. [Henry Bell. Fd by patrimony 28.6.1650.]

274. Nicholas Bowyer; Arthur (d); Pottersomersall, Derby; H; 7.5.1660; 7.5.1660; 2.7.1667; 7. Fd by Bell and George Purslowe.

BELL, Jane, Widow

275. Thomas Bowyer; William; Moreton, Staffs; Y; 4.2.1656; 4.2.1656; 5.2.1672; 7. Fd as Boyer.

276. Thomas Harefinch; Thomas; Bridewell precinct, M'sex; Upholsterer; 26.10.1653; 26.10.1653; - ; 7. Entry deleted; m.n. 'this Appr. surrendred his Indrs & went beyond ye Sea & is by ord of Court (4° Feb. 55) crossed out'.

277. John White; Guise; Hellington, N'hants; Cl; 26.10.1653; 26.10.1653; 3.12.1660; 7.

BELL, Moses

278. John Clarke; Thomas; Hampton Lucey, War; H; 2.8.1647; 2.8.1647; 7.8.1654; 7.

279. James Randall; xpofer; Blackfryers, London; T; 26.3.1646; 26.3.1646; 4.4.1653; 7.

280. Samuell Randall; Christopher; Blackfryers, London; T; 6.10.1645; 6.10.1645; - ; 7.

BELLAMY, John

281. Steven Bowtell. Fd by Bellamy 30.7.1642. Bd to him 16.7.1635.

282. Nathaniell Ekins; John; Ringsted, N'hants; G; 7.7.1641; 24.6.1641; 2.7.1649; 8.

283. Thomas Newbery; Thomas; Portsmouth, S'hants; Gunner; 6.10. 1645; 25.3.1645; 26.3.1653; 8.

284. Edward Spurdance. Fd by Bellamy 3.5.1675. Bd to him 30.3.1631.

BELLINGER, John

285. Arthur Baldero; John (d); London; C & Ha; 4.4.1664; 4.4.1664; 3.7.1671; 7. Fd as Baldro.

286. John Barsham; John (d); London; C & Go; 2.12.1668; 2.12.1668; - ; 7.

287. John Beech; John; Redburne, Herts; Y; 4.11.1672; 4.11.1672; - ; 7.

288. Richard Billinger. Fd by patrimony 7.12.1685.

289. Lionel Gosnold; Lionel; Otley, Suff; Cl; 5.8.1689; 5.8.1689; - ; 7.

290. John Henley. Fd by Bellinger 26.6.1682. Apparently never formally bd.

291. George Marriott; Richard; London; C & St; 7.10.1661; 29.9.1661; 7.10.1668; 8.

292. Robert Melsam; Geo (d); Oxford; G; 2.2.1652; 1.12.1651; - ; 8.

293. John Parker; John; Lutterworth, Leics; I; 3.3.1684; 3.3.1684; - ; 7.

293. John Parker; John; Lutterworth, Leics; I; 3.3.1684; 3.3.1684; - ; 7.

294. Thomas Sisson; Cuthbert; Westrenton, Dur; G; 7.12.1657; 1.8. 1657; - ; 8.

295. Robert Vincent; Edward; London; C & Bu; 6.12.1680; 6.12.1680; 9.1.1688; 7.

BELLINGER, Richard

296. Nicholas Harrison; Anthony;

London; C & Clothier; 7.12.1685; 7.12.1685; - ; 7.

BENBRIDGE, William

297. Edward Hawkins. Fd by Benbridge 7.7.1684. Bd to Langley Curtis (q.v.) 7.7.1684.

BENNETT, Henry

298. Robte Tym. Fd by Bennett 2.9.1644. Bd to him as Thomas Tym 27.3.1637.

BENNETT, John I.

299. [John Bennett. Fd by patrimony 20.1.1645.]

300. Edward Pelley; Nich; Amtill, Beds; Y; 20.1.1645; 29.9.1644; - ; 8.

BENNETT, John II

301. John Hastings; John; Chalbury, Oxon; Y; 4.12.1693; 6.11.1693; - ; 7.

BENNETT, Joseph

302. Edward Berrington; Elias (d); London; Mch; 17.11.1688; 17.11.1688; - ; 7.

303. James Gardner. Fd by Bennett 7.2.1681. Apparently never formally bd.

304. Charles Maddison; Charles; Parish of St Martin in the Feilds, M'sex; Tiremaker; 5.12.1681; 5.12. 1681; 4.3.1689; 7.

305. John Powell; Thomas (d); Parrish of St Giles in the feilds, M'sex; Mr; 4.2.1684; 4.2.1684; - ; 7.

306. Hen Swaile; Stephen (d); York; G; 3.5.1680; 3.5.1680; - ; 7.

BENNETT, Margaret, Widow

307. John Bowes. Bd to David Edwards (q.v.) 10.9.1694; t.o. to Margaret Bennett 6.2.1699.

308. Thomas Howlatt; Thomas; parish of St Giles in the Feildes, M'sex; T; 2.4.1694; 2.4.1694; 6.6.1709; 7.

309. Andrew Norman; John; London; C & Bl; 1.7.1700; 1.7.1700; - ; 7.

310. Thomas Turner; Francis; parish of St James Westmr, M'sex; Pumpmaker; 7.11.1692; 7.11.1692; - ; 7. Mrs Bennett is described as the widow of Joseph Bennett.

BENNETT, Thomas

311. Francis Bennet; John; Westmr; Mch; 7.9.1691; 7.9.1691; - ; 7.

312. Jonah Bowyer; Jonah; Sandbach, Ches; Mr; 6.4.1696; 6.4.1696; 8.11.1703; 7.

313. Noell Phillips; Richard (d); St Ismael, Pembroke; G; 6.8.1688; 6.8.1688; - ; 7.

314. William Ward; Francis (d); Leicester; Bs; 7.3.1698; 7.3.1698; 4.6.1705; 7.

315. James Wilson; John; Rochdale, Lancs; Gr; 7.10.1689; 7.10.1689; - ; 7.

BENSKIN, Thomas

316. Andrew Bell; James (d); Edenburgh in the Kingdome of Scotland; Mch; 2.4.1683; 2.4.1683; 4.3.1695; 7. Fd by Benskin and Benjamin Webster.

BENSON, John

317. Roger Bell; Roger; London; C & Cd; 22.11.1649; 29.9.1649; - ; 8.

318. William Bennison; Robt; Haughton, Westchester; Y; 3.12.1655; 3.12.1655; 1.6.1663; 7.

319. Thomas Collins. Fd by Benson 14.1.1641. Bd to him 2.12.1633.

320. John Playford. Fd by Benson 5.4.1647. Bd to him 23.3.1640.

321. Edward Way; Edward; Bradford, Wilts; Clothier; 1.5.1648; 1.5.1648; - ; 7.

BENSON, William

322. Robert Benson. Fd by patrimony 10.6.1684.

323. George Farthing; George; London; C & Dy; 30.4.1659; 30.4.1659; - ; 8.

BENTLEY, Richard

324. Edmond Rumbold; Edmond (d); Newgate Street, London; Mealman; 6.4.1691; 6.4.1691; 5.6.1699; 7.

BERESFORD, Edmond

325. John Beresford. Fd by patrimony 6.11.1682.

326. Edmond Beresford. Fd by patrimony 8.6.1691.

327. John Phillips; John (d); London; C & Throwster; 8.4.1700; 8.4.1700; 7.7.1707; 7. Originally bd to John Shrimpton (q.v.) 1.10.1694. Fd by Beresford.

BERESFORD, John

328. Joseph Harper; John (d); Wapping, M'sex; T; 2.11.1696; 2.11.1696; 5.2.1705; 8.

BERESFORD, Thomas

329. Latheus Edwards; Griffith; Stannerden of the Wood, Shrops; - ; 8.5.1665; 8.5.1665; - ; 8.

330. Thomas Goodwin; Nicholas; Abingdon, Berks; Gl; 2.4.1660; 2.4.1660; - ; 9.

331. Strangeways Mudd; Thomas; Bishopricke of Durham; Physician; 2.6.1656; 2.6.1656; 5.10.1663; 7.

BERNEHAM, Martin

332. Peter Richmond. Said to have been bd to Berneham, but there is no formal entry of binding. T.o. to Charles Spicer alius Helder 8.11.1675. Fd by Berneham 3.7.1676.

BEST, John

333. John Ashbridge; Thomas; London; C & Sk; 6.8.1660; 6.8.1660; - ; 7.

334. Thomas Hayley. Fd by Best 8.1.1667. Apparently never formally bd.

335. Tho Marriott; Willm; Eley, [Cambs]; Distiller; 5.10.1664; 5.10.1664; - ; 7.

BEST, Richard

336. George Dawes; Thomas; Litchfield, Staffs; G; 5.6.1654; 5.6.1654; 1.7.1661; 7.

337. Thomas Firbury; John; Carthrop, Yorks; Y; 23.6.1646; 23.6.1646; 29.6.1653; 7. Fd as Thomas Firby.

338. John Holmes; Christopher; Bentham, Yorks; G; 29.10.1651; 29.10. 1651; - ; 7.

BETTY, Parr

339. James Hobland; John (d); London; St; 16.3.1648; 16.3.1648; 1.10.1655; 8.

340. Henry Lee. Fd by Betty 4.3. 1650. Apparently never formally bd.

BILLINGSLEY, Benjamin

341. George Ball; Adam; London; C & Cu; 6.11.1676; 6.11.1676; - ; 7.

342. John Billingsley; Benjamin; [London]; [C & St]; 7.7.1690; 7.7. 1690; - ; 7. Bd to his father.

343. Edward Croft; Lyonell; Sutton vnder Brayles, Glos; Y; 11.4.1670; 11.4.1670; 18.6.1677; 7.

344. William Mason; William (d); parish of St Leonards Shoreditch, M'sex; - ; 6.7.1696; 6.7.1696; - ; 8.

BINE, John

345. Edward Fleming; Nicholas (d); Burnham, Bucks; Y; 6.3.1682; 6.3. 1682; - ; 8.

BIRCH, William

346. Jonathan Greenwood; James; Melton, W'land; Cl; 22.6.1670; 22.6. 1670; 24.3.1680; 7. Fd by Thomas Cockerill.

BIRD, George

347. Ferdinando Clinton; Robert; - , - ; E; 6.3.1671; 6.3.1671; 5.9.1681; 7. Bird is described as a Linendraper.

348. Richard Lowe; Francis; Stukely, Hunts; E; 18.6.1677; 18.6.1677; - ; 7.

349. Christopher Mohun; Michael; - , - ; G; 22.2.1675; 22.2.1675; - ; 8.

350. Francis Petre; Augustin; Ingerstone, Essex; E; 4.9.1676; 4.9.1676; - ; 7.

351. Valentine Saunders; Valentine; Citty of Norwich; E; 8.11.1675; 8.11. 1675; - ; 8.

BIRD, Henry

352. Richard Lannaway; John; parish of Farneham, Surr; Y; 12.7.1648; 12.7.1648; - ; 7.

353. James Marshall; Thomas; Crandall, Hunts; Y; 2.12.1650; 2.12.1650; - ; 7.

354. Jeremy Ramsey; John; Shelley, Essex; Webster; 29.3.1641; 29.3.1641; - ; 10.

355. James Winde. Fd by Bird 29.3. 1641. Bd to him 22.2.1633.

BIRD, Robert

356. Thomas Underhill. Fd by Bird 1.3.1641. Bd to him 5.3.1632.

BISHOP, George

357. Samuell Drafgate; Richard; Lichfeild, Staffs; Apothecary; 5.12.1642; 21.12.1642; 4.3.1650; 7. Fd by Bishop and Robert White.

358. Thomas Rosse; John; Braben, Kent; Cl; 15.1.1645; 15.1.1645; 19.1. 1652; 7. Fd by Bishop and Thomas Maxey.

BISHOP, Jane, Widow

359. John Bishop; Wm (d); London; C & St; 5.3.1677; 5.3.1677; - ; 8. Bd to his mother.

BISHOP, John

360. Richard Jennaway; Richard (d); Ransthorp, N'hants; H; 5.12.1659; 5.12.1659; 2.7.1667; 8.

361. John Meakes; Will; Steeple Cleydon, Bucks; Grazier; 6.4.1663; 6.4.1663; 5.2.1672; 8.

BISHOP, Richard

362. Henry Ander; Hatton; London; C & MT; 26.9.1646; 26.9.1646; - ; 7.

363. Richard Bannister; William (d) Churchdoone, Glos; Y; 21.10.1650; 21.10.1650; - ; 8.

364. Rich Dawlman; John; London; C & Whitebaker; 30.8.1641; 25.12.1641; - ; 7.

365. Wm Edwards; Wm (d); London; G; 3.5.1647; 3.5.1647; - ; 8.

366. Joseph Fry; Richard (d); London; C & Brownbaker; 19.8.1644; 20.4.1644; - ; 9.

367. Francis Twyn; Robte; Gilden Moreden, Cambs; Y; 5.12.1642; 5.12.1642 - ; 7.

BISHOP, William

368. William Amey; Benjamine; London; C & Cw; 5.6.1671; 5.6.1671; 7.5.1688; 7.

BISSELL, James

369. Joseph Blisse; William (d); parish of St James Clerkenwell, M'sex; Gardener; 3.8.1691; 3.8.1691; - ; 7.

BLACKMORE, Edward

370. Francis Dowse; Thomas; Hampshire; G; 5.12.1653; 5.12.1653; - ; 7.

371. John Mitchell; John; Begall, Yorks; G; 7.7.1662; 7.7.1662; - ; 7.

372. William Sledd; Lawrence; London; J; 2.8.1647; 29.9.1647; - ; 7.

373. Samuell Speed; Samuell (d); London; C & MT; 8.10.1649; 29.9.1649; 5.10.1657; 8.

BLACKWELL, Jonathan

374. George Blackwell. Fd by Blackwell 8.6.1653. Bd to him 7.7.1634.

BLADEN, William

375. William Bladen. Fd by patrimony 2.8.1641.

376. Nath Thompson. Fd by redemption 6.12.1669, paying 20s. Presented by Bladen.

377. John Winter; Richard; London; Lorimer; 7.7.1651; 7.7.1651; 26.3.1666; 10.

BLAGRAVE, Obadiah

378. Edward Candell; Tho; Syrencester, Glos; H; 1.8.1670; 1.8.1670; 1.10.1677; 7. Fd as Condell.

379. Katherine Cawdell; Thomas; Cirencester, Glos; [H]; 1.2.1675; 1.2.1675; - ; 7. Bd as Cawdell but probably sister of preceding.

380. Richard Fenn; Richard (d); Hossell, Surr; Y; 6.9.1675; 6.9.1675; - ; 7.

BLAGUE, Daniel

381. Daniel Blague. Fd by patrimony 26.3.1680.

382. Thomas Bond; George; Lusam, Kent; H; 5.9.1670; 5.9.1670; - ; 7.

383. John Bullord; John; - , M'sex; Cabinetmaker; 11.10.1680; 11.10.1680; 19.11.1695; 7.

384. Benjamine Needham; John; - , - ; - ; 7.5.1660; [7.5.1660]; 2.8.1669; -.

385. Thomas Walter; Thomas; Abington, Berks; Barber; 4.9.1671; 4.9.1671; - ; 7.

BLAIKLOCKE, Joseph

386. Joseph Cater; Gabriell; Leicester; T; 22.1.1646; 22.1.1646; 4.4.1653; 7. Fd as Carter.

387. Henry Gale; Robte; Longley, Wilts; H; 20.1.1645; 25.12.1644; - ; 8.

388. Thomas Ley; Robert; St Clements Danes, M'sex; G; 17.1.1659; 17.1.1659; - ; 7.

389. John Mallory; William; London; C & St; 7.10.1661; 7.10.1661; - ; 7.

BLAIKLOCKE, Lawrence

390. Samuell Smith. Fd by Blaiklocke 10.1.1655. Bd to him 3.2.1640.

391. George Manfeild; John; Bentley, S'hants; Y; 6.12.1647; 6.12.1647; - ; 8.

BLASHFIELD, Thomas
392. William Milward. Fd by Blashfield and William Terrey 7.3.1653; Bd to Terrey 2.3.1646.

BLOOME, Jacob
393. Richard Bloome. Fd by patrimony 6.8.1660.
394. Thomas Shaw; James (d); London; C & Woodmonger; 3.9.1660; 29.9.1660; - ; 7.
395. John White; Richard; London; C & Bu; 6.12.1658; 29.9.1658; 8.7.1668; 8.

BLOOME, Richard
396. Richard Palmer. Fd by Bloome 6.8.1677. Apparently never formally bd.

BLUNDEN, Humphrey
397. Nath Brookes. Fd by Blunden 6.4.1646. Bd to him 7.8.1637.
398. Timothy Smart; Timothy; London; C & Cd; 2.7.1646; 24.6.1646; 1.8.1653; 8. Fd by Blunden and Thomas Pierrepoint.

BLYTH, Francis
399. James Fowler; - ; - , - ; - ; 20.12.1687; 20.12.1687; - ; 7.
400. Francis Jewster. Fd by Blyth 6.7.1691. Originally bd to Edward Powell (q.v.) 5.4.1684.

BOATE, Francis
401. Isaac Boate. Fd by patrimony 4.10.1641.

BODINGTON, George
402. John Yelson; Henry (d); London; J; 1.5.1648; 1.4.1648; - ; 8.

BODDINGTON, Nicholas
403. Richard Colledge; Geo; Church Over, War; Farrier; 7.8.1676; 7.8.1676; 1.10.1683; 7.

404. Richard Danchey; Dennis; Lighthall, War; H; 2.10.1693; 2.10.1693; - ; 7.
405. William Warren; William; Citty of Exiter, [Dev]; Confectioner; 7.7.1690; 7.7.1690; - ; 7.
406. Richard Waterton; John (d); Harborough, War; H; 3.7.1682; 3.7.1682; 7.10.1689; 7.
407. John Webb; John; Churchover, War; L; 3.4.1693; 3.4.1693 - ; 7.

BODVILE, Peter
408. John Minshall; Randoll; City of Chester; I; 4.9.1671; 4.9.1671; - ; 7.

BOGGIS, Robert
409. Samuell Brookes; Edward; Onelip, Leics; Cook; 10.6.1650; 10.6.1650; 2.8.1658; 8.

BOLDEROE, Arthur
410. Robert Calcott; George; London; C & Silkman; 12.8.1671; 12.8.1671; 5.8.1678; 7.
411. John Woodgate; John; Horsham, Sussex; G; 2.7.1677; 2.7.1677; - ; 7.

BOLER, James
412. [James Boler. Fd by patrimony 5.4.1642.]
413. Thomas Luxford; Thomas (d); London; C & S; 5.12.1642; 25.12.1642; - ; 7.
414. George Sly; John (d); Windsor, Berks; G; 24.5.1647; 24.5.1647; - ; 7.

BOLLIFANT, Edmond
415. [Edmond Bolliphant. Fd by patrimony 1.6.1657.]

BOLT, John
416. [John Bolt. Son of Marmaduke Bolt; fd by patrimony 7.10.1672.]

BOLTER, William
417. Peter Bolter. Fd by patrimony 11.6.1655.

418. William Bolter. Fd by patrimony 7.3.1653.

BONWICK, Henry

419. James Bonwick; Benjn; Rygate, Surr; G; 4.5.1691; 4.5.1691; 4.7.1698; 7.

420. William Carter; Martin; Seiling, Essex; G; 5.6.1699; 5.6.1699; 9.9.1706; 7. Fd by Rebeccah Bonwick.

421. William Peck; Henry (d); Parish of St Margaretts Westminster, M'sex; G; 3.4.1682; 3.4.1682; - ; 7.

422. Launcelott Walton; Launcelott (d); London; C & -; 6.12.1697; 6.12.1697; - ; 7.

423. Richard Willington; Richd (d); London; G; 7.12.1685; 7.12.1685; 3.7.1693; 7.

BOOKER, William

424. William Bosden; William (d); London; G; 26.3.1683; 26.3.1683; - ; 7.

BOONE, Ralph

425. Nicholas Boone; George (d); parish of St Andrews Holborne, London; Victualler; 7.11.1659; 7.11.1659; - ; 7.

BOOTH, Francis

426. Thomas Cockett; Thomas (d); parish of St Giles without Cripplegate, London; G; 4.7.1687; 4.7.1687; - ; 7.

427. Richard Hancox; Thomas (d); Citty of Hereford; Bs; 4.5.1696; 4.5.1696; - ; 7.

BOSTOCKE, Robert

428. Wm Cowley. Fd by Bostocke 2.8.1641. Bd to him 1.9.1634.

429. Robert Harison; Robert; Allhollowes Barking, London; Cl; 1.9.1645; 1.9.1645; 5.12.1653; 8. Fd as Harrison.

430. Richard Rawlyn; Wm; London; C & MT; 8.11.1641; 8.11.1641; - ; 7.

BOSVILE, Alexander

431. Charles Pittard. Bd to Roger Clavell (q.v.) 7.12.1696; t.o. to Bosvile 4.7.1698. The note of turnover wrongly dates the binding to Clavell as 7.12.1697.

BOULTER, John

432. [John Boulter. Fd by patrimony 23.12.1652.]

BOULTER, Robert

433. James Ball; Nathaniell; Chiswell, Essex; Cl; 9.10.1666; 9.10.1666; - ; 7.

434. Samuel Eddowes; Ralph; Whitchurch, Shrops; Ironmonger; 3.8.1674; 3.8.1674; 2.10.1682; 7.

435. Abell Swalle; Abraham (d); London; C & Weaver; 5.12.1670; 5.12.1670; 20.12.1677; 7.

BOUND, Benjamin

436. Elizabeth Chamberlain; John; Stratton, Herefs; G; 6.12.1697; 6.12.1697; - ; 7.

437. Henry Dingley; John; Henley Castle, Worcs; G; 5.9.1692; 5.9.1692; - ; 7.

438. Henry Lee; Henry; Northampton, N'hants; G; 6.7.1685; 6.7.1685; 7.11.1692; 8.

BOURDEN, William

439. Robert Smith. Fd by Bourden and William Sherrington 1.5.1654. Bd to Sherrington 27.4.1646.

BOURMAN, John

440. Francis Durfy; Severinus; St Andrewes Holborne, [M'sex]; G; 6.11.1648; 6.11.1648; - ; 7.

441. Walter Hamond; Walter (d); London; C & St; 6.5.1659; 6.5.1659; 6.9.1669; 7.

442. William Place; John (d); Ardington, Berks; Cl; 6.10.1645; 6.10.1645; 3.7.1654; 7. Fd by Bourman and John Place.

BOURNE, Nicholas
443. Thomas Farley; Humphrey (d); London; C & Gr; 1.4.1645; 25.12.1644; - ; 9.
444. Robert Horne; Thomas (d); Elstoe, Beds; 4.6.1649; 4.6.1649; 3.7.1657; 8.
445. Roger Ive. T.o. to Bourne from Robert Burrough 4.12.1643. Bd to Samuel Petty 5.3.1638; fd by Burrough and Petty 10.3.1645.
446. John Jellis; Francis; Cambridge, Cambs; Gr; 13.7.1657; [13.7.1657?]; - ; 10.
447. John Millett; John; Alisbury, Bucks; Cl; 20.9.1644; 24.6.1644; - ; 8.
448. John Moirriell. Bd to Godfrey Edmondson (or Emerson) 26.6.1637; t.o. to Nicholas Bourne 6.12.1641.
449. Symon Peck; Symon; Dartchworth, Herts; Cl; 23.6.1646; 24.6.1646; - ; 8.
450. George Whittington. Fd by Bourne 2.9.1644. Bd to him 3.12.1632.

BOURNE, Samuel
451. John Meakins; John (d); London; Turner; 20.12.1672; 20.12.1672; 11.10.1680; 7.
452. John Monke; Wm; London; C & Cw; 6.10.1679; 6.10.1679; 6.12.1686; 7.

BOURNE, Thomas
453. William Collins. Fd by Bourne 23.12.1657. Bd to him 4.11.1639.
454. Thomas Dowce; Augustine; Long-stoke, S'hants; G; 15.9.1647; 15.9.1647; 16.10.1654; 7.

BOWEN, John
455. Peter Moreton; John; London; C & S; 5.10.1691; 5.10.1691; 7.2.1704; 7.

BOWLES, Oliver
456. Edward Godfery; Edward; Ware, Herts; G; 4.10.1658; 24.6.1658; - ; 8.

457. Benjamin Le Gay; Isaack (d); London; C & Gr; 5.8.1668; 5.8.1668; - ; 7.

BOWMAN, Francis
458. [Francis Bowman. Fd by redemption 2.4.1642.]
459. John Crosley. Fd by Bowman 19.9.1679. Apparently never formally bd.

BOWTELL, Steven
460. John Walker. Bd to Thomas Nicholls (q.v.) 4.5.1641; t.o. to Bowtell 5.12.1642. Fd by patrimony 16.3.1646.
461. Samuell Ward; Robte (d); Wethersfeild, Essex; G; 7.12.1646; 24.6.1646; - ; 8.

BOWTELL, William
462. John Marsh. Fd by Bowtell 8.11.1680. Apparently never formally bd.

BOWYER, Thomas
463. Edward Bowyer; Thomas; parish of Cripple Gate, London; - ; 3.6.1678; 3.6.1678; - ; 7.

BOWYER, William
464. James Bettenham; John; Ashford, Kent; - ; 6.5.1700; 6.5.1700; 9.6.1707; 7.
465. Thomas Jones; John (d); Gallis, Den; Cl; 7.8.1699; 7.8.1699; 3.3.1707; 7.

BOYDELL, Robert
466. Wm Walker; John; Tower hill, London; Victualler; 16.2.1646; 16.2.1646; - ; 8.

BRADDYLL, Thomas
467. Joseph Andrews. Bd to Henry Hills Junior (q.v.) 26.3.1683; said to have been t.o. to Braddyll (n.d.), but fd by Hills 7.4.1690.
468. David Edwards; Thomas; Pottfarry, Den; Y; 2.7.1683; 2.7.1683; 6.4.1691; 7. Fd as Thomas Edwards.

469. John Letts; John; London; C & B; 5.8.1700; 5.8.1700; 1.9.1707; 7. m.n. 'This Letts though presented in Court never bound by Indents'.

470. Henry Lloyd; Robert; Denbigh, Den; Ca; 7.12.1691; 7.12.1691; 3.4. 1699; 7.

471. Josias Long; George (d); Citty of Bath, Som; - ; 5.5.1679; 5.5.1679; - ; 7.

472. Edward Midwinter; Daniell; London; C & Tallowchandler; 27.9. 1695; 27.9.1695; 2.11.1702; 7.

473. Robert Ponder; Nathaniel; London; C & St; 5.8.1689; 5.8.1689; 5.2.1694; 7. Fd by patrimony.

BRADFORD, John

474. Richard Griffin; John (d); Citty of Oxford; Cd; 5.10.1696; 5.10. 1696; 2.4.1705; 7.

BRADLEY, Alice, Widow

475. Richard Beale; Geo; Woolescott, War; Cl; 3.11.1651; 3.11.1651; 6.12.1658; 7.

BRADLEY, George

476. Michael Bradley. Fd by patrimony 2.3.1674.

477. Andrew Johnson; Andrew; London; C & D; 13.8.1649; 24.8.1649; - ; 7.

478. John Towse; Nicholas (d); London; C & Mr; 14.1.1641; 14.1.1641; 7.5.1649; 8.

BRADLEY, William

479. Henry White; Willm; Stepney, M'sex; Chandler; 7.10.1668; 7.10.1668, - ; 7.

BRADSHAW, John

480. Richard Streete; George; Guilford, Surr; D; 6.5.1695; 6.5.1695; - ; 7.

BRAMPTON, Katherine, Widow

481. Charles Butler; John; Reygate, Surr; G; 7.5.1677; 7.5.1677; 7.9.1685; 7.

482. George Wigmore; Thomas; Bishop Upton, Herefs; G; 26.6.1682; 26.6.1682; - ; 7. Katherine Brampton is described as the widow of William Brampton.

BRAMPTON, William

483. Geo Bedford; Geo (d); London; G; 1.12.1651; 1.12.1651; - ; 7.

484. Richard Bradgate; Robert; Little Peatly, Leics; G; 5.9.1653; 5.9. 1653; - ; 7.

485. Joseph Bullin; James; Citty of Chester; G; 3.12.1655; 3.12.1655; - ; 7.

486. Faithfull Ivatt; Thomas; Clouelly, Dev; G; 3.11.1662; 3.11.1662; - ; 7.

487. Richard Parry; George; Llandevalocke, Brecknock; E; 7.2.1659; 7.2.1659; - ; 7.

488. Henry Twiford; Thomas; London; G; 2.11.1663; 2.11.1663; - ; 7.

BRAMSTON, Fish

489. Edmund Scofeild; William (d); Newington Butts, Surr; Y; 6.11.1699; 6.11.1699; 3.11.1712; 7. Fd by John Science.

BRANCH, John

490. John Sly; Edward; Citty of Oxford; Fuller; 7.12.1646; 7.12.1646; 6.2.1654; 7.

BRANCH, William

491. Randolph Abbott; John; Kingston, Dors; Y; 27.3.1648; 27.3.1648; - ; 7.

492. Richard Clavill; Edward; Vinfreth Neabor, Dors; G; 4.7.1642; 4.7. 1642; - ; 7.

493. Francis Cleavely; Gerrard; Harfordwarren, War; J; 11.2.1661; 11.2.1661; - ; 7.

494. Thomas Williams; John; London; C & Salter; 5.9.1653; 5.9.1653; - ; 7.

BRANSON, John

495. Robert Lamport; Henry; parish of Redding, Berks; Ironmonger; 3.6.1678; 3.6.1678; - ; 7.

496. Joseph Reynolds; Thomas; Parish of St Magdalens Bermondsey, Surr; Cornfactor; 1.4.1672; 1.4.1672; - ; 7.

497. Henry Stockwell; Henry; Camerwell alius Camberwell, Surr; Y; 1.3.1686; 1.3.1686; - ; 7.

BRAY, Edward

498. Richard Batten; Richard; Bemister, Dors; Sh; 6.11.1648; 6.11.1648; - ; 7.

499. John Bray; Marke; Bigglesworth, Beds; Y; 6.9.1647; 6.9.1647; - ; 7.

500. Thomas Darley; Thomas; Lambeach, Cambs; Y; 2.11.1663; 2.11.1663; - ; 7.

501. Beniamin Harris; William; London; C & BSg; 6.4.1663; 6.4.1663; 1.8.1670; 9.

502. Thomas Holmwood; Edw (d); London; G; 7.7.1651; 7.7.1651; 4.10.1658; 7.

BRETT, Adam

503. Charles Hide; John (d); Brumpton, Berks; Y; 7.5.1677; 7.5.1677; - ; 7.

BREWSTER, Edward

504. Valentine Acton; Valentine; Elkington, N'hants; G; 10.1.1670; 10.1.1670; 18.6.1677; 7.

505. Lawrence Aldworth; Thomas; Wantage, Berks; G; 6.11.1676; 6.11.1676; - ; 7.

506. Richard Harwick; Parsvall (d); Lynne Regis, Norf; Woollendraper; 1.8.1687; 1.8.1687; - ; 7.

507. William Keeblewhite; William; Newport, Isle of Wight; St; 29.3.1680; 29.3.1680; 4.4.1687; 7.

508. Giles Meddows; Thomas; Aston Magna, Worcs; H; 6.6.1659; 6.6.1659; 18.6.1666; 7.

509. Nathaniell Ranew. Fd by Brewster and Christopher Meredith 13.6.1659. Bd to Meredith (q.v.) 6.5.1652.

510. James Richardson; James; London; C & Apothecary; 10.9.1694; 10.9.1694; 6.10.1701; 7.

511. George Sawbridge. Fd by Brewster 14.4.1645. Bd to him 19.2.1638.

BREWSTER, Ellen

512. Thomas Bassett; Richard; Rugbey, War; G; 4.3.1650; 4.3.1650; 26.3.1657; 7.

BREWSTER, Thomas

513. William Babington; William (d); Ogle Castle, N'land; E; 4.11.1661; 4.11.1661; - ; 7.

514. Peter Bodnell; Jno; Cardeo, Caernarvon; - ; 4.2.1656; 4.2.1656; 6.4.1663; 7.

515. John Horsley; Ralph; Rubdee, War; Hatmaker; 5.3.1649; 5.3.1649; - ; 8.

516. Henry Moreclocke. Fd by Brewster and Robert Howes 3.3.1656. Bd to Howes (q.v.) 8.6.1648.

BRIDGE, Samuel

517. John Fisher; John (d); London; C & Ha; 8.4.1700; 8.4.1700; - ; 7.

518. William Osborne; John; Bromley neare Bow, M'sex; Bricklayer; 1.3.1697; 1.3.1697; 5.2.1705; 7.

BRISCOE, John

519. Edward Beard; Henry (d); London; C & Glazier; 2.7.1655; 2.7.1655; - ; 8.

BRISCOE, Samuel

520. John Willis; John; South-Hinksey, Berks; G; 8.8.1694; 8.8.1694; - ; 7.

BRISCOE, Thomas

521. John Briscoe. Fd by patrimony 30.6.1651.

522. Thomas Hodgson. Fd by Briscoe and Lawrence Leech 3.12.1646. Bd to Leech 1.2.1635.

BROAD, Thomas
523. James Boyle; Henry; - ,
Herts; Cl; 3.2.1651; 3.2.1651; - ; 7.

BROCKETT, Mary, Widow
524. Michael Buckland; William (d);
parish of St Martin in the Feilds, M'sex;
Victualler; 7.3.1692; 7.3.1692; - ;
7. Mary Brockett is described as the
widow of Thomas Brockett.

BROCKETT, Thomas
525. John Bennett. Fd by Brockett
6.2.1693. Bd to Nicholas Hooper (q.v.)
7.12.1685.
526. William Burroughs; William;
- , Shrops; Y; 6.7.1678; 6.7.1678;
22.12.1685; 7.
527. Dorsett Surby; Henry; London;
Sc; 6.11.1682; 6.11.1682; 12.11.1694;
7.

BROGDEN, Daniel
528. Richard Blount; Charles; parish
of St Margaret Westmr, M'sex; G;
6.6.1698; 6.6.1698; - ; 7.
529. John Caucking; Ralph; Donum
on the Hill, Ches; Weaver; 4.6.1694;
4.6.1694; - ; 7.

BROME, Charles
530. Edward Bunchley; Samuel;
Bourne, Cambs; Cl; 7.12.1685; 7.12.
1685; 4.6.1694; 7. Fd as Samuell
Bunchley.
531. William Cherrett; William (d);
Hurst, Berks; Cl; 26.3.1700; 26.3.1700;
- ; 8.
532. William Fursse; Wm (d); Wells,
Som; Cl; 3.2.1690; 3.2.1690; - ; 7.

BROME, Henry
533. Wm Bachelor; Nicholas; Forn-
ham, Surr; I; 14.1.1679; 14.1.1679;
1.2.1686; 7. A note, 'for not being turned
over at ye Hall ij:vj', is misplaced—it
refers to Charles Peregrine two entries
earlier.
534. Charles Broome. Fd by patrimony 10.6.1684.

535. [Henry Brome. Admitted to the
freedom of the Company 4.11.1678
'Gratis'.]
536. Jonathan Edwyn. 'Servant to
Henry Broome of the Company of
Haberdashers,' made free of the Stationers' Company 2.10.1671. m.n. 'Free
from the Haberdashers Company'.
537. George Gibson; John (d); Salisbury, [Wilts]; - ; 1.12.1679; 1.12.
1679; - ; 7.

BROME, Joanna
538. John Beddingfeild; John; London; C & Gr; 2.10.1682; 2.10.1682;
- ; 7. Bd to the widow of Henry
Brome.

BROMWICH, William
539. John Beale; Edward; Woolescott, War; G; 10.9.1677; 10.9.1677;
- ; 7.

BROOKE, John
540. James Brooke; Richd; Deptford, Kent; Bl; 25.6.1688; 25.6.1688;
1.2.1697; 7.
541. George Toft; Joshua; Godalming, Surr; Clothier; 6.5.1695; 6.5.1695;
- ; 7.
542. Charles Walkden; John; parish
of St James in the Liberty of Westmr,
M'sex; Cook; 5.6.1699; 5.6.1699; - ;
7.

BROOKE, Roger
543. Thomas Alsop; Robte; Chesterfeild, Derby; G; 14.6.1647; 14.6.1647;
27.6.1654; 7.
544. Edward Blackmore; Rich; Col-
lingborne-Jucy, Wilts; H; 10.4.1641;
10.4.1641; 16.4.1649; 7.
545. Thomas Brookes; Jeffery;
Berry, Lancs; Bu; 2.7.1655; 2.7.1655;
- ; 7.
546. Walte[r] Wilkes. Bd to Thomas
Whittlesey (q.v.) 4.4.1664; t.o. on
Whittlesey's death to Roger Brooke
12.3.1667.

BROOKES, Christopher

547. Joseph Brookes. Fd by patrimony 1.3.1683.

548. Mathew Wattleworth; Robert (d); Castle Towne, Isle of Man; Bl; 22.10.1656; 22.10.1656; 2.11.1663; 7. Fd as Mattleworth.

BROOKES, James

549. James Burden; Richard; London; C & MT; 6.5.1700; 6.5.1700; 2.8.1708; 7.

BROOKES, NATHANIEL

550. Obadiah Blagrave; Rich (d); London; C & Ha; 2.7.1655; 24.6.1655; 1.8.1664; 9.

551. Samuell Bolton; Adam (d); Blackborne, Lancs; Cl; 23.12.1652; 1.12.1652; 21.1.1662; 9. Rebd to John Wright (q.v.) 6.11.1655. Fd by Brookes and Wright.

552. Tho Greene; Thomas; Tanworth, Staffs; G; 2.12.1661; 2.12.1661; - ; 7.

553. George Hall; Robert; Renberry, Ches; T; 1.10.1655; 1.8.1655; - ; 8.

554. Robert Harford; Robert; Portsmoth, S'hants; Bs; 5.5.1668; 5.5.1668; 12.2.1677; 7.

555. John Heiern; Joseph; London; C & Mr; 3.2.1669; 3.2.1669; 6.3.1676; 7. The apprentice's name is entered as 'Heiern', the father's as 'Heiron'; fd as Heiorn.

556. Willm Leech; Richard; Horncastle, Lincs; Woollendraper; 3.10.1670; [3.10.1670]; - ; 7.

557. James Morrice; Richard; neer Leominster, Herefs; H; 6.6.1670; 6.6.1670; - ; 8.

558. Phillip Rotheram; Thomas; St Albans, Herts; -; 3.8.1663; 3.8.1663; - ; 7.

BROOKSBY, Phillip

559. Thomas Downes; John; parish of St. Martins Le Grand, M'sex; G; 3.11.1673; 3.11.1673; - ; 7.

560. John Foster; John; Braunston, Rut; Victualler; 3.3.1690; 3.3.1690; 7.2.1699; 7. Fd as Forsterby.

561. Richard Shuter; Thomas; Parish of St Giles without Cripplegate, M'sex; Gl; 5.12.1681; 5.12.1681; - ; 8.

562. John Walter; Thomas; Farum, S'hants; S; 1.2.1697; 1.2.1697; 5.2.1705; 7.

BROWNE, Benjamin

563. John Brookesbanke; Abraham; Reding, Berks; Cl; 2.10.1699; 2.10.1699; - ; 7.

564. Joshua Fulford; John; Newport Pagnell, Bucks; Brazier; 7.6.1697; 7.6.1696; 12.6.1704; 7.

BROWNE, Charles

565. Benjamin Mynd. Fd by Charles & John Browne 8.4.1695. Bd (as Mind) to John Browne (q.v.) 5.3.1688.

566. Edward Scoles; William (d); parish of St Sepulchres, London; L; 6.6.1692; 6.6.1692; - ; 7.

BROWNE, Christopher

567. [Christopher Browne, 'haveing served 5 yeares of his time to a member of the Merchantalers Company', fd 2.7.1688 by order of the Mayor and Court of Aldermen, paying 28s. 2d.]

568. John Dennis; Arthur; Stoney Stratford, Bucks; Cd; 7.8.1693; 7.8.1693; 2.12.1700; 7.

569. George Miller; Mathew; Stony Stratford, Bucks; I; 6.4.1696; 6.4.1696; - ; 7.

BROWNE, Daniel

570. Thomas Browne; Daniell; London; C & St; 8.4.1700; 8.4.1700; - ; 7. Bd to his father.

571. Francis Coggan. Bd to William Miller (q.v.) 7.10.1689; t.o. on Miller's death to Browne 10.9.1694.

572. Tobias Collyer; Tobias (d); London; C & Ha; 6.8.1688; 6.8.1688; - ; 8.

573. Amos Coppleston. Fd by Browne and Benjamin Webster 7.10. [1700]. Bd to Webster (q.v.) 3.10.1692.

574. Nicholas Cox; Nicholas; London; C & St; 4.9.1693; 4.9.1693. - ; 7.

575. John Lowdom; Stephen (d); Rumford, Essex; Y; 1.6.1674; 1.6.1674; 6.3.1682; 7.

576. Francis Mills; Francis; London; C & Gr; 4.7.1687. 4.7.1687; - ; 7.

577. Stephen Pidgeon; Jno; Chidley, Sussex; G; 6.8.1683; 6.8.1683; - ; 7.

BROWNE, Henry

578. John White. Fd by Browne 4.5.1641. Bd to him 19.1.1620.

BROWNE, John, I

579. John Browne. Fd by patrimony 3.7.1654.

580. Daniell Scamodyn; Robte; Barnesley, Yorks; Tn; 4.5.1641; 4.5.1641; - ; 7.

BROWNE, John, II

581. Edward Fowkes; Robt; Llanvehan, Mont; Cl; 6.11.1654; 6.11.1654; 16.12.1661; 7.

BROWNE, John, III

582. Benjamin Mind; John (d); Dublin, Ireland; Mch; 5.3.1688; 5.3.1688; 8.4.1695; 7. Fd by John and Charles Browne.

BROWNE, Nathaniel

583. [Nathaniell Browne. Fd by patrimony 3.8.1646.]

584. John Tedd; Francis; City of Coventrey, [War]; I; 6.10.1673; 6.10.1673; - ; 7.

BROWNE, Phillipp

585. [Phillipp Browne. Son of Nicholas Browne; fd by patrimony 1.8.1687.]

BROWNE, Robert

586. Richard Paine; Richard; Bramston, N'hants; Y; 2.4.1655; 2.4.1655; 7.4.1662; 7. Fd by Browne and Mathias Thurston.

BROWNE, Samuel

587. Humphrey Lorkin; John; Rochester, Kent; Cl; 22.3.1642; 22.3.1642; - ; 7.

588. Arthur Otway. Bd to Nicholas Fussell 7.12.1635; t.o. to 'Mr Browne' 29.3.1641 to serve out his time 'Except the last yeare'. Fd by Fussell 3.8.1646. There is no record of Browne's christian name.

589. Richard Richardson. Fd by Browne and Thomas Maud 5.3.1655. Bd to Maud (q.v.) 4.10.1647.

BRUDNELL, Elizabeth, Widow

590. Richard Man; Thomas; Isbrooke, Staffs; Cl; 7.1.1656; 7.1.1656; 19.1.1663. 8.

BRUDNELL, John

591. John Brudenell. Fd by patrimony 1.9.1690.

592. Moses Brudenell. Fd by patrimony 4.9.1699.

593. Clement Williams; Richard; London; C & Cw; 10.6.1661; 10.6.1661; 26.6.1668; 7. Fd by Brudnell and Ann Maxwell.

BRUDNELL, Thomas

594. Henry Barrow; Anthony; Citty of Worcester; Clothier; 14.6.1647; 14.6.1647; 27.6.1654; 7.

595. John Brudnell. Fd by patrimony 7.2.1659.

596. Anthony Brundnell; William (d); Stratford, Suff; Clothier; 4.12.1648; 4.12.1648; 7.1.1656; 8. Fd as Brudnell.

597. Robert Guss; Robert; London; L; 4.8.1651; 4.8.1651; - ; 8.

598. John Rud; John; London; C & Ca; 6.2.1643; 6.2.1643; - ; 7.

BRUEN, Thomas

599. Daniel King; Daniel; Esson, Glos; T; 7.3.1687; 7.3.1687; - ; 7.

600. Walter Yates; William; Aston, Ches; Y; 6.6.1687; 6.6.1687; - ; 7.

BRUGIS, Henry
601. Richard Brugis. Fd by patrimony 7.3.1692.
602. John Harrison; John; Marlow, Bucks; Y; 3.12.1683; 3.12.1683; 2.10.1693; 7. Fd by Alexander Milbourne.
603. Richard Meade; Richard; London; C & D; 3.9.1660; 3.9.1660; 8.10.1667; 7. Fd by Brugis and Henry Lloyd.
604. John Palmer; John; London; C & Ha; 6.3.1671; 6.3.1671; - ; 7.
605. Nathaniel Warden; Benjamin; London; C & Ca; 6.8.1677; 6.8.1677; 3.2.1685; 7. Fd by Henry Hills Junior.

BUCK, Peter
606. Richard Browne; Richard; Milbourne Wick, Som; G; 5.2.1694; 5.1.1694; - ; 7.

BUCKLER, Christopher
607. William Barlowe; William; London; C & Gr; 7.4.1671; 7.4.1671; - ; 7.
608. Leonard Huttchinson; Alexander; Chancery Lane, [London]; Plasterer; 3.8.1663; 1.7.1663; - ; 8.

BUCKLER, William
609. Christopher Buckler. Fd by patrimony 4.7.1663.
610. Joseph Gwillym; Stephen; Isleworth, M'sex; G; 23.6.1651; 23.6.1651; - ; 7.

BULKERY, John
611. [John Bulkery. Fd by patrimony 3.5.1680.]

BULLEN, John
612. [John Bullen. Fd by redemption 6.3.1676.]

BURDETT, John
613. Charles Burdett. Fd by patrimony 13.3.1693.
614. Francis Burdett; John; London, C & St; 8.11.1669; 8.11.1669; - ; 7. Bd to his father.
615. William Hall; Robt; London; C & MT; 2.8.1658; 24.6.1658; - ; 8.

616. Samuell Hoyle; Robt; Almonbury, Yorks; Y; 11.6.1655; 25.6.1655; 7.7.1662; 7.
617. Geo Squire; Wm; London; Porter; 24.5.1647; 24.5.1647; - ; 7.

BURGIS, Michael
618. Stephen Bateman; Hen; Strickland Kettle, W'land; Y; 26.3.1657; 26.3.1657; 6.12.1669; 8.
619. John Burton; Richard; Swinton, Yorks; Y; 4.10.1652; 4.10.1652; - ; 7.

BURGIS, Simon
620. Wm Dagnell; Wm (d); Barkhamsted, Herts; G; 2.12.1689; 2.12.1689; - ; 7.

BURREL, Thomas
621. John Gay. Fd by Burrel 3.5.1680. Bd to Francis Smith (q.v.) 3.2.1673.

BURROUGH, Robert
622. Thomas Burrow. Fd by patrimony 18.6.1689. Robert Burrough is described as 'a late member of this Company'.
623. Lyonell Daniell; Lyonell (d); London; C & Ha; 1.10.1650; 24.6.1650; - ; 8.
624. Edward Spence; Robte; Barkham, Sussex; G; 21.6.1645; 24.6.1645; - ; 8.
625. Roger Ive. Fd by Burrough and Samuel Petty 10.3.1645. Bd to Petty 5.3.1638; t.o. from Burrough to Nicholas Bourne 4.12.1643.
626. William Vezey; William; Tanton, Oxon; G; 13.11.1650; 13.11.1650; - ; 7.

BURROUGHS, John
627. John Blague; Wm (d); London; C & BSg; 30.10.1642; 1.11.1642; 4.11.1650; 8.
628. James Cole; Jonas; London; Pavier; 6.4.1653; 6.4.1653; 26.4.1661; 8.

629. Thomas Deakills; Wm (d); London; C & MT; 4.5.1641; 1.5.1641; - ; 9.

BURTON, Richard
630. James Hampson. Fd by Burton 6.7.1671. Apparently never formally bd.
631. Richard Hardy; Nicholas (d); Peterburough, N'hants; Bs; 8.10.1669; 8.10.1669; 6.11.1676; 7. Fd as Harding.
632. Andrew Hawkesworth; Thomas; London; Y; 5.9.1653; 5.9.1653; 26.3. 1661; 7. Originally bd to William Tyton (q.v.) 25.4.1650. Fd by Burton.
633. Richard Motherby; Henry; Cowick, Yorks; Y; 13.1.1642; 13.1. 1642; - ; 8.

BURTON, Simon
634. John Alford; James; London; C & Gr; 2.9.1661; 2.9.1661; - ; 7.
635. Simon Burton. Fd by patrimony 1.4.1672.
636. William Clayton; Thomas; London; G; 4.5.1674; 4.5.1674; 11.4.1681; 7. The entry of freedom describes Burton as deceased and Clayton as t.o. to Richard Barwell.
637. John Dier; John; Greewich, Kent; T; 4.11.1672; 4.11.1672; - ; 7.
638. Richard Taylor; Rich; Ramsey, Essex; Cl; 6.11.1655; 6.11.1655 - ; 7.

BUSH, Edward
639. Charles Combes; - ; - , - ; - ; 22.6.1697; 22.6.1697; - ; 7.

BUTTER, John
640. John Bradford; William (d); Waldston, Leics; Y; 6.3.1676; 6.3.1676; - ; 7.
641. Thomas Butter; George; Newent, Glos; Y; 6.10.1673; 6.10.1673; - ; 7.
642. William Fowkes; William; St Giles Cripplegate, London; L; 2.8. 1680; 2.8.1680; - ; 7.

BUTTER, Nathaniel
643. Robte Duke. Fd by Butter 21.4.1645. Bd to him 10.11.1635.
644. Richard Moore. Bd to Butter 4.4.1636; t.o. to Henry Twiford 4.5.1641.

BYFIELD, Adoniram
645. William Blackerby; Francis; London; C & V; 5.1.1657; 5.1.1657; - ; 8.
646. Thomas Taylor; Thomas; Burbidge, Wilts; Cl; 2.4.1660; 2.4.1660; - ; 7.

CADMAN, William
647. William Clark; James; Stoke, N'hants; Cl; 8.1.1672; 8.1.1672; - ; 7.
648. Gilbert Coundley; Gilbert; St Martins in ye Feilds, M'sex; - ; 3.11.1679; 3.11.1679; - ; 7.
649. Willm Hough; Thomas (d); Creston, Lancs; H; 16.9.1668; 16.9. 1668; - ; 7. Cadman's name is wrongly given as Gadman, Preston as Creston.
650. John Roffey; John; St Brides, London; G; 6.8.1677; 6.8.1677; - ; 7.
651. James Wardlow; Andrew; Edenburge in ye Kingdome of Scotland; Mch; 4.12.1682; 4.12.1682 - ; 7.

CADWELL, John
652. Mathias Sherwood; Robt; London; C & Cu; 28.3.1659; 28.3.1659; - ; 8.

CALCOTT, Robert
653. John Boucher; John; London; Sc; 5.8.1678; 5.8.1678; - ; 7.

CALVERT, Elizabeth, Widow
654. Thomas Corbett; Waties; Elton, Herefs; G; 9.2.1674; 9.2.1674; - ; 7.
655. Richard Pinder; John (d); Ashfeild, Rut; G; 12.6.1666; 12.6.1666; - ; 7.

656. Daniell Silver; Willm; high Wickham, Bucks; Y; 7.4.1668; 7.4. 1668; - ; 7.

657. Samuell Steele; Richard; late of Betley, Staffs ('now of London'); Cl; 4.7.1670; 4.7.1670; - ; 7.

658. Joshua Waterhouse. Fd by Mrs Calvert and John Hancocke 2.8.1669. Bd to Hancocke (q.v.) 5.5.1662.

CALVERT, George

659. Owen Braddy; William; Wells, Som; Y; 7.8.1654; 7.8.1654; - ; 7.

660. Simon Burges; Simon; Taham, Oxon; Pw; 6.2.1682; 6.2.1682; 4.3. 1689; 8. Fd by Thomas Sheppard and fined 2s. 6d. 'for his being turned over'.

661. Nathaniell Calvert. Fd by patrimony 5.10.1663.

662. Samuell Ferrice; Samuell; Beverly, Yorks; Cl; 11.6.1655; 11.6. 1655; 7.7.1662; 7. Fd as Herrice.

663. Stephen Foster. Bd to William Shrewsbury (q.v.) 6.11.1671; t.o. to Calvert 9.2.1674. Fd by Mrs. Taylor 2.12.1678.

664. William Grantham; Hugh; Southampton, [Hants]; 18.6.1677; 18.6.1677; 10.6.1684; 7.

665. Christopher Hussey; Christopher (d); Winchester, S'hants; G; 7.8.1666; 24.6.1666; 1.9.1673; 7.

666. Henry Roades; Henry; St Mary Overies, Southwark [Surr]; Cd; 19.5.1675; 19.5.1675; - ; 7.

667. Samuell Sprint; John (d); Hampsted, M'sex; Cl; 1.3.1659; 1.3. 1659; 2.4.1666; 7.

668. John Symms. Fd by Calvert and Christopher Reisold 16.1.1656. Bd to Reisold (q.v.) 10.1.1649.

669. Ralph Symson; Thomas; Chalbury, Oxon; Sh; 5.7.1669; 5.7.1669; 4.9.1676; 7. Fd as Simpson.

670. Francis Tindall; Felix; Plumsted, Kent; Y; 4.11.1644; 4.11.1644; - ; 7.

671. Elisha Wallis; Tho; London; C & BSg; 23.6.1646; 1.6.1646; 4.7. 1653; 9.

CALVERT, Giles

672. Thomas Brewster. Fd by Calvert 3.11.1647. Bd to him 28.9.1640.

673. Henry Millyn; Lewis; Coventry, [War]; Clothier; 6.6.1653; 6.6. 1653; 27.6.1660; 7.

674. Richard Moone; Richard; City of Bristoll; Farrier; 12.9.1645; 12.9. 1645; 11.10.1652; 9.

675. Gregory Moule. Bd to Joseph Hunscott (q.v.) 14.5.1642; t.o. to Calvert 22.5.1644. Fd by Hunscott 23.6.1649.

676. Mathias Stephenson; Richard; London; C & Gr; 3.3.1662; 3.3.1662; - ; 7.

677. Samuell Tailor; John; Ipswich, Suff; G; 5.9.1653; 5.9.1653; - ; 7.

678. Mathias Walker; Will; Darnell, Yorks; Cu; 3.12.1655; 3.12.1655; 3.8. 1663; 7. Fd as Mathew Walker.

679. Daniell White; Daniell; Hatfeild, Herts; G; 2.9.1650; 2.9.1650; 7.9.1657; 7.

CANNING, William

680. John Williams; John; parish of St Andrew Holborne, M'sex; I; 10.8.1686; 10.8.1686; - ; 7.

681. Bryan Wilson; Bryan; London; C & Waxchandler; 6.6.1687; 6.6.1687; - ; 7. T.o. (as William Bryan) 2.3.1691 to Joseph Raven.

CAPE, Simon

682. John Amery. Fd by Cape 8.10. 1669. Apparently not formally bd.

CAREY, Edward

683. John Lee; William (d); Oldstreete, M'sex; Bl; 5.9.1664; 4.7.1664; - ; 7.

CARPENTER, Thomas

684. Richard Ingersole; Edw (d); Hitchin, Herts; Br; 4.9.1676; 4.9.1676; - ; 7.

CARR, John

685. John Hudgibutt. Fd by Carr 7.10.1672. Apparently never formally bd.

686. Samuel Scott. Fd by Carr 6.6.1687. Fined 2s. 6d. 'for not being turned over ye Hall'.

CARR, Samuel

687. James Blackwell. Bd to John Place (q.v.) 4.9.1682; t.o. to Carr 3.10. 1687. Fd by Place 7.10.1689.

688. Jeremiah Bowes; Robert (d); London; C & Go; 6.7.1678; 6.7.1678; - ; 7.

689. Timothy Child; Timothy; London; C & Draper; 4.8.1679; 4.8.1679; 1.12.1690; 7. T.o. to Abel Swale (n.d.) and fd by him, but fined 2s. 6d. 'For not being turned over at the Hall'.

CARTER, Henry

690. William Chapman; William; Stanstead, Herts; Y; 8.6.1696; 8.6. 1696; 1.7.1706; 7.

691. Thomas Franklyn; Richard; Wilsdon, M'sex; H; 2.4.1694; 2.4.1694; 9.2.1702; 7.

692. Benjn Hill; Benjamin (d); London; C & Ha; 3.3.1690; 3.3.1690; - ; 7.

693. William Hunt; William; St Albans, Herts; Tobacco-pipe-maker; 5.2.1700; 5.2.1700; - ; 7.

694. Philip Reding; Henry; Langley, Bucks; G; 3.10.1687; 3.10.1687; - ; 7.

695. William Smith; Peter; St Gyles in the Fields, M'sex; Bricklayer; 7.11.1687; 7.11.1687; 7.11.1698; 8.

696. Wm Watson; William (d); Cullingham, Notts; - ; 1.8.1692; 1.8.1692; 7.8.1699; 7.

CARTER, John

697. John Ball; Wm (d); litle Horsley, Essex; G; 3.8.1646; 3.8.1646; 5.9.1653; 7.

698. John Dormer; John; Kaigworth, Leics; G; 17.1.1650; 17.1.1650; 7.6.1658; 7.

699. William Chedley; Willm; Odiham, S'hants; G; 3.11.1656; 3.11.1656; - ; 7.

700. Francis Lovell; John; Ilford, Essex; G; 3.5.1658; 3.5.1658; 20.5. 1668; 7.

701. Michaell Markham; Michaell; Rumford, Essex; B; 4.8.1656; 4.8.1656; 4.4.1664; 7.

702. Andrew Pennington; Anthony; Northweald-Bassey, Essex; Y; 29.3. 1641; 29.3.1641; - ; 7.

703. Clement Saywell. Fd by Carter 6.8.1649. Bd to him as Isaac Saywell 12.11.1638.

704. Richard Snart; Thomas (d); London; C & Gr; 7.7.1656; 7.7.1656; - ; 7.

CARTWRIGHT, Richard

705. Wm Carr; Wm; Rausby, Lincs; G; 1.7.1647; 1.7.1647; - ; 7.

CARTWRIGHT, Samuel

706. Samuell Cartwright; Samuell; London; C & St; 30.6.1645; 30.6.1645; 2.4.1655; 7. Bd to his father.

707. Richard Collins. Fd by Michael Sparkes 8.11.1641. Bd to Cartwright 27.10.1634.

708. Thomas Walrond; John; litle Hinton, Wilts; G; 7.6.1641; 7.6.1641; - ; 7.

CARTWRIGHT, William

709. John Dallow; Thomas (d); Coventry, War; - ; 2.11.1663; 2.11. 1663; - ; 7.

CASTLE, George

710. [George Castle. Fd by redemption 2.3.1685. In addition to the usual admittance fee of 3s. 4d. Castle paid a fine of £5. 5s.]

CATER, Joseph

711. Hen Evans; Henry (d); London; C & St; 3.11.1679; 3.11.1679; 2.4.1688; 8. Fd by 'Joseph Carter' and fined 2s. 6d. 'for not being turned over at the Hall'. Probably fd by Joseph Cater Junior who was fd by Henry Evans Senior (q.v.) 7.7.1679.

712. John Gifford; John (d); London; C & Cd; 5.7.1675; 5.7.1675; 7.8.1682; 7. Fd as Robert Gifford.

713. Nathaniell Hilliard; Mathew (d); London; C & Upholder; 1.12.1662; 1.12.1662; 7.8.1671; 8. Bd to 'Joseph Coates', otherwise unknown and clearly an error for Cater. Fd by Cater.

714. Benjamine Machen; William; Sutton, Notts; H; 12.8.1671; 12.8.1671; - ; 8.

715. Thomas Martyn; Samuell; Burrough of Leicester; D; 6.2.1682; 6.2.1682; 5.12.1698; 7. T.o. to Andrew Sowle (n.d.). Fd by Cater and Sowle.

716. John Newton; John; Burrough of Leicester; T; 2.6.1656; 2.6.1656; 26.3.1670; 8.

CERTAINE, William

717. Thomas Blyton; Samuell; London; Silkweaver; 2.8.1647; 2.8.1647; - ; 7.

718. George Flood; Isaac (d); London; Surgeon; 29.3.1641; 29.3.1641; 4.12.1648; 7.

719. Robert Shephard; Richard (d); London; C & Cw; 2.3.1657; 2.3.1657; - ; 7. Certaine's name is given as Sartaine.

720. George Thomas; William (d); Martins in the feilds; Y; 16.5.1645; 16.5.1645; - ; 8.

CHAMNEY, John

721. Anthoney Boyce; Anthoney; Petworth, Surr; H; 3.10.1670; 3.10.1670; - ; 7.

722. Samuell Pollard; Ralph; Hallifax, Yorks; Clothier; 8.6.1668; 8.6.

1668; - ; 8. Chamney's name is given as Chamley.

CHANDOS, James

723. [James Lord Chandos. 'The right honoble James Lord Chandos Baron of Suedly admitted to the Freedome of This Company' 5.8.1690. No charge.]

CHANTLER, James

724. Ralph Burrell; Timothy (d); Newcastle vpon Tyne; Mch; 14.2.1649; 25.3.1649; - ; 7.

CHAPLAINE, Sampson

725. Richard Hiller. Fd by Chaplaine 7.7.1690. Bd to John Rix (q.v.) 8.11.1680. T.o. to Chaplaine (n.d.), but fined 2s. 6d. 'for not being turned ouer att the Hall'.

CHAPMAN, Lawrence

726. Thomas Hutchens; John (d); St Andrews Holborne, London; G; 2.11.1646; 29.9.1646; 13.12.1654; 8. Fd by Chapman and John Field.

CHAPMAN, Livewell

727. Nathaniell Crouch; Thomas; Lewes, Sussex; T; 5.5.1656; 5.5.1656; 7.11.1664; 7.

CHAPMAN, Peter

728. Joseph Moore. Fd by Chapman and Francis Jones 26.3.1644. Bd to Chapman 6.3.1637.

CHAPMAN, William

729. William Chapman. Fd by patrimony 7.2.1676.

730. Christopher Tod; Robte; Pickering, Yorks; Y; 3.11.1647; 3.11.1647; 4.12.1654; 7.

CHAPPELL, John

731. Wm Brampton; John (d); London; C & Dy; 10.10.1642; 10.10.1642; 28.4.1651; 9.

732. Wm Chappell; John; London; C & St; 3.11.1645; 3.11.1645; - ; 8. Bd to his father.

733. John Hooper. Fd by Chappell 31.12.1649. Bd to him 19.12.1634.

CHARLES, William

734. Aaron Loveday; Moses; Brackley, N'hants; M; 4.10.1669; 4.10.1669; - ; 7.

735. Henry Thompson; John (d); City of Westmr; I; 4.7.1692; 4.7.1692; - ; 7.

CHARLETON, Francis

736. [Francis Charleton. Fd 'Gratis' 7.10.1689.]

CHARNLEY, Thomas

737. Thomas Charnlee. Fd by patrimony 5.12.1692.

738. William Coltman. Fd by Charnley 30.5.1687. Apparently never formally bd, unless this is the man bd to William Leybourne (q.v.) 1.12.1651.

CHASE, Henry

739. James Chase. Fd by patrimony 3.7.1693.

740. Thomas Jones. Fd by Chase 7.11.1664. Apparently never formally bd, but a Thomas James was bd to a Thomas Chase (q.v.) 5.10.1657.

741. John Penn. T.o. from Chase to Edmond Paxton 3.5.1669, but there is no record of the original binding.

742. Richard Walker; Thomas; Peterfeild, S'hants; G; 2.3.1663; 2.3. 1663; - ; 7.

CHASE, James

743. Thomas Chessell; Samuell; St Giles in the Feildes, M'sex; Cd; 1.7. 1695; 29.9.1694; - ; 7.

CHASE, Thomas

744. Thomas James; Henry (d); Awer, Glos; Cl; 5.10.1657; 5.10.1657; - ; 7. This entry is probably meant to refer to a Thomas Jones, fd by Henry Chase (q.v.) 7.11.1664.

CHATFIELD, Stephen

745. Samuell Burroughs; Samuell (d); London; C & Mr; 5.5.1656; 5.5. 1656; - ; 8.

CHEESE, Richard

746. Richard Cheese; Richard; London; C & St; 5.12.1681; 5.12.1681; 6.5.1685; 7. Bd to his father. Fd by patrimony.

CHEESE, Tace, Widow

747. Edward Saunders; Richard; Wendress, Glos; H; 4.6.1694; 4.6.1694; 3.11.1701; 7.

CHILDE, Thomas

748. Thomas Daniell. Fd by Childe and Francis Leach 7.7.1662. Bd to Leach (q.v.) 2.7.1655.

749. William Godwin; Ralph; London; C & D; 13.6.1659; 13.6.1659; 10.1.1670; 7.

750. John Shadd; Rich (d); London; - ; 11.4.1673; 11.4.1673; 3.5.1680; 7.

CHILDE, Timothy

751. William Kempster; William; London; C & Mason; 4.10.1697; 4.10. 1697; - ; 7.

CHISWELL, Richard

752. [Richard Chiswell. Admitted to the freedom of the Company 4.11.1678 'Gratis'.]

753. Benjn Cowse; William (d); London; C & St; 1.8.1692; 1.8.1692; 3.2.1701; 8. Bd 'Gratis'.

754. John Hawys; Wm (d); Norwich; Mch; 1.3.1680; 1.3.1680; - ; 8.

755. Jacob Huse; Abraham; Oakingham, Wilts [sic for Berks]; G; 6.8. 1683; 6.8.1683; - ; 8.

756. Daniel Midwinter; Daniel; London; C & Leatherseller; 9.9.1689; 9.9.1689; 7.2.1698; 8.

757. Nathaniel Rolls. Fd by Chiswell 3.2.1680. Apparently never formally bd.

758. Humphrey White; Peter; London; C & Ha; 1.2.1686; 1.2.1686; - ; 8.

CHOLMLEY, John

759. Phillipp Cholmley. Fd by patrimony 6.11.1693.

[29]

760. John Greene; John; Itam, Berks; Y; 3.11.1684; 3.11.1684; 9.2. 1702; 7. Fd by Cholmley and Samuel Walshall.

761. John Kingston; John (d); St Giles Cripplegate, [London]; Ca; 4.10.1675; 4.10.1675; - ; 7.

762. Moreton Peale; Moreton; London; G; 2.10.1682; 2.10.1682; 2.11. 1691; 8. Fd by Robert Gifford.

CHURCHILL, Awnsham

763. John Everingham; William; Navenby, Lincs; G; 3.7.1682; 3.7.1682; 5.8.1689; 7.

764. Edward Morey; Edwd; Michel Dever, Hants; Cl; 1.3.1683; 1.3.1683; 3.3.1690; 7.

765. Wm Moulton; Thomas; parish of St Martins, M'sex; G; 20.12.1689; 20.12.1689 - ; 7.

CHURCHILL, William

766. Peter Buck; John (d); Cobham, Kent; Minister; 6.10.1684; 6.10.1684; 2.11.1691; 7. T.o. to Christopher Wilkinson 22.12.1685. Fd by Churchill.

767. No entry.

CLARKE, Andrew

768. John Flower; Seth; St Martyns in the Feilds, [M'sex]; Barber; 5.6.1671; 5.6.1671; 1.7.1678; 7. Fd by Mary Clarke.

769. Mathew Morrice; Mathew; London; C & St; 5.9.1670; 5.9.1670; 1.10.1677; 7.

770. John Plyer; John (d); London; - ; 2.8.1675; 2.8.1675; - ; 7.

771. James Thrift; Edward (d); Gorsham, Wilts; Y; 8.11.1669; 8.11. 1669; - 7.

CLARKE, Benjamin

772. Fish Branston; Richard (d); Bowden Magna, Leics; Poulterer; 2.4. 1677; 2.4.1677; 2.3.1685; 7.

773. Samuell Manship; John; Gilford, Surr; - ; 5.8.1678; 5.8.1678; 6.9.1686; 7.

774. Thomas Northcott. Fd by Clarke 3.12.1684. Apparently never formally bd.

CLARKE, Francis

775. Thomas Clarke; Thomas (d); Witney, Oxon; Y; 7.11.1681; 7.11.1681; - ; 7.

776. Robert Crofts. Fd by Clarke 1.8.1687. Fined 2s. 6d. 'For his not being bound at the Hall' and a further 2s. 6d. 'For his not being turned over at the Hall'.

777. Lawrence Veze; John; London; C & Sk; 4.7.1687; 4.7.1687; 6.8.1694; 7. Fd by Clarke and Freeman Collins.

CLARKE, Hannah, Widow

778. John Barber. Fd by Hannah Clarke and George Larkin 6.6.1696. Bd to Larkin (q.v.) 6.5.1689.

779. Peter Clarke; Henry (d); parish of St Bennetts Pauls Wharfe, [London]; Printer; 11.11.1695; 11.11.1695; 5.7. 1714; 7.

780. James Davis; James; London; C & Weaver; 9.9.1700; 9.9.1700; 12.4.1708; 7.

781. John Greswell; John (d); Princes Street in Covent Garden, M'sex; Glazier; 7.12.1691; 7.12.1691; - ; 8.

782. Luke Weedon; John; Citty of Oxford; Printer; 6.7.1696; 6.7.1696; 5.7.1703; 7.

CLARKE, Henry

783. Richard Awnsham; Rich; London; V; 2.7.1677; 2.7.1677; - ; 7.

784. Thomas Boddington; Edward; Colebrook, Bucks; G; 22.1.1670; 22.1. 1670; 12.2.1677; 7.

785. Charles Brower; John (d); Abbots Langley, Herts; Y; 8.7.1668; 8.7.1668; - ; 7.

786. Thomas Burditt. Fd by Clarke 1.10.1688. Originally bd to Mary White; t.o. to John Heptinstall; t.o. again to Henry Clarke. Fined 2s. 6d.

'for his not being turned over at this Hall'. There is no formal entry of binding.

787. John Clark; Francis; Barkhairstead, Herts; G; 2.5.1670; 29.9.1669; 1.10.1677; 8.

788. Joseph Clerke; Edward; Hemel Hampstead, Herts; Y; 21.1.1662; 29.9.1661; - ; 8.

789. William Hall; Henry; ye Parish of St. Andrews Holborne, M'sex; Cu; 7.5.1683; 7.5.1683; - ; 7.

790. John Hooker; John; Masworth, Bucks; Cl: 4.9.1682; 4.9.1682; - ; 7.

791. Nathaniell Jenner; Sir Thomas; London; Knight, Sergeant at Law and Recorder of the City of London; 1.6.1685; 1.6.1685; - ; 7.

792. Thomas Kerby; Tho (d); London; C & Gr; 6.8.1655; 6.8.1655; 3.8.1663; 8.

793. Wm Moulson. Fd by Clarke 7.12.1691, and fined 2s. 6d. for being bd by a foreign indenture.

794. James Oades; William (d); Reading, Berks; Clothier; 5.10.1663; 5.10.1663; 7.11.1670; 7.

795. James Stone; John (d); Hemellhempsted, Herts; G; 5.5.1673; 5.5.1673; - ; 7.

796. Francis Thornborrow; George; parish of Tuxford, Notts; I; 13.5.1678; 13.5.1678; 6.5.1686; 7.

797. Benjamin Wilcocks; Joseph; Harrow on the Hill, M'sex; Vicar; 2.4.1688; 29.6.1688; - ; 7.

CLARKE, John, I

798. Wm Chapman. Fd by Clarke 5.10.1646. Bd to him 1.10.1638.

799. John Clarke. Fd by patrimony 6.9.1641.

800. Thomas Clarke; Willm; Shaperwicke, Som; Y; 11.7.1650; 11.7.1650; 14.6.1658; 8.

801. Jonathan Deeves. Fd by Clarke 6.4.1657. Bd to him 4.12.1637.

802. Samuell Franklyn; George; London; C & Cw; 7.5.1666; 7.5.1666; - ; 8.

803. John Vaston; John; Dukes place, London; G; 2.11.1658; 2.11.1658; - ; 8.

CLARKE, John, II

804. Samuel Amy; - ; St Giles Cripplegate, [London]; Apothecary; 3.5.1675; 3.5.1675; - ; 8.

805. William Carrington; Tho; Clifton, Beds; G; 2.10.1654; 2.10.1654; 4.11.1661; 7.

806. John Clark; Jeremiah (d); London; C & Poulterer; 6.9.1675; 6.9.1675; - ; 7.

807. Peter Dring; Mathias; Highworth, Wilts; D; 4.10.1652; 25.3.1652; 2.4.1660; 8.

808. John Dutton; Richard; Croell, Oxon; Y; 5.9.1687; 5.9.1687; 3.12.1694; 7.

809. Nathaniel Eyton; Sampson (d); Spond, Herefs; G; 1.9.1684; 1.9.1684; - ; 7.

810. Thomas Greene; Roger; London; C & MT; 3.9.1688; 3.9.1688; - ; 8.

811. Thomas Guy; Thomas (d); London; C & Ca; 3.9.1660; 24.6.1660; 7.10.1668; 8.

812. Richard Kell; Richard (d); London; C & Weaver; 3.7.1682; 3.7.1682; - ; 7.

813. John Lazenby; Robert; St Aubins, Herts; Y; 3.2.1679; 3.2.1679; - ; 7.

814. John Man. Fd by Clarke 1.8.1687. Fined 2s. 6d. 'For not being turned over at the Hall'.

815. Thomas Meades; Thomas (d); Warwick; G; 1.5.1676; 1.5.1676; - ; 7.

816. Timothy Nost; Willm; Thames Dytton, Surr; H; 4.6.1667; 24.6.1667; - ; 7.

817. Thomas Parkehurst; John; litle watring, Essex; Cl; 1.9.1645; 24.6.1645; 3.7.1654; 9.

818. Ruben Terrywest; William; Owndle, N'hants; - ; 3.7.1671; 3.7.1671; - ; 7.

819. Nathaniell Wolfe; Nathaniell; London; C & V; 7.4.1668; 7.4.1668; 7.6.1675; 7.

820. Nicholas Woolfe. Fd by John Clarke 3.5.1675. Apparently never formally bd. Presumably distinct from the preceding.

CLARKE, Mary, Widow

821. William Browne; William (d); London; Sh; 6.6.1681; 6.6.1681; 15.6. 1688; 7. Mary Clarke is described as 'late wife of Andrew Clarke'.

822. Charles Crafford; Richard; Citty of Oxon; Cd. T.o. to Mary Clarke 8.5.1682, and described as originally bd to Henry Hall, but there is no other entry of binding. Fd by Mary Clarke 1.2.1686.

823. John Flower. Fd by Mary Clarke 1.7.1678. Bd to Andrew Clarke (q.v.) 5.6.1671.

824. Charles Robinson; John (d); London; G; 8.5.1682; 8.5.1682; 29.5. 1689; 7. Mary Clarke is described as the widow of Andrew Clarke.

825. Morice Thellwell; Symon (d); London; C & Draper; 1.7.1678; 1.7.1678; - ; 7.

826. Tho Tristram; Edlin (d); Hertford; T; 3.5.1680; 3.5.1680; - ; 7.

827. Robert Whip; John; parish of Hinton Parva, Wilts; - ; 5.8.1678; 5.8.1678; 1.2.1686; 7.

CLARKE, Richard, I

828. Thomas Clarke. Fd by Clarke 25.10.1647. Bd to him 4.5.1640.

829. Thomas Clarke. Fd by patrimony 1.5.1671.

830. Stephen Cope; Stephen; Pidley, Hunts; Y; 2.3.1646; 2.3.1646; 5.3.1655; 9.

CLARKE, Richard, II

831. Thomas Chamberlayne; Edward; Ockelepitchard, Herefs; - ; 12.8.1671; 12.8.1671; 4.11.1678; 7.

832. Edward Rakins; Edward; Moreclocke, Surr; Waterman; 7.11. 1659; 7.11.1659; 12.11.1667; 7. Fd as Rawkins.

833. William Richardson; William; London; C & St; 11.10.1680; 24.6.1680; 3.7.1693; 8.

834. Richard Sambach; Wm; Broadway, Worc; Y; 6.3.1654; 1.1.1654; 3.3.1662; 8. Fd as Sambage.

CLARKE, Robert

835. [Robert Clarke. Fd by patrimony 4.6.1649.]

CLARKE, Samuel

836. [Samuell Clarke. Fd by redemption 6.4.1696.]

CLARKE, Thomas, I

837. Wm Bathoe; Tho; Duckington in the County Palatine, Ches; G; 20.12.1647; 20.12.1647; - ; 7.

838. William Bishop; John; East haddon, N'hants; T; 4.12.1654; 4.12. 1654; 1.9.1662; 8. Fd by Clarke and Robert Fletcher.

CLARKE, Thomas, II

839. Thomas Dunkin; Thomas; Canterbury, Kent; Mch; 11.5.1685; 11.5. 1685; - ; 7.

840. John How; George; St Martin in the Feilds, M'sex; Milliner; 1.8.1692; 1.8.1692; - ; 7.

841. William Kingsford; John; Canterbury, [Kent]; Milliner; 6.9.1680; 6.9.1680; - ; 7.

842. John Royley; Timothy; London; C & D; 4.11.1689; 4.11.1689; - ; 7.

CLARKE, William

843. William Clarke; Wm; London; C & St; 4.5.1641; 4.5.1641; - ; 7.

844. Richard Greenup. Fd by Clarke 15.1.1645. Bd to him 1.8.1637.

845. George Hadgley; Nath; Raydon, Essex; G; 7.3.1659; 7.3.1659; 26.3.1666; 7.

CLAVELL, Robert
846. Thomas Baker; Batholomew; Citty Worcester; G; 6.5.1700; 6.5.1700; - ; 7.

847. Benjamin Baldwin; Francis; London; Founder; 2.8.1680; 2.8.1680; 5.9.1687; 7.

848. Benjamin Crayle; Richard (d); Newark vpon Trent, Notts; G; 1.5.1676; 1.5.1676; 4.6.1683; 8.

849. Elias Givers; Thomas; parish of St Andrews Holbourne, M'sex; Tallowchandler; 6.8.1688; 6.8.1688; - ; 7.

850. Wm Hawes; John (d); Church Bedfont, M'sex; G; 29.5.1691; 29.5.1691; 6.6.1698; 7.

851. Edmond Lewis; Francis; Worth, Dors; Cl; 3.5.1658; 25.3.1658; - ; 8.

852. Jacob Samson; Ptolomeus; Totness, Dev; - ; 3.7.1671; 3.7.1671; 6.10.1678; 7.

853. John Senex; John; Ludlow, Shrops; G; 5.8.1695; 1.7.1695; 4.3.1706; 7.

854. Thomas Walker; William; Grantham, Lincs; Schoolmaster; 20.12.1682; 20.12.1682; 3.3.1690; 7.

CLAVELL, Roger
855. [Roger Clavell. Son of Roger Clavell; fd by redemption 24.10.1693.]

856. Charles Pittard; Robert; Tittenhall, Som; Cl; 7.12.1696; 2.11.1696; - ; 7. T.o. to Alexander Bosvile 4.7.1698.

CLAYTON, William
857. John Ausiter; Thomas (d); Norwood in the parish of Hayes, M'sex; G; 3.10.1681; 3.10.1681; 3.6.1689; 7.

CLEAVE, Isaac
858. John Bayley; John; London; C & St; 3.10.1698; 5.9.1698; 1.12.1707; 8.

859. James Lawrence; Henry; Long Ashton, Som; G; 4.3.1695; 4.3.1695; - ; 7.

860. Benja Southwood; Benjamine (d); London; C & St; 8.5.1682; 8.5.1682; - ; 7.

861. John Sturton; John; London; C & F; 5.8.1689; 5.8.1689; - ; 7.

CLEAVER, John
862. [John Cleaver. Fd by patrimony 27.3.1648.]

863. Gregory Poole; Willm; Cockerum, Lancs; H; 6.6.1659; 6.6.1659; 12.6.1666; 7.

CLEAVER, Samuel
864. Richard Barnes; Richard (d); London; C & St; 8.12.1656; 8.12.1656; 2.12.1668; 7.

865. Henry Cleaver. Fd by patrimony 2.12.1661.

CLERDUE, Francis
866. [Francis Clerdue. Son of Timothy Clerdue; fd by patrimony 6.4.1663.]

CLERKE, John
867. Joseph Button; John (d); Newcastle vpon Tyne, N'land; Bs; 2.10.1693; 2.10.1693; - ; 7.

868. [John Clerke. Fd 7.5.1688 'by Order of the Lord Major and Court of Aldern'.]

869. James Howard; John; Marson Trussell, N'hants; Cl; 2.12.1700; 2.12.1700; - ; 7.

870. Francis Prosser; John; Towne of Snowden in the parish of Peter Church, Herefs; G; 2.3.1696; 2.3.1696; - ; 7.

CLERKE, William
871. [William Clerke, 'Forrainer', fd by redemption 2.4.1688, paying £5.]

CLIFTON, Fulke
872. Josua Clifton. Fd by patrimony 3.10.1642.

873. Hezechias Usher. Fd by Clifton 7.2.1648. Bd to him 6.12.1630.

CLOWES, John
874. [John Clowes. Son of William Clowes; fd by patrimony 30.6.1645.]

875. Thomas Finch; Joseph (d); Cheston, Herts; Collarmaker; 1.10.1660; 1.10.1660; - ; 7.

876. Samuell Haughton. Fd by Clowes and Jane Coe 23.6.1652. Bd to Coe (q.v.) 5.5.1645.

CLUTTERBOOKE, Richard

877. John Mathewes. Fd by Clutterbooke and Richard Whitaker 17.1.1642. Bd to Clutterbooke 2.9.1633.

COCKERILL, Thomas, I

878. John Clarke; Thomas (d); [London]; C & Cw; 2.6.1679; 2.6.1679; - ; 8. A dense ink smudge obscures the entry.

879. Thomas Cockerill; Daniel; Collingtree, N'hants; Y; 7.5.1688; 7.5.1688; 3.6.1695; 7.

880. Thomas Glenister; John; London; C & Distiller; 6.5.1700; 6.5.1700; 3.11.1712; 7. Fd by John Wyatt.

881. Jonathan Greenwood. Fd by Cockerill 24.3.1680. Bd to William Birch (q.v.) 22.6.1670.

882. John Salisbury; Robert; Galtrinan, Den; G; 6.8.1677; 6.8.1677; 3.11.1684; 7.

883. Saml Wade; John; Hamersmith, M'sex; Cl; 3.12.1683; 3.12.1683; - ; 7.

884. Herbert Walwayne; Herbert; Bredwardine, Herefs; G; 7.7.1690; 7.7.1690; 6.6.1698; 7.

COCKERILL, Thomas, II

885. Richard Pampion; William; Escutt, N'hants; Y; 3.8.1696; 3.8.1696; - ; 7. Bd to Thomas Cockerill Junior.

COE, Andrew

886. [Andrew Coe. Fd by patrimony 2.2.1662.]

COE, Jane, Widow

887. Samuell Haughton; Lawrence; Mousley, Leics; Y; 5.5.1645; Easter Day 1645; 23.6.1652; 8. Fd by Jane Coe and John Clowes.

888. Leonard Hill; John (d); London; D; 24.5.1647; 24.5.1647; 5.2.1655; 8. Fd by Jane Coe and John Macocke.

COLE, James

889. [A James Cole was translated to the Weavers' Company 1.3.1666 (Court-Book D).]

890. Charles Burroughs; John (d); London; G; 7.6.1675; 7.6.1675; - ; 8.

891. Richard Holland; Nicholas; Haverford West, [Pembroke]; G; 1.9.1673; 1.9.1673; - ; 7.

892. James Holdrup; Henry (d); London; C & Weaver; 4.6.1667; 4.6.1667; - ; 7.

COLE, Peter

893. Stephen Chatfield; Thomas; Isefeild, Sussex; Y; 20.1.1645; 30.11.1644; 2.8.1652; 8.

894. Thomas Dingley; Thomas; Southampton; E; 1.3.1661; 1.3.1661; - ; 8.

895. Symon Dover; Symon; Bassenwaite, Cumb; Y; 14.6.1652; 14.6.1652; 5.3.1660; 7. Rebd to Gertrude Dawson (q.v.) 5.2.1655. Fd by Cole and Dawson.

896. Nathaniell Howell. Fd by Cole and John Hide 7.6.1658. Bd to Hide (q.v.) 2.6.1651.

897. James Nuthall. Fd by Cole 18.1.1647. Bd to him 2.12.1639.

898. Dixey Page. Fd by Cole and George Golborne 27.6.1664. Bd to Golborne (q.v.) 4.8.1656.

COLEBY, John

899. Humphrey Haward. Fd by Coleby 5.10.1646. Bd to him 11.5.1639.

COLEMAN, Henry

900. John Ward. Bd to William Cooper (q.v.) 6.5.1685; t.o. to Henry Coleman, 'Cittizen and Blacksmith of London', 6.9.1686.

COLES, Francis

901. Samuell Buncher; John (d); Paulers Perrey, N'hants; Y; 31.5.1650; 31.5.1650; - ; 7.

902. Henry Edsall; Henry; London; C & Turner; 2.4.1660; 1.5.1660; - ; 7.

903. Nicholas Gamage. Fd by Coles 7.7.1641. Bd to him 7.7.1634.

904. John Hose; Thomas; London; C Tiler and Bricklayer; 7.5.1666; 25.3.1666; 6.4.1674; 8.

905. Wm Rebold; John; Kynvare, Staffs; Y; 6.9.1641; 25.3.1641; 1.4.1650; 9.

906. William Waters; William; St Mary Islington, M'sex; Parish Clerk; 9.7.1663; 24.6.1663; - ; 8.

COLLINS, Freeman

907. Thomas Bowen. Fd by Collins 4.9.1693. Bd to Job King (q.v.) 2.8.1686.

908. Francis Burges; Francis (d); the Tower Liberty, London; Cl; 7.11.1692; 7.11.1692; 4.12.1699; 7.

909. Thomas Cooke; Richard (d); Wheely, Essex; Cl; 14.1.1679; 14.1.1679; 1.2.1686; 7. T.o. 'at Guild Hall to Ralph Holt who this day made him free paid [2s. 6d.] for not being turned over at this Hall'.

910. John Dermer. Fd by Collins 11.11.1700. Bd to his father John Dormer (q.v.) 2.10.1693.

911. Nathaniel Dover. Fd by Collins 4.3.1689. Bd to Thomas Moore (q.v.) 5.12.1681.

912. William Eyres; John; parish of St James Clarkenwell, M'sex; Br; 2.10.1699; 2.10.1699; 6.10.1707; 7.

913. Samuel Farlow; Edwd; Twining, Glos; Y; 6.5.1689; 6.5.1689; 4.9.1699; 8.

914. John Garret; John; Parrish of St Sepulchers, M'sex; Br; 3.3.1684; 3.3.1684; 4.5.1691; 7.

915. Richard Jones; Richard (d); London; C & B; 2.11.1685; 29.9.1685; - ; 8.

916. Thomas Urry; Thomas; parish of St Sepulchres, London; Br; 6.5.1700; 6.5.1700; - ; 7.

917. Lawrence Veze. Fd by Collins 6.8.1694. Bd to Francis Clarke (q.v.) 4.7.1687.

918. William Walrond; Henry; parish of Abbott Soyle, Som; G; 2.12.1695; 2.12.1695; - ; 7.

COLLINS, Gabriel

919. [Gabriel Collins. Son of Thomas Collins; fd by patrimony 7.12.1685.]

COLLINS, Henry

920. St John Harding; St John (d); London; C & Shipwright; 2.3.1691; 2.3.1691; - ; 7.

921. John Winde; Charles; Tewkesbury, Glos; G; 6.7.1696; 6.7.1696; 8.11.1703; 7.

COLLINS, James

922. George Conniers; John; Rippon, Yorks; G; 4.3.1678; 4.3.1678; 1.2.1686; 7. Fd as Conyers. Earlier t.o. (n.d.) to 'John Wright decd: this day made free pd [2s. 6d.] for not being turned over at this Hall.'

923. John Marden; John; Warfeild, Berks; G; 3.3.1668; 3.3.1668; - ; 7.

COLLINS, Lawrence

924. [Lawrence Collins. Fd by redemption 6.9.1675.]

COLLINS, Richard

925. John Calton; Hubert; Winterborne Kingston, Dors; Y; 20.12.1645; 27.10.1645; - ; 8.

926. Wm Harrison; Mathew; Reeth, Yorks; Y; 24.6.1650; 24.6.1650; - ; 7.

COLLINS, William

927. Thomas Greene; Thomas; Tanworth, War; G; 1.3.1658; 1.3.1658; - ; 7.

COLLIS, Robert
928. Thomas Lewis; Thomas; London; C & Ha; 6.4.1657; 6.4.1657; 6.6.1664; 7. Fd by Collis and William Stephens.
929. William Stephens; John; - , Bucks; H; 3.10.1653; 3.10.1653; 6.11.1660; 7. The entry of freedom notes Collis as deceased.

COLWELL, William
930. Edmond Peast. Fd by Colwell 11.4.1643. Bd to him 5.5.1634.
931. Edwyn Roberts. Fd by Colwell 11.4.1643. Bd to him 4.4.1636.

CONINGSBY, Christopher
932. Phillip Barrett; Michael; Pycomb, Sussex; Cl; 4.5.1691; 4.5.1691; 6.6.1698; 7.
933. Samuel Bartlett; Samuel; Citty of Oxford; Milliner; 3.9.1688; 3.9.1688; 11.11.1695; 7.
934. James Merest; John; Woking, Surr; Cl; 6.6.1698; 6.6.1698; - ; 7.

CONSTABLE, Richard
935. John Wager; Abraham (d); Finchley, M'sex; Tn; 20.2.1667; 20.2.1667; - ; 8.

CONSTABLE, Robert
936. James Gray. Fd by Constable 7.7.1641. Bd to him 7.7.1634.

CONYERS, George
937. Thomas Ballard; John; Parish of St. Buttalphs Aldersgate, London; T; 25.9.1690; 25.9.1690; 4.10.1697; 7.
938. Marke Conyers; John (d); Sernton, Yorks; G; 5.12.1687; 5.12.1687; - ; 7.

CONYERS, Joshua
939. James Baldwer; Willm; Long Sutton, Lincs; G; 4.7.1670; 4.7.1670; - ; 7.
940. Joshua Conyers. Fd by patrimony 7.11.1692.

COOKE, George
941. Wm. Cresbey; John (d); Badbery, Wilts; Y; 4.2.1650; 4.2.1650; 2.3.1657; 7. Fd as Crosby.
942. John Keene; John; HighWickam, Bucks; H; 6.6.1642; 6.6.1642; - ; 8.
943. Richard Leake; Richard; Wymswold, Leics; W; 7.6.1641; 7.6.1641; - ; 7.
944. John May; Will; London; Looking-glass maker; 6.8.1655; 6.8.1655; - ; 7.
945. William Simpson; Jno; Scales, Lancs; H; 6.8.1655; 6.8.1655; - ; 8.
946. Edward Ward; Edward; Hendon, M'sex; H; 29.11.1641; 24.6.1641; 7.2.1676; 8.
947. Samuell Widmer; Michaell; Chipping Wickham, Bucks; Chandler; 3.10.1642; 'from [blank] day last'; - ; 8. Rebd to John Wright (q.v.) 6.4.1646?
948. Joseph Wilkinson; Thomas; London; Br; 3.8.1646; 3.8.1646; 5.9.1653; 7.

COOKE, Josias
949. John Norman, Fd by Cooke 15.1.1645. Bd to him 6.11.1637.

COOKE, Samuel
950. Samuel Drury; John (d); Towne of Nottingham; Flaxdresser; 4.4.1687; 4.4.1687; 2.3.1702; 8.
951. William Flower; Adam; Lavington, Wilts; - ; 7.1.1678; 7.1.1678; - ; 7.
952. Wm Gathorne; Wm; parish o Shoreditch, M'sex; Y; 3.11.1679; 3.11.1679; 7.11.1687; 8.
953. Geo Marshall; John (d); London; C & St; 12.4.1692; 12.4.1692; 9.9.1700; 8.
954. Mathew Peble; John (d); Tottenham, M'sex; H; 8.5.1699; 8.5.1699; - ; 8.
955. John Plumpton; John; London; T; 2.8.1680; 2.8.1680; - ; 8.

956. Jonothan Prichard; David; Holt, Den; H; 5.5.1668; 1.5.1668; 6.10.1678; 8. Fd as Pritchard by Samuel Clarke, but this is almost certainly an error for Cooke.

957. Richard Rumball; Thomas (d); London; C & Bl; 3.4.1671; 3.4.1671; 5.5.1679; 8.

COOKE, Simon

958. John Atkinson; Robert; Hampstead, M'sex; Bricklayer; 1.3.1686; 1.3.1686; - ; 7.

959. Jonas Malsbery; John; Morton Pinkoney, N'hants; Cd; 5.2.1694; 5.2.1694; - ; 7.

960. David Selander; John; Whitechappell, M'sex; Smith; 7.6.1680; 7.6.1680; - ; 7.

COOKE, Thomas

961. William Curtis; John; Ratcliffe, M'sex; Gunner; 7.10.1650; 7.10.1650; 1.6.1657; 7. Originally bd to Samuel Rand (q.v.) 10.1.1650; fd by Rand.

962. Timothy Gander; Timothy; Ratcliffe; Mariner; 26.3.1666; 26.3.1666; - ; 7.

COOKE, William

963. John Smales; Marke; Beverley, Yorks; V; 4.7.1642; 4.7.1642; - ; 8.

COOPER, William

964. Mathew Allam; Mathew; Loughborough, Leics; Y; 2.8.1680; 29.9.1680; 3.10.1687; 7. Fined 2s. 6d. 'For not being turned over at the Hall'. But this note against the entry of freedom may be an error, since Allam was bound in the normal way to Cooper.

965. John Cooper. Fd by patrimony 1.2.1697.

966. Thomas Hargrave; Henry; Borough of Leicester; G; 2.5.1681; 2.5.1681; 7.5.1688; 7.

967. Charles Tooker; Henry; City of Winchester, [Hants]; G; 12.8.1671; 12.8.1671; 2.12.1678; 7.

968. John Ward; William; Sheeresby, Leics; Farmer; 6.5.1685; 6.5.1685; - ; 7. T.o. to Henry Coleman, 'Cittizen and Blacksmith of London', 6.9.1686.

COPE, Jonathan

969. [Jonathan Cope Esqr. Admitted to the freedom of the Company 5.8.1690. No charge.]

COPE, Steven

970. Daniell Austed; Daniell (d); London; C & Bu; 3.3.1668; 3.3.1668; - ; 7.

971. John Jones; Robert (d); Southwarke, Surr; Dy; 2.5.1664; 2.5.1664; - ; 7.

972. Thomas Tatnell. Fd by Cope and John Webb 10.11.1668. Bd to Webb (q.v.) 6.11.1660.

COPE, Thomas

973. William Kitchiner; Richard; - , Bucks; Schoolmaster; 6.11.1693; 6.11.1693; 4.10.1703; 7.

COPPING, George

974. Thomas Atkins; Tho; St Andrews Holborn, [M'sex]; - ; 7.6.1675; 7.6.1675; - ; 7.

975. Richard Beheathland; William; London; C & F; 26.3.1685; 1.12.1684; - ; 8.

976. Daniell Evance; Thomas; Camphill, War; Cl; 12.8.1671; 24.6.1671; 7.7.1679; 8.

977. Hammond Menheire; John (d); Kingston upon Thames, Surr; G; 7.7.1673; 7.7.1673; - ; 7.

978. Thomas Offley; Stephen; London; C & MT; 7.5.1666; 7.5.1666; 6.4.1674; 7.

979. Nicholas Smith; Kenelm; London; C & Ha; 1.7.1661; 1.7.1661; 5.5.1671; 8.

980. John Thurlby; Robert (d); London; G; 2.6.1679; 2.6.1679; 1.3.1688; 8.

COSSINETT, Francis

981. John Wilfeild; Phillip; London; C & B; 5.4.1658; 5.4.1658; 8.5.1665; 7. Fd as Winfeild.

COTES, Eleanor, Widow

982. Thomas Almond; Christopher; Ensam, Oxon; H; 7.12.1657; 7.12.1657; 6.2.1665; 7.

983. James Astwood; James; New England; Mch; 7.8.1654; 7.8.1654; 3.3.1662; 7.

984. Andrew Cotes; Richard (d); London; C & St; 7.3.1660; 7.3.1660; - ; 7. Bd to his mother.

985. Richard Dolman. Fd by Mrs Cotes 7.11.1653. Bd (as Richard Dawlman) to Richard Cotes (q.v.) 5.9.1642.

986. Robert Higgins. Fd by Mrs Cotes 7.1.1678. Apparently never formally bd.

987. John Love. Fd by Mrs Cotes, Henry Weston and Michael Sparkes 7.7.1662. Bd to Sparkes (q.v.) 4.10.1652.

988. Benjamin Mott; John; St Albons, Herts; Gl; 8.7.1668; 8.7.1668; 2.8.1675; 7. Mrs Cotes is described as the widow of Richard Cotes.

COTES, Francis

989. Sam Crispe; Nich; London; S; 30.3.1652; 25.3.1652; 7.5.1660; 8.

COTES, Richard

990. Isaac Bartholomew; Richard; -, -; -; 6.3.1648; 25.3.1648: 2.4.1655; 7.

991. Andrew Clarke; Andrew; Chelsey, M'sex; T; 4.6.1649; 2.2.1649; 1.3.1658 9.

992. Wm Codbid; Wm; London; Weaver; 27.4.1646; 27.4.1646; 4.5.1653; 8. Bd and fd as Codbid in error for Godbid.

993. Richard Dawlman; John; Alderwaise, Staffs; Y; 5.9.1642; 5.9.1642; 7.11.1653; 7. Fd (as Richard Dolman) by Mrs Cotes.

994. Symon Heinth. Fd by Cotes

and Henry Hall 1.3.1652. Apparently never formally bd.

995. Robte Ibitson. Fd by Cotes 21.10.1644. Bd to him 16.10.1637.

996. Thomas Newcomb. Fd by Cotes and Gregory Dexter 6.11.1648. Bd to Dexter 8.11.1641.

997. Wm Nuthead; Thomas (d); London; C & Go; 1.7.1644; 1.7.1644; 5.7.1652; 8.

COTGRAVE, Thomas

998. Thomas Cotgrave. Fd by patrimony 6.11.1671.

999. Benjamine Fish; Benjamine (d); London; C & Gr; 14.4.1656; 14.4.1656; - ; 7.

COTTERELL, James

1000. William Bradley; John (d); Norton, Shrops; Cl; 7.3.1681; 7.3.1681; - ; 7.

1001. James Dawson; Thomas; St Andrews Holborne, M'sex; BSg; 4.5.1674; 4.5.1674; 6.6.1681; 7.

1002. Vincent Engham; Vincent; Belthea, Ireland; - ; 4.11.1678; 4.11.1678; 25.6.1688; 7.

1003. Adam Islip; Kenelme (d); London; St; 2.5.1653; 2.5.1653; - ; 7.

1004. Robert Lamborn; Robt; St Giles in the Fields, M'sex; Victualler; 4.10.1658; 4.10.1658; 5.2.1666; 7.

1005. George Larkin; Benjamine (d); London; G; 1.12.1656; 1.12.1656; 6.6.1664; 7.

1006. Ralph Lee; Jo (d); London; C & Shoemaker; 6.9.1669; 6.9.1669; 1.10.1677; 8. Fd as Ralph Lett.

1007. Willm Onely; John (d); London; C & MT; 3.10.1681; 3.10.1681; 4.3.1689; 7.

1008. John Pennington; William; St Andrewe Holborne, [M'sex]; T; 6.5.1671; 6.5.1671; 6.5.1678; 7.

1009. Thomas Rainer; William (d); London; Ha; 1.7.1678; 1.7.1678; 6.7.1685; 7. Fd by Thomas Hodgkins.

1010. Edward Shybrough; William (d); Distaffe Lane, Parish of St Nich Cole Abby, -; Wine Cooper; 7.9.1663; 7.9.1663; - ; 7.

1011. Thomas Smith; John; Londonderry, North of Ireland; - ; 6.11.1654; 6.11.1654; 4.9.1676; 8.

1012. William Walton; Richard (d); Drayton, Shrops; Mr; 7.11.1681; 7.11.1681; 3.12.1688; 7. T.o. to Henry Hills Senior 2.11.1685. Fd by Hills.

COTTRELL, Henry

1013. Thomas Wigmore; Mich; Wickham, Bucks; Chandler; 7.2.1648; 24.8.1648; - ; 7.

COURTHOPE, Brian

1014. [Brian Courthope, 'Clerke to Mr Recorder of Lond By vertue of an Order of the Lord Mayors Court made ye 8th of September 1681', fd by redemption 6.2.1682.]

1015. William Holland; John (d); East Bourn, Sussex; Y; 30.9.1684; 30.9.1684; 4.7.1692; 7.

1016. Thomas Jamett; Ranee (d); London; Confectioner; 4.9.1693; 4.9.1693; - ; 7.

COWPER, Daniel

1017. George Wilford. Fd by Cowper 17.11.1645. Bd to him 13.11.1637.

COWSE, William

1018. Samuell Edmonds; Robert; Lewsom, Kent; Tn; 3.7.1671; 24.6.1671; 7.7.1679; 8. Cowse is described as a Scrivener in Wood Street.

COX, Gabriel

1019. David Barney; Thomas; Dalbanks, Yorks; E; 2.9.1661; 2.9.1661; - ; 7.

1020. Robert Bodnam; Roger; Rotherwais, Herefs; E; 7.5.1667; 25.3.1667; - ; 7.

1021. George Burd; Theophilus (d); St Giles in the feilds, [M'sex]; G; 2.11.1663; 2.11.1663; 6.2.1670; 7. Fd as Bird.

1022. William Harnedge; Edward; Belzerdine, [Shrops.]; - ; 1.10.1660; 1.10.1660; 8.10.1667; 7.

1023. Charles Skinner; Charles; Susted, Norf; E; 4.10.1669; 4.10.1669, - ; 7.

COX, George

1024. John Cox; George; London; C & St; 6.3.1654; 6.3.1654; - ; 7. Bd to his father.

1025. John Duley. Fd by Cox 4.10.1647. Bd to him 1.4.1639.

1026. John Fromantle; John; London; C & Cw; 4.10.1658; 24.6.1658; - ; 8.

1027. John Hall; Rich (d); Dawking, Surr; I; 12.6.1666; 12.6.1666; 4.8.1673; 7.

1028. Wm Lowen; Hen; Bromham, Beds; Y; 5.4.1652; 5.4.1652; 30.4.1659; 7.

1029. John Moore; Thomas; London, C & Mason; 2.3.1657; 4.2.1657; 7.7.1664; 8.

1030. John Newington; Willm (d); Beckingfeild, Bucks; I; 2.8.1669; 2.8.1669; 4.9.1676; 7.

1031. John Pratt; John; Burrough of Southwark, [Surr]; Y; 2.9.1661; 2.9.1661; 5.8.1668; 7. Fd by Mrs Maxwell.

1032. Thomas Reynolds; Miles; Winslow, Yorks; H; 18.1.1647; 21.10.1646; - ; 8.

1033. Richard Story. Fd by Cox and John Mould 1.9.1662. Apparently never formally bd.

1034. John Tomlinson; Peter; Thame, Oxon; Y; 6.9.1647; 6.9.1647; 2.10.1654; 7.

COX, Nicholas

1035. Jacob Marsh; Radi; parish of St Michael Oxford; 9.2.1674; 9.2.1674; - ; 7.

COX, Robert

1036. James Dowly; Thomas; Aldridge, Staffs; Cl; 3.12.1677; 3.12.1677; 3.5.1686; 8.

1037. John Maston; Thomas; St Albons, Herts; Y; 8.11.1669; 8.11.1669; 5.3.1677; 7. Fd as John Mason.

1038. Edward Moore; Edward; West Horsley, Surr; Y; 5.6.1665; 5.6.1665; 1.12.1673; 8.

1039. Thomas Stocker; John; Godmanchester, Hunts; Lighterman; 7.11.1670; 7.11.1670; 2.12.1678; 8.

1040. William Webster; Robert (d); Doncaster, Yorks; Whitesmith; 7.5.1683; 7.5.1683; - ; 8.

1041. William Wilkins. Bd to Brabazon Aylmer (q.v.) 5.7.1680. Fd by Cox 7.11.1687 and fined 2s. 6d. 'for not being turned over a[t] Hall'.

COX, William

1042. Wm Barroughes. Fd by Cox 25.2.1642. Bd to him 4.8.1634.

1043. Francis Beesley; John; Mooreton-Baggage, War; T; 6.9.1641; 6.9.1641; - ; 7.

CRANFORD, Joseph

1044. William Oliver; Sam (d); Wells, Som; Cl; 13.12.1654; 29.9.1654; - ; 8.

1045. Marke Pardo; Marke; Fotheringham, N'hants; G; 1.6.1663; 1.6.1663; 6.12.1675; 8. Fd by John Martin.

CRAWLEY, William

1046. Richard Baley; George; Fisherton, Wilts; Cl; 22.12.1646; 22.12.1646; 4.12.1654; 8. T.o. to George Dennis 17.4.1648. Fd (as Baily) by Crawley and Dennis.

1047. Thomas Coleman; John; Alborne, Wilts; Y; 14.7.1645; 14.7.1645; - ; 7.

1048. Edward Crawley. Fd by Crawley 1.5.1648. Bd to him 1.10.1638.

1049. William Turrey. Fd by Crawley 21.1.1644. Bd to him 3.6.1633.

1050. Steven Wells; Wm; Alborne, Wilts; T; 1.7.1644; 24.6.1644; - ; 9.

CRAYLE, Benjamin

1051. Wm Watts; William; parish of St Martin, M'sex; Victualler; 3.11.1690; 3.11.1690; 7.2.1699; 7.

CRAYLE, James

1052. Benjamin Browne; John (d); London; C & Painterstainer; 1.10.1688; 1.10.1688; 7.10.1695; 7.

1053. Thomas Hall; John; Rector of the parish of St Christophers, London; Cl; 3.2.1696; 7.1.1696; 1.2.1703; 7.

CREAKE, Thomas

1054. Richard Bockham. Fd by Creake, George Purslowe and John Hardestie 8.5.1665. Bd to Hardestie (q.v.) 5.4.1658.

1055. Robt Creak. Fd by patrimony 15.1.1667.

1056. William Walker; George; Thoroton, Notts; Y; 2.6.1656; 2.6.1656; 30.6.1663; 7.

CRIPPS, Henry

1057. William Cripps; Henry; Oxford, Oxon; Bs; 6.2.1654; 6.2.1654; - ; 7. Bd to his father.

1058. Peter Parker. Fd by Cripps 6.1.1665. Bd to Daniel White (q.v.) 2.8.1658.

1059. Samuell White. Fd by Cripps (his name is given as Crispe) 6.12.1697. Bd to Charles Garret (q.v.) 6.11.1682.

CRISPE, Samuel

1060. James Coles; John; Moulton, N'hants; H; 7.9.1663; 7.9.1663; - ; 7.

CROFTS, John

1061. Henry Carter; David; Kings Langley, Herts; Y; 7.11.1681; 7.11.1681; 4.3.1689; 7.

1062. Mathew Gregory; - ; parish of St Gregory, London; - ; 7.10.1689; 7.10.1689; - ; 10.

1063. Mannuel Mathews; Richard; Parrish of Whittburr, Herts; Y; 6.11.1683; 6.11.1683; 6.10.1690; 7. Fd as Emanuel Mathews.

CROFTS, Robert
1064. Isaac Gould; John; London; C & Bu; 28.6.1658; 28.6.1658; - ; 7.

CROOKE, Andrew
1065. William Bishop. Fd by Crooke 3.3.1645. Bd to him 5.2.1638.
1066. Thomas Court; Tho; Tanworth, War; H; 3.2.1673; 3.2.1673; 4.2.1684; 7.
1067. William Crooke; William; Kingston Blount, Oxon; Y; 24.1.1656; 24.6.1655; 2.11.1663; 9.
1068. James Davis; Samuell (d); London; Girdler; 6.11.1648; 24.6.1648; 7.7.1656; 8.
1069. Samuell Enderby; Samll; London; C & St; 5.12.1664; 5.12.1664; - ; 7.
1070. Mathew Gilliflower; John (d); City of Oxford; Cl; 6.4.1657; 6.4.1657; 7.5.1666; 9.
1071. Thomas Grover; Thomas; St Giles Cripplegate, London; Founder; 3.4.1671; 3.4.1671; 3.5.1680; 8.
1072. Robert Harwood; Robt; Kensington, M'sex; Bu; 6.11.1660; 6.11.1660; - ; 7.
1073. Symon Miller; George; London; C & St; 24.4.1645; 25.3.1645; 3.4.1654; 9.

CROOKE, John
1074. Robert Fletcher. Fd by Crooke and Thomas Allott 3.4.1654. Bd to Allott (q.v.) 4.10.1641.
1075. Allexander Hume; Thomas; Westminster, M'sex; G; 28.3.1659; 28.3.1659; - ; 7.
1076. Thomas Jackson. Fd by Crooke and Thomas Warren 17.11.1645. Bd to Crooke 12.11.1638.
1077. Theodore Sadler; Mountague; Fillongly, War; G; 1.3.1652; 1.3.1652; 1.3.1659; 7.
1078. Benjamine Tucke; Edmond (d); London; C & Ha; 7.9.1657; 7.9.1657; 5.2.1666; 8.
1079. Joseph Wilde; Samuell;

Roachdale, Rochester; Mr; 2.5.1664; 2.5.1664; - ; 7.

CROOKE, Mary, Widow
1080. John Humphreys. Fd by Mary Crooke 5.5.1690. Fined 2s. 6d. 'For being bound by a Forraigne Indr'.
1081. Daniel Reighly. Fd by Mary Crooke 2.4.1683. Apparently never formally bd.
1082. George Thompson. Fd by Mrs Crooke 5.9.1692. Apparently never formally bd.

CROOKE, William
1083. Richard Bassett; Thomas; London; C & St; 7.4.1690; 7.4.1690; 3.5.1697; 7.
1084. John Jackman; William (d); Slapton, N'hants; Y; 7.10.1689; 7.10.1689; - ; 7.
1085. Thomas Lilley; Gilbert; Purton, Oxon; G; 7.2.1670; 7.2.1670; - ; 7.
1086. James Norris; John; Alburn, Wilts; Cl; 2.8.1675; 2.8.1675; - ; 7.

CROOME, George
1087. [George Croome, 'Printer and Freeman of the Company of Leathersellers London', fd 2.4.1688, paying 21s. 6d.]

CROSBEY, Edward
1088. [Edward Crosbey. Fd by redemption 2.5.1687, his fine being £10.]

CROSLEY, Henry
1089. [Henry Crosley. Son of John Crosley; fd by patrimony 6.9.1641.]

CROSSE, William
1090. Isaac Gun; Isaac; parish of St Giles in the Feilds, M'sex; T; 8.6.1691; 8.6.1691; 3.10.1698; 7.
1091. John Saltmarsh; John; Enfeild, M'sex; Y; 6.3.1699; 6.3.1699; 3.2.1707; 7.

CROUCH, Edward
1092. Robert Chowne; Mich; Plumtree, Dev; Y; 3.11.1652; 3.11.1652; 7.7.1662; 7.

1093. William Palmer; Edward; St Albans, Herts; G; 25.6.1673; 25.6.1673; - ; 7.

1094. Adam Powell; Abraham; St Clement Daines, M'sex; Porter; 5.12.1670; 5.12.1670; - ; 7.

1095. Thomas Royston. Fd by Crouch 3.2.1680. Bd to Richard Hodgkinson (q.v.) 6.11.1671.

CROUCH, John

1096. George Crouch; Thomas; Ware westmill, Herts; Y; 3.10.1642; 3.10.1642; 12.11.1649; 7.

1097. John Crouch. Fd by patrimony 3.2.1673.

CROUCH, Nathaniel

1098. Samuell Crouch; Thomas; parish of St Thomas Southwarke, [Surr]; T; 3.3.1669; 3.3.1669; - ; 7. A Samuel Crouch was fd by redemption, by order of the Lord Mayor, 7.9.1674.

1099. Elizabeth Guard; Tho; Norton, Sussex; G; 5.10.1674; 5.10.1674; - ; 7.

CROUCH, Robert

1100. Tymothy Cole; Anthony; Longstanton, Cambs; Farrier; 5.6.1654; 24.6.1654; 8.7.1668; 9.

1101. Samuell Driver; Samuell; London; Silkthrowster; 6.10.1645; 24.8.1645; 7.11.1653; 8.

1102. Tobias Wickers; Tobias; Colchester, Essex; Clothier; 1.9.1656; 8.9.1656; 7.9.1663; 8.

1103. Edward Wotton; Hen; Chipman, Wilts; Y; 6.12.1647; 29.9.1647; 3.9.1655; 8.

CROUCH, Samuel

1104. [Samuel Crouch. Fd 7.9.1674 by redemption, by order of the Lord Mayor. Possibly the apprentice bd to Nathaniel Crouch (q.v.) 3.3.1669.]

1105. John Harrison; John (d); London; C & Ironmonger; 6.11.1676; 6.11.1676; 7.1.1684; 7. Fd as Thomas Harrison.

1106. Thomas Milnes; William; Ashford in the Peake, Derby; Y; 6.6.1681; 6.6.1681; - ; 7.

1107. James Townsend; Edward (d); Leicester; Br; 6.10.1684; 6.10.1684; 2.11.1691; 7.

CRUMP, James

1108. Roger Bassett. Fd by Crumpe 21.10.1646. Bd to him 12.11.1638.

1109. John Fletcher; John; Combe, Herefs; G; 21.10.1646; 21.10.1646; 7.11.1653; 7.

1110. John Marlow; John; Coventry, War; —; 28.6.1658; 28.6.1658; 3.7.1671; 7.

CRUMP, John

1111. Thomas Boomer; Thomas; - , Surr; G; 1.10.1677; 1.10.1677; 6.12.1686; 7.

1112. Samuell Sap; Thomas; London; C & Ha; 4.5.1674; 4.5.1674; - ; 7.

CRUTTENDEN, Henry

1113. Edward Bush. Fd by Cruttenden 7.7.1690. Fined 2s. 6d. 'For being bound by a Forraigne Indentr'.

1114. John Garetson. Described as servant to Cruttenden, but fd by Robert Jole 7.8.1684. Bd to Obedience Gellibrand (q.v.) 5.3.1677.

1115. Jonathan Heathfeild; Richard; Cittie of Oxon; Printer; 4.7.1681; 4.7.1681; 10.8.1688; 7.

1116. John Rame. Fd by Cruttenden 20.12.1684. Apparently never formally bd.

CUMBERLAND, Richard

1117. Edmund Holloway; John; Lavington, Wilts; I; 6.8.1694; 6.8.1694; 2.11.1702; 7.

CURTIS, Langley

1118. Thomas Benskin; Richard; Hartshorne, Derby; G; 4.3.1672; 21.12.1671; 7.7.1680; 8.

1119. Nathaniell Dancer; Nathaniell; Alesbury, Bucks; Bricklayer; 6.9.1669; 6.9.1669; 10.9.1677; 7.

1120. Edward Hawkins; Wm; Newton, War; G; 4.12.1676; 4.12.1676; 7.7.1684; 7. Fd by William Benbridge.

1121. John Neale; John; - , - ; Cl; 7.4.1679; 7.4.1679; - ; 8.

CURTIS, William

1122. Wm Abbott; Wm (d); Portsmouth, S'hants; Ca; 3.2.1690; 3.2.1690; - ; 7.

1123. John Ford; Richard (d); London; C & MT; 31.8.1668; 31.8.1668; 7.2.1687; 8.

1124. Anthony Risby; John (d); Saffronhill, M'sex; Schoolmaster; 5.7.1669; 5.7.1669; 2.4.1677; 8.

CUSHIE, Thomas

1125. Alexander Boorne; Alexander; Woodbridge, Suff; Salesman; 7.10.1689; 7.10.1689; 2.11.1696; 7. Fd as Bourne.

1126. John Cooke; John (d); Barking, Essex; H; 7.10.1668; 7.10.1668; - ; 7. Cushie is described as a Vintner.

1127. Thomas Noyes; Samuell; Hatherden in the parish of And[over], Hants; - ; 23.12.1663; 23.12.1663; - ; 7.

1128. John Parr; William; Siston, Leics; Y; 7.10.1661; 7.10.1661; - ; 7.

CUTLER, Robert

1129. Samuell Bourne; James (d); London; C & Co; 7.4.1662; 25.3.1662; 6.6.1670; 8. Fd as Samuell Browne.

1130. Josuah Conniers; Josuah; Brabrooke, N'hants; G; 2.10.1654; 1.7.1654; 4.11.1661; 8.

1131. John Eyloe; Richard; London; G; 1.2.1675; 1.2.1675; 2.10.1682; 7.

1132. John Grover; William; Redding, Berks; Bu; 6.12.1658; 5.11.1658; 6.6.1670; 8.

1133. John Hooke; Charles; Rutherfeild, Sussex; Iron founder; 10.8.1676; 10.8.1676; 1.10.1683; 7.

1134. Jonas Howard; Mathew (d); St Steevens, Herts; H; 11.2.1668; 25.12.1667; - ; 8.

1135. John Willmott; Willm; Abbington, Berks; G; 7.6.1669; 7.6.1669; 3.7.1676; 7.

DAGNALL, Stephen

1136. Thomas Bazen; John; Tewksbury, Glos; M; 1.6.1674; 1.6.1674; 1.2.1686; 7.

1137. Mathias Dagnall; Stephen; London; C & St; 23.5.1673; 23.5.1673; - ; 7. Bd to his father.

DAINTY, John

1138. Thomas Browne; Wm; London; MT; 3.5.1652; 3.5.1652; - ; 7.

1139. [John Dainty. Son of Robert Dainty; fd by patrimony 30.3.1652.]

1140. Thomas Lamprey; Tho; St James Clarkenwell, M'sex; Br; 1.6.1663; 1.6.1663; - ; 7.

DAINTY, Thomas, I

1141. Francis Cogan; Tho (d); Citty of Oxford; I; 6.12.1647; 6.12.1647; 6.10.1656; 8.

1142. Joseph Daintie. Fd by patrimony 7.3.1664.

1143. Thomas Dainty; Thomas; London; C & St; 22.6.1642; 22.6.1642; 17.4.1648; 7. Bd to his father. Fd by patrimony.

1144. Phillip Daunsey; Wm; Vley, Glos; G; 10.6.1650; 10.6.1650; 7.9.1657; 7.

1145. Thomas Ely. Fd by Dainty 13.11.1647. Bd to him 1.6.1640.

1146. Henry Flesher; Isaac (d); London; C & MT; 1.3.1644; 25.12.1643; 28.10.1651; 8. The father's name is given as Fletcher. Fd as Fletcher.

1147. Francis Hall; Francis; London; Go; 1.12.1651; 24.6.1651 - ; 8.

1148. Mathew Leake. Fd by Dainty 1.7.1644. Bd to him 27.3.1637.

1149. John Milborne; Robte (d); London; C & St; 3.2.1645; 25.12.1644; 2.6.1651; 8. Fd by patrimony.

1150. John Senior; Tho; Salisbury, Wilts; Go; 5.2.1649; 5.2.1649; - ; 7.

DAINTY, Thomas, II

1151. Samuell Mendwell; Willm (d); Throlsworth; Leics; Cl; 5.8.1661; 5.8.1661; - ; 7.

1152. James Tillyer; Christopher; London; C & Salter; 30.6.1663; 30.6.1663; - ; 7.

1153. Edward Wild; Robert; Citty of Worcester; G; 6.1.1651; 6.1.1651; 5.4.1658; 7.

DALLOM, John

1154. Cuthbert Fetherstone. Fd by Dallom 17.1.1642. Bd to him 14.1.1635.

1155. Thomas Maning; Thom; London; C & Woodmonger; 5.12.1653; 5.12.1653; - ; 8.

1156. Francis Mathewes; Robte; Buckton, Herefs; Y; 28.6.1641; 28.6.1641; 2.7.1649; 8.

1157. John Richardson; Robert; Higham, Leics. G; 2.3.1657; 2.3.1657; 4.4.1664; 7.

1158. Mathias Thurston; Richard (d); London; Gr; 3.8.1646; 3.8.1646; 5.9.1653; 7. Fd by Dallom and Richard Tomlyns.

DALTON, Thomas

1159. John Buchanan; James (d); Appleby, W'land; Cl; 7.5.1694; 7.5.1694; 4.10.1703; 7.

1160. Francis Crampton; Francis (d); Stafford, Staffs; G; 6.5.1685; 6.5.1685; - ; 7.

1161. John Pratt; John; Aylsbury, Bucks; G; 7.8.1699; 7.8.1699; - ; 7.

1162. Samuel Welchman; Edwd (d); Banbury, Oxon; B; 2.7.1688; 2.6.1688; 5.10.1696; 8.

DAME, Walter

1163. Edward Gee. Fd by Dame and Richard Westbrook 1.12.1662. Bd to Westbrook (q.v.) 6.11.1655.

DANCER, Nathaniel

1164. John Michell; John (d); parish of St Martins in the Feilds, M'sex; Coachman; 3.7.1686; 3.7.1686; - ; 7.

DANIELL, John

1165. William Norris; George; Mabbison Redway, Staffs; Y; 2.2.1662; 2.2.1662; 6.6.1670; 8. Fd as Willm Morrice.

DANIELL, Thomas

1166. Humfrey Salt; Humfrey; Rolston, Staffs; Sh; 3.3.1669; 3.3.1669; 2.4.1677; 8.

DARBY, Clement

1167. Charles James; Thomas; Starton, Glos; G; 2.5.1664; 25.3.1664; - ; 8.

DARBY, John, I

1168. John Darby. Fd by patrimony 4.3.1695.

1169. Edward Davenport; Henry; Waltham Crosse, Herts; Y; 6.11.1671; 6.11.1671; 4.8.1678; 7.

1170. Stephen Ewer; Obediah; Harron, M'sex; Y; 9.2.1680; 9.2.1680; 7.3.1687; 7.

1171. Thomas Gibbs; Thomas; Towne of Bath, Som; G; 6.4.1696; 6.4.1696; 11.2.1706; 7.

1172. David Hay; Hugh (d); Murray, Scotland; G; 6.6.1687; 6.6.1687; 12.11.1694; 7.

1173. John Humfrey; Daniel; London; C & MT; 7.5.1688; 7.5.1688; 3.6.1695; 7.

1174. Thomas Rowland; Richard (d) St Margaretts Westminster; G; 1.10.1683; 1.10.1683; - ; 7.

1175. George Royden; Robert; Okey, Surr; G; 27.9.1695; 27.9.1695; 1.3.1703; 7.

1176. William Smith. Fd by Darby and James Astwood 2.12.1700. Bd to Astwood (q.v.) 2.10.1693.

1177. Daniel Towgood; Mathew; Flint Mill, Dors; Cl; 7.8.1676; 7.8.1676; 1.10.1683; 7. Fd as Twogood.

DARBY, John, II

1178. John Darby. Fd by patrimony 4.10.1697.

1179. Samuell Humphry; Daniell; London; C & MT; 2.10.1699; 2.10. 1699; - ; 7.

1180. John Money; John; London; C & Lorimer; 11.11.1700; 11.11.1700; 1.12.1707; 7.

DARKER, Samuel

1181. Thomas Moyce; John; Shaldon, S'hants; Cl; 3.10.1698; 3.10.1698; - ; 8.

1182. John Smith; Wm (d); London; C & Weaver; 1.8.1692; 1.8.1692; 5.8.1700; 7.

DARRELL, Edward

1183. Thomas Brewer; Ralph (d); London; C & Girdler; 12.11.1694; 1.10.1694; 4.5.1702; 7.

1184. Edward Darrell; Edward; London; C & St; 7.6.1697; 29.5.1697; - ; 7. Bd to his father.

1185. Oliver Elliston; Peter (d); Gestingthorp, Essex; ?; 1.3.1680; 1.3.1680; 7.3.1687; 7. Trade indecipherable.

1186. William Thursby; Downhall; London; C & Gr; 1.8.1687; 1.8.1687; - ; 7.

DAVENPORT, Ralph

1187. Robert Everingham; Robert; Allerton, Yorks; H; 2.9.1661; 2.9.1661; 5.8.1668; 7. Fd by Davenport and John Macocke.

1188. Jeremiah Leadbetter; Joshua; City of Westminster; G; 4.6.1660; 4.6.1660; - ; 7.

DAVIES, Thomas

1189. Francis Hawes; Francis; London; C & D; 5.10.1657; 5.10.1657; - ; 7.

DAVIS, -, Widow

1190. John Lipscomb. Fd by Widow Davis 13.3.1693. Originally bd to George Eversden (q.v.) 26.3.1683.

DAVIS, Edward

1191. Wm Davis; John; Bitton, Shrops; Ca; 9.2.1691; 9.2.1691; - ; 7.

1192. Stephen Hillman; Stephen; the Devizes, Wilts; Gunsmith; 2.11.1691 2.11.1691; - ; 7.

1193. Francis Oldfeild; Henry (d); Bradeley, Staffs; Farrier; 7.4.1690; 7.4.1690; - ; 7.

1194. Samuel Wingfeild; Sam; parish of St Martin in the Feilds, M'sex; Cook; 7.10.1689; 7.10.1689 - ; 7.

DAVIS, Joseph

1195. James Penroy. Fd by Davis and Walter Powell 1.2.1664. Bd to Powell (q.v.) 6.11.1654.

DAWES, George

1196. John Heathcote; Willm; Potsworth, War; Schoolmaster; 8.7.1668; 8.7.1668; - ; 7.

1197. John Walthoe. Fd by Dawes 16.6.1684. Apparently never formally bd.

DAWKES, Ichabod

1198. Daniell Brogden. Fd by Dawkes 2.10.1693. Apparently never formally bd.

1199. John Chadwick; John (d); London; C & St; 2.3.1696; 2.3.1696; - ; 7.

1200. Joseph Haynes; Richard; Parish of St Martins Le grand, London; Sh; 5.8.1700; 5.8.1700; 3.11.1707; 7.

1201. Hugh Meere; John (d); Stratford Sea, S'hants; Y; 8.6.1696; 8.6. 1696; 2.8.1703; 7.

1202. Richard Peacock; William; London; C & MT; 3.10.1698; 3.10. 1698; 1.10.1705; 7.

DAWKES, Thomas

1203. Icabod Dawkes. Fd by patrimony 6.11.1682.

1204. [Thomas Dawkes. Fd by patrimony 6.8.1655.]

1205. Thomas Dawkes. Fd by patrimony 3.3.1684.

1206. Ralph Silverton; Ralph (d); London; C & Weaver; 5.2.1683; 5.2. 1683; - ; 7.

1207. Wm Spire. Fd by Dawkes 4.6.1683. Apparently never formally bd.

DAWSON, Ephraim

1208. George Bodington. Fd by Dawson 1.7.1647. Bd to him 5.6.1637.

1209. Thomas Egglesfeild. Fd by Dawson 15.1.1646. Bd to him 5.2.1638.

DAWSON, Gertrude, Widow

1210. Jasper Brensall; Nicholas; London; C & Cw; 3.10.1664; 3.10.1664; - ; 7.

1211. Thomas Charles; Thomas (d); London; C & Ca; 4.5.1657; 4.5.1657; 3.10.1664; 7.

1212. Symon Dover; Symon; Basthenthwaite, Cumb; Y; 5.2.1655; 5.2. 1655; 5.3.1660; 7. Originally bd to Peter Cole (q.v.) 14.6.1652. Fd by Dawson and Cole.

1213. John Gane. Fd by Mrs Dawson and Felix Kingston 5.12.1653. Bd to Kingston (q.v.) 3.12.1646.

1214. John Patteson; Thomas; Bassenquit, Cumb; Fuller; 6.11.1655; 6.11.1655 - ; 7.

1215. John Parkins. Fd 7.4.1651 by Mrs Dawson 'widdow of Jo: the elder per Test: Mr John Williams'. Bd to John Dawson Senior 26.3.1628.

DAWSON, John

1216. William Coates. Fd by Dawson 5.8.1647. Bd to him 20.1.1640.

1217. Richard Jones; Stephen; Shenley, Herts; Cl; 6.10.1645; 6.10.1645; 8.11.1652; 7.

1218. Stephen Lee; Edward; Goswell streete, [London]; Printer; 3.10. 1648; 29.9.1648; 1.6.1657; 8.

1219. Joy Phillips. Fd by Dawson 7.10.1644. Bd to John Dawson Senior 4.8.1634; t.o. to Dawson Junior 3.7.1637.

1220. Samuell Wade; Richard; Bocking, Essex; Y; 2.5.1643; 25.3.1643; - ; 8.

1221. John Whateley; Hugh; Dudston, Shrops; Y; 15.1.1646; 15.1.1646; - ; 7.

1222. Nathaniell Whitehead; Elias; Daintrey, N'hants; Sh; 6.6.1644; 6.6. 1644; - ; 7.

DAWSON, Samuel

1223. Wm Bragg; Richard; London; C & Go; 2.12.1644; 2.12.1644; - ; 8.

1224. Richard East; Gabriell; Chesterfeild, Derby; Tn; 6.9.1647; 6.9.1647; 2.10.1654; 7.

1225. Jasper Harmer; Jasper (d); Maydenhead, Berks; I; 8.10.1667; 8.10.1667; 22.2.1675; 7.

1226. Stephen Harris; Jno; London; C & Tallowchandler; 2.10.1654; 2.10. 1654; - ; 7.

1227. Carew Spragg. Fd by Dawson 18.1.1647. Bd to him 2.4.1638.

DEACON, Jonah

1228. Charles Bates; Richard; London; C & St; 4.6.1683; 4.6.1683; 7.7. 1690; 7.

DEANE, Nicholas

1229. Wm Meycock. Fd by Deane 4.7.1642. Bd to him 21.6.1634.

DEAVER, John

1230. Edward Thew; Henry; Hogstrap, Lincs; Y; 5.10.1646; 29.9.1646; - ; 8.

DEAVES, Robert

1231. Thomas Astley; Thomas; London; C & Cw; 6.5.1672; 6.5.1672; 4.8.1679; 7.

1232. William Fullerton; John; Bath, Som; H; 5.12.1664; 29.9.1664; - ; 9.

1233. Edmund Patshall; Edmund; London; C & Salter; 5.5.1656; 25.3. 1656; - ; 8.

DELL, Joseph

1234. William Ord; Thomas (d); Longridge, Dur; G; 4.12.1671; 4.12. 1671; 14.1.1678; 7.

DELVES, Elizabeth, Widow
1235. John Williamson; Richd (d); London; G; 26.6.1682; 26.6.1682; - ; 7.

DELVES, Ralph
1236. Edward Deare; Tho; Stratford, Wilts; Y; 3.12.1655; 3.12.1655; - ; 8.
1237. Henry Hewett; Henry; Ashmainsworth, Hants; G; 7.12.1657; 1.11.1657; - ; 8.
1238. William Lashley; William (d); London; C & Cu; 3.6.1672; 3.6.1672; - ; 7.
1239. Robert Ogglethorpe; George; London; T; 8.10.1649; 29.9.1649; 1.3.1658; 9.
1240. William Poynton; Ed; Little Hacklow, Derby; Y; 4.3.1661; 4.3.1661; - ; 7.

DENITT, Gerrard
1241. John Chalener; William; Steple Clayden, Bucks; G; 5.12.1698; 5.12.1698; 2.12.1706; 7.

DENNIS, George
1242. Richard Baley, bd to William Crawley (q.v.) 22.12.1646, t.o. to Dennis 17.4.1648. Fd (as Baily) by Dennis and Crawley 4.12.1654.
1243. Richard Wosald; Lawrence; Smithcott, Shrops; Y; 7.3.1664; 24.6.1663; 4.7.1670; 8.

DESBURROUGH, Christopher
1244. Tho Desburrough; Robte; BrigStock, N'hants; Y; 30.6.1651; 30.6.1651; 12.7.1658; 7.

DEWE, Eleanor, Widow
1245. Charles Fisher; Thomas; Moulsey, Surr; Y; 4.2.1689; 4.2.1689; 2.11.1696; 7. Eleanor Dewe is described as the 'late wife' of Richard Dewe.

DEWE, Richard, I
1246. William Corant; James; London; C & Cd; 1.6.1657; 1.6.1657; 3.4.1665; 7.

1247. Richard Dew. Fd by patrimony 9.2.1657.
1248. Francis Law; Francis; Great Steepy, Lincs; G; 12.7.1658; 12.7.1658; - ; 8.
1249. Edward Marston; Edward; Ypswich, Suff; Gr; 3.10.1648; 3.10.1648; - ; 7.
1250. John Walthorpp; Wm; London; C & St; 15.1.1646; 15.1.1646; 7.3.1653; 7.

DEWE, Richard, II
1251. Thomas Alderson; John (d); Detfordstrand, Kent; Schoolmaster; 3.5.1669; 3.5.1669; 7.8.1676; 7.
1252. William Gunboy; John (d); Little Dunham, Norf; Cl; 3.7.1682; 3.7.1682; 8.6.1691; 7. Fd (as Gunby) by Richard Dewe's widow.
1253. George Shell; George; Rugby, War; G; 22.2.1675; 22.2.1675; 4.12.1682; 7.
1254. William Sparke; John (d); London; C & MT; 1.8.1681; 1.8.1681; 2.11.1691; 7.
1255. John Spicer; William (d); Northampton, N'hants; Woollendraper; 6.8.1660; 6.8.1660; 8.7.1668; 7.
1256. Benjamin Webster; Edward; Derby; Cd; 6.4.1674; 6.4.1674; 2.10.1682; 7.
1257. Thomas Wood; Jonathan (d); Preston Bissett, Bucks; Minister; 8.5.1665; 3.4.1665; - ; 7.

DEXTER, Gregory
1258. Thomas Newcomb; Thomas; Dunchurch, War; Y; 8.11.1641; 8.11.1641; 6.11.1648; 8. Fd by Dexter and 'Mr Coates', presumably Richard Cotes.

DICAS, Thomas
1259. Humphry Lloyd; Humphry; Aston, Flint; G; 7.5.1666; 7.5.1666; - ; 7.

DICKINS, Robert
1260. William Dickins. Fd by patrimony 7.2.1676.

DIESTER, Francis
1261. John Collington; Jonathan; London; C & Ha; 13.7.1657; 13.7.1657; - ; 7.
1262. James Head; James (d); Cambridge; T; 19.1.1663; 19.1.1663; - ; 7.
1263. William Stringfellow. Fd by Diester 1.2.1664. Apparently never formally bd.

DIMONDSELL, Samuel
1264. Joseph Browne; Robert; London; C & MT; 7.3.1692; 7.3.1692; - ; 7.
1265. John Johnson; John (d); Parish of St Mary Savoy alius Stany, M'sex; Victualler; 7.11.1687; 7.11.1687; 6.5.1695; 7.

DOCHEN, Henry
1266. Edward Jelley. Fd by Dochen 4.10.1652. Apparently never formally bd.
1267. Wm Lightfoot; Wm (d); Hull, Yorks; Ironmonger; 1.9.1645; 1.9.1645; 4.10.1652; 7.

DOCHEN, Rebecca, Widow
1268. William Beke; William; Cuddington, Bucks; G; 3.3.1651; 3.3.1651; 7.11.1658; 7.

DOD, Edward
1269. Joseph Cranford. Fd by Dod 6.9.1652. Bd to Charles Greene (q.v.) 27.9.1645.
1270. Stephen Lincolne; Stephen; Burrough of Leicester; Bs; 14.4.1656; 14.4.1656; - ; 7.

DOLMAN, Isaiah
1271. [Isaiah Dawlman. Son of Robert Dolman; fd by patrimony 5.10.1657.]

DOLMAN, John
1272. Richard Hatchman; Phillip; Dorchester, Oxon; Cd; 7.8.1699; 7.8.1699; 3.11.1712; 7.

DOOLEY, John
1273. Thomas Batchelor; Tho; Far-

neham, Bucks; H; 7.11.1670; 7.11.1670; 6.6.1681; 7.

DORMER, John
1274. Edmond Botting; Edmond (d); East Grimstead, Sussex; G; 3.9.1660; 3.9.1660; - ; 7.
1275. John Dermer; John; [London]; [C & St]; 2.10.1693; 2.10.1693; 11.11.1700; 7. Bd to his father (properly Dormer). Fd by Freeman Collins.

DORRELL, Edward
1276. John Baskett; Roger; Sarum in Salisbury, [Wilts]; G; 4.12.1682; 4.12.1682; 5.5.1690; 7.
1277. [Edward Dorrell. Fd by redemption 24.10.1676.]

DOVER, James
1278. Edward Beale; Edward; parish of St Mary Matfellon alius White Chappell, M'sex; Chandler; 3.8.1696; 3.8.1696; 9.9.1706; 7.
1279. William Garrett. Fd by [James?] Dover and Job Killington 7.2.1698. Bd to Killington (q.v.) 4.3.1689.
1280. John Goodchild; Christopher (d); Crookham, S'hants; Y; 5.8.1700; 5.8.1700; - ; 7.

DOVER, Simon
1281. Thomas Adlington; Will; Bath, Som; Plumber; 21.1.1662; 21.1.1662; - ; 8.
1282. James Dover. Fd by patrimony 3.10.1681.

DOWLEY, James
1283. Joseph Bourne; Samuell; London; C & St; 4.3.1689; 4.3.1689; 26.3.1696; 7.
1284. John Randall; Thomas (d); parish of St Sepulchres, London; Gardener; 7.3.1687; 7.3.1687; - ; 7.

DOWNES, George
1285. John Weld; John; Newcastle Vpon Tyne, [N'land]; Cl; 12.11.1677; 12.11.1677; 6.4.1685; 7.

DOWNES, Ralph

1286. Richard Owfall. Fd by Downes, John Rawson and Edward Jelley 3.4. 1665. Bd to Jelley (q.v.) 1.3.1658.

DOWNES, Thomas

1287. Henry Lee. Fd by Downes 2.11. 1646. Bd to him 12.11.1638.

1288. Beniamyn Rogers; John (d); Beare Regis, Dors; Cl; 14.6.1647; 14.6.1647; - ; 7.

DOWNHAM, Thomas

1289. [Thomas Downham, 'Freeman of the Company of Haberdashers', fd by redemption 1.3.1688, paying £5.]

DOWNING, Thomas

1290. Thomas Mills. Fd by Downing 2.6.1684. Apparently never formally bd.

DOWNING, William

1291. Joseph Brookeland; Richard; Suningwell, Berks; H; 7.6.1697; 7.6. 1697; - ; 7.

1292. Wm Downing; Wm; London; C & St; 2.4.1683; 2.4.1683; 7.5.1694; 7. Bd to his father.

1293. James Read; George (d); London; Cornchandler; 2.4.1683; 2.4.1683; 7.4.1690; 7.

1294. Edward Steele; Edward (d); Great Nesson, Westchester; Cl; 3.10. 1692; 3.10.1692; - ; 7.

1295. Lawrance Thompson; Willm; Newport Pannell, Bucks; Tallowchandler; 9.9.1700, 9.9.1700; 1.12.1707; 7. Fd by Anne Downing.

DOWSE, Anthony

1296. Adiell Mill. Fd 5.8.1672 by redemption from the Company of Haberdashers, paying 46s. 8d. Presumably Mill was servant to Dowse at the time.

DOWSE, John

1297. James Crayle. Fd by Dowse 4.6.1683. Apparently never formally bd.

DRANT, Thomas

1298. Joshua Browne; Richard (d); Islington, M'sex; G; 4.12.1671; 4.7. 1671; - ; 7.

1299. Richard Head. Fd by Drant and Samuel Thompson 4.6.1660. Bd to Thompson (q.v.) 5.9.1653.

1300. William Hosge. Fd by Drant 1.3.1658. Apparently never formally bd.

DREWE, Mathias

1301. William Barloe. Fd by Drewe 2.10.1676. Bd to Peter Lillicrop (q.v.) 6.9.1669.

1302. [Mathias Drewe. Fd 6.11.1671 by redemption by order of the Lord Mayor dated 17.10.1671.]

DRING, Peter

1303. Richard Clement; John; Citty of Peterborough, [N'hants]; G; 7.12. 1674; 25.3.1674; 7.8.1682; 7.

1304. Rowland Reinolds; Thomas (d); London; C & Sk; 3.9.1660; 3.9. 1660; 8.10.1667; 7. Fd as Reynolds.

DRING, Thomas

1305. Robert Crofts; Tho; Tilminster, Kent; G; 10.1.1650; 10.1.1650; 26.3.1657; 8.

1306. Daniel Dring; Daniel; London; C & S; 5.12.1687; 5.12.1687; 4.2.1695; 7.

1307. Thomas Dring; Thomas (d); Spawlding, Hunts; Y; 5.10.1657; 25.12. 1656; 1.3.1665; 8.

1308. William Ewrey; William (d); - , Notts; G; 5.9.1681; 5.9.1681; - ; 7.

1309. William Freeman; Bipps froome, Herefs; G; 4.5.1674; 4.5.1674; 6.6.1681; 7.

1310. John Leete; John; Midlow, Hunts; G; 20.6.1662; 20.6.1662; 4.7. 1670; 8. Fd by Dring but also described as servant to Thomas Bassett.

1311. Willm Ryley; Willm (d); Morley, Derby; G; 1.3.1667; 1.3.1667; - ; 7.

1312. James Vade; James (d); London; C & MT; 4.7.1670; 4.7.1670; 6.8.1677; 7.

1313. John Wilson; Richard; Clement Danes, M'sex; G; 3.11.1656; 3.11.1656; - ; 7.

DRIVER, Samuel

1314. John Bankes; Francis (d); Great sheepy, Leics; L; 6.11.1655; 6.11.1655; - ; 7.

1315. John Dale; Zach; Harliston, Lincs; Y; 6.8.1655; 6.8.1655; - ; 8.

1316. Hugh Sparke; Henry (d); Torrington, Herefs; H; 1.12.1656; 1.12.1656; - ; 7.

DUGARD, William

1317. John Brainthwaite. Fd by Dugard and James Young 3.12.1655. Bd (as Banthwaite) to Young (q.v.) 7.10.1644; t.o. to Dugard 8.6.1648.

1318. [William Dugard. Fd by redemption 10.2.1648.]

1319. William Hill; William; Fulletby, Lincs; H; 22.12.1655; 22.12.1655; 1.2.1664; 8.

1320. Mathias Inman. Bd to James Young (q.v.) 2.11.1646; t.o. to Dugard 8.6.1648. Fd by Young and Dugard 6.2.1654.

DUKE, Robert

1321. Miles Gibson; Robert (d); Denbigh, Derby; Cl; 7.11.1659; 29.9.1659; - ; 8.

1322. William Morrice; Roger; London; C & Embroiderer; 9.7.1663; 24.6.1663; 8.

1323. Abraham Roe; Abraham; Golding lane, M'sex; Apothecary; 1.7.1650; 24.6.1650; 4.7.1659; 9.

DULY, Thomas

1324. [Thomas Duly. Son of John Duly; fd by patrimony 2.6.1684.]

DUNCOMB, Charles

1325. Leonard Bartlett; Robert (d); Twittingham, M'sex; - ; 6.3.1671; 6.3.1671; 4.11.1678; 7.

1326. [Charles Duncon. Fd by patrimony 4.6.1667.]

1327. Christopher Meggs; Peverall; Bradford, Dors; G; 6.12.1669; 6.12.1669; 12.2.1677; 7.

DUNN, Walter

1328. John Bannister; John; Isleworth, M'sex; G; 9.2.1674; 9.2.1674; - ; 7.

1329. Humphrey Baskervile; Humphrey; Longhope, Glos; Y; 6.2.1682; 6.2.1682; - ; 7.

1330. Edward Burges; Edmond (d); Cittie of Canterbury, [Kent]; 2.5.1681; 2.5.1681; - ; 7.

1331. William Evans; Thomas; Clapton, N'hants; H; 7.12.1663; 7.12.1663; 9.1.1671; 7.

DUNSCOMB, Margaret, Widow

1332. Sarah Wathing; Wm; London; C & Ha; 10.9.1677; 10.9.1677; - ; 7.

DUNSCOMB, Robert

1333. Thomas Bellamy. Fd by Dunscomb 2.12.1644. Bd to him 7.12.1635.

1334. Henry Perkins; Richard; Broughton, Leics; G; 2.9.1650; 2.9.1650; - ; 7.

1335. John Pettit; Lewis; Ringsted, N'hants; Y; 2.8.1641; 2.8.1641; 6.11.1648; 7.

1336. John Rayner; Edmond; Deptford, Kent; Shipwright; 1.10.1660; 25.3.1660; - ; 8.

1337. John Sowton; Will; Chichester, Sussex; Mch; 3.8.1664; 3.8.1664; - ; 8.

DUNTON, John

1338. Saml Palmer; Nicholas; [Bath, Som?]; Cl; 5.2.1683; 5.2.1683; - ; 8. Town and county are entered as 'of the County of Baths'.

1339. Richard Wright; Robert (d); St Neatts, Hunts; G; 4.3.1689; 4.3.1689; - ; 7.

EAST, Richard

1340. Benjamin Bond; - ; - , - ; - ; 6.8.1677; 6.8.1677; 1.9. 1684; 7. Fd as Bowne.

1341. Francis Bough; Richard; Tibberton, Worcs; G; 5.7.1669; 5.7.1669; 4.7.1676; 7. Fd as Baugh.

1342. Thomas Kerke; Tho; Chesterfeild, Derby; Mr; 1.10.1655; 1.10.1655; 3.11.1662; 7.

1343. Hen Perris; John; London; C & Ha; 3.12.1683; 3.12.1683; 9.2.1691; 7.

1344. Anthony Poole; Michll; Chesterfield, Derby; G; 1.4.1661; 1.4.1661; 2.6.1668; 7.

1345. Henry Prior; Will; Elkston, Glos; Cl; 4.8.1690; 4.8.1690; - ; 7.

ECCLESTON, Christopher

1346. George Palmer; Sam (d); Warwick, War; G; 9.7.1663; 9.7.1663; - ; 7.

ECCLESTON, Edward

1347. Francis Blyth. Fd by Eccleston 2.8.1686. Fined 2s. 6d. 'for not being bound at ye Hall'.

EDLYN, Richard

1348. Christopher Gale; Chri; Sunning, Berks; G; 3.6.1647; 3.6.1647; - ; 7.

1349. Nathaniell Ofill; Henry; Chersham, Bucks; - ; 1.9.1656; 1.9.1656; 27.6.1666; 7. Fd as Ofeild.

1350. Savill Wright; Ralph (d); London; C & MT; 8.6.1648; 8.6.1648; - ; 7.

EDMONDS, Samuel

1351. Mercy More; John (d); London; C & Mr; 4.8.1679; 4.8.1679; - ; 7.

EDMONDSON, Godfrey

1352. Thomas Hucklefoote; Wm (d); great Peadling, Leics; Cl; 24.1.1642; 29.9.1641; 8.10.1649; 8. Fd as Huckle.

1353. John Moirriell. Bd to Edmondson 26.6.1637; t.o. to Nicholas Bourne 6.12.1641.

EDWARDS, David

1354. Thomas Baily; Stephen (d); London; C & Gr; 4.7.1698; 4.7.1698; - ; 7.

1355. John Bowes; Jasper; parish of St Clement Danes, M'sex; T; 10.9.1694; 10.9.1694; - ; 7. T.o. to Margaret Bennett 6.2.1699.

EDWARDS, George

1356. John Collins. Fd by Edwards 2.2.1648. Bd to him 19.4.1630.

1357. Richard Edlyn. Fd by Edwards 1.9.1645 (possibly an error for 1.12.1645). Bd to him 6.8.1638.

1358. William Edwards; Thomas (d) Sibbeard Ferris, Oxon; Y; 6.12.1641; 25.12.1641; - ; 8.

1359. Francis Hearne; Fran; Burmington, War; H; 17.11.1645; 17.11. 1645; - ; 7. Possibly the Francis Heiron fd by redemption 12.11.1649.

1360. Joseph Nevill; Wm; Havering, Essex; Y; 5.5.1645; 5.5.1645; 4.5. 1653; 7. T.o. on the death of Edwards to John Wright 13.4.1648. Fd by Wright and Edwards.

1361. Christopher Tatnall. Fd by Edwards 6.12.1647. Bd to him 19.12. 1634.

EDWARDS, Ralph

1362. John Barrett; Francis; Doddington, Hunts; Cl; 27.9.1650; 27.9. 1650; 5.10.1657; 7. Fd by Edwards and Samuel Mearne.

1363. George Powell; Wm; Brayles, War; Y; 4.2.1650; 4.2.1650; 6.4.1657; 8. Fd by Edwards and Francis Hearne.

1364. Thomas Salmon; Tho; Mashfield, Glos; G; 4.4.1653; 4.4.1653; - ; 7.

1365. Edward Wynniard; James (d); London; T; 2.3.1646; 20.10.1645; 7.3. 1653; 9.

EDWYN, Jonathan

1366. Edward Burroughes; John (d); London; C & St; 7.10.1672; 7.10.1672; 17.10.1679; 7. Fd as Burrowes.

1367. Luke Meredith; John; Rutchin, Den; G; 7.5.1677; 7.5.1677; 13.5.1684; 7. Fd by Richard Royston.

EGGLESFIELD, Francis

1368. Justinian Angell; Robert; Giles Cripplegate, M'sex; E; 6.12.1652; 1.3.1653; - ; 7.

1369. William Bowler; John; London; C & MT; 7.3.1664; 29.9.1663; - ; 8.

1370. Edward Cleave. Fd by Francis Archer 13.1.1642. Bd to him 20.12.1633; t.o. to Egglesfield 1.10.1638.

1371. John Egglesfeild. Fd by patrimony 7.2.1681.

1372. Thomas Johnson; Edward; Reading, Berks; Ha; 2.11.1646; 2.11.1646; 5.12.1653; 7.

1373. Joshua Phillips. Fd by Egglesfield 1.9.1679. Bd to Benjamin Hurlock (q.v.) 5.8.1672.

1374. Jervas Randall alius Mole; Jervas; Bromsgrave, Worcs; Dr of Physick; 26.7.1658; 25.3.1658; - ; 8.

1375. Francis Redman; Edmund (d); London; C & St; 1.5.1654; 1.5.1654; - ; 8.

EGGLESFIELD, Thomas

1376. William Cadman; Willm (d); Preston, Lancs; Y; 6.4.1657; 6.4.1657; 2.5.1664; 7.

1377. Thomas Clopton; William; Grotton, Suff; E; 21.12.1650; 21.12.1650; 6.9.1658; 7.

1378. Henry Smith; Henry; - , Sussex; G; 16.1.1665; 16.1.1665; - ; 7.

EKINS, Nathaniel

1379. Joseph Spencer; Wm; Scaldwell, N'hants; Cl; 5.4.1652; 5.4.1652; - ; 7.

ELLIS, Francis

1380. [Francis Ellis. Fd by patrimony 7.6.1676.]

ELLIS, John

1381. Sachariah Done; John; Asellotby, Lincs; Mch; 8.6.1646; 8.6.1646; - ; 7.

1382. Joseph Jackson; Edmond (d); Boston, Lincs; Gr; 17.9.1651; 17.9.1651; 25.11.1664; 7.

1383. George Snodon. Fd by Ellis 3.8.1674. Apparently never formally bd.

ELLIS, Thomas

1384. Thomas Hawson. Fd by Ellis and Lawrence Udall 5.4.1642. Bd to Ellis 6.5.1634.

ELLIS, William

1385. Richard Cutler; Richard (d); Citty of Westmr; Cheesemonger; 6.9.1647; 6.9.1647; - ; 7.

1386. Willm Ellis. Fd by patrimony 1.12.1662.

1387. Henry Taylor; James; Dalton, Lancs; Y; 21.1.1644; 21.1.1644; - ; 7.

ELLISTON, Edward

1388. John West; Thomas; St Margaretts Westmr; St; 1.3.1680; 1.3.1680; 23.3.1687; 7.

ELLISTON, Oliver

1389. Phillipp Guidee; Phillipp; London; Doctor of Physic; 4.2.1695; 4.2.1695; - ; 7.

1390. Roger Reeve; Thomas (d); London; C & Salter; 8.6.1691; 8.6.1691; - ; 7.

ELMES, Robert

1391. Vezey Hastlefoote; Tho; Messing, Essex; G; 1.7.1695; 1.7.1695; - ; 7.

1392. Agar Warren; Samuell; London; G; 5.12.1698; 5.12.1698; 3.6.1706; 7.

1393. John Wright; George; Brandon, Suff; Cl; 6.8.1694; 6.8.1694; - ; 7.

ELY, Thomas

1394. William Baker; William; Tanton, Som; Ha; 2.12.1650; 29.9.1650; - ; 9.

1395. Francis Waddington; John; London; Poulterer; 1.3.1651; 1.3.1651; 1.3.1658; 7.

EMERY, Jasper

1396. Thomas Emery. Fd by patrimony 9.2.1674.

1397. Luke Love. Fd by Emery 5.4.1642. Bd to him 1.12.1634.

EMERY, Thomas

1398. Arthur Ashton; Tho; St Andrews Holborn, London; G; 7.9.1674; 7.9.1674; 10.8.1686; 8.

ENDERBY, Samuel

1399. Thomas Bridges; Walter; London; Cl; 1.12.1645; 1.12.1645; - ; 7.

ENGLISH, Joseph

1400. John Birde; Wm; Hackney, M'sex; Mch; 4.1.1690; 4.1.1690; - ; 7.

ESNEAD, Charles

1401. [Charles Esnead, 'forrainer', fd 2.4.1688, paying £5.]

EVANCE, Daniel

1402. Martin Calthorp; Christopher (d); London; C & Girdler; 7.6.1680; 7.6.1680; - ; 7.

1403. Walter Hardyman; Tho; Lydyard, Wilts; G; 1.3.1680; 1.3.1680; - ; 7.

1404. Joseph Hunt; James (d); Farneham, Surr; Mr; 3.7.1682; 3.7.1682; - ; 7.

1405. Henry Pease; Joseph (d); Moreton, Parish of Anderby, Yorks; G; 26.3.1683; 26.3.1683; - ; 7.

1406. Robert Wright; Robt; St Neotts, Hunts; G; 5.3.1688; 5.3.1688; - ; 7.

EVANS, Henry

1407. Joseph Cater; Joseph; London; C & St; 3.6.1672; 3.6.1672; 7.7.1679; 7.

1408. Bartholomew Davison; Willm; ye Burrough of Leicester; Spectaclemaker; 6.4.1657; 6.4.1657; - ; 7.

1409. William Earnly; Thomas; Byddyford, Dev; Y; 7.8.1666; 7.8.1666; - ; 7.

1410. Richard Fletcher. Bd to Jane Pattison (q.v.) 17.4.1648; t.o. to Evans 3.2.1651. m.n. 'This should have been entred the third of Febru'. In the note of the turnover the name of Fletcher's former master is given as John Pattison.

1411. John Gethin; Humfrey; Eglesbaugh, Den; G; 2.8.1669; 2.8.1669; 2.4.1677; 7.

1412. John Hollis; Robert; London; C & Leatherseller; 2.11.1658; 2.11.1658; - ; 7.

1413. Robte Neale; Henry (d); Berry St Edmonds, Suff; 3.5.1647; 3.5.1647; - ; 8.

1414. Roger Nealer; Roger; Manchester, Lancs; Mr; 3.7.1676; 3.7.1676; - ; 7.

1415. Doyley Quarles; Charles; Wansted, Essex; G; 4.2.1650; 4.2.1650; 3.8.1657; 7.

1416. John Veasey; John; Southwark, Surr; Ca; 2.12.1672; 2.12.1672; 11.10.1680; 7.

EVANS, John

1417. [John Evans. Son of Roger Evans; fd by patrimony 6.3.1654.]

1418. Thomas Palyn; Thomas; Shocklitch, Ches; Y; 18.12.1658; 18.12.1658; - ; 7.

EVANS, Sampson

1419. John Mountfort; William; Kederminster, Worcs; Y; 5.12.1681; 5.12.1681; - ; 7. Indentures allowed to be sealed at Worcester (Court-Book E, 5.12.1681).

1420. John Price; John; Nantmell, Rad; Y; 3.10.1670; 3.10.1670; - ; 7.

EVANS, William

1421. Willm Holford; Elitzer; St Giles Cripplegate, [London]; Y; 4.12. 1676; 4.12.1676; - ; 7.

EVERINGHAM, John

1422. John Hunt; Anthony; Parish of Stepny, [M'sex]; Weaver; 1.9.1690; 1.9.1690; 5.9.1698; 7.

1423. Henry Reeve; Henry (d); parish of St Andrew Holbourne, M'sex; Ca; 6.3.1699; 6.3.1699; 6.10.1707; 7.

EVERINGHAM, Richard

1424. Thomas Smith Cowell; John; Tuexbury, Glos; Y; 5.8.1695; 1.7.1695; 1.3.1703; 7.

1425. David Kite; Nicholas; Honnyborne, Glos; Y; 3.6.1695; 3.6.1695; - ; 7.

EVERINGHAM, Robert

1426. Thomas Cockatt. Fd by Everingham 7.10.1689. Bd (as Crockatt) to Thomas Hayley (q.v.) 4.9.1682, and fined 2s. 6d. 'For not being turned over at ye Hall'.

1427. Ben Corbett; Watis; Elton, Herefs; G; 4.11.1678; 4.11.1678; 5.7. 1686; 7.

1428. William Everingham. Fd by patrimony 5.8.1689.

1429. John Harlow; John; St Martins in the Feilds, [M'sex]; Y; 6.10. 1679; 6.10.1679; 5.12.1692; 7.

1430. Richard Joseph; Richard (d); Enfeild, M'sex; I; 5.10.1691; 5.10.1691; 7.2.1699; 7.

1431. Andrew Meires; Richard (d); London; C & Salter; 7.10.1689; 7.10. 1689; 2.5.1698; 7.

1432. Thomas Smith. Fd by Everingham 13.3.1693, and fined 2s. 6d. for being bd by a foreign indenture.

1433. William Sudworth; William; Clare, Suff; Y; 6.12.1697; 8.11.1697; 5.2.1705; 7.

1434. Joseph Usqhart. Fd by Everingham 9.2.1691. Apparently never formally bd.

1435. John Watts; William (d); parish of St Martin in the feilds, M'sex; Victualler; 3.10.1698; 3.10.1698; 9.6. 1707; 7. Fd by William Watts.

EVERINGHAM, William

1436. Marmaduke Norfolke; John (d); Hounslett, Yorks; Salter; 2.5.1692; 2.5.1692; 2.10.1699; 8.

EVERSDEN, George

1437. Richard Baldwin; Thomas (d); Wickham, Bucks; Hempdresser; 5.8. 1668; 5.8.1668; 25.8.1675; 7.

1438. William Church; John; 'now in parts beyond the Seas'; - ; 5.12.1681; 5.12.1681; - ; 8.

1439. Thomas Eglesfeild; Rich; St James Clarkenwell, M'sex; G; 1.6.1663; 1.6.1663; - ; 7.

1440. Humphrey Foster; Nath; -, Wilts; Cl; 22.2.1675; 22.2.1675; - ; 7.

1441. Francis Haley; Francis; London; C & Mason; 4.10.1658; 4.10.1658; 31.1.1666; 7. Fd by Eversden and Simon Waterson.

1442. John Hewett; Mathew (d); Helton, Dors; Cl; 5.6.1654; 5.6.1654; 2.9.1661; 7.

1443. John Lipscomb; John; Reading, Berks; Tn; 26.3.1683; 26.3.1683; 13.3.1693; 7. Fd by Widow Davis.

1444. Anthony Medcalfe; Anthony; Redding, Berks; Dr of Physick; 7.12. 1657; 7.12.1657; - 7.

1445. Thomas Owen; Thomas; Whight Chappell, M'sex; Gl; 4.9.1671; 4.9.1671; - ; 7.

1446. John Shelmerdine; Ralph; Manchester, [Lancs]; Bs; 25.8.1675; 25.8.1675; 4.9. 1682; 7.

1447. Israell Smart; Richard; Sturbridge, Worcs; G; 5.9.1664; 5.9.1664; 6.11.1671; 7.

1448. Thomas Wild; Tho (d); Shipton, Glos; Cl; 20.5.1650; 20.5.1650; 1.6.1657; 7. Fd by George and Henry Eversden.

[54]

EVERSDEN, Henry

1449. Thomas Drant. Fd by Eversden 2.9.1650. Bd to him 4.8.1640.

1450. Simon Evernden; Robt; Bright Hempsted, Sussex; Cl; 3.10.1659; 3.10.1659; 9.10.1666; 7. Fd as Eversden.

1451. George Eversden. Fd, probably by patrimony, 23.6.1648. Apparently never formally bd.

1452. Beniamin Foster; Solomon; Mayfeild, Sussex; - ; 3.8.1663; 3.8.1663; 3.10.1670; 7.

1453. Samuell Walsoll; John (d); Barking, Essex; G; 4.12.1671; 4.12.1671; - ; 7.

1454. Thomas Wild. Fd by George and Henry Eversden 1.6.1657. Bd to Henry Eversden (q.v.) 20.5.1650.

EVETTS, Edward

1455. John Booth; Valentine (d); Clay-Coaton, N'hants; Cl; 1.2.1697; 1.2.1697; 5.10.1713; 7.

1456. Robt Lowden; Francis; parrish of St Margaretts Westminster, M'sex; E; 5.5.1684; 5.5.1684; - ; 7.

1457. Robert Thoroton; Henry (d); London; Milliner; 6.8.1688; 6.8.1688; 6.9.1697; 7.

EYLOE, John

1458. Samuel Horne; Thomas; Aston, Glos; Y; 7.7.1684; 7.7.1684; - ; 7.

FABIAN, Thomas

1459. Saml Clement; Phillip; London; C & Embroiderer; 4.6.1683; 4.6.1683; 9.2.1691; 7.

1460. [Thomas Fabian. Fd by redemption 2.8.1675.]

FAGE, Edward

1461. Richard Young; Michaell (d); Rawcliffe, Yorks; H; 5.7.1669; 5.7.1669; 2.4.1677; 7.

FALCONER, Francis

1462. Wm Wenburne. Fd by Falconer 26.6.1643. Bd to him 7.12.1635.

FANN, Freeman

1463. Robert Ryles; Willm; Highgate, M'sex; Gardener; 7.4.1668; 7.4.1668; - ; 7.

FARNHAM, Edward

1464. William Birch; Willm; Kington, Worcs; Cl; 3.9.1660; 3.9.1660; 11.2.1668; 7. Fd (as Burch) by Farnham and John Sims.

FARWELL, Simon

1465. John Daffie. Fd by Farwell 30.8.1641. Bd to him 31.3.1634; rebd to John Haviland 6.11.1637.

FAWCETT, Thomas

1466. Humphrey Charme; Richard (d); Brace-Mill, Shrops; Y; 3.8.1646; 3.8.1646; - ; 7.

1467. Robert Cunningham; John; London; C & Ha; 5.9.1642; 5.9.1642; 5.9.1649; 8.

1468. Richard Fawcett. Fd by patrimony 6.10.1679.

1469. Thomas Greene; Thomas; Westminster, M'sex; G; 7.11.1659; 7.11.1659; - ; 8.

1470. Daniell Gregory; Edmond; London; C & Apothecary; 7.4.1662; 25.3.1662; 2.5.1670; 8.

1471. Edward Horton. Fd by Fawcett and Thomas Finch 7.9.1646. Bd to Finch 28.6.1638.

1472. Moses Hubbert; Robte; London; L; 7.8.1648; 7.8.1648; - ; 9.

1473. Thomas Morrell. Fd by Fawcett and Widow Hamon 1.7.1644. Bd to Judith Hamon 5.6.1637.

FAWNE, Luke

1474. Brabazen Aylmer; Anthony; London; G; 21.1.1661; 21.1.1661; 11.2.1668; 8.

1475. James Chantler. Fd by Fawne and William Aspley 2.12.1644. Bd to Aspley 6.11.1637; t.o. to Fawne 6.12.1641.

1476. Jonathan Robinson; Jno; Shorditch, M'sex; Mch; 6.8.1655; 6.8.1655; 3.11.1662; 7.

1477. Joseph Simonds; Jonathan (d); London; Cw; 7.3.1653; 7.3.1653; - ; 7.

1478. John Starkey. Fd by Fawne and John Saywell 6.11.1655. Bd to Saywell (q.v.) 9.11.1646.

1479. Robte Tutchin; Robte; Bridport, Dors; Cl; 5.12.1642; 29.9.1642; 2.9.1650; 8. Originally bd to Ralph Smith (q.v.) 22.3.1642. Fd by Fawne.

FELTON, Adam

1480. Thomas Dickson; John (d); Hawksworth, Yorks; G; 2.4.1688; 2.4.1688; - ; 7.

1481. Phinehas Harrison; Phinehas (d); Thames Ditton, Surr; Cl; 3.8.1685; 3.8.1685; - ; 7.

1482. John Lovekin; Thomas (d); Tylley, Shrops; G; 8.6.1668; 8.6.1668; - ; 7.

1483. Thomas Mather; Tho; Preston Gubbard, Shrops; G; 3.9.1672; 3.9.1672; 9.1.1688; 7. Fd by John Felton, probably in error for Adam.

1484. William Morrice; William (d); Burlaydam, Ches; G; 6.5.1671; 6.5.1671; - ; 7.

1485. Thomas Scott; Thomas (d); Shrewsbury, Shrops; D; 21.2.1682; 21.2.1682; - ; 7.

1486. Peter Tanner; Martin; Stockton, Wilts; G; 6.5.1678; 6.5.1678; - ; 7.

FELTON, Humphrey

1487. John Lucas; John; Eastdeane, Sussex; - ; 7.9.1663; 1.8.1663; - ; 7.

FENN, Elizabeth, Widow

1488. Humphry Elliott; Gray; Stratford, Herefs; G; 1.2.1697; 1.2.1697; - ; 7.

1489. John Lahunt; David (d); Baradon, Rut; G; 2.10.1699; 2.10.1699; - ; 7.

FENN, John

1490. John Brand; William (d); London; Go; 7.7.1690; 7.7.1690; - ; 7.

1491. Wm Hodges; Thomas; Marleborough, Wilts; Cd; 23.6.1680; 23.6.1680: - ; 7.

1492. Thomas Kirby; Richard; Sutton Hall, Derby; G; 29.1.1685; 29.1.1685; - ; 7.

1493. Oanadine James Messinger; John; - , Glos; G; 11.10.1680; 11.10.1680; - ; 7.

1494. Anthony Watts; Anthony; London; C & MT; 25.6.1688; 25.6.1688; - ; 7.

FERBANKE, Richard

1495. Henry Rogers; Edward; London; G; 1.2.1664; 1.2.1664; 25.6.1684; 7.

FERREY, William

1496. John Turnor; John; white Fryars, London; Victualler; 6.3.1676; 6.3.1676; - ; 8.

FERRICE, Samuel

1497. Richard Springall; Rich; Thame, Oxon; Bu; 4.8.1662; 4.8.1662; - ; 8.

FIELD, Henry

1498. [Henry Feild. Son of Richard Field; fd by patrimony 6.5.1646.]

1499. Wm White; John (d); Westarring, Sussex; Cl; 26.10.1646; 26.10.1646; - ; 7.

FIELD, Hester

1500. Elizabeth Bond; John; Reasbey, Lincs; G; 1.7.1689; 1.7.1689; - ; 7.

FIELD, John

1501. John Camden; John; NorthLynne, Oxon; Y; 3.11.1651; 1.11.1651; 30.4.1659; 8.

1502. John Davis; John; London; C & Ca; 7.2.1659; 7.2.1659; - ; 7.

1503. Hester Feild. Fd by patrimony 3.6.1689.

1504. Thomas Hutchins. Fd by Field and Lawrence Chapman 13.12.1654. Bd to Chapman (q.v.) 2.11.1646.

1505. Marmaduke Johnson; Wm; Rothwell, N'hants; T; 1.9.1645; 1.9.1645; 4.10.1652; 7.

1506. Thomas Johnson. Fd by Field 22.10.1656. Apparently never formally bd.

1507. Thomas Peckett. Fd by Field 7.6.1676. Apparently never formally bd.

1508. John Sprale; John; Winson, Som; Clothier; 21.1.1648; 24.6.1647; 5.2.1655; 8. Fd as Sprake.

1509. Henry Yerrington; Henry; London; C & MT; 2.11.1658; 2.11.1658; - ; 7.

FIFIELD, Alexander

1510. Alexander Fifield. Fd by patrimony 6.2.1671.

1511. Wm Harris; Wm; Ascott, Oxon; Mr; 26.9.1646; 26.9.1646; - ; 7.

1512. Godfrey Head; John; Peasmore, Berks; Cl; 5.8.1650; 1.8.1650; 6.9.1658: 8.

1513. Henry Kimberley; Willm; London; C & MT; 4.5.1657; 4.5.1657; - ; 7.

1514. Richard Kirrey; Edward; Barton, War; Y; 7.10.1644; 7.10.1644; 3.11.1651; 7.

1515. Richard Lewis. Fd by Fifield 8.11.1641. Bd to Thomas Wright 1.3.1630.

1516. George Sherwood. Fd by Fifield and Richard Adams 16.1.1643. Bd to Adams 14.1.1636.

1517. Isaac Sutton. Fd by Fifield 1.12.1645. Bd to him 7.5.1638.

FINCH, Thomas

1518. Edward Horton. Fd by Finch and Thomas Fawcett 7.9.1646. Bd to Finch 28.6.1638.

FIRBY, Syndonia, Widow

1519. Othniell Preston; Othniell; Selby, Yorks; Y; 19.1.1663; 19.1.1663; - ; 7.

1520. Thomas Randes; Willm; Netleham, Lincs; G; 7.5.1667; 29.1.1667; - ; 7. Mrs Firby is described as the late wife of Thomas Firby.

FIRBY, Thomas

1521. Edward Berrill; Will; Ather-ston, War; B; 6.11.1654; 6.11.1654; - ; 7.

FISH, John

1522. Thomas Mallard; Thomas; Westmr, M'sex; G; 4.8.1679; 4.8.1679; - ; 7.

FISHER, Benjamin

1523. William Pope. Fd by Fisher and William Leake 2.8.1641. Bd to Fisher 2.9.1633.

FISHER, William

1524. William Bradley; John; Ockingham, Berks; H; 5.9.1659; 2.8.1659; 5.8.1668; 9.

1525. Joseph Chubb; Richard (d); London; C & Cook; 3.4.1676; 3.4.1676; - ; 8.

1526. George Holliwell; George; London; C & Bricklayer; 8.1.1667; 1.1.1667; 9.2.1674; 7.

1527. Richard Mount; Ralph (d); Chislett, Kent; Y; 10.1.1670; 1.1.1670; - ; 8.

1528. Abraham Spencer; William; London; C & Leatherseller; 9.2.1657; 1.1.1657; - ; 8.

1529. Thomas Webb; Humphrey; Coventry, War; G; 6.3.1654; 6.3.1654; - ; 8.

FITZJAMES, George

1530. Troylus Turbervile; Troylus; Stratford vpon Avon, War; Knight and Baronet; 26.3.1662; 26.3.1662; - ; 7.

FLESHER, Elizabeth

1531. John Sharpe; John; Pawlespury, N'hants; Y; 2.11.1674; 2.11.1674; 7.10.1695; 7. Fd by Elizabeth Flesher and Thomas Snowdon.

1532. Thomas Walker; Isaack; London; C & V; 12.11.1677; 12.11.1677; - ; 7.

FLESHER, James

1533. Robert Addams; John; Oxford; Bs; 5.5.1656; 29.9.1655; 5.10.1663; 8.

1534. Archbold Ashburne; Richard (d); London; C & MT; 6.8.1667; 6.8.1667; - ; 7.

1535. William Beathwaite; John; Barrowdale, Cumb; Y; 6.11.1666; 6.11.1666; 7.2.1676; 8. Fd as Brathwaite.

1536. William Clerdue; John; Cricklard, Wilts; I; 15.1.1649; 25.3.1648; 26.3.1656; 8.

1537. Miles Flesher. Fd by patrimony 7.1.1678.

1538. Francis French; Thomas; Little Cressingham, Norf; Cl; 2.10.1654; 1.1.1654; - ; 8.

1539. Giles Gardner; Wm; Winston, Glos; Y; 17.1.1648; 17.1.1648; 17.1.1655; 7. Fd as Gardiner.

1540. Thomas Lambert; James; Cowick, Yorks; Y; 4.6.1667; 24.6.1667; 3.8.1674; 7.

1541. Thomas More; John; Parish of the Savoy in the Strand, M'sex; - ; 19.9.1670; 19.9.1670; 1.10.1677; 7.

1542. Edward Scarlett; Mathew; Finchfeild, Essex; Farmer; 5.6.1665; 25.3.1665; - ; 8.

1543. John Watson; Thomas (d); Lenton, Lincs; G; 1.8.1659; 25.3.1659; 2.4.1667; 8.

FLESHER, John

1544. Rich Weale; Willm; Cutson, Worcs; Y; 5.2.1672; 5.2.1672; - ; 7.

FLESHER, Miles

1545. Nathaniell Axen. Fd by Flesher 5.4.1647. Bd to him 2.3.1640.

1546. Robert Baker; Richard (d); Kelham, Notts; Y; 5.9.1681; 5.9.1681; 1.10.1688; 7.

1547. William Bartram; John; Henden, M'sex; Y; 24.3.1656; 1.1.1656; 18.1.1664; 8.

1548. Richard Beard. Fd by Flesher 7.12.1646. Bd to him 10.1.1639.

1549. Wm Bowyer; John; London; Gr; 1.9.1679; 1.9.1679; 4.10.1686; 7.

1550. Wm Burrough. Fd by Flesher

and John Legate 29.6.1646. Bd to Legate 16.10.1637.

1551. John Clifford; Edward (d); Oxford; Cook; 1.5.1654; 1.5.1654; 5.8.1661; 7.

1552. James Flesher. Fd by patrimony 5.10.1646.

1553. Bartholomew Fowler; James; Alhallowes Staining, London; - ; 7.6.1686; 7.6.1686; - ; 7.

1554. John Gouldingham; Tho; London; Embroiderer; 19.1.1652; 25.3.1652; 7.11.1659; 7. Fd as Goldingham.

1555. Francis Graythe; Raph (d); London; G; 22.6.1641; 22.6.1641; 10.1.1649; 8. Fd as Gray.

1556. John Grismond. Fd by Flesher 1.2.1641. Bd to him 7.10.1633.

1557. Edward Grove; Edward; London; C & Girdler; 14.4.1656; 1.5.1656; 4.5.1663; 7.

1558. Stanhop Harper; Robert; Beeston, Yorks; Cw; 2.8.1680; 2.8.1680; 5.9.1687; 7.

1559. Richard Harris; Robte (d); Westom, N'hants; Y; 18.8.1641; 18.8.1641; 12.11.1649; 7.

1560. Thomas Haviland; Thom; London; St; 2.8.1652; 2.8.1652; - ; 7.

1561. Edmond Jones. Fd by Flesher 16.3.1648. Bd to him 5.10.1640.

1562. Bryan Lambert. Fd by Flesher 17.8.1646. Bd to him 12.8.1639.

1563. Bryan Lambert. Fd by Flesher 4.11.1672. Apparently never formally bd. Son of preceding?

1564. Peter Lillicrop; Peter (d); Queatheack, Corn; G; 5.4.1647; 5.4.1647; 1.5.1654; 7.

1565. Edward Miller; Edw; Welford, Glos; Y; 4.5.1646; 4.5.1646; - ; 7.

1566. Walter Miller; Edward; Welford, Glos; Y; 1.3.1650; 25.3.1650; - ; 7.

1567. Richard Newcombe. Fd by Flesher, Thomas Newcomb, and Benjamin Mott 8.4.1695. Bd to Newcomb (q.v.) 5.3.1688.

1568. Thomas Parker; Reginald; Ellaston, Staffs; Y; 7.11.1687; 7.11. 1687; 8.4.1695; 7. Bd as Barker, but father's name Parker and fd as such by Flesher and John Heptinstall.

1569. Richard Pope; Richard; Stincomb, Glos; Clothier; 5.2.1655; 5.2. 1655; 3.3.1662; 7.

1570. Nicholas Spicer; Nicholas; London; Ha; 4.10.1641; 1.11.1641; - ; 7.

1571. Theodore Webb; Francis; Winston, Glos; Cl; 25.10.1647; 25.10. 1647; - ; 7.

FLESHER, Thomas

1572. Gabriell Cox; Edw; Kiddington, Oxon; G; 23.6.1652; 25.3.1652; 26.3.1660; 8.

1573. William Jelley; Richard (d); Richards-Castle, Herefs; Y; 3.3.1656; 21.12.1655; - ; 8.

1574. Silvester Kannedy; Walter; Dublin, Ireland; E; 13.6.1659; 24.6. 1659; 13.2.1667; 7. Fd as Kennedy.

1575. John Nicholson; Wm; Burleigh, Yorks; Y; 12.11.1677; 12.11.1677, 19.11.1695; 7.

1576. Benedict Winchcomb; Benedict; Cheame, Surr; G; 2.1.1660; 2.1. 1660; 8.10.1667; 7.

1577. Lawrance Wolfe; Francis; Maidley, Shrops; Y; 4.12.1648; 4.12. 1648; - ; 7.

FLETCHER, Henry

1578. John Craven; Isaac; Ware, Herefs [sic for Herts]; Cl; 7.2.1653; 1.12.1652; 3.12.1660; 8. Fd by Fletcher and John Richardson.

1579. Clement Darby; George; Fladbury, Worcs; G; 5.3.1652; 5.3.1652; 7.3.1659; 7.

FLETCHER, Richard

1580. William Charles; John; Blockley, Worcs; Woolman; 21.1.1661; 21.1. 1661; 6.9.1669; 7. Fd as John Charles.

1581. Thomas Staite; Edward; Block-ley, Worcs; Y; 3.12.1655; 3.12.1655; 6.4.1663; 7.

FLETCHER, Robert

1582. John Bishopp; John; Easthaddon, N'hants; Y; 20.12.1651; 20.12. 1651; 17.1.1659; 7.

1583. William Bishopp. Fd by Fletcher and Thomas Clarke 1.9.1662. Bd to Clarke (q.v.) 4.12.1654.

1584. Edward More; Edward; Lymehouse, M'sex; T; 1.3.1645; 1.3.1645; - ; 8.

1585. Solomon Poole; Richard; London; C & Bl; 17.1.1659; 17.1.1659; - ; 10.

1586. John Southen; John; London; Cw; 6.8.1649; 6.8.1649; 7.12.1657; 9.

1587. Phillip Wallis; Henry; Hull, Yorks; Mariner; 3.10.1648; 3.10.1648; - ; 8.

FLINSTONE, John

1588. John Finch; John; London; C & Armorer; 6.6.1698; 6.6.1698; - ; 7.

FLOOD, George

1589. Robert Bleaton; Samuell; London; C & Silkweaver; 10.1.1649; 10.1.1649; - ; 7. Entry deleted; m.n. 'This Appr. his mr. dyeing bound againe to Mr Tey for 7 yrs by order of Cort. dated 5th of Sept. 1649.' Bd to John Tey (q.v.) 5.9.1649 as Robert Blayton.

FOORD, Allen

1590. Robert Whitlidge; William; -, Lancs; Y; 11.10.1680; 11.10.1680; 7.11.1687; 7. Fd by Abel Rockall, and fined 2s. 6d. 'for not being turned over at the Hall'.

FORD, John

1591. William Charnock; Francis (d); London; C & V; 5.8.1700; 5.8. 1700; - ; 7.

1592. Charles Grist; John; Lacock, Wilts; Weaver; 6.12.1697; 6.12.1697; - ; 7.

FOST, Richard
1593. [Richard Fost. Fd 3.3.1684 by order of the Court of Aldermen.]

FOSTER, John
1594. [John Foster. Fd by patrimony 1.8.1648. Probably the son of Richard Foster, but the father's name is not given.]

FOSTER, Stephen
1595. Wm Bushnell; John Franfeild, Sussex; Minister; 1.3.1680; 1.3.1680; - ; 7.

FOWKES, Edward
1596. William Torrell; John; St Martin in the Feilds, M'sex; Y; 8.11.1675; 8.11.1675; - ; 7.

FOX, Thomas
1597. Thomas Betts; Thomas (d); London; G; 6.8.1688; 6.8.1688; - ; 8.
1598. Joseph Fox. Fd by patrimony 20.12.1687.

FRANK, John, I
1599. Thomas Bucknell; John; Shorditch, M'sex; E; 22.6.1642; 22.6.1642; 2.7.1649; 7. T.o. to Henry Harvey 22.8.1648. Fd by Frank and Harvey.

FRANK, John, II
1600. Thomas Dugdale; Thomas (d); Brainford, M'sex; H; 4.4.1687; 4.4.1687; - ; 7.
1601. John Locker; John (d); Ile of Portland, Dors; Mariner; 3.12.1688; 3.12.1688; 3.2.1696; 7.
1602. Thomas Spencer; Joseph; Istleworth, M'sex; Cook; 1.10.1694; 1.10.1694; - ; 7.

FRANKLIN, Michael
1603. Wm Combe; George (d); London; Bs; 5.4.1647; 5.4.1647; - ; 8.

FRANKLIN, Richard
1604. Henry Collins; Arnold (d); Bristoll, Glos; Gr; 4.9.1682; 4.9.1682; 7.10.1689; 7. Fd by Franklin but said to have been turned over to another master (unnamed) and fined 2s. 6d. 'For not being turned over at the Hall'.
1605. [Richard Francklin. Fd by redemption 1.7.1678.]
1606. Wm Francklyn; Henry; Willsley, Wilts; G; 2.6.1679; 2.6.1679; - ; 7.

FRANKLIN, Robert
1607. William Paman. Fd by Franklin and William Tibbs 6.10.1662. Bd to Tibbs (q.v.) 7.8.1654.

FRANKNELL, John
1608. Jotham Clarke; John; parish of St Martins in feilds, M'sex; T; 5.12.1687; 5.12.1687; - ; 7.
1609. John Shaw; Thomas; London; C & Cd; 6.5.1700; 6.5.1700; - ; 7.

FREEMAN, Samuel
1610. Thomas Nurse; Thomas (d); Yerdsley, Herefs; Ca; 1.5.1671; 1.5.1671; 6.5.1678; 8. Fd by John Hardney.

FREEMAN, William
1611. Richard Chinery; Richard (d); Kennett, Cambs; G; 1.10.1694; 1.10.1694; - ; 7.
1612. Richard Standfast; Thomas; Iland of Barbadoes beyond the Seas; Gr; 3.9.1688; 3.9.1688; 11.11.1695; 7.
1613. James Turner; James; Hitching, Herts; Maltster; 6.8.1683; 6.8.1683; - ; 7.

FRERE, Daniel
1614. John Cater. Fd by Frere 6.6.1659. Apparently never formally bd.
1615. John Saywell. Fd by Frere 4.3.1644. Bd to him 20.2.1637.
1616. Robert Scott; Arthur; Citty of Yorke; Cl; 10.1.1649; 10.1.1649; 31.3.1656; 7. T.o. 7.4.1651 to William Wells. Fd by Frere and Wells.
1617. Phillip Shirley; Edward (d); London; G; 8.6.1648; 8.6.1648; - ; 7.

FRERE, John

1618. Jonathan Maugham; John; Newton, Yorks; Y; 5.9.1698; 5.9.1698; - ; 7.

1619. John Newall; John; parish of St Ethelburgh, London; Y; 6.7.1691; 6.7.1691; - ; 7.

FRITH, Isaac

1620. Charles Gilbert; John (d); London; C & Dy; 6.6.1698; 6.6.1698; 6.8.1705; 7.

1621. James Marriner; Fd by Frith 26.3.1688. Bd to William Ord (q.v.) 7.3.1681, and fined 2s. 6d. 'for not being turned over at the Hall'.

1622. Joseph Oake; Henry (d); London; Mariner; 25.6.1688; 25.6.1688; 1.7.1695; 7.

1623. John Randall; John; Shrewsbury, [Shrops]; - ; 6.11.1693; 6.11.1693; 2.3.1702; 7.

FRYER, William

1624. John Bennett; Nicholas; Hamelton, Rut; Weaver; 7.6.1680; 7.6.1680; 6.4.1696; 7.

1625. William Bennett; Nicholas (d); Hambleton, Rut; Weaver; 8.5.1682; 8.5.1682; 2.10.1699; 7.

1626. Edward Davis; John; - , Shrops; Ca; 6.9.1680; 6.9.1680; 9.9.1689; 7.

1627. [William Fryer. Son of William Fryer; fd by patrimony 3.5.1680.]

1628. Thomas Pomfrett, William; Walden, Essex; Bl; 7.4.1690; 7.4.1690; - ; 7.

FUKES, Thomas

1629. Robte Bogges. Fd by Fukes 18.1.1646. Bd to him 4.6.1638.

1630. Thomas Coe; Thomas (d); Farneham, Surr; Tallowchandler; 5.6.1643; 5.6.1643; 2.9.1650; 7.

1631. Robert Sturt; Robte; Farnham, Surr; Gl; 3.8.1646; 3.8.1646; 3.10.1653; 7. T.o. 2.8.1652 to Isaac Herbert. Fd by Fukes.

1632. Michael Waler; Wm; London; MT; 1.9.1651; 1.9.1651; 4.10.1658; 7. Fd (as Waller) by Fukes and Thomas Matthews.

FUSSELL, Nicholas

1633. William James; William; Edmonton, M'sex; Bu; 6.4.1663; 6.4.1663; - ; 7.

1634. Arthur Otway. Fd by Fussell 3.8.1646. Bd to him 7.12.1635; t.o. 29.3.1641 to 'Mr Browne' to serve out his time 'Except the last yeare'.

FUSSELL, Richard

1635. John Fussell. Fd by patrimony 4.11.1672.

1636. Nicholas Fussell. Fd by patrimony 6.2.1682.

GAINE, John

1637. William Fisher; Michael; Citty of Leicester; Bl; 2.8.1680; 2.8.1680; - ; 8.

1638. Edward Goldstone; Robert (d); London; C & Plasterer; 3.12.1684; 3.12.1684; - ; 7.

GAMAGE, Nicholas

1639. Abraham Bradshaw; Abra (d); London; C & D; 1.5.1648; 1.5.1648; - ; 7.

1640. Symon Pawlins; Richard; Battersey, Surr; Bricklayer; 6.3.1654; 6.3.1654; 1.7.1661; 7.

GAMAGE, Richard

1641. Humphrey Bowrey; Thomas (d); London; C & St; 9.2.1642; 25.12.1641; - ; 8.

GARDNER, Thomas

1642. Thomas Fassett; Thomas; Kerby Lunsdale, W'land; Y; 1.4.1672; 1.4.1672; - ; 7.

1643. Richard Ockley; Richard (d); Witney, Oxon; Clothier; 3.3.1668; 3.3.1668; - ; 7.

GARE, Thomas

1644. William Candish; Edmond (d); Dublyn, Ireland; Cook; 14.6.1647; 14.6.1647; - ; 7.

[61]

1645. Mathew Cordwell; Richard (d); London; T; 3.7.1648; 3.7.1648; - ; 7.

1646. Thomas Gare. Fd by patrimony 26.6.1643.

1647. John Griffith; Francis; London; J; 6.5.1644; 25.3.1644; - ; 8.

1648. John Marsh; Michaell (d); London; Lorimer; 15.7.1644; 25.3.1644; - ; 9.

1649. William Turner; John; Harroll, M'sex; H; 5.12.1659; 5.12.1659; - ; 7.

1650. Henry Wardegar; Geo (d); - , Kent; G; 20.12.1649; 20.12.1649; - ; 7. The entry continues: 'dated the 2d of July 1648. This Indr was made by a Scrivener but allowed of in Cort.'

GARFIELD, John

1651. Joseph Price; David (d); St Dunstones in ye West, M'sex; I; 6.10.1656; 6.10.1656; - ; 7.

GARFORD, Richard

1652. [Richard Garford. Son of Richard Garford; fd by patrimony 19.1.1652.]

GARRET, Charles

1653. Samuell White; Samuell (d); Wansworth, Surr; Br; 6.11.1682; 6.11.1682; 6.12.1697; 7. Fd by Henry Cripps.

GARRETSON, John

1654. Edward Sea; Thomas (d); London; C & D; 7.10.1689; 7.10.1689; - ; 7.

GARTHWAITE, Timothy

1655. Joseph Clarke; Thomas; Welton, Lincs; Cl; 3.12.1655; 3.12.1655; 2.3.1663; 7.

1656. John More; Francis; City of Yorke; G; 3.3.1662; 3.3.1662; - ; 8.

1657. John North; Beniamyn; London; Ha; 16.5.1648; 16.5.1648; 11.6.1655; 7.

GAWILL, Edward

1658. Thomas Rider; [Richard] (d); Chelton, Wilts; Clothier; 12.10.1657; 12.10.1657; - ; 7. Rebd to Richard Bailey (q.v.) 1.8.1659.

GEE, William

1659. David Auvray; Jacob (d); London; C & G; 4.9.1671; 4.9.1671; - ; 7.

GELLIBRAND, Edward

1660. Charles West; Thomas (d); Northton, [N'hants]; Bs; 2.7.1677; 2.7.1677; - ; 7.

GELLIBRAND, Henry

1661. James Clarke; Giles; Stanton, Worcs; Y; 6.6.1698; 6.6.1698 - ; 7.

GELLIBRAND, John

1662. Saml Gellibrand; Henry (d); Linningston Lovell, Oxon [*sic* for Bucks]; Cl; 4.6.1683; 4.6.1683; 5.5.1701; 7.

GELLIBRAND, Obedience, Widow

1663. John Garrettson; Nich (d); Whitechappell, M'sex; - ; 5.3.1677; 5.3.1677; 7.8.1684; 7. Fd by Robert Jole, but described as servant to Henry Cruttenden.

1664. Thomas Hall; Isaac (d); St George Southwarke, Surr; Coffeeman; 2.12.1700; 2.12.1700; - ; 7.

1665. Wm Wilkinson; Simon; London; C & Weaver; 3.5.1680; 3.5.1680; - ; 7.

GELLIBRAND, Samuel

1666. Joseph Barber; Joseph (d); London; Embroiderer; 2.6.1645; 24.6.1645; 29.6.1653; 8.

1667. Daniell Foxcraft; James; Hallifax, Yorks; Oilman; 13.1.1642; 21.12.1641; 1.10.1677; 8.

1668. Edward Gellibrand. Fd by patrimony 6.12.1675.

1669. John Gellibrand. Fd by patrimony 7.6.1676.

1670. William Godfrey; William (d); London; C & Winecooper; 4.8.1656; 4.8.1656; - ; 8.

1671. Will Miller; Geo (d); London; C & St; 29.6.1653; 29.6.1653; 10.7.1660; 7.

1672. Samll Smith. Fd by Gellibrand 6.3.1682. Apparently never formally bd.

GENT, Samuel

1673. Saml Horne; Thomas; Parrish of St Mary WhiteChappl, [M'sex]; Cd; 1.10.1683; 1.10.1683; - ; 7.

1674. Joseph Pen; John; Grays Inn Lane, M'sex; Bricklayer; 4.11.1689; 4.11.1689; - ; 7.

GEORGE, Richard

1675. Robert Beard; Edward (d); Almsbury, Wilts; Y; 3.5.1686; 3.5.1686; - ; 8.

1676. William Boote; Joseph; London; C & MT; 6.11.1693; 6.11.1693; - ; 8.

1677. Thomas Eaton; Thomas; Parish of Whitechappell, M'sex; Mi; 7.10.1678; 7.10.1678; - ; 7.

1678. William Ewer; Richard (d); Heyworth, Wilts; - ; 7.2.1681; 7.2.1681; - ; 7.

1679. John George; John; Burford, Oxon; Y; 3.2.1673; 3.2.1673; - ; 7.

1680. Medrick Meade; Matthew (d); Enfeild, [M'sex]; Y; 6.10.1679; 6.10.1679; 2.5.1687; 7.

1681. Samuell White; Samuell; London; C & Cw; 2.11.1696; 2.11.1696; - ; 7.

GEORGE, Walter, alias WATKINS

1682. Stephen Keyes; Calver; Denham, Suff; Y; 8.11.1669; 8.11.1669; - ; 7.

1683. Francis Steevery; Rowland; Eckenton, Derby; G; 6.11.1676; 6.11.1676; - ; 7. Bd to 'Walter Watkins'.

GERRARD, Elizabeth

1684. John Gerrard; James; Wiggin, Lancs; G; 3.5.1686; 1.9.1685; - ; 7. See next entry.

GERRARD, John

1685. [John Gerrard. Fd by redemption 6.3.1689 by order of the Mayor and Court of Aldermen, paying 5s. 1od. See preceding entry.]

1686. Matthew Highstreete; Matthew; parrish of St Martins in the Feilds, M'sex; G; 6.2.1693; 6.2.1693; - ; 7.

1687. Charles Noy; Charles; Ailesbury, Bucks; Boddicemaker; 6.11.1699; 6.11.1699; - ; 7.

GERRARD, Robert

1688. Thomas Palmer; James; parish of Martock, Som; - ; 5.8.1678; 5.8.1678; 7.9.1685; 7.

1689. Thomas Sutton; Tho; - , Berks; - ; 2.8.1675; 2.8.1675; - ; 7.

GETTINS, Thomas

1690. Thomas Griffis; Abraham; Terrimoneth, Mont; Y; 1.2.1658; 21.12.1657; 7.8.1671; 8.

GIBBONS, Henry

1691. Thomas Baley; Thomas; Hickleng, Notts; Sh; 2.5.1642; 24.6.1642; 2.9.1650; 7.

GIBBS, Rebecca

1692. Martha Lock; John; Warneford, S'hants; Y; 4.9.1676; 4.9.1676; - ; 7.

GIBBS, Robert

1693. John Dalloway; John; London; C & Ha; 12.11.1649; 1.12.1649; - ; 8.

1694. Rebecca Gibbs. Fd by patrimony 28.6.1676.

1695. Robert Gibbs. Fd by patrimony 13.4.1698.

1696. Nathaniell Ponder; Jno; Rothwell, N'hants; Mr; 2.6.1656; 2.6.1656; 4.7.1663; 7.

1697. Daniell Storer; Issac; London; C & Ha; 2.2.1662; 2.2.1662; - ; 7.

GIFFORD, Robert

1698. Nicholas Collier; Richd (d); parish of St Giles without Cripplegate, London; Woodmonger; 6.12.1686; 6.12.1686; - ; 7.

1699. Jeremy Denton; Richard; Parrish of St Alhallowes Barking, M'sex; L; 3.3.1684; 3.3.1684; - ; 7.

1700. Morton Peale. Fd by Gifford 2.11.1691. Bd to John Cholmley (q.v.) 2.10.1682.

GILBERT, William

1701. Charles Blount. Fd by Gilbert 10.6.1684. Apparently never formally bd.

GILBERTSON, William

1702. Jonothan Arnold; Anthony; Epsam, Surr; - ; 7.12.1663; 7.12. 1663; - ; 8.

1703. George Emery; George; Islington, M'sex; Chandler; 5.9.1653; 5.9. 1653; - ; 8.

1704. William Ireland; Edw; Redburne, Herts; I; 16.3.1657; 16.3.1657; - ; 7.

1705. Charles Tyas; Charles; Guilford, Surr; Y; 8.10.1649; 8.10.1649; 22.10.1656; 7.

1706. William Whitwood; William (d); ye Strand, M'sex; T; 30.4.1659; 30.4.1659; 4.5.1666; 7. Fd by Gilbertson and Robert White.

GODBID, Anne

1707. Peregrine Huttoph; - ; - , - ; - ; 4.11.1678; 4.11.1678; - ; 7. See next entry.

1708. Charles Peregrine. The entry reads: 'Bound to Ann Godbidd and turned over to Benjamin Mott—this day [1.2.1686] made free. paid [2s. 6d.] for not being turned over at this Hall'. Fd by Mott 1.2.1686.

GODBID, William

1709. Symon Chamberlaine; John; Canke, Staffs; Y; 13.7.1657; 13.7.1657; 5.9.1664; 7.

1710. Richard Christmas; John; London; G; 6.8.1667; 29.9.1667; 5.10. 1674; 7.

1711. John Crutch; Richard; Oxford; Gl; 26.3.1674; 26.3.1674; 11.4.1681; 7.

1712. John Johnson; Willm; London; C & Weaver; 3.2.1673; 3.2.1673; 24.3.1680; 7.

1713. Rowland Johnson. Fd by Godbid and John Odell 1.7.1665. Bd to Odell (q.v.) 7.9.1657.

1714. John Playford; Mathew; Stanmore, M'sex; Cl; 6.11.1666; 6.11.1666; 1.12.1673; 7.

1715. John Thomas; Thomas; Grasford, Den; G; 7.7.1656; 7.7.1656; - ; 7.

1716. George Vnderhill; Samuel; Blackwell, Worcs; G; 18.6.1677; 18.6. 1677; - ; 7.

GOLBORNE, George

1717. Dixey Page; Oliver; London; C & Girdler; 4.8.1656; 24.6.1656; 27.6. 1664; 8. Fd by Golborne and Peter Cole.

GOODALL, Richard

1718. William Goodall. Fd by patrimony 5.9.1681.

1719. Samuell Rochf; Peter (d); St Martins in ye feilds, M'sex; Y; 1.12. 1662; 1.12.1662; - ; 7.

GOODWIN, Timothy

1720. Tobias Garbrand; Tobias; Abington, Berks; Doctor in Physic; 7.7. 1684; 7.7.1684; - ; 7.

1721. George Mowbray; Thomas; Headlam, Dur; G; 5.12.1692; 5.12. 1692; - ; 7.

1722. Edward Valentine; John; Manchester, Lancs; Mr; 3.8.1696; 3.8.1696; 8.11.1703; 7.

GORING, Elizabeth

1723. John Shuter; Thomas; Parrish of Cripplegate, London; Gl; 7.4. 1684; 7.4.1684; 4.5.1691; 7. The entry of freedom gives Shuter's original master as Edward Garing; t.o. to John

Millett (n.d.) and fd by him, but fined 2s. 6d. 'For not being turned over at the Hall'.

GORING, Jane, Widow

1724. Thomas Harrard; John; Sheere, Surr; T; 5.12.1664; 5.12.1664; - ; 7. This apprentice's indentures were stopped pending an explanation by Mrs Goring (Court-Book D, 5.12. 1664).

GORING, John

1725. John Browne; Thomas; parish of St Sepulchers, London; Sh; 3.9. 1660; 3.9.1660; 3.2.1669; 10.

1726. Thomas Goring; Thomas; Guilford, Surr; Bricklayer; 31.5.1650; 31.5.1650; 2.11.1657; 7.

1727. Richard Rash; Richard; London; T; 2.4.1649; 2.4.1649; - ; 7.

1728. John Sadler; Lawrence; London; C & Ha; 2.3.1657; 2.3.1657; 27.6.1664; 7.

1729. Richard Taylor; John (d); Broad Hinton, Wilts; Ca; 2.11.1657; 2.11.1657; - ; 7. Reported as having run away; crossed out by order 3.9.1660.

1730. Sebast Weme; Tho; parish of St Sepulchars, [London]; T; 2.8.1652; 2.8.1652; - ; 9.

GORING, Thomas

1731. John Levett; John (d); London; C & Dy; 7.11.1664; 7.11.1664; - ; 7.

1732. Robert Litleboy; Robte; Colebrooke, Bucks; - ; 7.10.1668; 7.10. 1668; 6.3.1676. Fd as Thomas Littleboy.

1733. Luke Skinner; Luke (d); - , - ; - ; 2.7.1677; 2.7.1677; 1.3.1686; 8.

GOSLING, John

1734. Henry Huggeford; Henry; Hyon, Staffs; G; 3.8.1663; 3.8.1663; - ; 7.

GOSSON, Henry

1735. Robte Purden. T.o. from Gosson to Francis Smethwicke 2.5.1642.

Bd to Gosson (as Robert Burden) 4.12. 1637.

GOUGH, Barbara

1736. [Barbara Gough. Fd by redemption 2.8.1680.]

GOUGH, Edward

1737. Edward Boyse; John; London; C & Girdler; 6.5.1661; 6.5.1661; - ; 8.

1738. Malcomb Feven; Robert; Thistleworth, M'sex; Gardener; 24.10. 1653; 24.10.1653; - ; 8.

1739. Thomas Gittens. Fd by Gough 22.3.1650. Bd to Richard Gough 30.6. 1634.

1740. Christopher Lingard; Richard; Higham-Ferris, N'hants; Surgeon; 6.12. 1647; 6.12.1647; 7.7.1662; 7.

1741. James Roulson; James (d); Tidbury, Staffs; Mason; 1.2.1658; 1.2.1658; - ; 7.

GOUGH, Richard

1742. Wm Dyos. Fd by Gough 15.2. 1647. Bd to him 2.9.1639.

GOULD, Thomas

1743. Edward Bradbourne; Hum (d); London; Cw; 22.1.1652; 22.1.1652; - ; 8.

1744. Ralph Delues. Fd by Gould 14.6.1657. Bd to him 3.12.1638.

1745. Robert Gibbs. Fd by Gould 6.11.1648. Bd to him 1.7.1640.

1746. Thomas Gould. Fd by patrimony 3.9.1660.

1747. Daniell Hater; John; Enford, Wilts; Y; 19.1.1663; 19.1.1663; 1.3. 1670: 7. Fd as Slater.

1748. Robte Mansell; Wm; Farnham, Surr; Y; 22.12.1646; 22.12.1646; - ; 8.

1749. John Overton; Tho; Covent Garden, M'sex; T; 30.6.1655; 30.6. 1655; 4.7.1663; 8.

1750. George Savile; George; Blaby, Leics; G; 11.2.1661; 11.2.1661; 11.2. 1668; 7.

1751. George Sewster; George (d); London; Go; 31.5.1650; 24.6.1650; - ; 7.

1752. Ferdinando Walmesley; James; London; C & Leatherseller; 22.8.1648; 22.8.1648; 12.10.1657; 9.

1753. Edward Yerwood; Willm; Petworth, Sussex; G; 4.6.1667; 4.6.1667; - ; 7.

GOULDHAM, John

1754. [John Gouldham. Son of Robert Gouldham; fd by patrimony 8.5.1665.]

GOULDING, John

1755. [John Golding. Son of John Goulding; fd by patrimony 10.6.1650.]

GRACE, John

1756. [John Grace. This name appears alone in the Book of Freedoms, with no note of master nor any other detail, under date 3.12.1677.]

GRADON, George

1757. Giles Greenhough; Geo; St Giles in the feilds, M'sex; G; 4.2.1650; 4.2.1650; 7.7.1662; 7.

1758. Jesse Silvester; Wm; Peterfeild, Hants; Y; 19.1.1652; 19.1.1652; - ; 7. The surname has been altered to Silvester from Silverstone.

1759. Symon Walcott. Fd by Gradon and Ferdinando Pennithorne 4.5.1657. Bd to Pennithorne (q.v.) 7.11.1642.

GRAFTON, George

1760. Robert Knell; Clement (d); London; C & St; 3.2.1696; 3.2.1696; 5.4.1703; 7. Fd by James Orme.

GRANGER, John

1761. Edward Ashcomb; Thomas; Stanhick, Oxon; L; 29.6.1646; 24.6.1646; - ; 8.

1762. Richard Brasington; Robte; St Mary Overies, Southwark, [Surr]; Y; 14.10.1641; 14.10.1641; - ; 8.

1763. Jon Francklyn. Fd by Granger 3.8.1646. Bd to him 4.4.1636.

1764. Henry Gisborne; Henry; Eiston Vnderhill, —; Ship's Carpenter; 3.11.1652; 3.11.1652; - ; 7.

1765. John Jowkin; Robert; Newington, Surr; H; 1.3.1642; 1.3.1642; - ; 9.

1766. William Pinker; John; Bray, Berks; H; 6.11.1654; 6.11.1654; - ; 7.

1767. John Williams; John; Glasborough, Rad; Weaver; 7.1.1656; 7.1.1656; - ; 7.

GRANGER, Thomas

1768. Thomas Oldoms; Willm (d); Coventry, War; Tiler; 1.6.1657; 1.6.1657; - ; 7.

GRANTHAM, John

1769. Richard Feilding. Fd by Grantham 6.8.1688. Fined 2s. 6d. 'for being bound by a Forraine Indrs'.

1770. [John Grantham. Son of Bernard Grantham; fd by patrimony 7.10.1672.]

1771. Henry Lawrence; Richard (d); London; C & D; 6.6.1681; 6.6.1681; 1.10.1688; 7.

GRANTHAM, William

1772. John Browne. Fd by Grantham and Christopher Meredith 4.5.1653. Bd to Meredith (q.v.) 27.4.1646.

1773. Richard Creswell; Robt; Alisbury, Bucks; Musician; 4.6.1660; 4.6.1660; 2.6.1668; 8.

1774. Anthony Delacourt; Anthony; Tilshead, Wilts; Cl; 6.9.1669; 25.3.1669; - ; 8.

GRAY, James

1775. [James Gray. Fd, probably by patrimony, 1.6.1663.]

GREENE, Charles

1776. Joseph Cranford; James; parish of St Christophers, London; Cl; 27.9.1645; 1.9.1645; 6.9.1652; 8. Fd by Edward Dod.

GREENE, Christopher
1777. William Blunke; Will; Lambeth, Surr; T; 6.10.1656; 6.10.1656; - ; 8.

GREENE, George
1778. Edward Dod. Fd by Greene and Phillip Nevill 29.6.1646. Bd to Nevill 4.12.1637.
1779. Thomas Edwards; Alexander (d); Hampmothill, War; Y; 15.1.1646; 15.1.1646; - ; 8.
1780. George Greene. Fd by patrimony 18.1.1647.
1781. Samuel Greene. Fd by patrimony 5.10.1691. Son of preceding?
1782. John Saben; Richard; Chakum, N'hants; Y; 1.7.1644; 1.7.1644; 14.6.1652; 8.
1783. Thomas Seare; Thomas; Redford, Glos; Cl; 1.5.1654; 1.5.1654; 3.3.1662; 8. In the entry of freedom Greene is noted as deceased.
1784. Beniamyn Wells; Richard (d); Chakum, N'hants; Y; 3.12.1649; 29.9.1649; 4.4.1664; 8.
1785. Wm Wells; Richard (d) Chakum, N'hants; Y; 10.8.1646; 10.8.1646; - ; 7.

GREENE, Richard
1786. [Richard Greene. Fd by redemption 2.3.1685. In addition to the usual admittance fee of 3s. 4d. Greene paid a fine of £6.6s.]

GREENHILL, Nicholas
1787. Edward Bray. Fd by Greenhill and John Hinson 14.7.1645. Bd to Greenhill 2.11.1635.

GREENUP, Richard
1788. Abraham Allen; Stephen; Southwarke, [Surr]; Silkthrowster; 1.12.1645; 1.12.1645; - ; 7.
1789. Edward Carr; Jo; Whitechappell, [M'sex]; Stockingseller; 2.2.1652; 2.2.1652; 7.11.1659; 7.
1790. John Harison; Adam; parish of St Olaves, Southwark, [Surr]; Silk-weaver; 5.10.1646; 5.10.1646; - ; 11.
1791. John Kitchen; John; Annowseed, Cumb; Y; 4.2.1650; 4.2.1650; 5.4.1658; 9.
1792. George Maxwell; Wm; London; Cl; 4.10.1652; 4.10.1652; 7.11.1659; 7.
1793. Austen Nelson; James; Wapping, M'sex; Hosier; 1.10.1655; 1.10.1655; - ; 7;

GREENWOOD, Jonathan
1794. Adam Chandler; Francis (d); Cooper's Sale, Essex; Cl; 3.7.1682; 3.7.1682; 5.8.1689; 7. Fd as Abraham Chandler.

GRIFFIN, Anne, Widow
1795. David Mallett; David; Henley on Thames, Oxon; M; 13.7.1657; 25.3.1657; 7.2.1676; 8. Fd by Sarah Griffin.

GRIFFIN, Bennet
1796. John Beadle; Henry; parish of St Mary Overs Southwarke, [Surr]; Cd; 25.6.1688; 25.6.1688; - ; 8.
1797. John Brocas. Fd by Griffin 5.12.1692. Apparently never formally bd.
1798. Stephen Bryan; Mathew; —, Som; Cl; 8.5.1699; 8.5.1699; 3.6.1706; 7. Fd by Lewis Thomas.
1799. Thomas Dawgs; Thomas; St Martin in ye Feilds, [M'sex]; G; 2.4.1677; 2.4.1677; 5.5.1684; 7.
1800. William Griffitts; William; Queenhill, Worc; Y; 6.6.1681; 6.6.1681; 1.7.1689; 8.
1801. John Hornesby; John; Ousby, Cumb; Y; 6.9.1680; 6.9.1680; - ; 7.
1802. Henry Lovell; Henry (d); Parish of Wells, Som; H; 3.6.1700; 3.6.1700; 9.6.1707; 7. Fd by Gilham Hills.
1803. Thomas Redding; Daniell; Cliffords Inne, London; G; 27.3.1693; 27.3.1693; - ; 7.

1804. Nevill Simmons; Tho; Stockwith, Notts;   -   ; 12.9.1692; 12.9.1692; 4.12.1699; 7. The father is also described as Citizen and Stationer of London. Fd as Simonds.

1805. Thomas Wood; Paul (d); parish of Over, Ches; Cl; 2.5.1698; 2.5.1698; 9.2.1708; 7. Fd by Christian Griffin, Widow.

GRIFFIN, Edward

1806. Thomas Ashton; Rich; Leigh, Lancs; Y; 8.6.1648; 1.5.1648;   -   ; 8.

1807. Andrew Crawley; Wm; London; C & St; 29.3.1641; 29.3.1641; 17.4.1648; 7.

1808. Wm Goodale; Arthur; Overton, S'hants; Y; 3.11.1647; 29.9.1647; - ; 8.

1809. Bernard Grantham. Fd by Griffin 3.11.1647. Bd to him 1.10.1638.

1810. Bennett Gryffin. Fd by patrimony 4.5.1666.

GRIFFIN, Sarah, Widow

1811. Edward Cart. Fd by Sarah Griffin 24.3.1680. Apparently never formally bd.

1812. John Curtis; Henry; Pepper, Oxon; Y; 5.12.1670; 5.12.1670;   -   ; 8.

1813. John Dickenson; Richard; Kings thorp, N'hants; Y; 4.8.1662; 24.6.1662; 7.11.1670; 8.

1814. Marcus Long; William; parish of St James Clerkewell, M'sex; Y; 9.2.1674; 9.2.1674; 11.4.1681; 7.

1815. David Mallett. Fd by Sarah Griffin 7.2.1676. Bd to Anne Griffin (q.v.) 13.7.1657.

1816. Thomas Mills; Tho; London; Pavier; 5.8.1672; 5.8.1672;   -   ; 8.

1817. John Searles; Richard (d); St Mary Otray, Dev; Weaver; 8.11.1669; 8.11.1669;   -   ; 8.

1818. Thomas Waterworth; Thomas; St Martins in the Feilds, M'sex; G; 5.6.1654; 25.3.1654; 7.4.1662; 8.

1819. Thomas Westrey; Thom; Cleater, Cumb; Cl; 4.8.1656; 4.8.1656; 7.9.1663; 7.

1820. John Wood; William; Witney, Oxon; Clothier; 5.6.1654; 25.3.1654; - ; 8.

GRIFFITH, Paul

1821. David Lees; Adam; parish of St Andrews Holbourne, [M'sex]; St; 3.11.1690; 3.11.1690;   -   ; 7.

GRIGMAN, George

1822. Edward Owens; James; Orton Madock, Flint; Shopkeeper; 1.5.1671; 1.5.1671;   -   ; 7.

1823. Willm Tuckerman; John (d); Chinkford, Essex; H; 3.9.1667; 3.9.1667;   -   ; 9.

GRISMOND, John

1824. Robert Battersby; William; Wells, Som; Y; 7.6.1658; 7.6.1658; 1.7.1665; 7.

1825. Randolph Bustard; Anthony; Kerbywharfe, Yorks; H; 20.6.1655; 25.3.1655; 6.4.1663; 7.

1826. Robert Chapman. Fd by Grismond and Robert Austen 5.8.1661. Bd to Austen (q.v.) 3.7.1654.

1827. Edward Grismond; Tho; Aston, Herefs; Y; 4.5.1657; 4.5.1657; - ; 7.

1828. John Hyllary; John; London; C & Cd; 22.8.1648; 25.7.1648; 4.8.1656; 8.

1829. Peter Kent; William; Stanlocke, Oxon; G; 6.1.1651; 6.1.1651; 7.12.1657; 7.

GROANE, John

1830. Nicholas Hooper; Thomas; London; C & Combmaker; 2.9.1661; 2.9.1661; 2.8.1669; 7.

1831. Thomas King; Willm; Hackington alius St Steevens, Kent; Cl; 4.10.1669; 4.10.1669;   -   ; 7.

1832. Wm Terry; George; Fulham, M'sex; E; 2.12.1661; 2.12.1661; 6.12.1678; 8.

GROVE, Francis

1833. John Andrewes; John; Ledbury, Herefs; Y; 12.4.1647; 12.4.1647; 1.5.1654; 7.

1834. Samuell Heath; Thomas; Ludlow, Shrops; —; 3.11.1662; 3.11.1662; - ; 8.

1835. William Thackray; London; C & BSg; 13.7.1657; 25.12.1656; 5.9.1664; 8. Fd by Grove and William Kendrick.

1836. Edward Williams. Fd by Grove 14.7.1645. Apparently never formally bd.

1837. John Wind; John; Biggleswade, Beds; Ha; 6.5.1650; 6.5.1650; 7.6.1658; 7.

1838. Francis Yeowell; Robert; Epsam, Surr; Cl; 1.5.1654; 1.5.1654; - ; 8.

GROVE, John

1839. Robert Miles; Thomas; London; C & Upholsterer; 12.7.1655; 12.7.1655, - ; 9.

GROVER, Alice, Widow

1840. William Beall; Ralph; Winchcomb, Glos; Y; 4.9.1682; 4.9.1682; - ; 7. Bd to the widow of James Grover.

1841. Thomas Tilliard; Edward; Parrish of St Sepulchers, M'sex; G; 3.3.1684; 3.3.1684; - ; 7.

GROVER, James

1842. Robert Fowler; John; London; C & Armorer; 5.5.1679; 5.5.1679; 6.6.1687; 7.

1843. Richard Webster. Fd by Grover 7.5.1683. Apparently never formally bd.

GROVER, John

1844. Edward Bell; Edward (d); Abington, Berks; Y; 6.8.1683; 6.8.1683; 8.6.1696; 7.

1845. John Worrall; John; Reading, Berks; Apothecary; 2.3.1674; 2.3.1674; 8.5.1682; 7.

GROVER, Thomas

1846. Randall Burton; Robert (d); London; C & Stockingmaker; 6.2.1682; 6.2.1682; - ; 7.

1847. Robert Middlewright; Robt (d); parish of St Margaretts Westmr; Clockmaker; 9.9.1689; 9.9.1689; 7.7.1701; 7.

1848. Robert Mitchell; Andrew; parish of St Andrew Holbourne, M'sex; T; 6.9.1697; 6.9.1697; 3.2.1707; 8.

1849. John Phillpott; Timothy; parish of St Bennett pauls Wharfe, London; L; 7.8.1693; 7.8.1693; 9.9.1700; 7.

1850. Joseph Slade; Richard; London; C & Ca; 6.12.1680; 6.12.1680; 2.7.1688; 7.

GUNBY, William

1851. John Fletcher; John; Hampsted, M'sex; H; 4.9.1699; 4.9.1699; - ; 7.

GUNN, Isaac

1852. Thomas Sanders; John (d); Tower Hill, London; Sk; 2.12.1700; 2.12.1700; - ; 7.

GURNEY, Henry

1853. [Henry Gurney. Fd by patrimony 1.5.1676.]

GUY, Thomas

1854. Samuel Burroughs; Thomas (d); Towne of Leicester, Leics; Y; 1.8.1687; 1.8.1687; 3.12.1694; 7.

1855. Christopher Hurt; Thomas; Coventry, [War]; Pipemaker; 5.9.1670; 5.9.1670; - ; 7.

1856. Thomas Hurt; John; Vttoxeter, Staffs; G; 14.1.1679; 14.1.1679; - ; 7.

1857. Edmund Parker; Edmund; Burrough of Darby, Derby; G; 6.7.1696; 6.7.1696; 7.2.1704; 7.

1858. Thomas Vernam; John (d); Tamworth, War; Mr; 2.6.1684; 2.6.1684; 7.5.1694; 7. Fd as Varnam.

HADDOCK, Robert
1859. [Robt Haddock. Son of Symon Haddock; fd by patrimony 22.12.1691.]

HADDON, William
1860. Joseph Bush; John; Bareford, Herts; H; 1.10.1694; 1.10.1694; 2.3. 1702; 7.
1861. John Morgan; Richard; Hitchin, Herts; Y; 8.4.1700; 8.4.1700; - ; 7.
1862. Thomas White; Francis (d); Letheridge, Surr; T; 6.11.1699; 6.11. 1699; 7.7.1707; 7.

HALES, Lawrence
1863. Phinees Atkinson; Thomas; Yorke, Yorks; G; 7.7.1641; 1.5.1641; 23.2.1654; 8.
1864. Randolph Catterall; Randolph (d); Swetnum, Ches; Cl; 6.4.1657; 25.3.1657; - ; 8.
1865. Richard Hewett; Richard; Waltham, Berks; Turner; 11.4.1643; 2.2.1643; 1.7.1650; 9. Fd as Nich Hewett.
1866. Henry Nicholls; Silvester; Claybrooke, Leics; Y; 10.6.1650; 10.6. 1650; - ; 7.
1867. John Singleton; Nathaniell; London; C & Pw; 4.7.1642; 1.2.1642; - ; 8.

HALEY, Francis
1868. Thomas Cossens; Willm; Ware, Herts; G; 4.10.1669; 4.10.1669; 6.11.1676; 7. T.o. 2.6.1673 to William Lee. Fd by Haley.

HALEY, Thomas
1869. Thomas Crockatt; John; London; G; 4.9.1682; 4.9.1682; 7.10.1689; 7. Fd (as Cockatt) by Robert Everingham and fined 2s. 6d. 'For not being turned over at ye Hall'.
1870. Ben Mawson. Fd by Haley 3.12.1684. Bd to Anne Purslowe (q.v.) 12.11.1677; t.o. on her death to Haley 22.9.1680.
1871. Caleb Millet; John; Walton

vpon Thames, Surr; Y; 6.6.1681; 6.6. 1681; 25.6.1688; 7.

HALL, Henry
1872. Charles Crafford; Richard; Citty of Oxon; Cd. So described when t.o. from Hall to Mary Clarke 8.5.1682, but there is no formal entry of binding to Hall. Fd by Mary Clarke 1.2.1686.
1873. Robert Dodd. Fd by Hall 10.3.1651. Apparently never formally bd.
1874. Edward Ewstace. Fd by Hall 1.10.1679. Apparently never formally bd.
1875. Henry Hall. Fd by patrimony 2.9.1661.
1876. Richard Hall. Fd by patrimony 2.11.1674.
1877. Symon Heinth. Fd by Hall and Richard Cotes 1.3.1652. Apparently never formally bd.
1878. Joseph Jackson. Fd by Hall 7.5.1660. Apparently never formally bd.
1879. Richard Plant. Fd by Hall 4.8.1662. Apparently never formally bd.
1880. Charles Read. Fd by Hall 1.10. 1679. Apparently never formally bd.
1881. John Seller; William (d); Canden, Glos; Cooper; 3.8.1663; 3.8. 1663; 5.9.1670; 7.
1882. Church Symons. Fd by Hall 3.8.1663. Apparently never formally bd.

HALL, Richard
1883. Gunter Morrell; Gunter; London; C & Go; 4.5.1663; 4.5.1663; - ; 7.

HAMMERSHAM, John
1884. Samuell Freeman. Fd by Hammersham, Thomas Alsop and Roger Bartlett 7.12.1663. Bd to Bartlett (q.v.) 1.12.1656.

HAMON, John
1885. William Sherrington. Fd by Hamon 17.7.1641. Apparently never formally bd.

HAMON, Judith, Widow
1886. Thomas Morrell. Fd by Mrs.
Hamon and Thomas Fawcett Junior
1.7.1644. Bd to Judith Hamon 5.6.1637.

HAMOND, Ralph
1887. [Ralph Hamond. Fd by patrimony 7.2.1653. The father's christian
name is not given.]

HAMOND, Thomas
1888. [Thomas Hamond. Son of
William Hamond; fd by patrimony
10.1.1649.]

HAMPSON, James
1889. Thomas Colls; Thomas (d);
Crowland, Lincs; G; 27.7.1671; 27.7.
1671; 2.12.1678; 7.

HAMPTON, Adam
1890. Edward Blundell; Edward (d);
Ashby Folvile, Leics; Ca; 5.12.1681;
5.12.1681; - ; 7.
1891. Richd Gillson; John; Great
Everton, N'hants; Millwright; 3.11.
1690; 3.11.1690; - 7.
1892. William Watts; Thomas; parish of Draycott, Staffs; H; 4.7.1698;
4.7.1698; - ; 7.

HANCOCKE, Edward
1893. Humphrey Tuckey. Fd by
Hancocke 29.3.1641. Bd to him (as
Humphrey Tuckley) 4.3.1633.

HANCOCKE, John
1894. John Booker; Zacheriah (d);
C & Cd; 3.3.1656; 1.3.1656; - ; 8.
1895. Mathew Brookes; Edward;
Onelip, Leics; Y; 16.8.1647; 8.6.1647;
- ; 8.
1896. John Hancock; John; London;
C & St; 8.5.1665; 8.5.1665; 7.6.1669;
7. Bd to his father; fd by patrimony.
1897. Francis Pearse; William; —,
Dev; Cl; 6.12.1680; 6.12.1680; - ; 7.
1898. Joshua Waterhouse; Joshua;
London; C & Ha; 5.5.1662; 5.5.1662;
2.8.1669; 7. Fd by Hancocke and
Elizabeth Calvert.

HARBIN, Thomas
1899. John Cordell; Thomas (d);
Stanford, Lincs; Upholsterer; 7.3.1687;
7.3.1687; - ; 7.
1900. Walter Dill; John; Corfe Mul-
len, Dors; Y; 11.4.1681; 11.4.1681;
- ; 8.
1901. Bryant Hartgill; John; Kil-
mington, Som [sic for Dev]; G; 5.6.
1699; 5.6.1699; - ; 7.
1902. Henry Sherring; Thomas;
Charminstow, Dors; Y; 25.6.1683;
25.6.1683; - ; 7.
1903. Wm Yeo; John (d); parish of
St Clemt Danes, M'sex; T; 2.11.1691;
2.11.1691; 7.

HARDESTIE, John
1904. Richard Bockham; John (d);
New Sarum, Wilts; J; 5.4.1658; 5.4.
1658; 8.5.1665; 7. Fd by Hardestie,
Thomas Creake and George Purslowe.

HARDING, John
1905. Shadrick Beale; Robert; Winchester, Hants; —; 7.5.1688; 7.5.1688;
- ; 7.
1906. Alexander Charnelhouse; Alexander; Sarford, Oxon; Cl; 11.4.1690;
11.4.1690; - ; 7.
1907. Alexander Cleave; —; Moore-
feilds, M'sex; D; 6.7.1678; 6.7.1678;
- ; 8.
1908. Richard Cooper; Thomas (d);
Nunington, Yorks; H; 3.8.1685; 3.8.
1685; - ; 7.
1909. William Cooper; John; Westminster; Patternmaker; 5.8.1700; 5.8.
1700; - ; 7.
1910. Nathaniel Farmer; Samuel (d);
Chipping Norton, Oxon; Apothecary;
6.9.1686; 6.9.1686; - ; 7.
1911. Allyn Ford; Thomas; Len-
ham, Kent; Turner; 5.9.1670; 5.9.
1670; 1.10.1677; 7.
1912. Barnaby Bernard Lintott. Fd
by Harding and Thomas Lingard 18.3.
1700. Bd to Lingard (q.v.) 1.12.1690.

1913. John Parker; John; parish of Colingane, Essex; Cl; 8.11.1697; 8.11. 1697; - ; 7.

1914. William Sutton; William (d); Detling, Kent; Cl; 7.6.1675; 7.6.1675; - ; 7.

1915. Richard Temple; Thomas; Salisbury, Shrops [*sic* for Wilts]; G; 7.9.1691; 7.9.1691; - ; 7.

HARDING, Oliver
1916. James Seguin. Fd by Harding 7.7.1684. Bd by foreign indentures.

HARDNEY, John
1917. Thomas Nurse. Fd by Hardney 6.5.1678. Bd to Samuel Freeman (q.v.) 1.5.1671.

HAREFINCH, Henry
1918. Richard Smith. Fd by Harefinch 4.3.1689. Bd to John Redmaine (q.v.) 3.10.1681.

HARFORD, Rapha
1919. Isaac Janeway; Wm (d); Vlting, Essex; Cl; 4.10.1641; 24.6.1641; - ; 8.

HARFORD, Robert
1920. Wenman Izode; Hen; Staunton, Glos; G; 1.3.1680; 1.3.1680; 5.9. 1687; 7.

HARGRAVE, Thomas
1921. Tho Bentley; Thomas; London; C & D; 4.7.1692; 4.7.1692; - ; 7.

HARMER, Jasper
1922. Saml Baker; Saml (d); parish of St Margaret Westmr; Tallowchandler; 3.2.1690; 3.2.1690; - ; 7.

1923. Wm Birtch; Edward; Erdington, War; G; 7.9.1691; 7.9.1691; - ; 7.

1924. William Orton; Richard; Great Peetling, Leics; - ; 2.12.1678; 2.12.1678; - ; 7.

1925. Robert Tristram; John (d); Hitching, Herts; M; 4.8.1684; 4.8. 1684; 2.11.1691; 7.

HARNAGE, William
1926. Mordant Cracherod; Mordant (d); Topsfeild, Essex; G; 5.6.1671; 5.6.1671; - ; 7. Harnage is described as a Linendraper.

1927. John Cuffande; Mathewe; Parish of Bramley, S'hants; E; 5.8.1668; 5.8.1668; - ; 7.

1928. James Danby; John; Leete, Yorks; E; 4.9.1676; 4.9.1676; - ; 7.

1929. Richard Davis; Robt (d); Brayles, War; G; 3.5.1669; 3.5.1669; - ; 7.

HARPER, Charles
1930. John Hore; Robert; Cuddington, Bucks; Y; 20.11.1671; 20.11.1671; - ; 7.

1931. Thomas Leigh; John (d); London; C & St; 4.5.1691; 4.5.1691; 6.6.1698; 7.

1932. Samuel Rickards; John; Presting, Radnor; G; 25.6.1684; 25.6.1684; - ; 7.

1933. John Rooke; John; Bradnich, City of Exon, [Dev]; G; 5.3.1677; 5.3. 1677; - ; 7.

1934. Charles Smith; John; London; C & D; 13.4.1698; 13.4.1698; 4.6. 1705; 7.

1935. Mathew Wotton; Thomas; Beaudley, Worcs; Gr; 20.12.1677; 20.12. 1677; 2.3.1685; 7.

HARPER, Richard
1936. Wm Beeston; Jno; Bow, M'sex; Ca; 23.5.1653; 23.5.1653; - ; 7.

1937. John Clarke; John; Long sutton, Lincs; G; 1.9.1645; 1.9.1645; 6.12.1652; 8.

1938. Edward Crouch. Fd by Harper 21.10.1646. Bd to him 14.1.1636.

1939. William Harper; Tho; great Bowden, Leics; Y; 14.1.1641; 1.11. 1640; - ; 8.

1940. Ralph Holt; Wm (d); London; G; 7.9.1646; 7.9.1646; 17.10.1653; 7. Fd by Thomas Harper.

HARPER, Thomas

1941. Henry Brugis; Tho; Rickmensworth, Herts; Dr in Physic; 23.5.1653; 23.5.1653; 4.6.1660; 7. In the entry of freedom Harper is noted as deceased.

1942. Ralph Davenport; Ralph; Edge in the County palatine, Ches; G; 20.12.1647; 20.12.1647; 10.1.1655; 7.

1943. Richard Dod. Fd by Harper 24.6.1648. Apparently never formally bd unless this is the apprentice bd to William Coxe 16.2.1607 and not otherwise fd.

1944. Thomas Durrant; John; Little Brickle, Bucks; G; 10.5.1654; 22.5.1654; 2.2.1662; 7. Fd by Harper but m.n. 'turned over to Tho: Newcombe' (n.d.).

1945. Ralph Holt. Fd by Harper 7. 10.1653. Bd to Richard Harper (q.v.) 7.9.1646.

1946. Wm Ibitson; Robert; Brotherton, Yorks; Bu; 10.5.1641; 10.5.1641; 8.6.1648; 7.

1947. Mathew Nelson. Fd by Harper 1.12.1645. Bd to him 6.8.1638.

1948. Thomas Tyman. Fd by Harper 2.5.1642. Bd to him 2.3.1635.

1949. John Wright. Fd by Harper 28.6.1641. Bd to him 6.5.1633.

HARRIGATE, John

1950. John Harrigate. Fd by patrimony 7.9.1657.

1951. Robte Harrigate; John; London; C & St; 28.3.1643; 28.3.1643; 8.6.1648; 7. Bd to his father; fd by patrimony.

1952. Henry Hurst. Fd by Harrigate 28.3.1643. Bd to him 4.5.1635.

HARRIS, Benjamin

1953. Edward Evans; Randall (d); parish of Markeweald, Den; Weaver; 7.11.1698; 7.11.1698; - ; 7.

1954. Benjamin Harris. Fd by patrimony 7.11.1698.

1955. Vavasor Harris. Fd by patrimony 7.11.1698.

1956. Arthur Hartwell; Arthur (d); London; C & Weaver; 1.2.1686; 1.2.1686; - ; 7.

1957. John How; Mary; London; Widow; 3.6.1672; 3.6.1672; 8.11.1680; 8.

1958. Thomas Norris; Tho; Islington, M'sex; - ; 7.4.1679; 7.4.1679; 6.6.1687; 7. 'bound to Ben: Harris for 7 yeares & afterwards turn'd ouer to Mary Harris.'

1959. Enoch Prosser; Walter; Carlion, Mon; H; 1.8.1670; 1.8.1670; 1.10.1677; 7.

1960. James Stanion; Charles; London; C & Salter; 6.12.1680; 6.12.1680; - : 7.

1961. Enoch Walter; Henry; Newport, Mon; G; 1.6.1674; 1.6.1674; - ; 7.

HARRIS, John, I

1962. Henry Barnard; Thomas (d); Pourtsmouth-Towne, S'hants; Upholsterer; 6.5.1685; 6.5.1685; 1.8.1692; 7.

1963. Daniell Meade; Richard (d); London; C & St; 6.8.1694; 6.8.1694; 2.3.1702; 7.

1964. Stephen Norgate; William; London; C & Gr; 4.5.1696; 4.5.1696; - ; 7.

HARRIS, John, II

1965. [John Harris. Fd by redemption 6.6.1692. Harris paid a 'Guiney to Poors Box'.]

HARRIS, William

1966. Thomas Crane; William; Kingstone vpon Thames, Surr; Y; 7.8.1682; 7.8.1682; 1.9.1690; 8. Fd by Sarah Harris.

1967. Nathaniell Dodd; Nathaniell (d); parish of St Leonard Shoreditch, M'sex; Pipemaker; 8.5.1699; 8.5.1699; 5.7.1708; 7. Fd by Benjamin Harris Senior.

1968. Tho Groves; Wm; Lambeth Marsh, Surr; Waterman; 2.11.1691; 2.11.1691; - ; 7.

1969. Benjamin Harris; William; London; C & St; 6.4.1696; 6.4.1696; 12.11.1705; 8. Bd to his father.

1970. Thomas Harris; James; parish of Cripple Gate, London; Ca; 3.6.1678; 3.6.1678; - ; 7.

1971. William Harris. Fd by patrimony 30.7.1677.

1972. Thomas Linegar; Thomas (d); Parrish of St Sepulchers, London; G; 1.10.1683; 1.10.1683; 7.12.1691; 8. Fd by George Larkin.

1973. Edward Pinnock; John; Skelton, Cumb; Drover; 12.11.1677; 12.11.1677; - ; 7.

1974. John Titchbourne; John; London; C & Weaver; 5.3.1688; 5.3.1688; 3.7.1699; 7.

1975. John Weekly; William; Ipsige, Suff; Bs; 6.12.1680; 6.12.1680; - ; 7.

HARRISON, Israel

1976. Abraham Ellis; John (d); Cambridge; Y; 1.9.1673; 1.9.1673; - ; 7.

1977. Israell Harrison; Israell; London; C & St; 3.4.1693; 3.4.1693; 5.8.1700; 7. Bd to his father.

1978. Wm Lindsey; William; London; C & Plasterer; 3.5.1686; 3.5.1686; 3.7.1693; 7.

1979. William Meers; Leonard; Feversham, Kent; Mariner; 9.9.1700; 9.9.1700; 6.10.1707; 7.

1980. Thomas Parry; Thomas; London; C & Ha; 2.6.1679; 2.6.1679; - ; 7.

1981. George Powell. Fd by Harrison 6.4.1685. Apparently never formally bd.

1982. Joseph Raven; Joseph; —, War; H; 6.12.1680; 6.12.1680; 26.3.1688; 7.

1983. Thomas Sturmy; William (d); Clements Inn, M'sex; G; 3.8.1691; 3.8.1691; - ; 7.

HARRISON, John, I

1984. Richard Arton; James (d); London; C & St; 18.1.1647; 18.1.1647; - ; 8.

1985. Samuell Browne; Sam (d); London; C & Cu; 17.1.1648; 17.1.1648; - ; 7.

1986. John Dorrington. Fd by Harrison 6.4.1646. Bd to him 13.2.1637.

1987. Edward Rogers; Thomas (d); Bedford, Beds; T; 1.9.1645; 1.9.1645; - ; 8.

1988. Thomas Rookes; John; Wickhambrooke, Suff; G; 2.9.1650; 2.9.1650; 7.9.1657; 7.

HARRISON, John, II

1989. John Grace; John; Abbington, Berks; Victualler; 5.10.1674; 5.10.1674; - ; 7.

1990. [John Harison. Fd by patrimony 23.6.1647. The father's christian name is not given.]

1991. Thomas Lacey; Wm (d); High=Wickham, Bucks; Mason; 3.7.1652; 3.7.1652; 7 4.1668; 7.

1992. John Shrimpton; Hugh; High Wickham, Bucks; Tallowchandler; 3.11.1656; 3.11.1656; 7.4.1668; 7.

HARRISON, Ralph

1993. [Ralph Harrison. Son of Edward Harrison; fd by patrimony 8.12.1645.]

HARRISON, Thomas

1994. Nathaniell Delaporte; Gabrielle (d); London; Mch; 5.8.1695; 5.8.1695; - ; 7.

HARRISON, William

1995. Peirson Blechinden; Richard; London; C & MT; 6.10.1662; 6.10.1662; - ; 7.

1996. William Murfin; Richard; Sachoose, Yorks; H; 11.2.1661; 11.2.1661; - ; 7.

1997. William Price; John (d); Hollowell, Oxon; Smith; 10.1.1655; 10.1.1655; - ; 7.

HARROGATE, Florentia, Widow
1998. John Harrogate; John (d);
— , — ; — ; 3.6.1672; 3.6.1672;
- ; 7. Bd to his mother, probably the
widow of John Harrigate.

HART, Matthew
1999. John Hart; Mathew; Cowley,
M'sex; Y; 4.5.1657; 4.5.1657; 9.2.1674;
7.

HARTFORD, Ralph
2000. Richard Westbrooke. Fd by
Hartford and Edward Stanley 20.12.
1645. Bd to Hartford 7.11.1638.

HARTLEY, John
2001. Fletcher Giles; Walter; London; C & MT; 4.3.1700; 4.3.1700;
- ; 7.

HARTUS, Henry
2002. Thomas Leming; Edmund;
Blackborne, Lancs; Y; 7.8.1682; 7.8.
1682; - ; 7.
2003. Roger Rymer; Ralph; Cittie
of Yorke; G; 4.7.1681; 4.7.1681; - ; 7.

HARVEY, Henry
2004. Thomas Bucknell. Bd to John
Frank (q.v.) 22.6.1642; t.o. 22.8.1648
to Harvey. Fd by Frank and Harvey
2.7.1649.

HARVEY, William
2005. Joseph Davies; London; C &
Cd; 2.10.1699; 2.10.1699; - ; 7.

HARWARD, Humphrey
2006. Tho Waite; John; Wigginton,
Yorks; — ; 1.3.1652; 1.3.1652; - ;
7.

HARWOOD, Stephen
2007. Thomas Knowles; Thomas;
Newington, Surr; Turner; 5.6.1671;
5.6.1671; 4.11.1678; 7.
2008. Walter Wright; William;
Whiston, N'hants; Y; 6.10.1673; 6.10.
1673; - ; 8.

HATSELL, Lawrence
2009. Timothy Bedford; Wm (d);
Donstable, Beds; Cl; 7.11.1698; 7.11.
1698; - ; 7.
2010. Samuell Clark; Wm; London;
C & BSg; 6.5.1689; 6.5.1689; 1.2.1697;
7.
2011. Francis Dove; Thomas; Parish of St George in Southwarke, Surr;
G; 8.5.1682; [8.5.1682?]; - ; 8. The
entry gives the term as '8 yeares from
the Date of ye Indentr'.

HAVILAND, John
2012. John Daffie. Fd by Simon Farwell 30.8.1641. Originally bd to Farwell 31.3.1634; rebd to Haviland
6.11.1637.
2013. Jeffery Provender. Fd by Haviland 14.1.1641. Bd to him 15.9.1634.
2014. Francis Sowle. Fd by Haviland 7.9.1646. Apparently never formally bd.
2015. Francis Wortley. Fd by Haviland 10.5.1641. Bd to him 3.4.1633.

HAWES, William
2016. Emanuell Read; James; parish of St Clemt Danes, M'sex; G; 2.10.
1699; 2.10.1699; - ; 7.

HAWKINS, Edward
2017. William Gamball; John; London; Capmaker; 4.8.1684; 4.8.1684;
- ; 7.
2018. Robert Willoughby; Joseph;
Crayford, Kent; - ; 5.9.1698; 5.9.
1698; 4.3.1706; 7. Fd by Mark Forster.

HAWKINS, Thomas
2019. John Richardson; John; Malburrough, Wilts; Y; 2.3.1685; 2.3.1685;
- ; 8. A John Richardson was fd by
Thomas Horne 3.5.1714.

HAWKINS, William
2020. Wm Cross; Richard; parish of
Spelsbury, Oxon; Bookbinder; 3.11.
1679; 3.11.1679; 6.12.1686; 7.

2021. Thomas Horne; Thomas; Vp-nold, Glos; Y; 1.8.1687; 1.8.1687; - ; 7.

2022. Joseph Piddock; William (d); London; G; 2.7.1677; 2.7.1677; - ; 8.

2023. William Rockall. Fd by Hawkins 4.9.1693. Bd to Abel Rockall (q.v.) 1.3.1686.

HAYES, John

2024. James Beechenoe; Edward; Cambridge; Bs; 16.12.1668; 16.12.1668; 7.2.1676; 7.

2025. Thomas Cooke; Robert; Sowdley, Shrops; G; 7.6.1658; 7.6.1658; 6.11.1666; 7.

2026. John Grumball; Robt; Cambridge; Freemason; 4.2.1689; 25.3.1688; 6.4.1696; 8.

2027. James Haddy; James; Barnewell, Cambs; — ; 1.5.1676; 1.5.1676; - ; 8.

2028. John Harding. Fd by Hayes and John Legate 6.4.1663. Bd to Legate (q.v.) 3.3.1656.

2029. Brampton Lowry; Beniamine (d); Cambridge; Mch; 21.4.1670; 21.4.1670; 7.5.1677; 7.

2030. John Petit; John; Cambridge; L; 1.5.1676; 1.5.1676; - ; 8.

2031. Wm Smith; Wm; Cambridge; Chandler; 4.2.1684; 25.3.1683; - ; 8.

2032. John Woodfeild; Simon; — , Beds; H; 6.11.1676; 6.11.1676; - ; 7.

HAYHURST, Robert

2033. William Tracy; Edward; London; Ca; 8.5.1682; 8.5.1682; 1.7.1689; 8.

HAZARD, Thomas

2034. John Gun; William (d); Westminster, M'sex; Cook; 5.1.1657; 5.1.1657; - ; 8.

2035. Thomas Pitts; James; London; C & Bu; 27.4.1646; 27.4.1646; - ; 7.

2036. Edward Rogers; Edward; Hat-feild, Herts; Y; 3.7.1654; 3.7.1654; - ; 7.

2037. Francis Smith; Francis; Bradford, Yorks; Farrier; 3.5.1647; 3.5.1647; 5.5.1654; 7.

HEAD, Godfrey

2038. William Dew; William; Oxford; Y; 7.6.1676; 7.6.1676; 4.6.1683; 7.

2039. Richard Fisher; Willm; St Pulthers, London; Tollman; 2.5.1670; 2.5.1670; - ; 8.

2040. John Haynes; John (d); New Chapple, [Staffs?]; Cl; 2.10.1682; 2.10.1682; - ; 7.

2041. Charles Hobbs; Christopher; Fetter lane, London; G; 1.6.1685; 1.6.1685; - ; 7.

2042. Francis Page; Fra (d); London; C & Tallowchandler; 2.10.1676; 2.10.1676; 3.12.1683; 7.

2043. Nicholas Reynolds; Nicholas; Parrish of St Margaretts Westminster; Y; 7.2.1681; 7.2.1681; - ; 7.

2044. John Wild; William; London; C & Swordcutler; 1.10.1683; 1.10.1683; - ; 7.

HEAD, Mary

2045. Stephen Gilbert; Stephen; London; C & MT; 5.2.1694; 5.2.1694; 5.5.1701; 7.

HEARNE, Francis

2046. John Crofts; Willm; Doncaster, Yorks; Bs; 22.6.1670; 22.6.1670; 5.5.1679; 7. Hearne's name is given as Heiron.

2047. John Grimes; John; Sherrington, Glos; H; 1.9.1656; 1.9.1656; - ; 7.

2048. Mich Harris; John; Admonton, Glos; H; 4.8.1662; 4.8.1662; - ; 7.

2049. [Francis Heiron. Fd by redemption 12.11.1649. Probably the Francis Hearne bd to George Edwards (q.v.) 17.11.1645.]

2050. Samuel Mason; John; Hill, War; Y; 10.9.1677; 10.9.1677; - ; 7.

2051. Daniel Michael; Daniel; London; C & Gr; 18.6.1677; 18.6.1677; - ; 7.

2052. George Powell. Fd by Hearne and Ralph Edwards 6.4.1657. Bd to Edwards (q.v.) 4.2.1650.

HEARNE, Richard

2053. Joseph Pack; Joseph; St Martyns in the feilds, M'sex; J; 29.3.1641; 29.3.1641; 24.5.1648; 7.

2054. Thomas Turner. Fd by Hearne 15.2.1647. Bd to him 3.2.1640.

HEBB, Andrew

2055. Henry Jackson. Fd by Hebb 23.3.1644. Bd to him 7.9.1635.

2056. James Nuthall; James (d); Cannondon, Essex; Cl; 4.5.1641; 25.3.1641; - ; 10.

HELME, Richard

2057. [Rich Helme. Son of John Helme; fd by patrimony 20.2.1652.]

HENDRY, Samuel

2058. Joseph Stockwell; Thomas; Newberry, Berks; Ha; 6.10.1679; 6.10.1679; - ; 7.

HENSMAN, William

2059. William Beale; William (d); London; Weaver; 5.9.1698; 5.9.1698; 7.6.1708; 7.

2060. John Helmes; Nathaniell; London; C & Apothecary; 2.8.1697; 2.8.1697; 1.7.1706; 7.

HEPTINSTALL, John

2061. Thomas Burditt. Originally bd to Mary White; t.o. by her to Heptinstall, and by him to Henry Clarke. Fd by Clarke 1.10.1688, and fined 2s. 6d. 'for his not being turned over at this Hall'. There is no formal entry of binding.

2062. Phillip Crosse; John; East

Malling, Kent; Cl; 5.12.1698; 5.12. 1698; - ; 7.

2063. William Heptinstall; John; Saint Albans, Herts; Cd; 7.7.1684; 7.7.1684; - ; 7.

2064. Howard Kettlewell; Robert; London; C & St; 11.11.1700; 11.11. 1700; - ; 7.

2065. David Oakes; Abraham; Ellaston, Staffs; Y; 6.6.1692; 6.6.1692; 3.7.1699; 7.

2066. Thomas Parker. Fd by Heptinstall and Miles Flesher 8.4.1695. Bd to Flesher (q.v.) 7.11.1687.

2067. William Peirson. Fd by Heptinstall 8.5.1693. Apparently never formally bd.

2068. Robert Powell; Robert; Malmsbury, Wilts; T; 11.11.1695; 11.11.1695; 3.7.1704; 8.

HERBERT, Francis

2069. Ralph Emmerton; William; Bishoprick of Durham, [Dur]; G; 3.4. 1693; 3.4.1693; - ; 7.

HERBERT, Isaac

2070. Francis Abbay; Fran; Stonifeild, Oxon; — ; 6.11.1655; 6.11. 1655; 1.12.1662; 7.

2071. Wm Barlow; Wm; Hardingstone, N'hants; Y; 6.9.1647; 6.9.1647; 6.11.1655; 7.

2072. John Gaddes; Thomas; Berwick, N'land; Y; 3.11.1662; 3.11.1662; - ; 7.

2073. Wm Russell; — ; Northton, [N'hants]; — ; 5.7.1652; 29.9.1652; - ; 8.

2074. Richard Simpson; Thomas; — , Oxon; Sh; 5.12.1653; 5.12.1653; 21.1.1661; 7.

2075. Robert Sturte. Bd to Thomas Fukes (q.v.) 3.8.1646; t.o. 2.8.1652 to Herbert. Fd by Fukes 3.10.1653.

HERRINGMAN, Henry

2076. John Herringman; John (d); Cashalton, Surr; G; 7.6.1669; 7.6.1669; - ; 7.

[77]

2077. Hobart Kemp; Tho; Citty of Norwich; E; 1.9.1662; 1.9.1662; 6.3. 1671; 8. Fd as Hubbard Kempe.

2078. Christofer Long; Willm; London; C & Hosier; 4.3.1672; 4.3.1672; - ; 8.

2079. John Playfere; Tho (d); London; C & MT; 6.8.1655; 24.6.1655; 3.8.1663; 8.

2080. Francis Saunders. Fd by Herringman 19.12.1683. Bd to Abel Roper (q.v.) 4.12.1676.

HEWETT, John

2081. Ephraim Childe; Willm; Lambeth Marsh, Surr; G; 5.8.1668; 5.8. 1668; - ; 7.

2082. William Keyes. Originally bd to Richard Janeway (q.v.) 1.8.1670; t.o. 6.11.1671 to Hewett.

2083. Timothy Westley; John; Dorchester. [Dors]; Cl; 4.5.1674; 4.5.1674; - ; 7.

HEWETT, Richard

2084. Francis Hewett; Rich; Laurence Waltham, Berks; Turner; 7.2.1653 7.2.1653; - ; 7.

2085. John Hunt; John; Radnidge, Bucks; Gl; 5.8.1668; 5.8.1668; 6.9. 1675; 7. Fd by William Johnson.

2086. William Johnson; William; Brocknoll, Berks; Y; 7.10.1661; 7.10. 1661; 4.11.1668; 7.

2087. John Rowney; Jno; Ormescutt, Worcs; — ; 6.3.1654; 6.3.1654; 8.3. 1661; 7.

HEWSON, Richard

2088. George Ashby; Robert; Harefeild, M'sex; E; 6.4.1685; 6.4.1685; - ; 7.

2089. [Richard Hewson. Fd by redemption 30.7.1677.]

HEYRICK, Samuel

2090. John Deelle; John; Citty of Oxford; Printer; 2.10.1693; 2.10.1693; - ; 7.

2091. William Fitz-Jeoffrey; John (d); Bedford, Beds; G; 5.8.1672; 5.8. 1672; - ; 7.

2092. Sylvanus Hayes; Richard; Evesham, Worcs; Y; 2.12.1695; 2.12. 1695; - ; 7.

2093. Thomas Holbrooke; Richard (d); Manchester, Lancs; Cl; 8.11.1686; 8.11.1686; - ; 7.

2094. Benj Mills; Christopher; London; C & B; 6.11.1683; 6.11.1683; - ; 7.

2095. Edmund Poole; Thomas; Nothingame, [Notts]; G; 2.6.1679; 2.6.1679; 4.10.1686; 7.

2096. Richard Walker; Thomas (d); St Andrews Holborne, [M'sex]; Sh; 3.8.1664; 3.8.1664; 6.12.1675; 8.

2097. Samuell Walker; Richard; London; C & St; 8.5.1693; 8.5.1693; 2.8.1703; 7.

HICKMAN, Henry

2098. Nicholas Comferford; Thomas; London; Platemaker; 7.7.1679; 7.7. 1679; - ; 7.

HICKMAN, Spencer

2099. John Lowe; John; Denton, Lancs; Cl; 6.2.1671; 6.2.1671; - ; 7.

2100. Henry Mayos; Hen; Canon Dyon, Herefs; I; 6.8.1677; 6.8.1677; 4.8.1684; 7. Fd by Thomas Hodgkins.

HICKS, Benjamin

2101. [Benjamin Hicks. Son of Giles Hicks; fd by patrimony 8.11.1669.]

HIDE, John

2102. John Darby; John; Diseworth, Leics; H; 6.9.1647; 6.9.1647; 6.11. 1660; 7.

2103. Thomas Edmonds; John; Thurlinston, War; H; 6.6.1670; 6.6. 1670; - ; 7.

2104. John Franklin; John (d); London; C & St; 1.8.1659; 1.8.1659; - ; 7.

2105. Wm Hill; Wm; Guilford, Surr; Cl; 2.8.1641; 24.6.1641; - ; 8.

2106. Nath Howell; Hum; Citty of Oxford; Y; 2.6.1651; 2.6.1651; 7.6. 1658; 7. Fd by Hide and Peter Cole.

2107. Thomas Iley. Fd by Hide and Henry Huffen 7.7.1662. Bd to Huffen (q.v.) 11.6.1655.

2108. James Skelton; Henry; Braintwaite, Cumb; H; 3.5.1652; 25.3.1652; - ; 9.

HIGGENBOTHAM, Richard
2109. Raph Edwards. Fd by Higgenbotham and Thomas Fukes 2.5.1642. Bd to Higgenbotham 5.5.1634; t.o. 2.5.1636 to Fukes.

HIGGENS, Christopher
2110. Gerrard Irvine; Christopher; — ; Surgeon; 6.2.1665; 6.2.1665; - ; 7.

HILLER, Nathaniel
2111. Robert Burges; John; Stepney Parrish, M'sex; Chandler; 6.5. 1685; 6.5.1685; - ; 7.

2112. John Charrott; John; Godalming, Surr; Y; 10.9.1677; 10.9.1677; - ; 8.

2113. Daniel Ferman; Jonathan (d); London; C & Cooper; 4.5.1691; 4.5. 1691; - ; 7.

HILLER, Richard
2114. Samuel Hiller; John; Mircott in the parish of Crudwell, Wilts; Y; 6.7.1691; 6.7.1691; - ; 7.

HILLIARD, Thomas
2115. James Cunningham; Ninian (d); St Martyns in the Feilds, M'sex; G; 18.12.1666; 18.12.1666; - ; 7.

2116. Jeofferey Dauglas; Symon; Framington in Swale Dale, Yorks; Y; 6.2.1671; 6.2.1671; - ; 7.

2117. John Feild; Samuell (d); London; C; 1.1.1668; 1.1.1668; - ; 7.

2118. John Gosling; Tho; Thelton, Norf; G; 6.11.1655; 6.11.1655; 6.4. 1663; 7.

2119. Adam Hampton; William; Chiswick, M'sex; Cl; 6.3.1671; 6.3. 1671; 5.12.1681; 7.

2120. James Singleton; Thomas; Stayning, Lancs; G; 18.12.1658; 18.12. 1658; - ; 7.

HILLS, Gilham
2121. Samuell Bolton; Richard; Newcastle Under=Line, Staffs; Y; 4.2. 1695; 4.2.1695; 9.2.1702; 7. Fd as Boulton.

2122. Jonathan Edwin; Jonathan (d); London; C & St; 3.8.1691; 3.8. 1691; 5.9.1698; 7.

2123. Thomas Rowse; John (d); London; G; 1.8.1698; 1.8.1698; 12.11. 1705; 7.

HILLS, Henry, I
2124. John Boulton; Richard; NewCastle Vnderline, Staffs; Maltster; 5.2. 1683; 5.2.1683; 3.3.1690; 7. Fd by Hills' executors.

2125. Maurice Davis; Maurice; Hench, Den; Y; 12.11.1677; 12.11. 1677; - ; 7.

2126. Gillam Hills. Fd by patrimony 24.3.1680.

2127. [Henry Hills. Fd by redemption 7.10.1651.]

2128. Henry Hills. Fd by patrimony 7.7.1679.

2129. John Hills; Henry; Sevennokes, Kent; Mealman; 4.5.1657; 4.5. 1657; - ; 7.

2130. Ambros Hoskins; John; Hereford, Herefs; Cl; 3.4.1654; 3.4.1654; 6.5.1661; 7.

2131. Charles Jolliffe; Tho; Kidwelly, Carmarthen; G; 1.6.1674; 1.6. 1674; 4.7.1681; 9.

2132. John Joliffe; Thomas; Kidwelly, Carmarthen; G; 1.12.1673; 1.12.1673; 8.11.1680; 7.

2133. Griffith Thomas; Edward; LLangendaire, Carmarthen; Y; 8.11. 1669; 8.11.1669; - ; 7.

[79]

2134. Lewis Thomas; Morris; Parrish of Langadock, Carmarthen; G; 12.11.1683; 12.11.1683; 1.12.1690; 7. Fd by Hills' executors.

2135. John Wallis; John; London; C & Ha; 31.7.1655; 31.7.1655; - ; 7.

2136. William Walton. T.o. 2.11.1685 to Hills. Bd to James Cotterell (q.v.) 7.11.1681 for 7 years. Fd by Hills 3.12.1688.

HILLS, Henry, II

2137. Joseph Andrews; Thomas; Daventry, N'hants; Sh; 26.3.1683; 26.3.1683; 7.4.1690; 7. T.o. (n.d.) to Thomas Braddyll, but fd by Hills.

2138. John Coxall; John; London, C & Cooper; 23.6.1680; 23.6.1680; 4.7.1687; 7. Fd as Croxall.

2139. Ahasnerns Fromanteel; John; London; C & Clockmaker; 5.7.1680; 5.7.1680; - ; 7. Ahasnerns is presumably an error for Ahasuerus.

2140. John Science. Fd by Hills 7.5.1688. Bd to William Abbington (q.v.) 3.1.1681. Fined 2s. 6d. 'for not being turned over at the Hall'.

2141. John Slapl[e]; Thomas; London; C & Ca; 7.8.1682; 7.8.1682; 3.11.1690; 8. The father's surname is given as Slaple. Fd as Slape. T.o. (n.d.) to James Astwood and fd by him, but fined 2s. 6d. 'for not being turned over at the Hall'.

2142. Nathaniel Warden. Fd by Hills 3.2.1685. Bd to Henry Brugis (q.v.) 6.8.1677.

2143. Thomas Whitlidge. Bd to Thomas James (q.v.) 7.8.1682; t.o. (n.d.) to Hills and fd by him 9.9.1689.

HINCKSON, John

2144. [John Hinckson. Fd by patrimony 6.6.1653.]

HINDLEY, John

2145. Thomas Harriot; John; Brigstock, N'hants; Tn; 3.3.1684; 3.3.1684; - ; 7.

2146. Lewis Owen; Lewis (d); Havodtowill, Merioneth; G; 7.5.1683; 7.5.1683; - ; 7.

2147. Edward Wood; Edward (d); Pewsey, Wilts; Surgeon; 5.10.1685; 5.10.1685; - ; 7.

HINDMARSH, Joseph

2148. Rich Harris; Isaah; Buckingham Towne, Bucks; G; 1.10.1683; 1.10.1683; 5.10.1681; 7.

2149. Edward Poole; Robert; Gameborough, Lincs; Y; 4.11.1678; 4.11.1678; 7.12.1685; 7.

2150. John Stokes; John; Melton Mowbray, Leics; Mr; 6.5.1695; 6.5.1695; - ; 7.

2151. Geo. Strachin; John; parish of St Martin in the Feilds, M'sex; Doctor in Divinity; 1.2.1692; 1.2.1692; 7.9.1702; 7. Fd as Strahan.

2152. Thomas Trevor; James; London; C & Apothecary; 5.8.1689; 5.8.1689; - ; 7.

HINSON, John

2153. Edward Bray. Fd by Hinson and Nicholas Greenhill 14.7.1645. Bd to Greenhill 2.11.1635.

2154. Richard Lewis; Richard; Shelborne St Johns, S'hants; Bu; 4.10.1647; 25.7.1647; 6.11.1655; 8.

HODGKINS, Thomas

2155. Henry Brickwood; Samuell (d); Maldon, Essex; G; 4.12.1699; 4.12.1699; 3.2.1707; 7.

2156. Francis Catling; Jeremiah; London; C & D; 6.5.1678; 6.5.1678; 6.4.1685; 7.

2157. Tho Corchin; Thomas (d); Walpoole St Andrews, Norf; Y; 6.11.1683; 6.11.1683; 6.10.1690; 7. Fd as Corching.

2158. Simon Feild; John (d); Rowington, War; Cl; 9.2.1691; 9.2.1691; 2.5.1698; 7.

2159. William Hatch; Edward (d); Totteridge, Herts; Y; 7.11.1698; 7.11.1698; 12.11.1705; 7.

2160. Wm Mathews; John (d); Coventry, War; Sh; 7.12.1691; 7.12.1691; - ; 7.

2161. Henry Mayos. Fd by Hodgkins 4.8.1684. Bd to Spencer Hickman (q.v.) 6.8.1677.

2162. Abraham Parkines; Thomas (d); Much Badoe, [Essex]; G; 2.10.1699; 2.10.1699; 4.11.1706; 7.

2163. Thomas Rainer. Fd by Hodgkins 6.7.1685. Bd to James Cotterell (q.v.) 1.7.1678.

HODGKINSON, Elizabeth

2164. Richard Innocent. Tho; Mansfeild, Notts; M; 7.8.1676; 7.8.1676; - ; 8.

HODGKINSON, Richard

2165. Benjamine Bishop; John; Witney, Oxon; Weaver; 7.9.1657; 7.9.1657; - ; 7.

2166. Amos Coles. Fd by Hodgkinson and John White 7.12.1646. Bd to Hodgkinson 3.10.1639.

2167. Wanderton Cottrell; Michaell; Hope vnder Denmarke, Herefs; G; 6.12.1641; 25.12.1641; - ; 7.

2168. William Doewell; Thomas; London; C & Leatherseller; 1.7.1661; 26.3.1661; 2.8.1669; 8. Fd as Dowell.

2169. John Ferris; John; Morefeilds, London; — ; 12.8.1671; 12.8.1671; - ; 7.

2170. Francis Gill; Richard; London; Br. 3.2.1673; 3.2.1673; - ; 7.

2171. Ralp Hodgekinson. Fd by patrimony 3.2.1673.

2172. Thomas Hodgkins; Robt; Warwicke, War; Cook; 4.12.1654; 4.12.1654; 21.1.1662; 7.

2173. Richard Hodgkinson. Fd by patrimony 1.6.1657.

2174. Thomas Hodgkinson. Fd by patrimony 21.1.1662.

2175. Thomas Mabb. Fd by Hodgkinson 1.4.1647. Bd to him 11.1.1637.

2176. Thomas Royston; Ralph;

Kerby, Notts; Y; 6.11.1671; 6.11.1671; 3.2.1680; 7. Fd by Edward Crouch.

2177. Francis Wright; Richard; Tinmarsh, Berks; Cl; 4.5.1657; 4.5.1657; - ; 7.

HODGKINSON, Thomas

2178. Wm Botham; Jonathan (d); London; C & MT; 12.11.1683; 24.8.1683; 7.9.1691; 8.

HODGSON, Robert

2179. George Fitzjames; Robert; Vpway, Dors; G; 2.5.1653; 2.5.1653; 3.9.1660; 7.

2180. John Goodier; Thomas (d); Lenthall Starks, Herefs; G; 3.8.1657; 3.8.1657; - ; 7.

2181. John Lacy; William; Kempton, S'hants; G; 6.11.1660; 6.11.1660; 1.9.1673; 7.

HOLDEN, Henry

2182. Richard Holden; Henry; London; C & St; 6.8.1660; 6.8.1660; - ; 7. Bd to his father.

2183. Francis Hooper; Robte; Putney, Surr; Br; 20.12.1651; 20.12.1651; - ; 7.

2184. Richard Martin; Thomas (d); Parish of Stone, Island of Oxney, Kent; Cl; 7.5.1660; 7.5.1660; 2.7.1667; 7. Fd by Holden and Thomas Leach.

HOLDEN, John

2185. Thomas Dugard; Wm; London; St; 19.1.1652; 19.1.1652; - ; 7.

HOLDEN, William

2186. Thomas Davies; Humphrey; Cranbury, War; G; 8.11.1641; 8.11.1641; 3.12.1655; 7. Fd as Davis.

HOLFORD, John

2187. Edmund Saunders; George; Meiles, Berks; Farmer; 3.6.1678; 3.6.1678; - ; 7.

HOLFORD, Samuel
2188. [Samuel Holford, 'Free of the sadlers but trading in Bookes', fd by redemption 3.11.1690, paying £3. 4s. 6d.]

HOLLAND, William
2189. Richard Hyatt; Robert; parish of Marden, Wilts; Farrier; 6.4.1696; 2.3.1696; 6.10.1707; 7.

HOLMES, George
2190. Thomas Cotgrave. Fd by George Holmes 6.11.1655. Bd to him 4.6.1638.
2191. John Wade; John (d); Wilmington, Sussex; Y; 3.10.1642; 3.10. 1642; - ; 7.

HOLMWOOD, Thomas
2192. Thomas Smith; Thomas; London; G; 6.8.1660; 1.7.1660; - ; 8.

HOLT, Elizabeth
2193. Isaac Dalton; John; Parish of St Buttolph without Aldersgate, M'sex; Sh; 3.6.1700; 3.6.1700; 9.6.1707; 7.

HOLT, Ralph
2194. Thomas Cooke. Bd to Freeman Collins (q.v.) 14.1.1679, but t.o. (n.d.) to Holt and fd by him 1.2.1686.
2195. Michael Holt; Edward (d); Alford, Surr; Cl; 2.5.1681; 2.5.1681; 12.4.1692; 8. Fd by the executrix or administrator of Ralph Holt.
2196. Seth Mody; Seth (d); parish of St Martins in the Fields, M'sex; G; 3.11.1673; 3.11.1673; - ; 7.
2197. Sidney Roe; Thomas (d); London; C & V; 7.6.1686; 7.6.1686; - ; 7.
2198. Jeremiah Wilkins; Francis; Gaddesden, Herts; Y; 5.3.1677; 5.3. 1677; 7.4.1684; 7.

HOOD, Henry
2199. Herbert Jones; John; Citty of Hereford; Cl; 3.3.1651; 3.3.1651; - ; 7.
2200. Robte Taunton; Henry (d);

London; C & St; 6.3.1648; 6.3.1648; - ; 8.
2201. Francis Titon. Fd by Hood 9.3.1646. Bd to him 5.3.1638.

HOOKE, Nathaniel
2202. William Edwin. Servant to Cornelius Bee (q.v.) and Nathaniel Hooke. Fd 6.10.1673 by redemption from the Haberdashers' Company by order of the Lord Mayor and Court of Aldermen. m.n. 'Free from ye Haberdashers Company'.

HOOPER, Nicholas
2203. John Bennet; Thomas (d); little Worley, Essex; G; 7.12.1685; 7.12.1685; 6.2.1693; 7. Fd by Thomas Brockett.

HOPE, William
2204. Edward Archer; Tho; London; C & Cook; 6.4.1646; 1.3.1646; 3.4.1654; 8. Fd by Hope and John Saywell.
2205. Wm Hope; Wm; London; St; 14.6.1652; 1.5.1652; 4.3.1661; 8. Bd to his father.
2206. Richard Morkitt; Richard; C & Cooper; 1.7.1661; 20.5.1661; 11.4. 1670; 8. Fd as Northkitt.
2207. Thomas Richardson; Wm; Lusam, Kent; T; 1.4.1645; 25.12.1644; - ; 8.
2208. John Scott; John; Maidstone, Kent; Ha; 28.3.1643; 29.9.1642; - ; 9.

HOPPER, George
2209. George Hopper; Lancelot; St Katherines Tower, London; Victualler; 30.5.1687; 30.5.1687; - ; 7.

HORA, George
2210. James Hughes. Fd by Hora 6.2.1643. Bd to him 23.1.1636; t.o. 12.11.1638 to John Clifton.

HORNE, John
2211. Roger Wilford. Fd by Horne 11.4.1643. Bd to him 10.11.1635.

HORNE, Robert
2212. Oliver Cobb; John; Farnebrooke, Beds; G; 6.10.1673; 6.10.1673; - ; 7.
2213. Joseph Knight; John; London; C & Cw; 11.2.1668; 11.2.1668; - ; 7.
2214. William Saywell; William (d); London; C & Salter; 3.10.1659; 24.6.1659; 6.8.1667; 8.

HORNE, Thomas
2215. Henry Day; Mathew; Loleworth, Cambs; G; 4.11.1689; 4.11.1689; 7.12.1696; 7.
2216. [Thomas Horne. Fd by patrimony 9.9.1689.]

HORNE, William
2217. George Ball; John; London; C & Bricklayer; 3.7.1693; 3.7.1693; - ; 7.

HORTON, Edward
2218. Thomas Ashfeild. Fd by Horton 3.2.1680. Apparently never formally bd.
2219. Benjamine Beardwell; Benjamine (d); London; C & Bl; 2.5.1681; 2.5.1681; 9.2.1691; 7. Fd by Roger Norton.
2220. John Brudenell; John; London; C & St; 8.11.1686; 8.11.1686; 1.6.1690; 7. Fd by patrimony.
2221. William Clerke. Fd by Horton 2.4.1688, and fined 2s. 6d. 'for not being bound at the Hall'.
2222. William Pokins; John; Dainton, Oxon; G; 9.9.1678; 9.9.1678; 5.3.1688; 7.

HORTON, William
2223. Edwd Adlard; Saml; Whapload, Lincs; G; 6.4.1691; 6.4.1691; - ; 7.
2224. Thomas Ames; Thomas; ye Parish of St Andrews Holborne, M'sex; L; 7.5.1683; 7.5.1683; - ; 8.
2225. Alexander Ashburne; Solomon; Crowle, Lincs; Cl; 4.5.1691; 4.5.1691; 5.9.1698; 7.

2226. John Evans; Thomas; London; Glassgrinder; 6.6.1698; 6.6.1698; - ; 8. A John Evans, servant to Sarah Holt, was fd 6.8.1705.
2227. [William Horton. Fd by patrimony 7.6.1676.]
2228. Thomas Spencer; Thomas; London; C & Painterstainer; 7.11.1698; 7.11.1698; 5.5.1707; 7. Fd by William Downing.
2229. Richard Willmott; John; Citty of Oxford; Bs; 6.4.1696; 6.4.1696; - ; 7.

HOSKINS, Mary, Widow
2230. Richard Abbot; Jno; Stratford, Bucks; — ; 2.8.1652; 2.8.1652; - ; 7.
2231. John Abbott; John; Stony Stratford, Bucks; H; 2.6.1645; 2.6.1645; 14.6.1652; 7.
2232. Thomas Mascoll. Fd by Mrs Hoskins 1.3.1647. Bd to Robert Hoskins 3.9.1632.
2233. Samuell Norris; Wm; London; C & Cw; 2.7.1655; 2.7.1655 - ; 7.

HOSKINS, Robert
2234. John Streeter. Fd by Hoskins 6.6.1644. Bd to him 4.8.1635.

HOSYER, William
2235. Thomas Fitton; Francis (d); Auldery, Ches; Y; 10.7.1660; 10.7.1660; - ; 7.

HOTH, Thomas
2236. [Thomas Hoth. Son of John Hoth; fd by patrimony 4.11.1650.]

HOW, Job
2237. John Redish; Simon; Parrish of Bishops Gate, London; Br; 1.10.1683; 1.10.1683; 2.11.1696; 7.

HOW, John
2238. Elisha King; Lawrence; Citty of Oxon; Gl; 26.6.1682; 26.6.1682; - ; 7.

HOWES, Jeremiah
2239. Benjamin Gladman. Fd by
Howes 4.5.1691. Gladman is described
as a 'Forreigner'; the fee paid was 40s.
2240. Thomas Halford; Richard;
Fleckney, Leics; G; 7.10.1668; 7.10.
1668; - ; 7.
2241. Gregory Sylvester; Joshua;
Mansfeild, Notts; — ; 5.6.1671; 5.6.
1671; - ; 7.

HOWES, Robert
2242. Samuel Heiron; Edmond;
Netherhauen, Wilts; Y; 17.8.1646;
17.8.1646; - ; 7.
2243. Jeremiah Howes. Fd by patrimony 4.6.1667.
2244. John Howes. Fd by patrimony
15.1.1646.
2245. Joseph Howes. Fd by patrimony 10.9.1677.
2246. Henry Moreclock; Richard;
Stanton, Derby; G; 8.6.1648; 25.12.
1647; 3.3.1656; 8. Fd by Howes and
Thomas Brewster.

HOWES, Samuel
2247. Edward Cole; Edward (d);
East Barford, Suff; Mch; 6.3.1654;
6.3.1654; 8.3.1661; 9.

HOYLE, Samuel
2248. Richard Audsley; Robert; Ol-
manbury, Yorks; Y; 1.2.1664; 1.2.1664;
26.4.1672; 8.
2249. Francis Booth; Francis (d);
Almonbury, Yorks; Bl; 6.5.1672; 1.3.
1672; 3.5.1680; 8.
2250. George Clark; Thomas; Willoughby, War; Y; 23.3.1676; 23.3.1676;
- ; 7.
2251. Cristopher Crosland; Thomas;
Cobcroft, Yorks; G; 5.8.1678; 5.8.1678;
- ; 7.
2252. Lewis Davis; Hugh; Hampsted, M'sex; Cl; 1.6.1674; 1.6.1674;
- ; 8.
2253. James Gill; James (d); Parish
of St Andrew Holborne, M'sex; G;
7.8.1682; 7.8.1682; - ; 7.

2254. Thomas Kettle; Humphrey;
Southwarke, [Surr]; V; 5.9.1687; 5.9.
1687; - ; 7.
2255. George Stead; James; Surby
Streete, Yorks; Clothier; 2.4.1666;
2.4.1666; 4.8.1673; 7.

HUBBERT, Francis
2256. Francis Hide; William; Shin-
field, Berks; Y; 6.6.1687; 7.4.1687;
- ; 8.
2257. John Kindon; William; Chadsley, Worcs; Y; 4.12.1699; 4.12.1699;
3.12.1711; 7. Fd by John Nicholson.

HUCKLE, Robert
2258. Wm Bevan; John; Salop,
Shrops; Cw; 6.2.1643; 2.2.1643; 2.2.
1652; 9. Fd as Beband.
2259. Thomas Mew. Fd by Huckle
and John Neave 5.12.1642. Bd to
Neave 3.12.1632.
2260. Jo Samon; Wm; Dawncaster,
Yorks; Y; 19.1.1652; 29.9.1651; 7.3.
1659; 8.
2261. Giles Sussex; Thomas; Ilsley,
Berks; Bl; 1.3.1642; 1.3.1642; 6.5.
1650; 8.
2262. Edward Wilson; Edward;
Cambridge; Chandler; 6.5.1659; 25.12.
1658; - ; 8.

HUCKLESCOTT, Thomas
2263. John Smith; John; Haddam-
nash, Herts; Farrier; 7.7.1656; 7.7.
1656; - ; 7.

HUDGEBUTT, John
2264. Rice Jones; Thomas; Monmouth; Y; 2.8.1680; 2.8.1680; - ; 7.
2265. George Sutton; Ellys; Gwer-
sylt, Den; G; 7.12.1674; 7.12.1674;
- ; 7.
2266. Jasper Venner; Alexander (d);
London; C & MT; 3.11.1684; 3.11.
1684; - ; 7.
2267. James Withe; John; Norwich;
Weaver; 6.12.1680; 6.12.1680; - ; 7.

[84]

HUDSON, John
2268. Noah Barton; Thomas; Haggetts Broughton, Worcs; Y; 1.10.1677; 1.10.1677; - ; 7.
2269. Anthony Brotherick; Tho; Pierith, Cumb; Y; 6.12.1675; 6.12.1675; - ; 7.
2270. John Marpell; John (d); Bentley, Derby; — ; 6.10.1679; 6.10.1679; - ; 7.

HUFFEN, Henry
2271. Thomas Iley; Joseph; Foxon, Leics; Y; 11.6.1655; 11.6.1655; 7.7. 1662; 7. Fd by Huffen and John Hide.

HUGHS, James
2272. Clement Hardingham; Isaac; Norwalsham, Norf; G; 15.9.1657; 15.9. 1657; - ; 7.

HULL, William
2273. William Pinney; Wm; Huntsham, Herefs; G; 7.10.1689; 7.10.1689; - ; 7.

HUMPHREYS, John
2274. Richard Humphryes; Edmond; Bangor, Carmarthen [*sic* for Cards.]; G; 5.9.1698; 5.9.1698; 1.7. 1706; 7.

HUMPHREYS, William
2275. Thomas Cope. Fd by Humphreys 9.2.1691. Bd to Ann Norris (q.v.) 3.12.1683.
2276. Joel Desermew; Benjn; parish of St Mary White Chappel, M'sex; Victualler; 6.4.1691; 6.4.1691; - ; 7.

HUNBOLT, Gabriel
2277. [Gabriel Hunbolt. Fd by redemption 3.5.1675.]

HUNSCOTT, Joseph
2278. George Calvert. Fd by Hunscott 6.5.1644. Bd to him 6.2.1637.
2279. Robte Cutler; Geo; London; C & Go; 4.5.1646; 4.5.1646; 4.5.1653; 7.
2280. John Garfeild. Fd by Hunscott and Mrs Hannah Allen 10.1.1655. Bd to Mrs Allen (q.v.) 6.12.1647.
2281. John Hunscott. Fd by patrimony 28.6.1641.
2282. Gregory Moule; Gregory; Fowdon, Norf; G; 14.5.1642; 24.6.1642; 23.6.1649; 7. T.o. 22.5.1644 to Giles Calvert. Fd by Hunscott.
2283. John Norcott; John (d); Wing, Bucks; Farmer; 4.5.1646; 24.6.1646; - ; 7.

HUNT, Richard
2284. John Clapp; George; Hunnington, Dev; Y; 5.9.1687; 5.9.1687; - ; 7.
2285. George Harris; Wm; Helmden, N'hants; Y; 7.5.1677; 7.5.1677; - ; 7.
2286. William James; John; — , — ; Y; 18.6.1677; 18.6.1677; - ; 7.
2287. Andrew Maihew; Henry (d); Troutehed Fryers, London; Mariner; 6.10.1679; 6.10.1679; 8.11.1686; 7.
2288. John Shorthazell; John; parish of Eversham, Worcs; H; 7.2.1687; 7.2. 1687; 12.12.1695; 7.
2289. Henry Sturmy; Edmond; London; C & Gr; 8.11.1686; 8.11.1686; - ; 8.

HUNT, Thomas
2290. John Archer; Wm; London; C & Bricklayer; 1.7.1647; 25.3.1647; - ; 8.
2291. Thomas Durborne; William; London; C & Cu; 12.8.1671; 12.8.1671; - ; 7.
2292. Benjamine Evans; Benjamine; Shrewsbury; I; 7.1.1656; 7.1.1656; 7.3.1665; 9.
2293. John Farrow; Jno; James Dukes place, London; Clothier; 3.3. 1656; 1.1.1656; - ; 8.
2294. Robert Fukes; Tho; London; St; 14.6.1652; 14.6.1652; - ; 8.
2295. Wm Richardson; William; Lensham, Kent; H; 5.12.1642; 24.6. 1642; 19.1.1652; 9.

HUNT, William

2296. Adam Burridge; Adam (d); parish of St Buttolph Aldgate, London; Sawyer; 3.5.1697; 3.5.1697; 4.6.1705; 8.

2297. Peter Fox. Fd by Hunt and Felix Kingston 6.6.1659. Bd to Kingston (q.v.) 30.6.1651.

2298. William Grace; Nich; Desford, Leics; G; 4.8.1656; 4.8.1656; - ; 7.

2299. John Newby; Thomas; Marleborough, Wilts; Clothier; 1.5.1654; 1.5.1654; 6.5.1661; 7.

2300. John Purser; Rich (d); Witney, Oxon; Cw; 5.4.1647; 5.4.1647; 1.5.1654; 7.

2301. Thomas Richardson. Fd by Hunt 7.3.1698. Apparently never formally bd, but a man of this name was bd to William Hope (q.v.) 1.4.1645.

HURLOCK, Benjamin

2302. Nathaniell Jackman; Thomas; Newent, Glos; Cl; 1.5.1671; 1.5.1671; - ; 7.

2303. Charles Passenger; Thomas; Guilford, Surr; Gl; 2.10.1671; 2.10. 1671; 20.12.1677; 7.

2304. Joshua Phillips; George; Shadwell, Essex [*sic* for M'sex?]; Mariner; 5.8.1672; 5.8.1672; 1.9.1679; 7. Fd by Francis Egglesfield.

HURLOCK, George

2305. Francis Corsnett; Armell; Parshall, Worcs; Y; 16.3.1648; 16.3.1648; 26.3.1656; 8.

2306. Beniamine Hurlock. Fd by patrimony 21.4.1670.

2307. Thomas Johnson. Fd by Hurlock 6.7.1647. Bd to him 3.10.1639.

HURLOCK, Mary, Widow

2308. William Jackson; John (d); London; C & Cd; 3.5.1669; 3.5.1669; - ; 7.

HUSBANDS, Edward

2309. Rich Badeley. Fd by Husbands 3.4.1647. Bd to him 20.4.1640.

2310. Wm Sheilds; John (d); Rochester, Kent; G; 6.4.1646; 6.4.1646; 20.4.1653; 7.

2311. Gilbert Woort. Fd by Husbands 23.12.1641. Bd to him 4.11.1634.

HUSE, Thomas

2312. Phillip Hunt; Phillip; London; C & D; 8.4.1700; 8.4.1700; - ; 7.

2313. Elizabeth Kitcheyman; William; London; Coachman; 13.4.1698; 13.4.1698; - ; 7.

HUSSEY, Christopher

2314. John Pero; Edward; Brughton, Som; G; 7.7.1684; 7.7.1684; 1.2. 1692; 7.

2315. Thomas Shellmerdine; Daniell; Twyford, Derby; Cl; 8.4.1678; 8.4. 1678; 7.6.1686; 7.

HUTCHINSON, Joseph

2316. Richard Humphrey. Evidently bd to Hutchinson (although there is no formal entry of binding) and t.o. to Richard Baldwin. Fd by Baldwin 6.10.1690, but fined 5s. 'For being bound by a Forraine Indr & not being turned over at the hall'.

HUTTON, George

2317. Henry Lane. Fd by Hutton 4.3.1644. Bd to him 5.10.1635.

2318. Arthur Storar; Thomas; Northampton, N'hants; BSg; 5.9.1642; 5.9. 1642; - ; 7.

IBBITSON, Robert

2319. John Best; Stephen (d); Eansbury, Hunts; G; 24.5.1647; 24.5.1647; 5.6.1654; 7.

2320. Thomas England; Thomas; Pomfret, Yorks; H; 1.7.1661; 1.7.1661; 8.7.1668; 7. Fd as Ingland.

2321. Obadiah Gumbleton; John; New Sarum, Wilts; 7.5.1660; 7.5.1660; 7.1.1668; 7. Fd as Grombleton.

2322. Joseph Royse; Wm; London; C & Freemason; 10.1.1650; 10.1.1650; 9.2.1657; 7. Fd as Rash.

2323. Thomas Snodham; Jno; Wake-feild, Yorks; — ; 6.11.1655; 6.11.1655; 1.12.1662; 7.

2324. Roger Thomas; Tho; Bristow, — ; Bs; 6.11.1654; 29.9.1654; - ; 8.

ILES, William

2325. Peter Bearsley; Peter (d); London; C & Pw; 3.11.1673; 3.11.1673; - ; 7.

2326. Elias Hardcastle; Henry (d); London; C & MT; 1.6.1663; 1.6.1663; - ; 8.

2327. Willm Harris; James; London; C & Ca; 2.8.1669; 2.8.1669; 4.9.1676; 7.

2328. Leonard Hill; Humphrey; London; C & D; 18.12.1666; 18.12.1666; 4.5.1674; 7.

ILIVE, Thomas

2329. James Philpott; Timothy; parish of St Bennett Pauls Wharfe, London; L; 6.2.1699; 6.2.1699; 3.6.1706; Fd as John Philpott.

INGLISH, William

2330. Reynold Fox; Thomas; London; C & Cd; 4.4.1687; 4.4.1687; - ; 7.

INMAN, Mathias

2331. Solomon Shorter; Solomon; London; C & MT; 3.9.1660; 3.9.1660; - ; 7.

RELAND, William

2332. Wm Newcombe; Wm; Darby, Derby; Cw; 7.7.1641; 7.7.1641; - ; 8.

ISAAC, Abraham

2333. John Franknell, 'servant to Abraham Isaac Cittizen and Merchantailer of London', fd by Isaac 4.10.1686.

ISAAC, Jane, Widow

2334. Thomas Fisher; Mark; Ilson, Derby; H; 6.5.1661; 6.5.1661; - ; 7.

2335. John Handley; Robt; Burton, Yorks; B; 10.1.1654; 10.1.1654; 11.2.1661; 7.

ISAAC, Ralph

2336. Cornelius Beard; Abraham (d); Mch; 6.4.1646; 6.4.1646; 6.11.1654; 7.

2337. Gabriell Cornish; John; Tiverton, Dev; Y; 3.10.1648; 3.10.1648; - ; 7.

2338. Francis Glover; Thomas; Croyden, Surr; Y; 2.6.1645; 2.6.1645; 6.12.1658; 8.

2339. Peirse Langford; George (d); London; C & Tallowchandler; 24.1.1642; 24.1.1642; - ; 7.

2340. Henry Speake; Henry; York; Y; 6.9.1652; 6.9.1652; - ; 7.

2341. Thomas Stoneham; Thomas; Beddington, Surr; H; 1.6.1646; 'Wensday next'; 7.8.1654; 7.

ISAM, Henry

2342. Francis Wood; William (d); London; G; 1.2.1641; 1.2.1641; - ; 8.

ISBURNE, Thomas

2343. [Thomas Isburne. Fd by patrimony 2.11.1696.]

ISLIP, Adam

2344. William Hunt. Fd by Islip 1.2.1641. Apparently never formally bd.

2345. Mathew Morris. Bd to Thomas Badger 2.11.1640; t.o. 6.7.1646 to Islip. Fd by Badger 7.5.1649.

ISTED, Ambrose

2346. John Alcock; Lawrence; Tyllington, Sussex; G; 2.12.1668; 24.6.1668; - ; 8.

2347. Leonard Austyn; Edward; Pacham, Essex; T; 12.8.1671; 12.8.1671; - ; 7.

2348. John Clarke; Nicholas; London; Perfumer; 5.9.1664; 5.9.1664; - ; 7.

2349. William Hunt; William (d); London; C & St; 5.10.1674; 5.10.1674; 7.3.1687; 7.

2350. John Hurst; John; London; C & Gr; 7.8.1666; 24.6.1666; - ; 8.

2351. Henry Paine; John (d); Petworth, Sussex; E; 1.10.1677; 1.10.1677; - ; 7.

IVE, Roger

2352. Thomas Berisford; Mich; Borden, Kent; Cl; 15.1.1646; 15.1.1646; 17.1.1655; 9.

2353. John Comins; Humphry; Draycot, Derby; Y; 1.4.1661; 1.4.1661; - ; 7.

2354. Nathan Cooper; Thomas; Lewton, Beds; M; 4.9.1654; 4.9.1654; - ; 7.

2355. Wm Randall; Wm; Capell, Surr; G; 30.6.1651; 24.6.1651; - ; 8.

2356. John Roberts; John; Goorges Southwarke, [Surr]; Hostler; 6.11.1654; 6.11.1654; 2.12.1661; 8.

2357. Robte Slater; Richard (d); Mitcham, Surr; Cl; 2.3.1646; 2.3.1646; - ; 7.

2358. William Towersey; William; Woodford, Essex; H; 13.7.1657; 13.7.1657; - ; 7.

2359. Thomas Yates; William; St Saviours, Southwarke, Surr; Victualler; 27.6.1659; 27.6.1659; 3.2.1669; 7. Fd as Willm Yates.

IZARD, Anthony

2360. Anthony Izard; Anthony; [London]; [C & St]; 1.9.1679; 1.9.1679; - ; 8. Bd to his father.

JACKSON, Benjamin

2361. [Benjamin Jackson. Son of Ralph Jackson; fd by patrimony 2.4.1667.]

JACKSON, Edward

2362. Samuell Bayly; John; Rothersthrop, N'hants; - ; 28.9.1653; 28.9.1653; - ; 8.

2363. Ro Jones; John; Fernhill, Shrops; Bl; 5.7.1652; 1.6.1652; - ; 8.

JACKSON, John

2364. Thomas Horsman. Bd to Thomas Bassett (q.v.) 6.5.1659; t.o. 25.6.1662 to Jackson.

2365. Richard Preston; Thomas; Rothwell, Yorks; H; 4.2.1656; 4.2.1656; 4.5.1663; 7.

JACKSON, Joseph

2366. Thomas Gibson; Tho; Pinchbeck, Lincs; Y; 25.11.1664; 25.11.1664; - ; 8.

2367. Benjamin Whiting; Benjamin; Boston, Lincs; Woollendraper; 13.1.1669; 13.1.1669; - ; 7.

JACKSON, Thomas

2368. John Orchard; Walter; Chilcomb, Dors; Cl; 7.8.1648; 7.8.1648; - ; 7.

JACOB, William

2369. John Jacob; Edmond; Baskett, Berks; Y; 8.11.1669; 8.11.1669; - ; 7.

2370. James Pinfold; James; Holborn, [M'sex]; Coachman; 3.5.1675; 3.5.1675; 3.5.1686; 7. An earlier entry of 22.2.1675 binds Pinfold to Jacob for 7 years from 22.2.1675. Fd as James Pinford, and fined 2s. 6d. 'for not being turned over at ye Hall'.

2371. Roger Vaughan; Tho (d); London; C & BSg; 1.9.1679; 1.9.1679; - ; 7.

JAMES, Andrew

2372. David Evans; Robert; Offasire, Shrops; H; 3.3.1669; 3.3.1669; - ; 7.

2373. Richard Francklin; Richard; Cirencester, Glos; G; 6.4.1674; 6.4.1674; - ; 7.

2374. Nathaniell French; Richard (d); Danbury, Essex; G; 7.9.1646; 7.9.1646; 5.12.1653; 7.

2375. John James. Fd by patrimony 5.10.1685.

2376. Thomas Ockley; Thomas (d); Stocke Daborne, Surr; Y; 5.5.1668; 5.5.1668; - ; 7.

JAMES, Anne

2377. Thomas Mullins; Thomas; Fitchett Metravas, Dors; Y; 1.2.1675; 1.2.1675; - ; 7.

JAMES, John
2378. Charles Paine; Charles; parish of Woollavington, Som; Cl; 2.12.1695; 2.4.1692; - ; 7.

JAMES, Robert
2379. Robert Fellow; John (d); Reading, Berks; G; 6.9.1697; 6.9.1697; - ; 7.

2380. Ciprian Thompson; William (d); Rocksome, Lincs; G; 5.12.1698; 5.12.1698; - ; 7.

JAMES, Thomas
2381. Alexander Gibbs; James; parish of St Dunstan in the East, London; Gl; 7.6.1680; 7.6.1680; 2.7.1688; 8.

2382. John Petty; John; Shaftesbury, Dors; Clothier; 6.8.1677; 6.8.1677; 2.5.1687; 8.

2383. Joseph Stockley; John; London; L; 7.10.1700; 7.10.1700; - ; 7.

2384. Wm Swingler. Fd by James 26.3.1689, but fined 5s. 'For being bound by a Forraine Indr & turned over'.

2385. John Tharpe; Richd; London; C & F; 5.3.1688; 5.3.1688; - ; 8.

2386. Wm Wade; Wm; parish of St Saviours Southwarke, Surr; Victualler; 12.4.1692; 12.4.1692; 1.9.1701; 8.

2387. Thomas Whitlidge; William (d); Vp Holland, Lancs; Y; 7.8.1682; 7.8.1682; 9.9.1689; 7. T.o. (n.d.) to Henry Hills Junior and fd by him.

JANEWAY, Jonathan
2388. Abraham Sheppard; Abra; London; C & MT; 30.5.1687; 30.5.1687; - ; 7.

JANEWAY, Richard, I
2389. John Collyer; John; Great Holton, N'hants; Y; 4.11.1689; 4.11.1689; 1.2.1697; 7.

2390. Robert Dawson; Robert; London; C & Cd; 3.7.1682; 3.7.1682; 5.8.1689; 7.

2391. Richard Jannaway. Fd by patrimony 5.10.1691.

2392. Willm Keyes; James; Towne of Northamton; Victualler; 1.8.1670; 1.8.1670; — ; 8. T.o. 6.11.1671 to John Hewett.

2393. Richard Osgood; Richard (d); parish of Thetcham, Berks; Hatter; 13.5.1678; 13.5.1678; - ; 7.

2394. John Pickering; John (d); Little Eaton, Derby; Scythestone Picker; 4.10.1686; 4.10.1686; - ; 7.

2395. Richard Stephens; Richard; little Harridon, N'hants; H; 8.1.1672; 8.1.1672; 1.8.1681; 7.

2396. Caleb Swinnock; George; Maidston, Kent; Cl; 7.6.1675; 7.6.1675; - ; 7.

JANEWAY, Richard, II
2397. John Hawkins; William; London; C & St; 13.4.1698; 13.4.1698; 7.5.1705; 7.

2398. John Norman; John; Parish of St Giles in the Feilds, M'sex; L; 6.5.1700; 6.5.1700; - ; [7].

2399. Henry Peach; Henry (d); Hardingstone, N'hants; M; 1.2.1697; 1.2.1697; 4.9.1704; 7.

JAYE, Eliphall
2400. Phillipp Payne; Phillipp (d); London; C & Ha; 4.12.1693; 6.11.1693; - ; 7.

JELLEY, Edward
2401. John Andrews; John; Milbrooke, Beds; Sh; 2.3.1657; 2.3.1657; - ; 9.

2402. Henry Fowler; Roger; Hambleton, Rut; Y; 2.6.1656; 2.6.1656; - ; 7.

2403. Richard Owfall; Robert (d); Bretton, Flint; Y; 1.3.1658; 1.3.1658; 3.4.1665; 7. Fd by Jelley, Ralph Downes and John Rawson.

JEMSTON, William
2404. Samuell Pett; William; Chatham, Kent; — ; 7.9.1663; 7.9.1663; 27.3.1671; 8.

JENKINS, Thomas
2405. George Birch; John (d), London; C & Dy; 3.3.1656; 2.2.1656; - ; 8.

JENKS, John
2406. Thomas Bland; Thomas; Shefeild, Yorks; Smith; 2.11.1663; 2.11.1663; - ; 7.
2407. Richard Edwards; Wm (d); whoton conquest, Beds; G; 8.10.1649; 1.9.1649; - ; 8.
2408. Mathias Pratt; Rich; Harrowwild, M'sex; Y; 3.12.1655; 3.12.1655; 19.1.1663; 7.
2409. John Smith; Jno; Southmins, M'sex; B; 6.3.1654; 6.3.1654; - ; 7.

JENOUR, John
2410. Mathew Jenour; John; [London]; [C & St]; 1.8.1692; 1.8.1692; 7.8.1699; 7. Bd to his father.

JOHNSON, Benjamin
2411. Elizabeth Browne; Alexandr (d); London; C & Ca; 4.9.1699; 4.9.1699; - ; 7.
2412. John Grover; Tho (d); Burrough of Corfe Castle in the Isle of Purbeck, Dors; Woolcomber; 2.3.1691; 2.3.1691; 7.6.1703; 7.
2413. Andrew Johnson; William (d); Litchefeild, Staffs; Y; 3.12.1683; 3.12.1683; - ; 7.
2414. Edwd Short; Valentine; Citty of Chester; Mch; 3.3.1684; 3.3.1684; - ; 7.
2415. Richard Taylor; — (d); City of Chichester, [Sussex]; G; 2.5.1698; 2.5.1698; 7.6.1708; 7. Fd by Hester Johnson.

JOHNSON, Joshua
2416. Samuel Mence; Robt; Hembleton, Worcs; Y; 7.10.1672; 7.10.1672; - ; 7.
2417. Joseph Pike; Joseph (d); London; C & V; 3.12.1667; 3.12.1667; - ; 7.

JOHNSON, Michael
2418. Nathaniel Kent; Nathaniel (d); Warmecham, Ches; G; 9.9.1689; 9.9.1689; - ; 7.
2419. Jacob Miller; William; Curburrow, Staffs; Y; 3.5.1686; 3.5.1686; - ; 7.

JOHNSON, Rowland
2420. Thomas Bishop; Christopher; Pulloxhill, Beds; H; 7.2.1670; 7.2.1670; 7.5.1677; 7.
2421. John Christopherson; William (d); London; C & Cw; 7.4.1668; 7.4.1668; 3.5.1675; 8.

JOHNSON, Thomas
2422. John Crumpe; James; London; C & St; 7.5.1660; 25.3.1660; 4.6.1667; 8. Fd by patrimony.
2423. Henry Hardy; Henry; Loughborough, Leics; Ca; 1.8.1659; 25.3.1659; - ; 8. Entry deleted; m.n. 'This Apprentice is discharged by cancelling the Indentures. And raced out of this Booke by an Order of the 28th of June 1665.' Hardy was said to have gone to Virginia (Court-Book D).
2424. John Hickman; John; Westhaddon, N'hants; G; 28.6.1665; 1.1.1665; - ; 7.
2425. Samuell Johnson; Sam; Redding, Berks; Ha; 17.1.1648; 17.1.1648; - ; 7.
2426. Thomas Tennat; Edm; London; C & Cw; 19.3.1655; 1.1.1655; - ; 8.
2427. Barber Tooth; Jonathan; Strand, M'sex; Victualler; 18.6.1666; 18.6.1666; - ; 7.
2428. John Williams; Francis (d); Morton, Herefs; Y; 4.7.1670; 4.7.1670; 6.8.1677; 7.

JOHNSON, William
2429. John Hunt. Fd by Johnson 6.9.1675. Bd to Richard Hewett (q.v.) 5.8.1668.

2430. Samuell Johnson; William; Warfeild, Berks; Y; 6.2.1682; 6.2.1682; 3.6.1689; 7.

2431. Robte Pritchard. Fd by Johnson 1.7.1647. Bd to him 26.3.1635.

2432. Charles Turner; Arthur; Beconsfeild; Berks; G; 5.10.1674; 5.10.1674; - ; 7.

JOHNSON, Zachary

2433. Thomas Johnson. Fd by patrimony 10.6.1650.

2434. Zachary Johnson. Fd by patrimony 31.5.1650.

JOLE, Robert

2435. Elizabeth Beheathland; Henry (d); London; C & Ha; 3.7.1682; 3.7.1682; - ; 7.

2436. Henry Carter; William; St Martin in ye Feilds, M'sex; Ca; 5.3.1677; 5.3.1677; 7.4.1684; 7.

2437. John Coke; John; St Clements Danes in the Strand, M'sex; Mr; 12.8.1671; 12.8.1671; - ; 8.

2438. Jane Couly; Timothy (d); London; Mch; 5.8.1700; 5.8.1700; - ; 7.

2439. Margarett Deane; John; Manchester, Lancs; Y; 7.7.1679; 7.7.1679; - ; 7.

2440. John England; John; Marshfeild, Glos; Tn; 4.8.1690; 4.8.1690; 1.3.1703; 7. Fd by Joseph Tutle.

2441. Wm Haddon; John; Aston, N'hants; Y; 7.1.1684; 7.1.1684; 6.4.1691; 7.

2442. Daniell Jole; Christopher; Stratton St Margarets, [Wilts]; Cl; 5.12.1664; 24.6.1664; - ; 7.

2443. John Jole. Fd by patrimony 15.2.1700.

2444. Robert Jole. Fd by patrimony 4.12.1693.

2445. Thomas Manwaring; Andrew; London; C & Go; 3.7.1686; 3.7.1686; - ; 7.

2446. William Tegg; Edward; Pangbourne, Wilts [sic for Berks]; Y; 11.11.1695; 11.11.1695; - ; 7.

2447. Thomas Traford; Henry (d); Windlebury, Oxon; Y; 7.10.1689; 7.10.1689; - ; 7.

JONES, Benjamin

2448. [Beniamyn Jones. Son of William Jones; fd by patrimony 1.12.1645.]

JONES, Edward

2449. John Bayles; Robert; Bishop Prick of Durham, [Dur]; Gr; 4.2.1689; 4.2.1689; 6.4.1696; 7. Fd as Bales.

2450. Francis Dabb; Edward (d); Wooburne, Beds; Y; 9.2.1691; 9.2.1691; - ; 7.

2451. William Davis; Thomas; Lanfah, Glamorgan; Y; 6.2.1699; 6.2.1699; 4.3.1706; 7. Fd by Mary Jones.

2452. Saml Griffin; Thomas; Brise Norton, Oxon; Y; 25.6.1684; 25.6.1684; 7.12.1691; 7.

2453. Richard Harbin; John; Dorchester, Dors; Schoolmaster; 4.9.1699; 4.9.1699; - ; 7.

2454. Thomas Hooper; William; London, C & Combmaker; 3.4.1699; 3.4.1699; 6.5.1706; 7. Fd by Mrs Jones, Widow.

2455. John Morphew; Stephen; Casehaulton, Surr; Y; 2.12.1695; 2.12.1695; 1.2.1703; 7.

2456. John Smith; John; London; C & Embroiderer; 3.7.1693; 3.7.1693; - ; 7.

JONES, Francis

2457. Wm Cobbell; Ro; Lacock, Wilts; H; 8.9.1652; 8.9.1652; - ; 7.

2458. Francis Joanes. Fd by patrimony 4.10.1669.

2459. Joseph Moore. Fd by Jones and Peter Chapman 26.3.1644. Bd to Chapman 6.3.1637.

JONES, John, I

2460. John Joanes; John; London; C & St; 22.8.1667; 22.8.1667; - ; 7.

Bd to his father. Possibly the John Jones
fd by patrimony 24.4.1697.

2461. [John Jones. Fd by Widow
Jones 18.3.1647, probably by patrimony. Apparently never formally bd.]

JONES, John, II

2462. [John Jones. Fd by redemption
1.2.1697.]

JONES, John, III

2463. Thomas Baker; Bartholomew
(d); City of Worcester; G; 4.9.1699;
4.9.1699; 9.9.1706; 7.

2464. [John Jones. Fd by patrimony 24.4.1697.]

JONES, Richard

2465. Benjamin Alport. Fd by Jones
3.8.1685. Apparently never formally bd.
Jones is described as Citizen and Joiner.

2466. Thomas Tandy; John (d);
Stowe in the old, Glos; Ca; 6.6.1670;
6.6.1670; 5.5.1679; 7.

JORDAN, John

2467. [John Jordan. Fd by redemption 2.8.1680.]

JOYNER, John

2468. [John Joyner. Fd by patrimony 22.12.1691.]

JUSTICE, Thomas

2469. William Langleton; Will;
Lawnden, Bucks; Y; 11.6.1655; 1.5.
1655; 2.5.1664; 8. Fd as Laughton.

2470. William Peete; William (d);
Wimbolton, Hunts; G; 4.2.1656; 4.2.
1656; 2.3.1663; 7.

2471. Henry Stotesberry; Luke; Ev-
anly, N'hants; M; 1.4.1661; 23.2.1661;
- ; 8.

KEBLE, Samuel

2472. Alexander Bosvile; Thomas;
Breathwell, Yorks; Cl; 6.8.1688; 6.8.
1688; 11.11.1695; 7.

2473. Hugh Case; George (d); St
Dunstan in ye West, London; Barber;
1.3.1680; 1.3.1680; - ; 7.

2474. Robert Gosling; Robert (d);

London; C & MT; 7.8.1699; 7.8.1699;
4.11.1706; 7. Fd as Gostling.

2475. William Keble; Samuell; [Lon-
don]; [C & St]; 5.8.1695; 8.4.1695;
4.12.1704; 7. Bd to his father.

KEINTON, Joshua

2476. William Gilbert. Fd by Keinton 17.5.1671. Apparently never formally bd.

KEINTON, Matthew

2477. Benjamine Page; John; East-
ham, Essex; Cl; 7.9.1657; 24.6.1657;
- ; 9.

2478. Richard Warder; Richard;
Godsill, S'hants; Cl; 2.11.1658; 2.11.
1658; 7.5.1666; 7.

2479. Charnell Wolley; Robert; Hat-
feild, Herts; G; 26.3.1656; 26.3.1656;
6.5.1670; 8.

KELLAM, Charles

2480. William Austin. Fd by Kellam
3.8.1674. Apparently never formally bd.

KEMB, Andrew

2481. Morris Evans; Chri; Mirod,
Mont; — ; 5.3.1652; 5.3.1652; 21.1.
1662; 7.

2482. William Thompson. Fd by
Kemb 7.5.1655. Bd to him 11.4.1636.

KEMB, Thomas

2483. Thomas Williams. Fd by Kemb
4.3.1644. Bd to him 5.10.1635.

2484. John Woodhouse; Wm (d);
London; Gr; 4.3.1644; 4.3.1644; - ;
7.

KENDON, Francis

2485. Thomas Carpenter; John;
Bramsgrove, Worcs; Y; 19.1.1663;
19.1.1663; 4.7.1670; 7. Bd to 'Kendale',
fd by 'Kendon'.

2486. Nathaniell Gateward; Tho (d);
Ratcliffe, M'sex; Schoolmaster; 7.2.
1670; 7.2.1670; 1.10.1677; 7.

2487. William Lane; William; Kidderminster, Worcs; Scythesmith; 4.9.
1676; 4.9.1676; 16.6.1684; 7.

2488. William Shrewsberry; Wm; Wortley, Glos; H; 2.7.1655; 2.7.1655; 7.7.1662; 7.

KENDRICK, William
2489. William Thackery. Fd by Kendrick and Francis Grove 5.9.1664. Bd to Grove (q.v.) 13.7.1657.

KENNEDY, Silvester
2490. Henry Constable; Robert; Chediock, Dors; G; 4.6.1667; 4.6.1667; - ; 7.
2491. John Darnell; Phillip; Giles in the feilds, M'sex; G; 12.11.1667; 12.11. 1667; - ; 7.

KEQUICK, Thomas
2492. Willm Barker; Willm; City of Westminster; Victualler; 2.5.1670; 2.5. 1670; 18.6.1677; 7.
2493. Edward Gould; Ed; Reading, Berks; Br; 2.11.1663; 2.11.1663; - ; 7.
2494. John Littleton alius Tinker; John; Citty of Westmr; Cl; 2.6.1673; 2.6.1673; 7.7.1680; 7.
2495. John Sequence; Thomas; London; C & Tallowchandler; 1.7.1661; 1.7.1661; - ; 7.

KERSEY, John
2496. Alexander Kersey; John; London; C & St; 5.9.1687; 5.9.1687; - ; 7. Bd to his brother.

KETTLEBY, Walter.
2497. Samuell Clarke; Samuell; [Oxford]; Esquire Beadle of the University of Oxford; 8.11.1669; 8.11.1669; 3.12.1677; 7.
2498. Fincham Gardner; Abraham (d); London; C & F; 5.3.1677; 5.3. 1677; - ; 7.
2499. Samuell Twells; John; Newark, Notts; Schoolmaster; 6.2.1693; 5.12.1692; - ; 7.
2500. William Wells; Edward; Parrish of St Andrews Holborne, London; Cl; 2.5.1681; 2.5.1681; - ; 7.

2501. Richard Wilkins; William; Heathfeild, Sussex; Cl; 3.12.1683; 3.12.1683; 3.4.1693; 7.

KETTLEWELL, Robert
2502. John Clarke; Ralph (d); London; G; 1.9.1684; 1.9.1684; - ; 7.

KEYS, Stephen
2503. Richard Ashton; Richard (d); Westchester, Ches; I; 7.3.1692; 7.3. 1692; - ; 7.
2504. John Ballett; John (d); Westleton, Suff; Tn; 1.7.1695; 1.7.1695; - ; 7.
2505. Thomas Breven; Chester; Linendraper; 2.6.1679; 2.6.1679; 7.6.1686; 7. Fd as Bruen, the form of the father's surname.
2506. John Broadhurst; Thomas; Citty of Chester; G; 2.7.1694; 2.7.1694; - ; 7.
2507. Edward Clarke; Edward; parrish of St Andrews Holborne, M'sex; Perriwigmaker; 2.6.1684; 2.6.1684; - ; 7.
2508. John Johnson; Thomas (d); Debenham, Suff; Cl; 8.4.1700; 8.4.1700; - ; 7. A John Johnson was fd by Mrs Leas, widow of Charles Leas, 1.12.1712.
2509. Roger Kusick; Roger (d); Parish of St Giles in the Feilds, M'sex; G; 8.5.1682; 8.5.1682; - ; 7.
2510. Robert Perry; Thomas; Citty of Westchester, [Ches]; Tn; 2.8.1686; 2.8.1686; - ; 7.

KIDGELL, John
2511. Benjamine Cox; George (d); Withybrooke, War; G; 4.7.1681; 4.7. 1681; - ; 7.

KIFT, Henry
2512. David Arnold; Walter (d); Llangattocke Lingoed, Mon; Y; 6.6. 1687; 6.6.1687; 2.7.1694; 7.
2513. Joshua Davill; Thomas; Crake, Yorks; Cw; 6.2.1682; 6.2.1682; 3.3. 1690; 8.

2514. Robert Kifft; William (d); parish of Ninehead, Som; Y; 1.2.1697; 1.2.1697; 6.3.1704; 7.

2515. Thomas Turner; Wm; Warminster, Wilts; Y; 7.8.1693; 7.8.1693; 2.3.1702; 7.

KILLINGTON, Job

2516. Wm Garret; Wm (d); Citty of Oxon; G; 4.3.1689; 4.3.1689; 7.2.1698; 7. The entry of freedom describes Garret as having been t.o. to one [James?] Dover (n.d.). Fd by Killington and Dover.

KING, Job

2517. Tho Adams; Thomas (d); parish of St Thomas in Southwarke, [Surr]; Cl; 7.9.1691; 7.9.1691; 2.3. 1702; 8.

2518. Thomas Bowen; Thomas; Llangarthen, Carmarthen; G; 2.8. 1686; 2.8.1686; 4.9.1693; 7. Fd by Freeman Collins.

KINGSTON, Felix

2519. Christopher Desborough; Robte; Bennefeild, N'hants; Y; 22.6. 1641; 25.3.1641; 2.4.1649; 8.

2520. Jonas Elcom; Thomas (d); Hodgsdon, Herts; Cooper; 27.3.1645; 27.3.1645; - ; 7.

2521. Richard Fearbanck. Fd by Kingston 5.10.1646. Bd to him 5.2.1638.

2522. Peter Fox; Reynold; London; C & Bricklayer; 30.6.1651; 25.3.1651; 6.6.1659; 8. Fd by Kingston and William Hunt.

2523. John Gane; Edgar; Shastone, Dors; Y; 3.12.1646; 3.12.1646; 5.12. 1653; 7. Fd by Kingston and Mrs Dawson.

2524. Josua Johnson; Jefferey; Brewton, Som; Y; 30.6.1649; 30.6.1649; 4.8.1656; 7.

2525. John Owsley; Christopher; parish of Curry-evill, Som; Clothier; 3.10.1642; 3.10.1642; 3.12.1649; 7.

KIRBY, Thomas

2526. Jeremia Gazely; Thomas (d); London; C & Gr; 5.10.1663; 5.10.1663; - ; 8.

KIRKE, Thomas

2527. William Benning; Ambrose; Orwell, Cambs; G; 7.12.1663; 7.12.1663; - ; 7.

KIRKMAN, Francis

2528. Thomas Croskill. Fd by Kirkman 6.2.1682. Apparently never formally bd.

KIRTON, Joshua

2529. Richard Godfrey; Robte; Nuffield, Oxon; Cl; 22.12.1646; 22.12.1646; 6.2.1654; 7.

2530. Wm Jemsone; Wm; London; C & MT; 26.3.1652; 29.9.1651; 3.10. 1659; 8.

2531. William Kirton. Fd by patrimony 6.6.1664.

2532. Richard Randall; Rich; Bramfeild, Suff; G; 4.8.1656; 24.6.1656; 8.5.1665; 8.

KITCHELL, John

2533. Thomas Bowles; Wm (d); Abington, Berks; Y; 2.6.1645; 25.3. 1645; - ; 8.

KITCHIN, Francis

2534. Edmund Gutteridge; William (d); London; G; 4.10.1658; 4.10.1658; - ; 8.

2535. John Penne; Thomas (d); Warrington, Lancs; Go; 9.7.1663; 9.7. 1663; 6.11.1671; 7.

KNAPTON, James

2536. Robert Billing; Thomas; parish of Milton, N'hants; Y; 3.2.1696; 3.2.1696; 5.4.1703; 7.

KNELL, Clement

2537. Clement Knell. Fd by patrimony 7.2.1698.

2538. Thomas Knell. Fd by patrimony 1.2.1697.

KNIGHT, Joseph

2539. Edward North; Edward; parrish of St Martins in the Feilds, M'sex; G; 6.4.1685; 6.4.1685; - ; 7. T.o. 7.10.1689 to Francis Saunders.

KNOWLES, Peter

2540. [Peter Knowles. Son of Richard Knowles; fd by patrimony 7.8. 1671.]

KNOWLES, Thomas

2541. John Finch; Thomas; Guilford, Surr; H; 5.10.1696; 5.10.1696; - ; 7.

2542. Joseph Michell; Joseph; Cavarsham, Oxon; Gardener; 6.9.1680; 6.9. 1680; - ; 7.

KUNHOLT, Gabriel

2543. William Blackwell; William; London; C & Gr; 6.8.1677; 6.8.1677; - ; 7.

2544. William Marden; John; London; C & MT; 2.8.1675; 2.8.1675; 4.9.1682; 7.

LACEY, Thomas

2545. John Alchorn; John; Buxstead, Sussex; Y; 6.8.1677; 6.8.1677; 3.12.1684; 7.

2546. Anthony Bryant; Anthony (d); Peckham, Surr; G; 3.8.1691; 3.8.1691; - ; 7.

2547. Richard Hayle; Robert; London; C & Leatherseller; 6.3.1676; 6.3.1676; - ; 7.

2548. George Hindly; John; Horsham, Sussex; Mr; 2.6.1684; 2.6.1684; 5.2.1694; 7.

2549. Samuell Pope; George (d); White Chappell, M'sex; Doctor in Physic; 1.8.1698; 1.8.1698; - ; 7.

2550. Edward Randoll; Jonothan; Wickham, Bucks; G; 7.6.1669; 7.6. 1669; 4.3.1678; 7.

2551. John Usborne; Joseph; Brightelmston, Sussex; Y; 2.6.1684; 2.6.1684; 3.8.1691; 7.

LAIT, Ambrose

2552. Reynold Bagford; Walter; Bedfant, M'sex; — ; 1.3.1641; 25.12. 1640; - ; 8.

LAMAS, Jeremy

2553. John Harding; George; Widdenbrough, Ches; H; 1.8.1653; 1.8. 1653; 6.8.1660; 7.

2554. Thomas Lamas; Anthony; Isleworth, M'sex; Chandler; 6.10.1645; 29.9.1645; 3.10.1653; 8.

2555. Daniell Lammas. Fd by patrimony 7.8.1671.

2556. John Royse; Richard; Billiter Lane in Alhallowes, Stayning, — ; Cd; 7.9.1663; 7.9.1663; - ; 7.

2557. John Shephard; George; Ludlow, Shrops; G; 22.10.1656; 22.10.1656; 7.3.1670; 7.

LAMAS, Thomas

2558. William Compton; Will; Glocester, Glos; G; 2.7.1655; 2.7.1655; - ; 7.

2559. Charles Lea; Willm; London; G; 3.9.1667; 3.9.1667; 2.8.1686; 7.

2560. William Vining; William; Gillingham, Dors; H; 4.8.1656; 4.8.1656; - ; 7.

LAMBERT, James

2561. Leonard Smith; Leonard (d); London; Tidewaiter; 25.6.1683; 25.6. 1683; 3.4.1693; 7.

LAMBERT, John

2562. Richard Canninges; Richard; Fildinge, Wilts; Weaver; 4.9.1648; 4.9.1648; 1.10.1655; 7.

LAMBERT, Thomas

2563. William Battersby; Wm; Wells, Som; Cu; 6.11.1654; 6.11.1654; 2.12. 1661; 7.

2564. James Lambert. Fd by patrimony 1.6.1674.

2565. William Tinley; Henry; Wath, Yorks; — ; 1.7.1661; 1.7.1661; - ; 7.

LAMBORNE, Robert
2566. [Robert Lamborne. Fd by patrimony 1.9.1690.]

LANE, Isaac
2567. [Isaac Lane. Fd by patrimony 9.9.1700.]

LANGHAM, Edward
2568. Tymothy Raghett; Timothy (d); Berrey, Suff; Apothecary; 7.9.1646; 7.9.1646; - ; 7.

LANGLEY, John
2569. John Hews; John; Parish of St Thomas in Southwarke, [Surr]; Boddice-maker; 6.10.1690; 6.10.1690; - ; 7.

LARKIN, George, I
2570. John Barber; Morgan; Grays Inn Lane of the Parish of St Andrews Holbourn, [M'sex]; BSg; 6.5.1689; 6.5.1689; 6.7.1696; 7. Fd by Larkin and Hannah Clarke.
2571. Thomas Burt; Francis; Burnham, Bucks; Sh; 5.9.1681; 5.9.1681; - ; 7.
2572. Edward Ceny. T.o. from Larkin to Thomas Newcomb Junior 7.1. 1678. There is no entry of the binding to Larkin.
2573. George Larkin. Fd by patrimony 3.6.1689.
2574. Tho Linagar. Fd by Larkin 7.12.1691. Bd to William Harris (q.v.) 1.10.1683.
2575. Edward Reyner; Robert (d); London; G; 6.3.1682; 6.3.1682; 3.6. 1689; 7.

LARKIN, George, II
2576. Joseph Duehurst; Robert; London; Sugarbaker; 7.12.1696; 7.12.1696; - ; 7.

LATHAM, George
2577. Simon Gape; Simon (d); London; C & Cheesemonger; 26.7.1652; 24.6.1652; 7.5.1660; 8.
2578. Tymothy Garthwaite. Fd by Latham 1.7.1644. Bd to him 5.6.1635.

2579. Wm Gough. Fd by Latham 7.9.1646. Bd to him 30.4.1638.
2580. Elizabeth Latham. Fd by patrimony 16.12.1668.
2581. George Latham; George; London; C & St; 10.7.1646; 10.7.1646; 2.6. 1651; 7. Bd to his father. Fd by patrimony.
2582. Henry Marsh. Fd by Latham and Francis Titon 5.10.1657. Bd to Titon (q.v.) 1.7.1650.
2583. Thomas Palmer; Joseph; Croperdy, Oxon; Physician; 13.11.1647; 13.11.1647; - ; 7.

LAUGHTON, William
2584. William Lucas; Simon; Ratleigh, War; Y; 7.5.1677; 7.5.1677; 5.5. 1707; 7. The entry of freedom notes 'Lawton' as deceased.

LAW, Thomas
2585. John Cooke. Fd by Law 5.4. 1642. Bd to him 7.10.1633.
2586. Jonathan Law. Fd by patrimony 16.10.1644.
2587. Thomas Law. Fd by patrimony 5.4.1642.

LAWRENCE, John
2588. Whattoffe Boulter; Richard; London; C & Dy; 2.12.1695; 2.12.1695; 2.8.1703; 7.
2589. Robert Gaylard; Francis; Dorchester, Dors; Plumber; 16.6.1691; 16.6.1691; - ; 7.
2590. William Kenyon; William; Boynton, Yorks; Cl; 6.6.1687; 6.6.1687; - ; 7.

LAWSON, Anthony
2591. Cuthbert Burton; Arthur; Killinghall, Yorks; G; 25.6.1657; 25.6. 1657; 5.9.1664; 7.
2592. John Fillby; Edward; Farnham, Surr; G; 3.10.1687; 3.10.1687; - ; 7.
2593. Edward Fisher; William; Sumerton, Som; — ; 18.1.1664; 18.1. 1664; - ; 7.

2594. Anthony Lawson; Anthony; London; C & St; 3.10.1681; 3.10.1681; 7.11.1692; 8. Bd to his father.

2595. Thomas Newlin; John (d); Longwood, S'hants; Y; 5.10.1674; 5.10. 1674; - ; 7.

2596. Thomas Parke; John; Spofforth, Yorks; Y; 4.6.1667; 4.6.1667; - ; 7.

2597. Wm Parkins; Thomas; Sheffeild, Yorks; Ironmonger; 7.3.1692; 7.3.1692; - ; 7.

2598. Thomas Robinson; John; Stapleford Tawrey, Essex; G; 7.6.1669; 7.6.1669; 28.6.1676; 7.

LAWTON, James

2599. Edward Nott; Edward; Braden Forest, Wilts; — ; 5.1.1657; 5.1.1657; 18.1.1664; 7. Fd by Lawton and Edward Mann.

LEACH, Francis, I

2600. John Carey. Fd by Leach 1.4. 1650. Apparently never formally bd.

2601. Thomas Child; Richard; London; C & Bl; 6.3.1648; 6.3.1648; 31.3. 1656; 8.

2602. Thomas Daniell; Wm; Snath, Yorks; H; 2.7.1655; 2.7.1655; 7.7.1662; 7. Fd by Leach and Thomas Childe.

2603. Thomas Leach. Fd by patrimony 21.6.1658.

2604. William Leach. Fd by patrimony 5.10.1653.

2605. Francis Leech. Fd by patrimony 1.2.1664.

2606. Robert Newton; William; ye parish of Clemt Danes, M'sex; I; 25.6. 1657; 25.6.1657; - ; 8.

2607. Samuell Reeve; Wm; London; C & J; 2.6.1651; 2.6.1651; 6.12.1658; 7.

2608. Robert Seile; Robert; London; C & Tallowchandler; 10.1.1655; 10.1. 1655; 2.2.1662; 7. Fd by Francis and Thomas Leach.

2609. Richard Tennant; Nicholas; Lockland, Yorks; Y; 6.12.1641; 6.12. 1641; - ; 7.

LEACH, Francis, II

2610. Willm Godsaw; Willm (d); Croome Debitat, Worcs; Weaver; 20.7. 1670; 20.7.1670; - ; 7.

2611. Francis Leach. Fd by patrimony 6.11.1683.

2612. Benjamin Mettcalfe, Benjamin (d); Hogsdon, M'sex; T; 7.10.1700; 7.10.1700; 1.8.1709; 7.

2613. Richard Money; William; London; C & Weaver; 5.5.1684; 5.5. 1684; 6.7.1691; 7.

2614. James Nott; William (d); parish of St James Westminster; — ; 2.3.1696; 2.3.1696; 3.12.1705; 7.

2615. David Partridge; Daniel (d); London; C & Ha; 2.11.1691; 2.11.1691; - ; 7.

2616. John Plowright. Fd by Leach 7.12.1691, but fined 2s. 6d. for being bd by a foreign indenture.

2617. Mary Travers. Fd by Leach 1.8.1692, but fined 5s. for being bd by a foreign indenture.

LEACH, Thomas

2618. Richard Holland; Geo (d); London; C & MT; 7.3.1659; 7.3.1659; 2.4.1666; 7.

2619. John Kennell; John (d); Soleberry, Bucks; Grazier; 2.5.1670; 2.5. 1670; - ; 7.

2620. Jonothan Kinge; Richard; Langley, Derby; G; 5.5.1668; 5.5.1668; - : 7.

2621. Richard Martyn. Fd by Leach and Henry Holden 2.7.1667. Bd to Holden (q.v.) 7.5.1660.

2622. Robert Seile. Fd by Francis and Thomas Leach 2.2.1662. Bd to Francis Leach (q.v.) 10.1.1655.

LEACH, William

2623. William Duke; William; London; MT; 7.10.1678; 7.10.1678; - ; 7.

2624. Samuel Watson. Fd by Leach 3.12.1684. Apparently never formally bd.

LEAKE, John

2625. William Bartlett; Thomas (d); Eaton, Berks; Bs; 13.3.1693; 13.3.1693; - ; 7.

2626. William Butler; William; parish of St Sepulchers, London; Tobacconist; 12.11.1694; 1.10.1694; 9.2.1702; 7.

2627. Thomas Dunstan; Thomas (d); London; C & Bricklayer; 9.9.1689; 9.9.1689; 5.10.1696; 7.

2628. Christopher Hargrave; Richard; London; C & Cd; 6.7.1696; 6.7.1696; 7.8.1704; 8. Fd as Hargreaves.

2629. Robert Jenkinson. Fd by Leake 4.3.1689. Bd to John Playford (q.v.) 5.12.1681.

2630. William Kingston; Thomas; parish of Stebunheath alius Stepney, M'sex; Sawyer; 6.10.1684; 6.10.1684; - ; 7.

2631. John Marsh; Samuell (d); Thornford, Dors; G; 3.10.1698; 3.10.1698; - ; 7.

2632. Charles Price. Fd by Leake 6.9.1697. Apparently never formally bd.

LEAKE, William

2633. John Benson. Fd by Leake 7.9.1646. Bd to him 10.6.1639.

2634. Richard Gamon; Richard; Savoy, M'sex; G; 26.10.1653; 26.10.1653; 3.12.1660; 7.

2635. Charles Harper; Henry; Quebb, Herefs; G; 4.6.1660; 4.6.1660; 4.6.1667; 7.

2636. Charles Leake; Wm (d); London; C & St; 8.6.1646; 24.6.1646; - ; 7.

2637. John Leake; William; London; C & St; 7.5.1666; 7.5.1666; 4.8.1673; 7. Bd to his father.

2638. William Leake. Fd by patrimony 5.12.1670.

2639. George Monke; John; Honington, Suff; G; 4.7.1681; 4.7.1681; - ; 7.

2640. William Pope. Fd by Leake

and Benjamin Fisher 2.8.1641. Bd to Fisher 2.9.1633.

LEE, Charles

2641. John Johnson; Christopher (d); parish of St Sepulchres, London; Farrier; 2.12.1689; 2.12.1689; - ; 7.

2642. Thomas King; Bartholomew (d); Charlbury, Oxon; T; 7.2.1687; 7.2.1687; - ; 7.

LEE, Henry

2643. Charles Bolt; John; Eastborne, Sussex; Cl; 5.8.1650; 5.8.1650; - ; 7.

2644. Henry Halsey; Thomas; Cuddington, Beds; Y; 15.2.1647; 15.2.1647; - ; 7.

2645. Leonard Matson; Tho (d); East Smithfeild, M'sex; Weaver; 31.5.1650; 31.5.1650; - ; 7.

2646. James Pendred; Thomas; London; C & Farrier; 8.5.1693; 8.5.1693; 3.6.1700; 7. Fd by Lee and Henry Perris.

2647. Samuell Roberts; John; Barbwich, Leics; Y; 7.8.1666; 7.8.1666; - ; 7.

2648. Thomas Scriuell; John; City of Glocester; G; 1.8.1653; 1.8.1653; - ; 7.

2649. John Williams; Henry; London; C & Go; 6.3.1654; 6.3.1654; - ; 7.

LEE, Joseph

2650. John Applebury; Tho; Cleans, Worcs; H; 5.3.1660; 20.12.1659; - ; 8.

2651. [Joseph Lee. Son of William Lee Senior; fd by patrimony 17.9.1649.]

2652. John Shittlewood; Francis; London; Ha; 5.7.1652; 5.7.1652; 10.7.1660; 8. Fd as Shuttlewood.

2653. Richard Wyer; Abraham; Cripplegate, [London]; Tn; 3.8.1663; 1.7.1663; - ; 8. Lee's name is given as Leigh.

LEE, Richard
2654. [Richard Lee, 'a Freeman of the Citty of London', fd by redemption 2.4.1688, paying 50s.]

LEE, Stephen
2655. George Lee. Fd by patrimony 5.9.1692.
2656. Thomas Lee. Fd by patrimony 4.9.1699.
2657. Stephen Lee. Fd by patrimony 6.6.1687.

LEE, Thomas
2658. John Harris; John; Meastham, Surr; Cl; 26.3.1677; 26.3.1677; - ; 7.

LEE, William, I
2659. Charles Adams; Wm; Cliffords Lime in Fleet-street; G; 21.10.1644; 21.10.1644; 28.10.1651; 7.
2660. Allen Bancks; Willm; London; C & Cw; 30.4.1659; 30.4.1659; 4.5.1666; 7.
2661. George Everingham; Thomas; Winterton, Lincs; G; 16.8.1647; 24.8.1647; 28.8.1654; 7.
2662. John Fauconberge; Christopher (d); South Ottrington, Yorks; G; 1.9.1656; 1.9.1656; 7.9.1663; 7. Fd as Falconbarge.
2663. Joseph How. Fd by Lee 5.12.1642. Bd to him 19.1.1635.
2664. John Lee. Fd by patrimony 5.5.1668.
2665. Thomas Lee. Fd by patrimony 7.12.1674.
2666. Wm Lee; Wm; London; St; 6.10.1651; 6.10.1651; 12.10.1657; 7. Bd to his father. Fd by patrimony.
2667. Edward Peachell; John (d); Carletonscroope, Lincs; Cl; 21.10.1654; 29.9.1654; - ; 8.

LEE, William, II
2668. Samuell Butterfeild; Thomas; Woberne, Bucks; G; 6.6.1664; 6.6.1664; - ; 7.
2669. Tho Cossens. T.o. from Francis Haley to Lee 2.6.1673. Bd to Haley

(q.v.) 4.10.1669; fd by Haley 6.11.1676.
2670. Samuell Keble; Joseph (d); London; Mch; 4.6.1667; 4.6.1667; - ; 7.
2671. John Pardo; Richard (d); London; C & F; 1.2.1658; 1.2.1658; - ; 8.

LEECH, Lawrence
2672. Thomas Hodgson. Fd by Leech and Thomas Briscoe 3.12.1646. Bd to Leech 1.2.1635.

LEEDS, Richard
2673. James Waterman; James; Waltham Crosse, Herts; Silkweaver; 3.5.1658; 3.5.1658; - ; 7.

LEETE, John
2674. Richard Feilding; Richard (d); Parish of St James Clarkenwell, London; Victualler; 6.11.1682; 6.11.1682; - ; 7.

LEETE, Robert
2675. Edward Waller; Tho; Felsted, Essex; BSg; 7.5.1655; 7.5.1655; - ; 7.

LEETE, Thomas
2676. [Thomas Leete. Fd by patrimony 7.11.1653.]

LEGATE, John
2677. Richard Anderton. Fd by Legate 27.4.1646. Bd to him 5.3.1639.
2678. John Ballard; Daniell; Bisly, Glos; H; 4.9.1648; 4.9.1648; - ; 8.
2679. Wm Burrough. Fd by Legate and Miles Flesher 29.6.1646. Bd to Legate 16.10.1637.
2680. John Corbett; William; the Ree, Glos; G; 3.3.1656; 3.3.1656; - ; 7.
2681. John Harding; Samuell; London; C & Cooper; 3.3.1656; 3.3.1656; 6.4.1663; 7. Fd by Legate and John Hayes.
2682. Wm Harris; Wm (d); Ascott, Oxon; Mr; 14.6.1647; 14.6.1647; 27.6.1654; 7.

2683. William Rawlins; Edward; Arnesby, Leics; - ; 3.7.1654; 3.7. 1654; 5.8.1661; 7. T.o. 4.5.1657 to John Streater; fd by Legate and Streater.

2684. John Richardson; Wm (d); litle Haddam, Herts; Bricklayer; 2.11. 1646; 2.11.1646; 7.11.1653; 7.

2685. Thomas Singleton; Thomas; London; I; 7.3.1653; 7.3.1653; - ; 8.

2686. Edward Tay; Robte; London; C & Weaver; 7.12.1646; 25.12.1646; - ; 8.

LEIGH, John
2687. Thomas Lake; Richard; Layton Buzzard, Beds; Tn; 4.10.1669; 4.10. 1669; 2.6.1684; 8.

2688. Robert Lownds; Robt (d); Overton, Ches; G; 26.3.1683; 26.3.1683; - ; 7.

2689. Benjamine Needham; Thomas; London; C & Cw; 3.4.1682; 3.4. 1682; 4.8.1690; 7.

LEIGH, Thomas
2690. John Midwinter; Daniell; London; C & Leatherseller; 3.7.1699; 3.7. 1699; 26.9.1712; 8. Fd by Daniel Midwinter.

LETTICE, George
2691. Edward King; Francis; parish of St Giles without Cripplegate, [London]; Armorer; 6.3.1643; 6.3.1643; - ; 7.

2692. Richard Lilley. Fd by Lettice 8.11.1641. Bd to him 4.8.1634.

LEWCY, Richard
2693. [Richard Lewcy. Fd by patrimony 4.5.1663.]

LEWIS, Giles
2694. John Hamond; John; Marlebrough, Wilts; Bs; 2.4.1655; 2.4.1655; - ; 7.

2695. Stephen Lewis. Fd by patrimony 2.10.1654.

LEWIS, John
2696. [John Lewis. Son of George Lewis; fd by patrimony 5.2.1655.]

LEWIS, Richard
2697. John Fowkes; Nicholas; Cawcutt, N'hants; H; 4.1.1658; 4.1.1658; 5.2.1666; 8.

2698. John Lewis. Fd by patrimony 4.6.1683.

2699. Richard Lewis. Fd by patrimony 3.7.1671.

2700. Benjamine Wolley; Benjamine; London; C & Br; 10.9.1677; 10.9.1677; - ; 7.

LEWIS, Stephen
2701. Anthony Owen; John (d); Okam, Rut; V; 2.4.1655; 2.4.1655; - ; 7.

LEWIS, Thomas
2702. Francis Holden. Fd by Thomas Northcott 6.9.1697, but described as servant to Thomas Lewis. Bd to Edward Paine (q.v.) 4.8.1690.

2703. Thomas Lewis. Fd by patrimony 24.4.1697.

2704. William Mose; John; Covent Garden, M'sex; J; 2.11.1658; 2.11.1658; - ; 7.

LEYBOURNE, Robert
2705. Wm Elan; Robte; London; C & Gr; 13.12.1649; 29.9.1649; - ; 8.

2706. Richard Hampe; Richard; London; C & Ha; 2.10.1654; 2.10.1654; 7.10.1661; 7.

2707. Wm Leyborne. Fd by patrimony 1.7.1647.

2708. Thomas Peirce; Nathan (d); London; C & St; 1.8.1645; 24.8.1645; 11.6.1655; 8.

LEYBOURNE, William
2709. Wm Coltman; Christopher; London; Weaver; 1.12.1651; 1.12.1651; - ; 7. Possibly fd by Thomas Charnley (q.v.) 30.5.1687.

2710. John Croome; Thomas; London; C & MT; 31.5.1656; 31.5.1656; 1.6.1663; 7. Fd by Leybourne and Thomas Newcomb.

2711. Thomas James; Fran; Haies, M'sex; Cl; 4.12.1654; 4.12.1654; 16.12.1661; 7.

2712. John Leaborne; John; Northing, War; Y; 21.1.1661; 21.1.1661; 10.1.1670; 7. Fd as Leighbourne.

LIGHTFOOT, William

2713. William Benton; Jeremiah (d); White Chappell, M'sex; — ; 3.6.1678; 3.6.1678; 5.10.1685; 7.

2714. Isaack Frith; Willm (d); Southwark, [Surr]; Mealman; 3.3.1668; 3.3.1668; 2.8.1675; 7.

2715. William Gee; Thomas; Walkinton, Yorks; G; 3.3.1662; 3.3.1662; 3.7.1671; 7.

2716. Robert Lowe; Robert (d); London; C & Cw; 4.9.1654; 7.8.1654; - ; 9.

2717. Thomas Whittlesea; Jno; — ; Hunts; Weaver; 7.3.1653; 7.3.1653; 3.3.1662; 7.

LILLICROP, Peter

2718. Willm Barlowe; Willm; Herrington, N'hants; H; 6.9.1669; 6.9.1669; 2.10.1676; 7. Fd (as Barloe) by Mathias Drewe.

2719. Clement Knell; Clement (d); London; C & MT; 4.6.1660; 4.6.1660; 4.2.1678; 8. Fd by Mrs Maxwell.

2720. John Watson; John; Snath, Yorks; T; 3.5.1667; 3.5.1667; - ; 7.

LILLINGSTON, William

2721. John Barnard; John; Chelmsford, Essex; Mr; 6.6.1698; 4.4.1698; - ; 7.

LILLY, Benjamin

2722. Samuell Thomasman; Richard; London; C & Leatherdresser; 6.12.1680; 6.12.1680; - ; 7.

LILLY, Richard

2723. Richard Andrews; Richard; Hogsden, M'sex; Silktwister; 7.2.1648; 7.2.1648; 9.5.1655; 7.

2724. Ellis Duncombe; John; St Albons, Herts; Cooper; 5.12.1681; 5.12.1681; - ; 7.

2725. Thomas Hudson; Jno; London; C & Dy; 9.5.1655; 9.5.1655; - ; 8.

2726. Joseph Lilly. Fd by patrimony 2.10.1682.

2727. Steven Lilley; Henry; Burton Latimer, N'hants; Silktwister; 4.7.1642; 4.7.1642; - ; 7.

2728. John Marsh. Fd by Lilly 27.11.1688. Said to have been bd to Robert Missenden, and fined 2s. 6d. 'For being turned over'. There is no formal entry of binding.

2729. Henry Mountague; Thomas (d); London; C & V; 2.12.1689; 2.12.1689; - ; 7.

2730. Richard Paine; Richard (d); St Giles Cripplegate, London; Cd; 6.11.1676; 6.11.1676; - ; 7.

2731. Ralph Snow; Ralph; London; C & Cw; 5.9.1687; 5.9.1687; 8.4.1695; 7. Fd by Lilly and John Marsh.

2732. James Trewblood; William; St Giles without Cripplegate, [London]; Mealman; 7.6.1676; 7.6.1676; - ; 7.

2733. Richard Walker; Thomas; Brales, War; H; 7.7.1651; 7.7.1651; 5.12.1659; 8.

LIMPANY, Edward

2734. Charles Becket; William; Twitnam, M'sex; Y; 6.2.1665; 6.2.1665; - ; 7.

2735. Robert Limpany; Edward; London; C & St; 16.1.1656; 16.1.1656; 5.12.1664; 8. Bd to his father.

2736. James Wallis; James (d); Rickmansworth, Herts; Cornchandler; 4.6.1667; 29.4.1667; - ; 7.

LIMPANY, Humphrey

2737. Edward Limpany. Fd by patrimony 17.3.1651.

2738. Edward Lympany. Fd by Limpany 5.12.1664. Apparently never formally bd.

LIMPANY, Robert

2739. John Beauchamp; Christopher; Fulham, M'sex; Ca; 4.9.1699; 4.9. 1699; - ; 7.

2740. John Browne; Roger; Fulham, M'sex; T; 8.4.1700; 8.4.1700; - ; 7.

2741. John Dancaster; Ottowell, parish of St Batholomew, London; G; 4.3. 1678; 4.3.1678; - ; 7.

2742. George Grymes; Richard; Putney, Surr; Waterman; 5.9.1670; 5.9. 1670; 4.3.1678; 7.

2743. John Limpany; Edward; Fullham, M'sex; Y; 20.12.1684; 20.12.1684; - ; 7.

2744. Daniel Meads; Thomas; London; C & Waterman; 6.5.1689; 6.5. 1689; - ; 7.

2745. Abraham Odell; William; Newport Pannell, Bucks; Felmonger; 4.2.1695; 29.9.1694; - ; 7.

LINDSEY, William

2746. Thomas Booth; Samuell; London; C & Ha; 3.12.1694; 3.12.1694; - ; 7.

LINGARD, Christopher

2747. John Fowler; John; Wotton, N'hants; G; 6.6.1670; 6.6.1670; - ; 7.

2748. John Harrold; John; Islington, M'sex; Br; 6.9.1680; 6.9.1680; - ; 7.

2749. William Hasell; Edward; Steeple Claton, Bucks; Y; 2.4.1666; 25.3.1666; - ; 7.

2750. Thomas Hughs; Charles (d); London; Br; 11.4.1681; 11.4.1681; 6.4.1691; 8.

2751. Thomas Lingard; Christopher; [London]; [C & St]; 7.1.1678; 7.1.1678; 6.6.1687; 7. Bd to his father; fd by patrimony.

2752. John Moodey; John; London; Victualler; 5.8.1672; 5.8.1672; - ; 8.

2753. Henry Morace; Henry; parish of St Leonard Shoreditch, M'sex; Fringemaker; 25.6.1688; 25.6.1688; 8.11.1697; 7.

2754. Robert Wilson; Gowin; parish of St Buttolph without Aldersgate, London; G; 2.5.1687; 2.5.1687; 2.7. 1694; 7. Fd by Lingard, but fined 2s. 6d. for not being turned over at the hall. There is no record of Wilson having served another master.

LINGARD, Thomas

2755. John Clarkson; John; Burrough of Southwarke, Surr; B; 7.11. 1687; 7.11.1687; - ; 7.

2756. Barnaby Bernard Lintott; John (d); Horsham, Sussex; Y; 1.12. 1690; 1.12.1690; 18.3.1700; 7. T.o. (n.d.) to John Harding. Fd by Lingard and Harding.

LINNELL, Thomas

2757. John Lynnell. Fd by patrimony 6.8.1655.

2758. John Rawlins. Fd by Linnell 4.4.1653. Bd to him 2.11.1635.

LITGOLD, Nicholas

2759. Thomas Hill; John; Wem, Shrops; Y; 7.10.1661; 24.8.1661; - ; 8.

2760. Samuell Litgould; Nicholas; London; Sc; 2.11.1663; 25.3.1663; - ; 8.

2761. William Thompson; Lancelott; London; C & Cw; 17.9.1649; 24.8.1649; 4.1.1658; 8.

2762. Thomas Whitfeild; Richard; London; C & Mr; 1.12.1656; 15.9. 1656; - ; 8.

LITTLEBURY, George

2763. Thomas Doughty; Thomas; New Windsor, Berks; Cl; 4.5.1696; 20.3.1696; - ; 7.

2764. Anthony Eyre; Anthony (d); Tetney, Lincs; E; 6.6.1698; 6.6.1698; - ; 7.

2765. Lovett Saunders; Christopher; London; C & MT; 7.8.1699; 7.8.1699; - ; 7.

2766. John Stannard; John; Simpson, Bucks; Cl; 6.8.1694; 6.8.1694; - ; 7.

LITTLEBURY, John
2767. John Brigham; Thomas; parish of St Andrew Holbourne, M'sex; G; 7.10.1689; 7.10.1689; 1.2.1697; 7.

LITTLETON, John
2768. John Vernon; Edward; Westminster; Cabinetmaker; 7.7.1690; 7.7.1690; - ; 7. A John Vernon was fd by William Barker 26.9.1712.

LLOYD, Henry
2769. Willm Everet; John (d); Gainsbury, Lincs; Y; 8.11.1669; 8.11.1669; - ; 7.
2770. Richard Meade. Fd by Lloyd and Henry Brugis 8.10.1667. Bd to Brugis (q.v.) 3.9.1660.
2771. Mathew Orris; Daniell; - , - ; Milliner; 6.2.1671; 6.2.1671; 4.3.1678; 7.
2772. John Price; William; London; C & Wheelwright; 11.11.1700; 11.11.1700; - ; 7.
2773. Joseph Walker; Ambros; London; C & Cooper; 7.3.1659; 29.9.1659; 8.10.1667; 7.

LLOYD, Lodowick
2774. George Horne; Robert; London; C & Ha; 7.9.1657; 7.9.1657; - ; 9.
2775. Mathew Smelt; Willm; Rascelfe, Yorks; - ; 6.10.1656; 6.10.1656; 2.11.1663; 7.

LOCKE, John
2776. [John Locke. Fd by patrimony 3.9.1672.]

LOCKE, Thomas
2777. John Harrod; John; Harrington, N'hants; H; 6.3.1654; 6.3.1654; 7.10.1661; 7.
2778. Robert Roberts. Fd by Locke 4.8.1662. Apparently never formally bd.

LONG, Henry
2779. Robert Robinson; Jno; Sutton in holderness, Yorks; H; 7.6.1658; 7.6.1658; - ; 7.

LOVEDAY, Aaron
2780. William Loveday; Moses; Brackley, N'hants; M; 2.4.1677; 2.4.1677; - ; 7.

LOVELL, Henry
2781. [Henry Lovell. Fd 3.3.1684 by orders of the Court of Aldermen.]

LOWEN, William
2782. John Lowen; Henry (d); Brumham, Beds; Y; 1.4.1672; 1.4.1672; 15.2.1700; 7.

LOWNES, Richard
2783. Thomas Carlos; Will; Breewood, Staffs; G; 2.7.1655; 2.7.1655; - ; 7.
2784. William Hall; Lawrence; St Andrews Holborn, London; - ; 7.6.1676; 7.6.1676; 2.6.1684; 7.
2785. John Lownes. Fd by patrimony 5.7.1675.

LOWNES, Samuel
2786. Anthony Baskervile; Anthony (d); London; Bricklayer; 5.9.1681; 5.9.1681; 20.12.1689; 8.
2787. John Beekeman; Gabriell; Maidstone, Kent; - ; 3.5.1680; 3.5.1680; - : 7.
2788. John Bradbury; Willm; Mobely, Ches; Y; 4.3.1672; 4.3.1672; - ; 7.
2789. James Brand; David; London; Mch; 8.11.1697; 8.11.1697; - ; 7.
2790. George Harris; Edward (d); Epping, Essex; G; 27.9.1695; 3.7.1695; 8.11.1703; 7. Fd by Thomas Chapman.
2791. George Huddleston; George (d); Lincolne; G; 5.6.1690; 5.6.1690; 4.10.1697; 7.
2792. Eustace Ludford; Clement (d); Balls Hall, War; Cl; 2.12.1672; 2.12.1672; - ; 7.
2793. Richard Mather; John; Croston, Lancs; - ; 3.10.1670; 3.10.1670; - ; 7.

LUGGER, William
2794. Robte Boydell. Fd by Lugger 2.2.1646. Bd to him 6.2.1637.

2795. Wm Fisher; Godfrey (d); London; C & Cu; 3.11.1645; 29.9.1645; 4.10.1652; 8.

LUNN, Robert

2796. Edward Cavill; John; London; Go; 3.10.1648; 1.9.1648; 6.10.1656; 8. Fd as Gawill.

2797. Jonathan Evans; Stephen (d); London; C & Ca; 3.7.1656; 24.6.1656: 3.10.1664; 8.

2798 John Griffin. Fd by Lunn 3.11 1647. Bd to him 30.6.1634.

2799. Jonathan Wood; Jonathan; Preston Bissett, Bucks; Cl; 6.6.1664; 1.6.1664; - ; 7.

LUTTON, John

2800. John Peaseley; Barth; city of Oxon; Mason; 7.7.1673; 7.7.1673; - ; 7.

LYON, William

2801. Thomas Baley; Ralph; Shadamosse, Ches; Y; 9.2.1642; 9.2.1642; - ; 7.

2802. Samuell Dymensdell; John; Ratcliffe, - ; L; 26.3.1666; 26.3.1666; 20.6.1673; 7.

2803. Benjamin Hewes; Shadrack; London; C & Cd; 3.12.1660; 25.12.1660; - ; 7.

2804. John Huggans; Richard; London; C & Horner; 4.2.1656; 4.2.1656; - ; 7.

2805. Richard Hunt; Henry (d); Georges Cleft, Dev; Y; 5.8.1668; 5.8.1668; 6.12.1675; 7.

2806. Nicholas Steevens; Philip; London; C & Dy; 2.4.1667; 2.4.1667; - ; 8.

2807. Samuell Thomas; Stephen; London; C & Ha; 6.8.1660; 25.12.1660; - ; 7.

2808. James Thrup; James (d); Sparshall, Berks; Sh; 1.3.1647; 1.3.1647; - ; 7.

2809. Joseph Whetton; Thomas; Drempton, Dors; - ; 4.7.1670; 4.7.1670; 6.8.1677; 7.

2810. James Whitley; Lancelott; Magglesfeild, Ches; Y; 7.9.1674; 7.9.1674; - ; 7.

MABB, Thomas

2811. Lyonell Lennier; Clemt; East Greenwich, Kent; Musician; 5.12.1659; 5.12.1659; - ; 7.

2812. Ralph Shaw; Vincent; Westwitton, Yorks; Schoolmaster; 1.7.1650; 1.7.1650; - ; 7.

MACOCKE, John

2813. Gabriell Brookes; Thomas (d); Hornesey, M'sex; Y; 6.7.1667; 6.7.1667; 2.8.1675; 8.

2814. Joshua Churchill; William; Dorchester, Dors; St; 29.3.1680; 29.3.1680; 4.4.1687; 7.

2815. Robert Everingham. Fd by Macocke and Ralph Davenport 5.8.1668. Bd to Davenport (q.v.) 2.9.1661.

2816. Leonard Hill. Fd by Macocke and Jane Coe 5.2.1655. Bd to Coe (q.v.) 24.5.1647.

2817. Francis Jackman; Robert; Westminster, M'sex; G; 6.3.1665; 6.3.1665; - ; 7.

2818. John Leek; Wm; Blewill, Staffs; Y; 7.9.1674; 24.6.1674; 26.6.1682; 8.

2819. John Long; Cardeu; St Egidy in the Fields, M'sex; G; 9.2.1674; 9.2.1674; 3.10.1681; 7.

2820. Thomas Macock; Richard; Heyford Warren, Oxon; H; 18.12.1666; 18.12.1666; 9.2.1674; 7.

2821. John Mason; John (d); Piddington, N'hants; - ; 3.3.1673; 3.3.1673; 24.3.1680; 7.

2822. John Mathews; John (d); Wasperton, War; Sh; 7.8.1682; 7.8.1682; 9.9.1689; 7.

2823. Griffin Miller; Jno; Brackley, N'hants; - ; 6.6.1653; 6.6.1653; 3.11.1662; 8.

2824. Thomas Mosse; Thomas; Daventry, N'hants; G; 6.12.1658; 6.12.1658; 10.11.1668; 8.

2825. Thomas Oliver; Tho (d); St Martins in the Fields, Westminster; G; 3.7.1656; 29.9.1655; 7.11.1664; 9.

2826. Edmund Powell; Paul; London; C & Embroiderer; 7.11.1687; 7.11.1687; 12.11.1694; 7. Fd by Macocke and Benjamin Mott.

2827. Joseph Ray. Fd by Macocke 5.7.1675. Bd to John North (q.v.) 26.6.1668.

2828. George Stauely; Charles; Cauersham, Oxon; G; 3.9.1655; 3.9.1655; 27.6.1664; 9.

2829. Edward Tracy; Edward; London; C & Carman; 7.11.1681; 7.11.1681; 13.11.1689; 8.

2830. Thomas Webster; Rich; Pannell, Yorks; Linendraper; 17.11.1645; 17.11.1645; 6.12.1652; 7.

2831. Michael Whittle; Samuel (d); London; G; 1.5.1676; 1.5.1676; 13.5.1684; 8. Fd as White.

MADDISON, James
2832. [James Maddison. Son of Henry Maddison; fd by patrimony 1.3.1698.]

MADDOX, Katherine, Widow
2833. John Langley. Fd by Katherine Maddox 6.10.1690. Bd to Thomas Maddox (q.v.) 4.9.1682.

2834. Jeremiah Millner; Joseph (d); Notton, Yorks; Y; 7.11.1692; 7.11.1692; 3.12.1705; 7. Bd to the widow of Thomas Maddox.

2835. William Turner; Thomas (d); Kellamarsh, Derby; G; 6.6.1687; 6.6.1687; 4.7.1698; 7. Bd to the widow of Thomas Maddox.

MADDOX, Thomas
2836. George Evans; Thomas; London; C & MT; 3.8.1657; 3.8.1657; 31.1.1666; 8. Fd by Maddox and William Mason.

2837. John Langley; Samll; London; C & Woodmonger; 4.9.1682; 4.9.1682; 6.10.1690; 7. Fd by Katherine Maddox.

MAGNES, James
2838. Richard Bentley. Fd by Magnes 25.6.1684. Apparently never formally bd.

2839. John Smith. Fd by Magnes 10.6.1684. Apparently never formally bd.

MAIOR, John
2840. John Cooper. Fd by Maior 6.11.1643. Bd to him 15.10.1635.

2841. John Greene; William; Saltwich, Worcs; H; 2.8.1652; 2.8.1652; - ; 9.

2842. Christopher Lee; Chr; Woouerhampton, Staffs; Cl; 3.5.1647; 3.5.1647; - ; 7.

MAIOR, William
2843. John Davison. Fd by Maior 6.12.1647. Bd to him 3.6.1634.

MAIZEY, Francis
2844. John Feilder; Edward; Tedbury, Glos; Bl; 3.2.1645; 3.2.1645; - ; 7.

2845. John Piper. Fd by Maizey 3.2.1645. Bd to him 6.2.1637.

2846. Robert Reade; Robt; Leigh, Scotland; E; 6.11.1655; 6.11.1655; - ; 7.

MAJOR, Benjamin
2847. Edward Jones; John (d); parrish of St Clement Danes, M'sex; T; 2.3.1685; 2.3.1685; 2.4.1705; 7. T.o. 'by Endorsement' to John Penn 1.8.1687. Fd by Penn.

MAJOR, Daniel
2848. Benjamin Major; Gabriel; Leicr, [Leics]; Cl; 18.6.1677; 18.6.1677; 7.7.1684; 7. Fd by William Phillips.

MALLET, David
2849. Robert Vaughan; Robert (d); London; C & Leatherseller; 1.8.1681; 1.5.1681; 6.8.1688; 8.

MALLET, Elizabeth, Widow

2850. David Mallet; David (d); London; C & St; 7.5.1683; 7.5.1683; 29.1.1685; 7. Bd to his mother; fd by patrimony.

2851. Thomas Orum; Thomas; Parish of St Martins in the feilds, M'sex; Bricklayer; 4.6.1683; 4.6.1683; 9.2.1691; 7. T.o. to John Redmaine (n.d.) and fd by him, but fined 2s. 6d. 'for not being turned over at the Hall'.

MALLEY, James

2852. George Swinhowe; George; Millend, Parish of Rickmansworth, Herts; Cl; 6.6.1670; 6.6.1670; - ; 7.

MALLORY, William

2853. Samuell Woodliffe; Tho; Stumford, Lincs; Mr; 20.12.1645; 21.12.1645; - ; 8. The father's name is given as Woodcliffe; the entry is given under the date 20.12.1645 but reads 'Eight yeares from St. Tho: Day last. dated ye 6th of January 1645[-6]'.

MALTHURST, Thomas

2854. Richd Middlesop; John; Reddington, Berks; G; 4.12.1682; 4.12.1682; - ; 7.

MANN, Edward

2855. John Fish; Anthoney (d); London; C & Linendraper; 27.7.1671; 27.7.1671; 6.10.1678; 7.

2856. John More; Thomas (d); Oxford; G; 3.12.1667; 3.12.1667; - ; 8.

2857. Edward Nott. Fd by Mann and James Lawton 18.1.1664. Bd to Lawton (q.v.) 5.1.1657.

MANN, John

2858. Benjn Bartholomew; William; parish of Stepney, M'sex; Schoolmaster; 7.12.1691; 7.12.1691; 7.4.1701; 7. Fd by Isaac Bartholomew.

MANN, Samuel

2859. Thomas Ford; Richard; Maldon, Essex; Y; 14.5.1642; 14.5.1642; 4.6.1649; 7.

2860. Edward Man. Fd by patrimony 24.4.1655.

2861. Thomas Man. Fd by patrimony 4.10.1658.

MANSHIP, Samuel

2862. Wm Davis; Edward (d); London; C & Girdler; 9.2.1691; 9.2.1691; 7.3.1698; 7.

MARKHAM, Michael

2863. Robert Croker; Richard; Somning, Oxon; H; 6.6.1670; 6.6.1670; 6.5.1678; 7.

MARLOW, John

2864. Edward Maddox; Edwd; Coventry, War; G; 5.4.1684; 5.4.1684; 8.6.1691; 7. T.o. (n.d.) to John Richardson and fd by him, but fined 2s. 6d. 'For not being turned over at the Hall''.

MARRINER, James

2865. John Coulston; Thomas (d); parish of St Geo Southwarke, [Surr]; Watchmaker; 1.10.1688; 1.10.1688; 11.11.1695; 8. Fd as Colston.

2866. Thomas Wallis; Thomas; London; C & Mr; 2.3.1696; 2.3.1696; - ; 7.

MARRIOTT, George

2867. Wm Canning; Chareles (d); London; - ; 14.1.1679; 14.1.1679; 2.8.1686; 7. Fd by the executors of Francis Tyton.

2868. John Hill. Fd by Marriott 12.11.1677. Bd to Nathaniel Ponder (q.v.) 1.8.1670.

2869. Henry Lord; John; Salehurst, Sussex; Cl; 5.2.1672; 5.2.1672; 2.6.1684; 7.

MARRIOTT, John

2870. Giles Astley. Fd by Marriott 3.7.1654. Bd to him 21.6.1638.

2871. Whitguift Aylmer; Samuell; Bishopstarford, Herts; Dr of Physick; 7.12.1646; 7.12.1646; - ; 7.

MARRIOTT, Richard

2872. Edward Eggleston; John; Winchelsey, Sussex; Surgeon; 2.4.1649; 2.4.1649; - ; 7.

2873. Giles Johnson; Giles; Hamersmith, M'sex; G; 10.6.1651; 10.6.1651; - ; 7.

2874. Charles Lee; Benjamine (d); London; G; 12.7.1658; 12.7.1658; - ; 7.

2875. Richard Rodd; James; Hentlon, Herefs; H; 5.8.1661; 24.1.1661; - ; 8.

2876. Willm Warter; John; Inner Temple, London; G; 20.5.1668; 20.5.1668; 7.6.1675; 7.

MARSH, Henry

2877. Thomas Ames; John; great Chesterford, Essex; Weaver; 4.6.1649; 24.6.1649; - ; 9.

2878. John Ashenhurst; Edmond; Sedgley, Staffs; G; 10.6.1661; 10.6.1661; - ; 7.

MARSH, John

2879. John Boone; Stephen; London; C & Turner; 3.6.1695; 3.6.1695; - ; 7.

2880. Tho Grove; Henry; parish of St Giles Cripplegate, M'sex; Bl; 7.10.1689; 7.10.1689; 2.11.1696; 7.

2881. Christopher Hurt; Christopher; parish of St Mary Matfellon alius White-Chappell, M'sex; G; 1.10.1694; 1.10.1694; - ; 7.

2882. Thomas Mew; Thomas (d); London; C & Patternmaker; 7.12.1696; 7.12.1696; 3.2.1707; 7.

2883. John Petersverhesselt; Aron; London; T; 7.7.1690; 7.7.1690; - ; 8.

2884. Ralph Snow. Fd by Marsh and Richard Lilly 8.4.1695. Bd to Lilly (q.v.) 5.9.1687.

2885. James Twedy; William; parish of St Giles Criplegate, M'sex; Victualler; 2.8.1697; 2.8.1697; 6.11.1704; 7.

2886. Seth Wild; John; parish of St Giles Criplegate, London; Cl; 4.12.1699; 4.12.1699; 7.4.1707; 7.

MARSHALL, John, I

2887. William Boddington; Isaack; London; C & Weaver; 6.12.1680; 6.12.1680; - ; 7.

2888. Richard Dugard; Wm; London; C & St; 8.10.1649; 29.9.1649; - ; 8.

2889. Thomas Gardiner; Edward; Norly, Oxon; Clothier; 6.11.1655; 6.11.1655; 7.12.1663; 7. Fd as Gardner.

2890. John Marshall. Fd by patrimony 6.8.1677.

2891. Phillip Wathin; Roger; Langarren, Herefs; Y; 5.6.1654; 5.6.1654; - ; 7.

MARSHALL, John, II

2892. John Bladon; Willm; Utuxiter, Staffs; Ironmonger; 5.8.1700; 5.8.1700; - ; 7.

2893. Ebenaz Careless; John; Citty of Gloucester; G; 5.8.1695; 5.8.1695; - ; 7.

MARSHALL, William

2894. Wm Harris; Thomas; Charleberry, Oxon; Y; 12.11.1677; 12.11.1677; - ; 7.

2895. Willm Hawkins; Richard; Spelsbury, Oxon; H; 10.1.1670; 10.1.1670; 12.2.1677; 7.

2896. Eliphall Jaye; John; London; C & MT; 7.11.1681; 7.11.1681; 7.9.1691; 7.

2897. John Marshall; William; [London]; [C & St]; 5.9.1687; 5.9.1687; 4.3.1694; 7. Bd to his father.

2898. Nathaniel Stanton; Nathan; London; C & Bricklayer; 6.5.1689; 6.5.1689; - ; 7.

2899. Mark Theed; John; Wentmore, Bucks; Y; 3.11.1679; 3.11.1679; - ; 7.

MARSTON, John

2900. William Marston; Thomas; parish of St Aubins, Herts; Y; 3.6.1678; 3.6.1678; - ; 7.

MARTIN, John

2901. Henry Faithorne; William; London; C & Go; 6.5.1672; 6.5.1672; 2.6.1679; 7.

2902. Obediah Hughs; Humphry; - , Kent; G; 5.12.1664; 5.12.1664; - ; 8.

2903. John Kersey; John; parish of St Pauls Covent Garden; - ; G, 6.10.1673; 6.10.1673; 11.10.1680; 7.

2904. Mark Pardoe. Fd by Martin 6.12.1675. Bd to Joseph Cranford (q.v.) 1.6.1663.

2905. Richard Tauernor; Richard; Hoxton, Herts [*sic* for M'sex]; G; 3.11.1652; 24.6.1652; - ; 8.

2906. Thomas Thornicraft; Edward; Siddington, Ches; G; 3.7.1656; 1.8.1656; 3.8.1663; 7.

MASCALL, Elizabeth, Widow

2907. William Cope; Thomas; Yoxall, Staffs; H; 13.7.1657; 13.7.1657; 26.3.1670; 7.

2908. Richard George; Will; Stepney parish, M'sex; Coverletweaver; 3.10.1664; 3.10.1664; 6.11.1671; 7.

MASON, Giles

2909. George Brangwell; Daniell; London; C & V; 5.3.1655; 5.3.1655; - ; 7.

2910. Robte Lanning; Robte; Hamersmith, M'sex; Cd; 6.9.1641; 6.9.1641; - ; 9.

2911. John Worsly. Fd by Mason 6.9.1652. Bd to him 10.1.1639.

MASON, William

2912. George Evans. Fd by Mason and Thomas Maddox 31.1.1666. Bd to Maddox (q.v.) 3.8.1657.

MATHER, Thomas

2913. Samuel Manning; Saml; Newton Waterfeild, Bucks; Cl; 2.7.1688; 2.7.1688; - ; 7.

2914. Thomas Elrington; William (d); Wells, Norf; G; 9.1.1688; 9.1.1688; - ; 7.

MATTHEWS, Augustine

2915. John Whateley. Fd by Matthews 28.6.1641. Apparently never formally bd.

MATTHEWS, Emanuel

2916. William Bowmaker; John (d); parish of St Margarets Westmr; G; 5.9.1692; 5.9.1692; - ; 7.

2917. Thomas Turford; William (d); London; C & J; 6.5.1700; 6.5.1700; - ; 7.

MATTHEWS, John

2918. Thomas Wiggins; Thomas; parish of St Anne Westmr, M'sex; Heelmaker; 4.7.1698; 4.7.1698; 10.9.1705; 7.

MATTHEWS, Thomas

2919. Langley Curtis; Robert; Sotby, Lincs; H; 17.1.1659; 17.1.1659; 5.2.1666; 7.

2920. George Moore; Joseph (d); Buxton, Derby; Cl; 1.9.1645; 24.8.1645; - ; 9.

2921. Stephen Muggs; Edw (d); London; B; 3.5.1652; 1.5.1652; 4.6.1660; 8.

2922. Thomas Riland; John; Stratford vpon Avon, War; M; 22.8.1648; 22.8.1648; 1.2.1658; 9.

2923. Randolph Taylor. Fd by Matthews 7.5.1649. Bd to him (as Randall Taylor) 2.3.1640.

2924. Stephen Tothill; Stephen; London; C & Gr; 6.10.1662; 24.8.1662; - ; 8.

2925. Michael Waller. Fd by Matthews and Thomas Fukes 4.10.1658. Bd to Fukes (q.v.) 1.9.1651.

MAUD, Thomas

2926. Samuell Browne. Fd by Maud 4.12.1648. Bd to him 2.11.1640.

2927. Richard Richardson; Wm; London; Mch; 4.10.1647; 24.8.1647; 5.3.1655; 8. Fd by Maud and Samuel Browne.

MAWSON, Richard

2928. John Ford; John; parish of Christ-Church, Surr; Mariner; 24.10. 1694; 8.10.1694; - ; 7.

MAXEY, Thomas

2929. John Caluin; Peter; Colchester, Essex; Clothier; 10.1.1654; 10.1. 1654; - ; 7.

2930. Henry Kimberley; Wm; London; C & Cw; 4.2.1650; 4.2.1650; - ; 9.

2931. David Maxwell; William; London; Cl; 21.12.1650; 21.12.1650; 23.12. 1657; 7.

2932. Tho Putnam. Fd by Maxey 7.10.1661. Apparently never formally bd.

2933. Thomas Rosse. Fd by Maxey and George Bishop 19.1.1652. Bd to Bishop (q.v.) 15.1.1645.

MAXWELL, Anne, Widow

2934. Joseph Churchill; Josuah; Towne of Dorchester, [Dors]; Cl; 3.3. 1684; 3.3.1684; - ; 7.

2935. Henry Cruttenden; Henry (d); Tunbridge, Kent; Y; 7.4.1668; 7.4. 1668; 3.5.1675; 7.

2936. John Curtis. Fd by Mrs Maxwell 4.10.1675. Apparently never formally bd.

2937. John Elliott; Robert; Evershott, Glos; G; 6.8.1683; 6.8.1683; - ; 7.

2938. Job How; Mary; - , - ; Widow; 3.6.1672; 3.6.1672; 6.10.1679; 7. Bd to Anne Maxwell; fd by' Dorothy Maxwell'.

2939. Clement Knell. Fd by Mrs Maxwell 4.2.1678. Bd to Peter Lillicrop (q.v.) 4.6.1660.

2940. Michael Martin; Randal; - , Herts; Y; 7.4.1679; 7.4.1679; 3.3. 1690; 7. Said to have been t.o. to Robert Roberts (n.d.) but fd by Mrs Maxwell.

2941. Thomas Pokins; John; Denton, Oxon; Y; 4.5.1674; 4.5.1674; 6.6.1681; 7.

2942. John Pratt. Fd by Mrs Maxwell 5.8.1668. Bd to George Cox (q.v.) 2.9.1661.

2943. John Salisbury; John; London; C & MT; 6.10.1679; 6.10.1679; - ; 7.

2944. Robert Stafford; John (d); Dafford, Derby; Cl; 8.5.1682; 1.5.1682; 5.5.1690; 8. Anne Maxwell is described as the widow of David Maxwell. Stafford was t.o. (n.d.) to Robert Roberts and was fined 2s. 6d. 'For not being turned over at ye Hall'.

2945. Clement Williams. Fd by Mrs Maxwell and John Brudnell 26.6.1668. Bd to Brudnell (q.v.) 10.6.1661.

MAXWELL, David

2946. Mathew Duckett; Ambros; Northbellinger, Norf; H; 5.9.1659; 5.9. 1659; 6.11.1666; 7.

2947. John Mackmath; John; Harbourne, Staffs; Cl; 4.10.1658; 4.10. 1658; - ; 7.

MAYNARD, John

2948. Richard Adcock; John; Towne of Leicester; Y; 20.12.1689; 20.12.1689; 7.6.1697; 7.

MAYOS, John

2949. Theophilus Hastings; George (d); London; G; 2.8.1697; 2.8.1697; - ; 7.

2950. David Richmond; Christopher; London; C & MT; 3.6.1700; 3.6.1700; 9.6.1707; 7.

MEACHAM, John

2951. Robert Scott; John; St Giles Criplegate, M'sex; L; 7.3.1698; 7.3. 1698; - ; 7.

MEADE, Medriach

2952. Robert Allen; Thomas (d); Enfeild, M'sex; Bricklayer; 5.7.1697; 5.7.1697; - ; 7.

2953. William Sheffeild; William (d); Stapleford, Leics; Cl; 6.12.1697; 6.12. 1697; 6.8.1705; 7. Fd by Edward Hawkins.

MEADE, Richard

2954. Richard Mead. Fd by patrimony 5.9.1692.

2955. Thomas Mead. Fd by patrimony 5.9.1692.

MEADE, Robert

2956. John Burroughes. Fd by Meade 29.3.1641. Bd to him 3.6.1633.

2957. John Groane; Peter; Crofte, Lincs; T; 4.5.1641; 24.6.1641; 22.10. 1649; 8.

2958. Robert Guest; Stephen; London; C & St; 24.9.1649; 24.9.1649; - ; 9. Entry deleted; m.n. 'This Entrey was mistaken & therefore entred on the other side of the Leafe'. Two entries later the same details are given under the date 8.10.1649, the term of service also beginning from that day.

2959. Thomas Mead; Robte; London; C & St; 6.3.1643; 6.3.1643; - ; 7. Bd to his father.

2960. William Phillips; Wm; Weston Fauell, N'hants; Jersey Comber; 6.2. 1654; 6.2.1654; 4.3.1661; 7.

MEADE, Thomas

2961. Robert Walker; David (d); parish of St Cyrus, Mearns, Scotland; G; 3.7.1699; 3.7.1699; 2.12.1706; 7.

MEAKES, John

2962. Anthony Barker; John; Barmby on the Moore, Notts; Y; 6.12.1697; 6.12.1697; 5.3.1705; 7. Fd as Barber.

2963. John Bush; Francis (d); parish of Lambeth, Surr; G; 3.7.1686; 3.7. 1686; - ; 7.

2964. Charnell Gibbens; Thomas; Parish of St Giles in the Feilds, M'sex; G; 7.8.1682; 7.8.1682; - ; 7.

2965. Humphry Jackson; John; Reading, Berks; Cd; 1.10.1694; 1.10. 1694; 3.11.1701; 7. Fd by Meakes and John Beresford.

2966. John Phillips; John (d); London; C & MT; 3.7.1682; 3.7.1682; - ; 7.

MEAKINS, John

2967. Thomas Tebb; Thomas; Tamworth, Staffs; Hatter; 2.5.1687; 2.5. 1687; 11.6.1694; 7. Fd by Meakins and Peter Richmond, and fined 2s. 6d. for not being t.o. at the hall.

MEARNE, Samuel

2968. John Barrett. Fd by Mearne and Ralph Edwards 5.10.1657. Bd to Edwards (q.v.) 27.9.1650.

2969. Thomas Bernard; Willm (d); London; C & Turner; 6.6.1659; 6.6. 1659; - ; 7.

2970. James Bissill; James; St Buttolphs Aldersgate, London; Bu; 6.8. 1677; 6.8.1677; 4.7.1687; 8.

2971. William Colson; William; Citty of Winton, - ; G; 3.7.1682; 3.7. 1682; - ; 7.

2972. William Garfoote; Anthoney; Bishoprick of Durham; Bookbinder; 5.6.1665; 29.5.1665; 20.6.1673; 8.

2973. Gabriel Hedges; William; Newberry, Berks; Clothier; 3.5.1675; 3.5.1675; - ; 7. m.n. 'Discharged from his service' n.d.

2974. Robert Heyborne; Henry; London; C & Cw; 8.5.1665; 29.9.1664; - ; 8.

2975. Charles Mearne. Fd by patrimony 24.6.1682.

2976. Robert Reading; Nicholas; Desford, Leics; H; 5.9.1653; 25.12.1652; - ; 8.

2977. Robert Steele; John; Bartrumlee, Ches; Y; 7.10.1668; 7.10.1668; 8.11.1675; 7.

2978. Nathaniel Stevenson; John; Cleasby, Yorks; G; 9.2.1674; 9.2.1674; 7.3.1681; 7. Fd as Stephenson.

2979. William Willis; Jno; Pilkington, Dors; - ; 11.6.1655; 25.3.1655; 4.5.1663; 8.

MEDLEY, Thomas
2980. Giles Clement; Giles; Southampton; T; 23.12.1641; 24.8.1641; - ; 8.

MEGGS, Christopher
2981. John Odumes; Richard; Everston, War; Smith; 7.5.1683; 7.5.1683; - ; 7.
2982. John Pine; Saml; London; C & Go; 2.10.1682; 2.10.1682; - ; 7.

MEIGHEN, Richard
2983. James Coates. Fd by Meighen 4.5. 1641. Bd to him 31.3.1634.
2984. John Tey. Fd by Mrs Meighen 7.5.1649. Bd to Richard Meighen 28.6.1638.

MENDY, John
2985. John Clark; Willm; Daventry, N'hants; Y; 7.6.1676; 7.6.1676; 6.8. 1683; 7.
2986. John Fryar; William; Cuddington, Bucks; Y; 5.12.1681; 5.12. 1681; 7.4.1690; 7. Fd as Freer.
2987. Henry Hickman; Henry; Cuddington, Bucks; H; 3.2.1669; 3.2.1669; 6.3.1676; 7.
2988. John Mendy. Fd by patrimony 3.5.1697.
2989. Joseph Pool. Fd by Mendy 31.1.1679. Bd to Hannah Parkhurst (q.v.) 6.2.1671.
2990. William Rose; James; Owney, Bucks; Y; 6.6.1664; 6.6.1664; - ; 7.
2991. Adam Winch; John; Haddenham, Bucks; Cw; 4.7.1659; 4.7.1659; 7.8.1666; 7.

MENDY, William
2992. Wm Francklyn; George (d); Haddenham, Bucks; Y; 14.6.1652; 14.6.1652; - ; 7.
2993. John Mendie; John; Hadinham, Bucks; Y; 19.1.1652; 19.1.1652; 7.2.1659; 7.

MERCER, Thomas
2994. Richard Nicholson; Richard; London; C & Victualler; 7.4.1684; 2.2.1684; - ; 8.

MEREDITH, Christopher
2995. Edward Brewster; Edward (d); London, St; 24.5.1648; 24.5.1648; 5.12. 1653; 7. Fd by patrimony.
2996. John Browne; Sam (d); Shrewsbery, Shrops; Cl; 27.4.1646; 1.5.1646; 4.5.1653; 7. Fd by Meredith and William Grantham.
2997. Nathaniell Ranew; Nathaniell; Felsteed, Essex; Cl; 6.5.1652; 6.5.1652; 13.6.1659; 7. Fd by Meredith and Edward Brewster.
2998. Nathaniell Webb. Fd by Meredith 21.1.1644. Bd to him 14.1.1636.

MEREDITH, Luke
2999. John Butler; William; Alton, S'hants; Clothier; 4.10.1697; 4.10.1697; - ; 7.
3000. Phillip Monckton; John; Brenchley, Kent; Cl; 25.6.1688; 25.6. 1688; 2.11.1696; 7.
3001. Wm Wilmot; John; Oxford; Bs; 3.10.1692; 3.10.1692; - ; 7.

MEYCOCK, William
3002. Charles Howard; Henry; Kingston, Surr; G; 2.11.1646; 2.11.1646; - ; 7.

MIDDLETON, William
3003. John Loyd. Servant to William Middleton, Merchant Tailor, fd 7.7. 1673 by His Majesty's order.

MIDWINTER, Daniel
3004. William Jackson; John; Witcham, Isle of Ely, Cambs; Cl; 8.4.1700; 8.4.1700; 5.5.1707; 7.

MILBOURNE, Alexander
3005. Henry Duffe; John Malcome; St Giles in the Feildes, M'sex; G; 2.12. 1695; 2.12.1695; 7.12.1702; 7.
3006. John Harrison. Fd by Milbourne 2.10.1693. Bd to Henry Brugis (q.v.) 3.12.1683.

3007. Thomas Knight; John (d); St Andrews Holbourne, M'sex; Coachman; 9.9.1700; 9.9.1700; 1.9.1712; 7.

3008. Phillip Wood; Phillip (d); parish of Saint Andrews Holbourne, [M'sex]; G; 5.12.1687; 5.12.1687; 2.12.1695; 7.

MILBOURNE, John

3009. Wm Hookes; Willm; Conway, Caernarvon; E; 6.7.1661; 6.7.1661; - ; 7.

3010. Eusebius Kidder; Edward; Stockton, Shrops; G; 5.5.1662; 5.5.1662; - ; 7.

MILBOURNE, Robert

3011. Steven Pilkington. Fd by Milbourne 11.4.1643. Bd to him 4.4.1636.

MILBOURNE, Thomas

3012. Nathaniel Anderton; Richard (d); London; C & St; 9.1.1688; 9.1.1688; - ; 8.

3013. John Bayley; John; Barckley, Som; Cl; 13.1.1669; 13.1.1669; - ; 7.

3014. Henry Cosgrove; Patrick; Layton, Essex; Mch; 5.8.1700; 5.8.1700; - ; 7.

3015. Samuell Darby; Samuell (d); London; C & Cw; 6.7.1696; 6.7.1696; 4.2.1706; 7.

3016. William Downing; Willm; parish of St Dunstans in the West, London; Chandler; 1.8.1659; 1.8.1659; 3.12.1667; 7.

3017. Esra Edwards; John; parish of Abergavinny, Mon; - ; 4.3.1678; 4.3.1678; 3.11.1688; 7. In the entry of binding the master's name is left blank; fd by Thomas Milbourne.

3018. Robert Hayherst; Jonathan; Ribchester, Lancs; G; 5.10.1674; 5.10.1674; 5.12.1681; 7.

3019. William Heathcott; William; London; Ca; 7.8.1682; 7.8.1682; 9.9.1689; 7.

3020. Thomas Ilive. Fd by Milbourne 7.10.1689. Bd to Thomas Snowden (q.v.) 3.6.1678.

3021. Alexander Milborne. Fd by patrimony 6.12.1682.

3022. Thomas Milborne; Tho; London; C & St; 4.12.1643; 4.12.1643; 9.12.1650; 7. Bd to his father.

3023. Wm Milbourne; Thomas; London; St. 4.8.1651; 4.8.1651; - ; 7. Bd to his father.

3024. Edward Milburne. Fd by patrimony 5.12.1681.

3025. William Smythes; Isaac (d); London; C & Pw; 8.6.1696; 8.6.1696; 5.7.1703; 7. Fd as Smythers.

3026. John Timbrell; Joseph; London; C & Musician; 8.5.1693; 8.5.1693; - ; 7.

3027. Lewis Wettenhall; Christopher; Fingell, Yorks; G; 2.12.1672; 2.12.1672; 8.5.1682; 8.

MILL, Adiel

[The following note appears under date 5.12.1687: 'Mr Scotts man turned over to Adiel Mills'. It probably refers to Charles Hoffman.]

3028. George Brent; Daniell; Covent Garden, M'sex; G; 11.4.1681; 11.4.1681; - ; 7.

3029. Richard Butterfeild; John; London; C & Gr; 3.12.1688; 3.12.1688; 6.8.1711; 7.

3030. William Churchill; Wm; Dorchester, [Dors]; Bs; 7.5.1677; 7.5.1677; 13.5.1684; 7.

3031. Coppin Fanshaw; Francis; Hartlibb, Kent; Y; 6.4.1674; 6.4.1674; 6.6.1681; 7.

3032. George Littlebury; Robert; London; C & Ha; 6.3.1682; 1.2.1682; 6.5.1689; 8.

3033. Henry Perkins; Geo (d); London; G; 27.9.1672; 27.9.1672; - ; 7.

3034. John Swann; Robert; Plastow, Essex; G; 1.3.1680; 1.3.1680; - ; 7.

MILLER, Abraham

3035. John Axtell; Robert; Rushall, Staffs; Y; 6.11.1654; 24.6.1654; - ; 8.

3036. Joseph Bennett; Nich; London; C & Ha; 14.6.1647; 24.6.1647; 2.7. 1655; 9.

3037. Richard Butler. Fd by Miller and Thomas Underhill 30.6.1663. Bd to Underhill (q.v.) 6.8.1655.

3038. John Hayes. Bd to George Miller (q.v.) 6.5.1646; t.o. on Miller's death to Abraham Miller 5.10.1646. Fd by Abraham and George Miller 3.10.1653.

3039. Joshua Stodder; Lawrence; Southwarke, Surr; Leatherdresser; 30.6. 1663; 30.6.1663; - ; 9.

3040. John Warner; John; Sutton Cofield, War; H; 7.3.1653; 25.3.1653; 1.4.1661; 8.

3041. Peter Worgane; Peirce; London; Mr; 7.9.1663; 7.9.1663; - ; 8.

MILLER, Elizabeth

3042. Roger Tukyer; Charles (d); London; E; 2.5.1698; 2.5.1698; - ; 7.

MILLER, George

3043. John Draper; Henry; Kettring, N'hants; Cd; 7.6.1641; Easter Day 1641; 8.6.1648; 8.

3044. John Hayes; Edmond; Ashford, Kent; Cl; 6.5.1646; 25.12.1645; 3.10.1653; 8. T.o. on Miller's death to Abraham Miller 5.10.1646. Fd by George and Abraham Miller.

3045. Abraham Miller. Fd by patrimony 21.1.1644.

3046. Daniell Mogge. Fd by Miller 6.10.1645. Bd to him 2.10.1637.

MILLER, John

3047. Gilbert Beacham; John (d); Kidderminster, Worcs; H; 7.5.1694; 7.5.1694; - ; 7.

MILLER, Simon

3048. John Beaumont; Stephen (d); London; C & BSg; 6.6.1664; 1.3.1664; - ; 8.

3049. John Miller; Abraham (d); London; C & St; 7.3.1670; 7.3.1670; 18.6.1677; 7.

3050. James Pullen; Thomas; Islington, M'sex; Y; 3.12.1677; 3.12.1677; 5.9.1687; 7.

3051. Humphrey Wharton; Humphrey; Barton, - ; G; 2.4.1655; 2.4. 1655; 6.10.1662; 7.

MILLER, William

3052. Francis Coggan; John (d); Hull, Yorks; G; 7.10.1689; 7.10.1689; - ; 7. T.o. on Miller's death to Daniel Browne 10.9.1694.

3053. Vavasor Price; Charles; Hammersmith, M'sex; Cl; 6.10.1673; 6.10. 1673; - ; 8.

3054. Joseph Reekes; Robert; Alton Barnes, Wilts; Y; 6.10.1684; 6.10.1684; - ; 7.

3055. Henry Tilley. Fd 26.3.1686 by Miller as executor to Evan Tyler deceased. Bd to Tyler (q.v.) 5.8.1678.

3056. Joseph Watts; Joseph; Doulkin, Som; - ; 28.6.1676; 28.6.1676; 3.2.1685; 8.

MILLETT, John

3057. John Birdwistle; John; parish of St Sepulchres, London; Bu; 6.7.1691; 6.7.1691; - ; 8.

3058. Wm Hascar; William (d); London; G; 26.3.1683; 26.3.1683; 7.7. 1690; 7.

3059. John Quinney. Fd by Millett 6.7.1691. Apparently never formally bd.

3060. John Shuter. Fd by Millett 4.5.1691. Bd to Elizabeth Goring (q.v.) 7.4.1684.

3061. Follensby Thackeray; William; London; C & St; 8.6.1691; 8.6.1691; 5.9.1698; 7. Fd by William Onely.

MILLION, Henry

3062. Thomas Cartwright; James (d); Badgworth, Glos; G; 6.11.1671; 6.11.1671; 2.12.1678; 7.

3063. Jonathan Hampson; Phillipp (d); London; MT; 5.9.1664; 5.9.1664; - ; 7.

3064. Robert Jones; John (d); Wrix-on, Den; G; 7.8.1666; 24.6.1666; 7.2.1687; 8.

MILLS, Richard
3065. Ephraim Docray; Francis; London; C & Girdler; 7.6.1669; 7.6.1669; - ; 7.
3066. Beniamine Pate; Thomas; White Chappell, [M'sex]; Br; 5.9.1664; 5.9.1664; - ; 7.
3067. Nathaniel Wastell; Leonard; Hurworth, Bishoprick of Durham; Cl; 1.3.1676; 1.3.1676; - ; 7.

MILNER, John
3068. John Meech; John; Knighton, Dors; Y; 14.6.1647; 1.5.1647; - ; 8.
3069. John Staples; Richard (d); Citty of Worcester; Mr; 26.5.1646; 25.3.1646; - ; 8.
3070. Sam Wright; Sam (d); London; Cd; 6.5.1652; 25.3.1652; - ; 8.

MILNER, Joseph
3071. Walter Dunne; Wm; Bath, Som; Surgeon; 9.11.1646; 9.11.1646; 25.6.1657; 8. T.o. 1.7.1650 to John Underhill. Fd by Underhill and Milner.
3072. Richard Hicks; Geo; Wrighton, Shrops; Y; 6.9.1641; 6.9.1641; 5.8.1650; 7.

MILNER, Thomas
3073. [Thomas Milner. Fd by patrimony 5.9.1698.]

MILWARD, William
3074. James Fox; Thomas; Dullidge, Surr; Farrier; 2.4.1655; 2.4.1655; - ; 8.

MINORS, Thomas
3075. James Evans; Richard (d); Wooburne, Beds; Y; 21.11.1692; 21.11.1692; - ; 7.

MINSHALL, Thomas
3076. Danielle Crale; Richard (d); London; C & Bl; 6.11.1682; 6.11.1682; 2.12.1689; 7.
3077. Tho Eales; George; West Deane, Sussex; Cl; 9.2.1691; 9.2.1691; - ; 7.

3078. [Thomas Minshall. Son of William Minshall; fd by patrimony 12.6.1666.]
3079. Joanna Nye; John; Quindon, Essex; Cl; 7.8.1666; 7.8.1666; - ; 7.
3080. Peter Wallis; Thomas (d); Trewbridge, Wilts; Brazier; 2.3.1691; 2.3.1691; - ; 7.
3081. Wm Willis; Wm; London; C & St; 5.6.1690; 5.6.1690; - ; 7.

MISSENDEN, Robert
3082. John Marsh. Fd by Richard Lilly 27.11.1688 but said to have been bd to Missenden and fined 2s. 6d. 'For being turned over'. There is no formal entry of the binding.

MITCHELL, Thomas
3083. Charles Reade; George (d); London; G; 1.9.1684; 1.9.1684; 2.11.1691; 7.

MOGGS, Daniel
3084. John Baskerville; John; parish of St James Clarkenwell, M'sex; St; 1.7.1695; 1.7.1695; - ; 7.
3085. Samuel Miles; Thomas; Hunnibul, Worcs; T; 7.11.1692; 7.11.1692; - ; 7.
3086. [Daniel Moggs. Fd by patrimony 7.4.1679.]

MONGER, Richard
3087. [Richard Monger. Son of John Monger; fd by patrimony 3.11.1645.]

MOONE, Richard
3088. John Daniell; Barthus (d); Crookhorne, Som; D; 23.3.1653; 23.3.1653; 26.3.1660; 7.

MOORE, Edward
3089. John Farbrew; John (d); parish of St Martin in the Feilds, M'sex; Coachmaker; 5.7.1680; 5.7.1680; - ; 7.

MOORE, John
3090. [John Moore. Son of Richard Moore; fd by patrimony 10.5.1641.]

MOORE, Joseph

3091. John Spicer; Giles; stamford, Essex; Farmer; 7.7.1651; 7.7.1651; 2.8.1658; 7.

3092. Richard Stanniford; Richard; Cottingham, N'hants; Y; 7.1.1656; 7.1.1656; - ; 8.

3093. George Wilford; George (d); London; C & St; 5.8.1668; 5.8.1668; - ; 8.

MOORE, Robert

3094. [Robert Moore. Fd by redemption 10.6.1684. In addition to the usual admittance fee of 3s. 4d. Moore paid a fine of £15.]

MOORE, Thomas

3095. Nathaniell Dover; James; Parish of St James Clarkenwell, M'sex; T; 5.12.1681; 5.12.1681; 4.3.1689; 7. Fd by Freeman Collins and fined 2s. 6d. 'for being turned over'.

3096. Henry Pointing. Fd by Moore 9.5.1694. Bd by a foreign indenture and at first refused his freedom. The Court allowed it in response to arguments by other printers against the retention of excessive numbers of apprentices (Court-Book F, 9.5.1694).

3097. Mathias Thurston. Fd by Moore 6.3.1671. Apparently never formally bd.

MOREY, Edward

3098. John Chantry; John (d); Citty of Canterbury, Kent; - ; 3.6.1695; 3.6.1695; 6.7.1702; 7. Fd as Chauntry.

3099. John Penfold; John; Slinfold, Sussex; G; 5.12.1692; 5.12.1692; - ; 7.

MORGAN, Edward

3100. [Edward Morgan. Son of Richard Morgan; fd by patrimony 3.7.1648.]

MORRELL, Thomas

3101. Adam Ayres; Thomas (d); Darbey, Derby; G; 7.12.1646; 7.12.1646; - ; 7.

MORRIS, Henry

3102. William Cooke; John; parish of St Mary Overs Suddrick [sic, for Southwark, Surr?]; G; 6.5.1700; 6.5.1700; - ; 7.

MORSE, Thomas

3103. Francis Berkly; Sam (d); Clingingford, Shrops; Cl; 3.7.1676; 3.7.1676; - ; 7.

3104. John Brind; Bartholomewe; Roughton, Wilts; G; 5.7.1669; 5.7.1669; - ; 7.

3105. Robert Pedmore; Arthur (d); Hexton, Shrops; - ; 5.7.1680; 5.7.1680; 3.2.1690; 7. Fd as Podmore.

MORTIMER, George

3106. Thomas Burch; William; South Walbrough, S'hants; - ; 5.8.1700; 5.8.1700 - ; 7.

3107. Mary Hoult; Robert (d); parish of St James Clerkenwell, M'sex; Bodicemaker; 7.5.1688; 7.5.1688; - ; 7.

3108. Saml Hunt; John (d); Southwick, S'hants; Y; 2.6.1684; 2.6.1684; - ; 7.

3109. Robert London; John; Rapley, S'hants; Cl; 5.12.1692; 5.12.1692; - ; 8.

3110. Ralph Underwood; Henry (d); Irthingborough, N'hants; G; 2.3.1685; 2.3.1685; 7.8.1693; 7.

MORTLOCK, Henry

3111. Edward Castle; Henry (d); Cranborn, Dors; Mr; 7.3.1687; 7.3.1687; 4.3.1695; 7.

3112. George Coulston; George (d); Scevington, Notts; G; 12.11.1667; 3.9.1667; 22.2.1675; 7. Fd as Colson.

3113. Thomas Fox; Tymothy; Bicknell, Derby; Cl; 12.8.1671; 12.8.1671; 6.10.1678; 7.

3114. James Knapton; William; Brockenhurst, S'hants; - ; 2.8.1680; 2.8.1680; 5.9.1687; 7.

3115. Thomas Lister; Joseph (d); London; C & Drugster; 12.6.1693; [12.6.1693]; - ; 7. Bd for 7 years 'from the Date of his Indentures'.

3116. Randall Minshall; John; Citty of Chester; Bs; 2.3.1696; 2.3.1696; - ; 7.

3117. Edward Pepys. Fd by Mortlock 3.11.1690. Bd to Richard Royston (q.v.) 6.8.1683.

3118. Thomas Rennett; John (d); London; C & Bl; 9.9.1678; 9.9.1678; 4.10.1686; 8. Fd as Bennit.

3119. Henry Vernatty; Nathaniel Rames (d); parish of St Clemt Danes, M'sex; G; 8.6.1691; 8.6.1691; - ; 7.

3120. John Wheeler. Bd to Thomas Northcott (q.v.) 7.8.1693; t.o. 1.10.1694 to Mortlock.

3121. Henry Wright; Richard; Nottingham; G; 8.4.1695; 8.4.1695; 6.7.1702; 7.

MOSELEY, Humphrey

3122. Thomas Hunt. Fd by Moseley 29.6.1646. Originally bd to Thomas Alchorne 4.6.1638; rebd to Moseley 19.12.1639.

3123. John Langford; Fran; Tremab, Corn; E; 6.9.1658; 6.9.1658; - ; 7.

3124. Saint-John Osborne; Wm; Norrell, Beds; G; 21.3.1654; 26.3.1654; 27.6.1664; 8.

3125. Henry Pentor; Stephen (d); Winchester, S'hants; G; 2.11.1658; 2.11.1658; - ; 7.

3126. Robte Sparke; Thomas (d); Candever, S'hants; Cl; 16.8.1647; 24.6.1647; - ; 8.

3127. Charles Webb; Berington; London; C & Ha; 22.10.1649; 25.12.1649; 9.2.1657; 7.

MOSSE, Thomas

3128. Daniel Harding; John (d); Winchenham, Glos; Y; 2.5.1681; 2.5.1681; 7.10.1689; 7.

MOTT, Benjamin

3129. Thomas Catesby Atkins; Francis; London; C & F; 6.7.1696; 6.7.1696; - ; 8.

3130. Henry Buckridge; George;

London; Shipwright; 4.8.1690; 4.8.1690; 6.9.1697; 7.

3131. Nathaniel Harris; Isaah (d); - ; Bucks; Cl; 1.3.1686; 1.3.1686; 13.3.1693; 7.

3132. George James; John; Basingstoke, S'hants; Cl; 1.8.1698; 1.8.1698; 6.8.1705; 7.

3133. Edward Lewis; Phillipp; Morton vpon Lugg, Herefs; Cd; 6.9.1697; 6.9.1697; 6.11.1704; 7.

3134. Richard Newcombe. Fd by Mott, Thomas Newcomb and Miles Flesher 8.4.1695. Bd to Newcomb (q.v.) 5.3.1688.

3135. Charles Peregrine. Bd to Anne Godbid (q.v.) but t.o. (n.d.) to Mott and fd by him 1.2.1686.

3136. Edmund Powell. Fd by Mott and John Macocke 12.11.1694. Bd to Macocke (q.v.) 7.11.1687.

3137. Richard Sendall; Richard; London; C & Cd; 5.8.1700; 5.8.1700; - ; 7.

3138. James Slatter; James (d); City of Oxford; Cook; 3.7.1699; 3.7.1699; 3.2.1707; 7.

3139. Hector Thomas; Hector; London; G; 7.5.1683; 7.5.1683; 4.8.1690; 7. This entry is immediately followed by another for the same apprentice, again bd to Mott but giving the father's name as 'John Thomas late of Treoendech in the County of Pembroke Gent'. It is almost certainly a corrected form of the first entry.

3140. Robert Tooke; Benjn; London; C & St; 2.5.1692; 2.5.1692; 8.5.1699; 7.

MOTTERSHED, Edward

3141. Swithin Bing; Swithin; Owndle, N'hants; T; 13.7.1657; 13.7.1657; - ; 8.

3142. Thomas Collier; John; Kempsey, Worcs; Ca; 5.6.1654; 25.3.1654; - ; 8.

3143. Anthony Izard; Anthony; Lon-

don; C & Gr; 1.9.1656; 1.9.1656; 7.9.
1663; 7.

3144. John Joyner; Mathew; London; C & MT; 4.5.1663; 4.5.1663;
6.6.1670; 7.

3145. Leonard Parry; Ellis (d); London; C & S; 20.12.1647; 20.12.1647;
9.2.1657; 9.

3146. Samuell Turner; James (d);
London, C & Bricklayer; 30.6.1663;
30.6.1663; - ; 8.

MOULD, Benjamin

3147. Thomas Eve. Fd by Mould
6.8.1677. Apparently never formally bd.

3148. John Riddlesworth; John (d);
Stock, Essex; Y; 2.10.1676; 2.10.1676;
- ; 7.

MOULD, John

3149. Randall Baker. Fd by Mould
16.3.1646. Bd to him (as Randolph
Baker) 6.8.1638.

3150. Robte Dickens; Wm; Kennellworth, War; G; 16.3.1646; 16.3.1646;
- ; 7.

3151. John Frost; John; London; V;
1.3.1647; 25.12.1646; - ; 8.

3152. Richard Phelpes. Fd by Mould
5.2.1644. Bd to him 16.11.1635.

3153. James Procter; Michaell;
Ravenstone dale, W'land; H; 26.7.1652;
25.7.1652; - ; 8.

3154. William Stellington; Wm; Earith, Hunts; Y; 1.5.1654; 1.5.1654;
- ; 8.

3155. Richard Story; Xpofer; Ashby
Legers, N'hants; Y; 1.5.1654; 29.3.1654;
1.9.1662; 8. Fd by Mould and George
Cox.

3156. William Wiltshire; John (d);
Batcomb, Som; Clothier; 3.4.1654;
3.4.1654; - ; 9.

MOULD, Nathaniel

3157. James Brathwait; William;
Sara, Lancs; H; 2.9.1661; 2.9.1661;
- ; 7.

3158. Peter Gosse; Henry; Cole-

brook, Bucks; - ; 3.5.1669; 3.5.1669;
- ; 7.

3159. Richard Jones; Henry; Ruthen, Den; Y; 6.6.1659; 1.5.1659; - ; 8.

3160. Thomas Merrett; Thomas; Isffeild, S'hants [sic for Sussex]; Y; 2.12.
1668; 2.12.1668; - ; 7. Mould is
described as a Tallowchandler.

3161. Beniamin Mould; John; Billingsgate warde, [London]; Tallowchandler; 3.8.1664; 3.8.1664; 5.8.1672;
7.

3162. John Murden; Wm (d); Welford, N'hants; Chandler; 2.11.1646;
2.11.1646; 5.3.1655; 8.

3163. Thomas Purden; Daniell;
Stepney, M'sex; Y; 10.1.1654; 25.3.
1653; 2.9.1661; 8.

3164. Edward Tatam; Edward;
Chelmesford, Essex; Tallowchandler;
2.7.1655; 2.7.1655; - ; 7.

3165. Benjamin Waterfeild; Thomas
(d); London; C & B; 3.4.1671; 3.4.
1671; - ; 7.

MOUNT, Richard

3166. [Richard Mount. Son of Ralph
Mount; fd by patrimony 21.6.1693.]

3167. William Mount; Richard;
London; C & St; 7.11.1698; 7.11.1698;
26.3.1708; 9. Bd to his father.

MOUNTFORD, George

3168. Ro Day; Ro; Padbury, Bucks;
H; 6.9.1652; 5.1.1652; - ; 9.

3169. Henry Gloster; Peter; Croyden, Surr; Y; 2.7.1646; 2.7.1646; 17.10.
1653; 8.

3170. John Lambert; John; Buckingham, Bucks; G; 1.5.1648; 1.5.1648;
- ; 7.

3171. Richard Montford. Fd by
Mountford 2.7.1649. Bd to him 4.8.
1640.

MOWLE, Gregory

3172. Nath Barrow; Nathaniell; St
Giles in the Feilds, [M'sex]; Cu; 7.3.
1653; 1.4.1653; - ; 7. Entry deleted;

m.n., slightly obscured in binding: '[struck] out by order [of the] Corte . . .'.

MUDD, Strangeways

3173. John Bradshaw; Henry (d); London; C & MT; 27.6.1687; 27.6. 1687; 10.9.1694; 7.

3174. Robert Harcastle; Michaell; Warmouth, Dur; G; 4.7.1681; 4.7.1681; - ; 7.

3175. Willm Lawe; John; London; C & Tallowchandler; 3.3.1668; 3.3. 1668; - ; 7.

3176. Lewes Owen; William (d); Remham, Berks; Cl; 16.6.1671; 16.6. 1671; - ; 7. This entry comes between those for 5.6.1671 and 3.7.1671, but it actually appears beneath the date ':16: January: 1671:'. This is assumed to be an error for 16 June 1671.

MURDEN, John

3177. Charles Barker; Charles; little Over, Ches; G; 4.5.1666; 4.5.1666; 5.5.1673; 7.

3178. John Tilliard; John; Hornsey, M'sex; H; 6.5.1659; 6.5.1659; 3.12. 1667; 7.

3179. John Wood; Cornelius; - , N'hants; Y; 4.3.1672; 4.3.1672; - ; 7.

MUSTON, John

3180. John Hicks; Wm; Shewbury, Essex; Cl; 7.12.1691; 7.12.1691 - ; 7.

MYNN, Richard

3181. Wm Benson. Fd by Mynn 4.7. 1642. Bd to him 15.9.1634.

3182. Francis Myn. Fd by patrimony 6.5.1651.

NAPPER, Edward

3183. Mathew Butler; Mathias; London; C & Cook; 24.1.1642; 24.1.1642; - ; 8.

3184. Jeremy Lamas. Fd by Napper 7.10.1644. Bd to him 16.11.1635.

3185. Edward Nappier. Fd by patrimony 1.2.1664.

NASH, Samuel

3186. Daniell Clarke; Daniell; Tring,

Surr [sic for Herts]; G; 29.10.1696; 29.10.1696; - ; 7.

3187. Robert James; Robert; Redding, Berks; G; 4.11.1689; 4.11.1689; 3.5.1697; 7.

3188. Charles White; John; Thorney, Herts; G; 6.11.1682; 6.11.1682; 3.2.1690; 7.

NEALAND, Rebecca, Widow

3189. William Iles; William; London; G; 17.10.1653; 17.10.1653; 6.11. 1660; 7.

NEALAND, William

3190. [William Nealand. Son of Samuel Nealand; fd by patrimony 7.10. 1650.]

NEALE, Simon

3191. James Walkden; John; Reading, Berks; Woollendraper; 7.6.1675; 7.6.1675; - ; 7.

NEAVE, Alice, Widow

3192. Richard Barrett. Fd by Mrs Neave 6.9.1641. Bd to her 31.3.1634.

NEAVE, John

3193. Thomas Mew. Fd by Neave and Robert Huckle 5.12.1642. Bd to Neave 3.12.1632.

NEEDHAM, Ann

3194. Mary Wingfeild; Geo; Stratford le Bow, M'sex; G; 1.10.1688; 1.10. 1688; - ; 7.

NEEDHAM, Benjamin

3195. Edward Andrewes; Tobias; Uppingham, Rut; G; 4.6.1694; 4.6. 1694; - ; 7.

NEEDHAM, Lawrence

3196. Marmaduke Aplebey; Thomas; Washingbroffe, Lincs; G; 4.6.1649; 4.6.1649; 7.7.1656; 7.

NEEDHAM, Leonard

3197. George Dennis. Fd by Needham 2.8.1641. Bd to him 7.7.1634.

NEEDHAM, Ralph

3198. John Hunt; Robert; Lycester, Leics; Y; 6.11.1671; 6.11.1671; 2.12. 1678; 7.

3199. Ann Needham. Fd by patrimony 4.4.1687.

NEILE, Anne, Widow
3200. Roger Trendor; Roger (d); Whitchappell, M'sex; G; 1.9.1656; 1.9.1656; 10.1.1670; 7.

NEILE, Francis
3201. William Neile. Fd by patrimony 7.12.1657.
3202. Anthony Sellinger; Dudley (d); Isle of Tennett, Kent; G; 4.3.1650; 4.3.1650; - ; 7.

NETLESON, Andrew
3203. John Sturgeon; John (d); Holborne, M'sex; Gr; 6.9.1669; 29.6.1669; - ; 8.

NEVILL, Joseph
3204. John Nevill. Fd by patrimony 6.9.1697.
3205. Tymothy Sumster; Tymothy (d); London; C & Ca; 6.5.1672; 6.5.1672; 4.8.1678; 7.

NEVILL, Phillip
3206. Edward Dod. Fd by Nevill and George Greene 29.6.1646. Bd to Nevill 4.12.1637.
3207. Gifford Dalton. Fd by Nevill and Henry Overton 21.1.1644. Bd to Overton 5.5.1634.

NEWBERRY, Thomas
3208. Robert Cox; Edward; London; C & Cw; 2.3.1657; 24.8.1656; 5.9.1664; 8. Fd by Newberry and William Richardson.
3209. Theophilus Price; Richard; Shrewsbury, Shrops; D; 7.12.1657; 24.6.1657; 7.10.1672; 8. T.o. 6.12.1658 to John Baker and fd by him.
3210. Joseph Sledd; John; London; C & J; 6.11.1654; 6.11.1654; - ; 8.

NEWBOROUGH, Thomas
3211. Maurice Atkins; Maurice (d); London; C & St; 7.9.1696; 7.9.1696; 8.11.1703; 7.

NEWCOMB, Richard
3212. William Manforth; Edmund; parish of St Andrew Holborne, London; Mi; 4.5.1696; 25.3.1696; - ; 8.

NEWCOMB, Thomas, I
3213. William Argin; Anthony; Whitchford, War; Y; 5.8.1650; 5.8.1650; - ; 7.
3214. James Baldwin; John; St Giles in the Feilds, [M'sex]; - ; 5.7.1675; 5.7.1675; 7.8.1682; 7.
3215. Richard Boodle; Rich; City of Coventry, [War]; Bu; 3.10.1670; 3.10.1670; - ; 7.
3216. Richard Cheese. Fd by Newcomb and Thomas Paine 2.10.1654. Bd to Paine (q.v.) 2.8.1647.
3217. Freeman Collyns; Thomas; Exeter, Dev; Cl; 3.3.1669; 3.3.1669; 6.3.1676; 7.
3218. John Croome. Fd by Newcomb and William Leybourne 1.6.1663. Bd to Leybourne (q.v.) 31.5.1656.
3219. Thomas Durrant. Fd by Thomas Harper 2.2.1662, but m.n. 'turned over to Tho: Newcombe' (n.d.) Bd to Harper (q.v.) 10.5.1654.
3220. Edward Jones; Rich (d); London; C & St; 3.2.1673; 3.2.1673; 24.3.1680; 7.
3221. John Jones; Richard; Kidwelley, Carmarthen; - ; 6.7.1685; 6.7.1685; 1.8.1692; 7. Fd by Newcomb's executrix.
3222. John Lydiate; John; Alkerton, Oxon; H; 6.11.1671; 6.11.1671; - ; 7.
3223. Edward Newcomb; Tho; Dunchurch, War; I; 14.6.1652; 14.6.1652; 4.7.1659; 7.
3224. Thomas Newcomb; Thomas; London; C & St; 18.12.1666; 18.12.1666; 7.10.1672; 7. Bd to his father; fd by patrimony.
3225. John Nicks. Fd by Newcomb and George Purslowe 6.9.1658. Bd to Purslowe (q.v.) 30.6.1651.

3226. Thomas Sparrey; Tho; Coventrey, War; Sh; 4.2.1650; 4.2.1650; 1.3.1658; 8.

3227. John Weaver; Edward (d); London; C & Ha; 19.3.1658; 19.3.1658; 12.6.1666; 8.

3228. William Williams; Wm; Westbery, Wilts; Cw; 4.12.1654; 4.12.1654; 2.3.1663; 8.

NEWCOMB, Thomas, II

3229. Edward Ceny. T.o. from George Larkin to Newcomb 7.1.1678. There is no entry for the binding to Larkin.

3230. Thomas Farr; John; St Martin in ye Feilds, M'sex; G; 5.3.1677; 5.3.1677; 4.8.1684; 7.

3231. John Langley; Daniel; London; C & BSg; 20.12.1684; 20.12.1684; - ; 7.

3232. John Mayo; John; Burrough of Southwark, Surr; Hempdresser; 4.10.1676; 4.10.1676; 19.12.1683; 7.

3233. Richard Newcomb; John; South Hampton, War; Y; 5.3.1688; 5.3.1688; 8.4.1695; 7. Fd by Newcomb, Miles Flesher and Benjamin Mott.

3234. John Nuwtt; John; Kalne, Wilts; Y; 1.9.1684; 1.9.1684; 7.12.1691; 7. Fd (as John Nutt) by Thomas Newcomb's widow.

NEWELL, John

3235. [John Newell. Fd by patrimony 20.7.1670.]

NEWMAN, Dorman

3236. John Clarke; Willm; Grantham, Lincs; - ; 2.8.1669; 2.8.1669; - ; 7.

3237. John Lutton; Ralph (d); Napton, Yorks; - ; 7.7.1662; 7.7.1662; 2.8.1669; 7.

3238. Thomas Malthus; John (d); Reading, Berks; Clothier; 4.10.1675; 4.10.1675; 2.10.1682; 7.

3239. Hugh Newman; Hugh; Reading, Berks; Clothier; 4.8.1679; 4.8.1679; 7.11.1687; 7.

3240. Thomas Newman; Dorman; London; C & St; 7.11.1687; 7.11.1687; - ; 7. Bd to his father.

3241. Thomas Parker; Thomas (d); Edmunton, M'sex; - ; 4.9.1693; 4.9.1693; - ; 7.

3242. Moulson Radcliffe; Tho (d); Chalfont St Giles, Bucks; E; 21.10.1672; 21.10.1672; - ; 7.

3243. Thomas Speed; William; London; C & Leatherseller; 22.12.1681; 22.12.1681; 6.5.1689; 7.

3244. Jonothan Wilkins; Jonothan (d); London; C & Ha; 5.8.1668; 5.8.1668; 3.11.1679; 7.

3245. Joseph Wright; John; Leicingham, Lincs; Cl; 8.11.1669; 8.11.1669; - ; 7.

NEWTON, John

3246. John Ayers; John; Dagnham, Essex; H; 7.2.1687; 7.2.1687; - ; 7.

3247. Abraham Lewis; Tymothy (d); Martlesome, Suff; Bl; 2.7.1688; 2.7.1688; - ; 7.

3248. William Norrwood; Nathaniell; parish of St Giles Cripplegate, M'sex; Br; 4.5.1696; 4.5.1696; - ; 7.

NEWTON, William

3249. [William Newton. Fd by patrimony 1.3.1641.]

NICHOLLS, Arthur

3250. Thomas Flower; Thomas (d); London; Embroiderer; 4.7.1653; 4.7.1653; - ; 7.

NICHOLLS, Thomas

3251. John Walker; John (d); London; C & St; 4.5.1641; Easter Day 1641; 16.3.1646; 8. T.o. 5.12.1642 to Steven Bowtell to serve the residue of his term, remitting the last year. Fd by patrimony.

NICHOLSON, Andrew

3252. Thomas Cotterell; Thomas; London; C & MT; 16.12.1650; 16.12.1650; - ; 8.

3253. Wm Cowse; Simon; Parish o St Gyles Criplegate, M'sex; Engraver; 5.5.1662; 1.1.1662; 6.2.1671; 8.

3254. Robert Evance; Jno; Hordley, Oxon; H; 4.4.1653; 28.1.1653; 6.2.1660; 7. Fd as Evans.

3255. Thomas Swinerton; Thomas; West Thurrocke, Essex; Cl; 4.8.1656; 4.8.1656; 7.11.1664; 8.

NORFOLKE, Marmaduke

3256. William Littleboy; John; Highwickham, Bucks; Ca; 9.9.1700; 9.9.1700; 6.10.1707; 7. Fd by Richard Janeway.

NORMAN, John

3257. Francis Constable; Thomas (d); Broadhynton, Wilts; T; 28.6.1652; 28.6.1652; 3.12.1660; 7.

3258. Francis Diester; Thomas; Eeslam, Cambs; Cu; 3.11.1645; 3.11.1645; 5.12.1653; 8.

3259. Thomas Mitchell; Jeremiah; Burbidge, Leics; H; 4.9.1654; 1.8.1654; - ; 8.

3260. Thomas Norman. Fd by patrimony 6.10.1679.

3261. Thomas Parker; Thomas; Bosbery, Herefs; Ca; 3.12.1660; 3.12.1660; - ; 8.

3262. Christopher Stevenson; Plaitway; Carperbey, Yorks; Mason; 14.6.1647; 14.6.1647; - ; 7.

3263. James Warren; James; London; C & MT; 13.7.1657; 13.7.1657; - ; 7.

NORMAN, Thomas

3264. Stephen Blisse; Tobias; Strowdwest, Glos; Cw; 7.5.1688; 7.5.1688; - ; 7.

3265. Joseph Hazard; Joseph; London; C & Weaver; 12.6.1693; 12.6.1693; 7.7.1701; 7. Fd by Norman and Robert Whitledge.

3266. William Horne; William; Old Brandford, M'sex; Y; 7.5.1683; 7.5.1683; 5.10.1691; 7.

NORRINGTON, William

3267. [William Norrington. Fd by redemption 7.8.1648.]

NORRIS, Ann

3268. Thomas Cope; Samuel; Abbots-Brumley, Staffs; Tn; 3.12.1683; 3.12.1683; 9.2.1691; 7. T.o. to William Humphreys (n.d.) and fd by him, but fined 2s. 6d. 'for not being turned over at the Hall'.

NORRIS, Thomas

3269. Moses Gregory; Ambrose (d); Southwarke, Surr; G; 6.5.1695; 6.5.1695; 6.7.1702; 7.

NORRIS, William

3270. John Pennington; John; - , - ; Porter; 8.11.1680; 8.11.1680; 7.10.1689; 8. T.o. 2.5.1687 to Robert Steele. Fd by Norris.

3271. George Vnite; Philip; Litchfeild Close, [Staffs?]; G; 4.10.1675; 4.10.1675; 5.1.1683; 7.

NORTH, John

3272. Joseph Ray; Giles (d); London; C & Woodmonger; 26.6.1668; 26.6.1668; 5.7.1675; 7. Fd by John Macocke.

NORTHCOTT, Richard

3273. Gamaliel Carr; Gamaliel (d); Braintree, Essex; Cw; 6.9.1686; 6.9.1686; - ; 7.

3274. Thomas Jones; Thomas; London; C & Weaver; 2.6.1679; 2.6.1679; 3.11.1688; 8.

3275. Samuel Walfall; - ; - , Kent; Cl; 2.7.1677; 2.7.1677; - ; 7.

NORTHCOTT, Thomas

3276. Francis Holden. Fd by Northcott 6.9.1697, but described as servant to Thomas Lewis. Bd to Edward Paine (q.v.) 4.8.1690.

3277. Christopher Jackson; Richard (d); Thirsk, Yorks; Tn; 6.9.1686; 6.9.1686; - ; 7.

3278. John Wheeler; Thomas; Alder-shott, S'hants; Y; 7.8.1693; 7.8.1693; - ; 7. T.o. 1.10.1694 to Henry Mort-lock.

NORTON, John

3279. Richard Knowles. Fd by Thomas Warren 'for Mr Jo: Norton' 17.4.1648. Apparently never formally bd.

3280. John Norton. Fd by patrimony 19.1.1663.

3281. Roger Norton. Fd by patrimony 30.6.1651.

NORTON, Joyce

3282. Samuell Tompson. Fd by Joyce Norton and Richard Whitaker 17.1. 1642. Bd to Mrs Norton 3.2 1634.

3283. Thomas Whitaker. Fd by patrimony 30.8.1641. Bd to Joyce Norton 6.2.1637.

NORTON, Robert

3284. Mathew Bolton; William; London; C & Ha; 1.3.1686; 2.12.1685; - ; 8.

NORTON, Roger, I

3285. Roger Arthur; John; Bansted, Surr; L; 1.6.1657; 1.6.1657; - ; 15.

3286. John Burrow; John; Grimley, Worcs; H; 2.11.1646; 2.11.1646; 7.11. 1653; 7. Fd as Burrough.

3287. John Cadwell; Edward; London; D; 23.6.1646; 23.6.1646; 4.7.1653; 7.

3288. Simon Corbett; William; - , - ; - ; 3.1.1653; 3.1.1653; 6.2. 1660; 7.

3289. Francis Hughes; John; Kemps-scott, Oxon; Cl; 3.7.1654; 3.7.1654; 6.7. 1661; 7.

3290. George Hopper; John (d); Wolsingam, - ; - ; 23.10.1655; 23.10.1655; 2.11.1663; 8.

3291. William Langford; Gowen; London; C & Cloakmaker; 5.8.1661; 5.8.1661; 3.3.1669; 8.

3292. Roger Norton. Fd by patrimony 1.8.1653.

3293. William Powell; Thom; Breck-nocke, Brecknock; H; 4.5.1657; 4.5. 1657; - ; 7.

3294. William Thompson; Robert; Parish of St Benedict Pauls wharfe, London; G; 4.6.1660; 7.5.1660; - ; 7. Entry deleted; m.n. 'Crossed out by order of Cort. 3 Sept 1660. Indrs by consent of Father and Mr being cancelled'.

3295. Richard Wilkes; Richard; Ludlow, Shrops; G; 24.3.1648; 24.3. 1648; 1.10.1655; 8.

NORTON, Roger, II

3296. Charles Banebridge; Hen; Long Bellington, Lincs; Y; 4.11.1672; 4.11.1672; 1.12.1679; 7. Fd as Bem-bridge.

3297. Benjamin Beardwell. Fd by Norton 9.2.1691. Bd to Edward Horton (q.v.) 2.5.1681.

3298. Wm Beech; Wm; parish of St Sepulchres, M'sex; Plasterer; 5.7.1680; 5.7.1680; - ; 7.

3299. John Copeland; John; St Giles Cripplegate, M'sex; Bu; 2.11.1674; 2.11.1674; 3.7.1682; 8.

3300. Richard Kerrington; Richard (d); Weldrake, Yorks; Cl; 4.11.1668; 4.11.1668; 2.10.1676; 8. Fd as Kelling-ton.

3301. William Norton. Fd by patrimony 5.6.1699.

3302. Wm Payne; Edward; Whately, Oxon; Y; 3.12.1683; 3.12.1683; - ; 7.

3303. John Stubbs; William (d); Bishoprick of Durham, [Dur]; Cl; 5.9. 1692; 5.9.1692; 2.10.1699; 7.

NORTON, William

3304. Daniell Rogers; William; parish of St Andrew Holbourne, M'sex; Mi; 7.8.1699; 7.8.1699; 9.9.1706; 7.

NOWELL, Nathaniel

3305. Nathaniel Bisbie; Mathias; London; C & Ironmonger; 4.10.1686; 4.10.1686; - ; 7.

3306. Edward Crofts; Henry; Kingsdowne, Kent; G; 6.12.1647; 6.12.1647; 13.12.1654; 7.

3307. John Morfey; Daniel (d); St Margaretts Westminster; G; 4.6.1683; 4.6.1683; - ; 7.

3308. Nathaniell Nowell; Nathaniell; [London]; [C & St]; 12.11.1694; 12.11. 1694; - ; 7. Bd to his father.

NURSE, Thomas

3309. Edward Faulkner; Thomas; parish of St Martin in the Feilds, M'sex; - ; 7.6.1680; 7.6.1680; 4.7.1687; 7. Fined 2s. 6d. 'For not being turned over at the Hall', but there is no other indication of Faulkner's having been t.o. to another master.

3310. William Gwalter; James; Yearsley, Herefs; Y; 5.8.1678; 5.8.1678; - ; 7.

3311. Thomas Wright; John; Ackworth, Yorks; Y; 7.4.1679; 7.4.1679; 3.5.1686; 7.

NUTHALL, James

3312. Charles Cox; Wm (d); Malburrough, Wilts; M; 19.1.1652; 25.12. 1651; - ; 9.

3313. Edward Kent; Walter; Codsill, Staffs; H; 2.8.1652; 2.8.1652; - ; 7.

3314. James Nuthall. Fd by patrimony 7.10.1689.

3315. Fredericke Purchas; Samuell; sutton, Essex; Cl; 7.8.1654; 7.8.1654; 7.4.1662; 7.

3316. Jo Smith; Jo; Winsor, Berks; Cooper; 30.6.1651; 30.6.1651; - ; 7.

3317. Joseph Vaugham; Thomas (d); Aveley, Essex; Cl; 8.6.1668; 8.6.1668; - ; 7.

NYE, Henry

3318. Laurence Hatsell; Henry (d); Saltrain, [Dev]; - ; 4.8.1673; 24.6. 1673; 3.10.1681; 8.

3319. Thomas Rawson; John; Pickborne, Yorks; G; 3.2.1679; 3.2.1679; 2.11.1689; 8.

3320. Richd Ward; Richard; Vpton, Yorks; - ; 4.2.1684; 4.2.1684; - ; 7.

OADES, James

3321. Timotheus Bates; Thomas; London; C & Ha; 1.9.1673; 1.9.1673; 5.2.1683; 7.

3322. John Beamish; John; Stradbrock, Suff; G; 1.4.1672; 1.4.1672; - ; 7.

3323. John Brookes; Jeffery; Henley upon Thames, Oxon; Mr; 8.6.1696; 8.6.1696; - ; 8.

3324. Edward Dawgs; Thomas; Newgate street, Herts; G; 8.4.1700; 8.4.1700; - ; 7.

3325. Anthony Drury; Nich; London; E; 2.4.1688; 2.4.1688; - ; 7.

3326. Robert Hodges; William; parish of St Martin in the Feilds, M'sex; G; 3.4.1699; 3.4.1699; - ; 7.

3327. John Martin; Thomas; Lymehouse, M'sex; Mealman; 6.9.1686; 6.9.1686; - ; 7.

3328. Thomas Sheppard; Edmund; London; C & MT; 6.12.1680; 6.12. 1680; 2.7.1688; 7.

3329. Edward Stracey; John; London; C & Cu; 4.8.1684; 4.8.1684; - ; 7.

3330. Henry Yong; Phillip (d); Markett Overton, Rut; E; 14.1.1679; 14.1. 1679; 6.5.1686; 7.

ODELL, John

3331. George Holmewood; Robte (d); Petworth, Sussex; B; 4.10.1647; 4.10.1647; - ; 7.

3332. Rowland Johnson; John (d); Holborne, M'sex; T; 7.9.1657; 24.6. 1657; 1.7.1665; 8. Fd by Odell and William Godbid.

3333. Humphrey Penne. Fd by Odell 24.5.1648. Bd to him 27.6.1639.

OGLETHORPE, Robert

3334. John Tapley; William (d); Burrough of Southwark, [Surr]; Y; 5.8.1661; 5.8.1661; - ; 7.

OKES, Edward

3335. George Bartholomew; Robert (d); Christchurch, S'hants; Fisherman; 3.6.1672; 3.6.1672; 2.5.1681; 7.

3336. Thomas Foster. Fd by Okes 6.12.1675. Apparently never formally bd.

OKES, John

3337. Christopher Brooke. Fd by Okes 29.6.1648. Bd to him 19.12.1639.

3338. John Leicester. Fd by William Wilson for Okes 11.3.1650. Apparently never formally bd.

3339. Wm Leicester. Fd by Okes and William Wilson 1.7.1647. Bd to Okes 22.6.1640.

3340. Edward Oakes. Fd by patrimony 27.6.1664.

3341. John Okes. Fd by patrimony 7.4.1662.

OKES, Joseph

3342. Thomas Hudson; William; London; C & Ha; 6.6.1698; 6.6.1698; - ; 7.

OKES, Nicholas

3343. John Carpenter. Fd by Okes 1.8.1642. Bd to him 31.3.1634.

3344. Thomas Chapman; Thomas; Beudley, Worcs; Sh; 5.9.1642; 5.9.1642; - ; 9.

OKES, Roger

3345. Thomas Bourne. Fd by Okes 6.11.1643. Bd to him 4.4.1636.

3346. Richard Young. Fd by Okes 7.5.1655. Bd to him 4.4.1636.

OKES, Walter

3347. Wm Chetham. Fd by Okes 30.6.1645. Bd to him 2.4.1638.

3348. Wm Fox; John; Aston=Rogers, Shrops; Boxmaker; 3.10.1642; 28.10.1642; - ; 7.

3349. Wm Houghton. Fd by Okes 6.9.1641. Bd to him 14.1.1633.

3350. Richard Wilford. Fd by Oakes 20.1.1645. Bd to him 4.12.1637.

OLDFIELD, Nathaniel

3351. John Kingston; John; Westchester, Ches; Ca; 13.1.1669; 13.1.1669; 7.5.1688; 7.

ONELY, William

3352. Sherard Sheffeild; Wm (d); Stapleford, Leics; Cl; 7.9.1696; 15.6.1696; - ; 7.

3353. Follensby Thackery. Fd by Onely 5.9.1698. Bd to John Millett (q.v.) 8.6.1691.

ORD, William

3354. James Mariner; James; Lymehouse, M'sex; Mariner; 7.3.1681; 7.3.1681; 26.3.1688; 7. Fd by Isaac Frith and fined 2s. 6d. 'for not being turned over at the Hall'.

ORME, James

3355. Willm Nost; Thomas; London; C & Cw; 3.7.1693; 3.7.1693; 2.12.1700; 7. Fd by Orme and William Redmaine.

ORME, John

3356. Robte Browne; Robte; London; Coachman; 7.12.1646; 7.12.1646; 3.7.1654; 7. Originally bd to John Pattison (q.v.) 4.5.1646, and fd by Pattison.

3357. Benjamine Clarke; Math (d); Stretham, Isle of Ely; Cl; 5.1.1657; 5.1.1657; 7.11.1664; 7. Fd by Orme and Elisha Wallis.

3358. Peter Maplesden; Robert (d); Lid, Kent; G; 3.5.1658; 1.5.1658; 4.5.1666; 8.

OSBERSTON, Thomas

3359. [Thomas Osberston. Fd by patrimony 4.3.1661.]

3360. James Willowes; John; Edmondthorpe, Leics; Cook; 3.12.1667; 3.12.1667; - ; 7.

OSBOURNE, Charles

3361. Samuell Butler; George (d); parish of Aston, N'hants; G; 7.2.1698; 7.2.1698; 2.7.1705; 7.

3362. Roger Millert; John (d); parish of St Martin in the Feildes, M'sex; G; 4.2.1695; 4.2.1695; - ; 7.

OTLEY, Thomas

3363. John Samuel; John; St Martin in ye Feilds, [M'sex]; Coachsmith; 5.3.1677; 5.3.1677; - ; 7.

OULTON, Richard

3364. Robte Jennison. Fd by Oulton and John Wright 5.4.1647. Bd to Oulton 7.5.1638.

OVERTON, Henry, I

3365. John Broadstock; John; Ardington, Berks; Y; 26.3.1677; 26.3.1677; - ; 7.

3366. Henry Cripps. Fd by Overton 6.12.1647. Bd to him 3.10.1639.

3367. Edward Farneham; Adrian (d); Quarnden, Leics; G; 20.12.1647; 25.12.1647; 7.1.1656; 8. Fd by Overton and John Sweeting.

3368. Gifford Galton. Fd by Overton and Phillip Nevill 21.1.1644. Bd to Overton 5.5.1634.

3369. Samuell Howes; Robte; London; C & St; 21.1.1644; 29.9.1643; 3.2.1651; 9. Fd by Mrs Overton.

3370. Henry Overton. Fd by patrimony 18.6.1661.

3371. Thomas Wood; Tempest; Lenton alius Levington, Lincs; Cl; 28.6.1641; 1.5.1641; - ; 8.

OVERTON, Henry, II

3372. [Henry Overton. Son of Valentine Overton; fd by patrimon y 23.12.1663.]

OVERTON, John

3373. John Chatwin; John; Fennmore, Oxon; Y; 4.11.1689; 4.11.1689; 1.2.1697; 7.

3374. Thomas Cockrell. Bd (as Cockarell) to Philemon Stephens (q.v.) 7.8.1666; t.o. 2.5.1670 to Overton, but fd by Stephens 1.9.1673.

3375. Samuell More; Richard; East Barkholt, Suff; Cl; 8.11.1669; 8.11.1669; - ; 8.

3376. Phillipp Overton; John; [London]; [C & St]; 2.12.1695; 2.12.1695; - ; 7. Bd to his father.

3377. Jeremy Ratcliffe; Persivall; Carlile, Cumb; - ; 5.10.1663; 5.10.1663; - ; 7.

3378. Joseph Toppyn; John; Norton, N'land; - ; 11.4.1670; 11.4.1670; - ; 7.

3379. James Walker; James; Northton, [N'hants]; Hosier; 1.9.1679; 1.9.1679; 6.7.1691; 7. Fd by Overton but said to have been bd originally to Robert Walton; fined 2s. 6d. for not being t.o. at the hall.

3380. John Westley. Fd by Overton 8.1.1672. Apparently never formally bd.

OWSLEY, John

3381. Richard Hamerton; John (d); London; C & Waxchandler; 2.3.1657; 2.3.1657; - ; 7.

PAGE, Dixey

3382. Richard Smith; Richard; London; C & Dy; 7.8.1666; 24.6.1666; 7.9.1674; 8.

PAINE, Edward

3383. Francis Holden; John (d); Brandford, M'sex; Br; 4.8.1690; 4.8.1690; 6.9.1697; 7. Fd by Thomas Northcott but described as servant to Thomas Lewis.

PAINE, Thomas

3384. Richard Cheese; Wm; Maidstone, Kent; L; 2.8.1647; 2.8.1647; 2.10.1654; 7. Fd by Paine and Thomas Newcomb.

3385. Dominican Clifton; Richard (d); London; C & BSg; 13.4.1644; 13.4.1644; - ; 8.

PAKEMAN, Daniel

3386. Roger Pawlett; Moses; Melton Mowbray, Leics; Mr; 5.7.1652; 5.7.1652; 1.8.1659; 7. Fd as Robert Pawley.

3387. Thomas Poole; Robert; - , Ches; Y; 5.10.1646; 5.10.1646 - ; 8.

3388. Fabian Stedman; Fran; Youghton, Herefs; Cl; 7.7.1656; 7.7.1656; 4.7.1663; 7.

3389. Roger Wingate; Edmond; Grayes Inne, [London]; E; 4.5.1646; 4.5.1646; 5.6.1654; 8.

PALMER, Charles
3390. [Charles Palmer. Son of William Palmer; fd by patrimony 5.12. 1681.]

PALMER, Richard
3391. Joshua Thorpe; John; Sutterdon, Lincs; Y; 10.9.1677; 10.9.1677; - ; 7.

PAPE, Nicholas
3392. [Nicholas Pape. Son of Thomas Pape; fd by patrimony 4.11.1672.]
3393. Thomas Pape. Fd by patrimony 3.6.1695.

PARDOE, Mark
3394. Peter Burrell; John; Cookfeile, Sussex; G; 2.5.1681; 2.5.1681; - ; 7.

PARIS, Nathaniel
3395. Danielle Blague; Edward; London; C & Physician; 7.7.1641; 7.7.1641; 3.10.1648; 7.
3396. Thomas Bull; Thomas; Ainsbury, Hunts; Y; 6.8.1649; 6.8.1649; - ; 7.
3397. Thomas Helders; Richard; Great Storton, Hunts; G; 7.8.1654; 7.8.1654; - ; 7. A Thomas Spicer alias Helder was fd by a Matthew Paris 3.3.1662; he was almost certainly this apprentice of Nathaniel Paris.
3398. Henry Medlam; Henry; London; C & MT; 3.9.1655; 3.9.1655; 6.10.1662; 7.

PARKE, Robert
3399. John Place. Fd by Parke 6.11. 1648. Apparently never formally bd.

PARKER, Henry
3400. Thomas Brownknaffe; Tho; Newport=Bagnell, Bucks; B; 2.8.1641; 2.8.1641; - ; 7.

PARKER, John
3401. Henry Eversden; Henry; London; C & St; 4.5.1646; 4.5.1646; 4.5. 1653; 7. Fd by Parker and Stephens, probably Philemon Stephens.
3402. Peter Harsnett; Martin; Stretham, Surr; G; 13.4.1644; 13.4.1644; - ; 7.
3403. Christopher Higgins. Fd by Parker 4.7.1645. Bd to him 7.8.1637.
3404. Antixas Parker. Fd by patrimony 8.5.1665.
3405. Thomas Roycroft. Fd by Parker and John Beale 23.6.1647. Bd to Beale 4.12.1637.

PARKER, Peter
3406. John Cater; Thomas; Brill, Bucks; Brickmaker; 4.9.1682; 4.9.1682; - 7.
3407. John Cripps; Hen (d); London; St; 4.3.1678; 4.3.1678; - ; 7.
3408. Joseph Hindmarsh; Robert; Gainsborough, Lincs; Tn; 6.2.1671; 6.2.1671; 1.3.1678; 7.
3409. Henry Nelme; John (d); Shipton, Glos; Cl; 6.2.1682; 6.2.1682; 2.4. 1694; 7.
3410. Peter Parker; John; Altringham, Ches; Carrier; 6.8.1688; 6.8. 1688; 4.7.1698; 7.
3411. William Rawlins; Nester; - , Lancs; - ; 8.5.1665; 8.5.1665; 3.6. 1672; 7.
3412. Richard Thompson; Richard; Horley, Oxon; G; 27.9.1691; 27.9.1691; - ; 7.

PARKHURST, Hannah, Widow
3413. Joseph Poole; Joseph; Ipswich, Suff; B; 6.2.1671; 6.2.1671; 31.1.1679; 7. Fd by John Mendy.

PARKHURST, James
3414. Joseph Farneworth; Joseph; Prittlewell, Essex; Cl; 12.3.1667; 12.3. 1667; - ; 10.

PARKHURST, Thomas
3415. Lawrence Brinley; Samuel; Dedham, Essex; Cl; 3.12.1677; 3.12. 1677; - ; 7.

3416. Richard Burroughs; William; Chenish, Bucks; Cl; 7.6.1697; 7.6.1697; 12.6.1704; 7.

3417. William Chandler; Nathaniel; Soning, Berks; Br; 3.11.1684; 3.11.1684; 7.12.1691; 7.

3418. Nathaniell Cliss; Robert (d); Matlock, Derby; Mch; 1.2.1697; 1.2. 1697; 7.2.1704; 7.

3419. Joseph Collier; Richard; Farnham, Surr; Mr; 7.6.1669; 7.6.1669; 7.6.1676; 7.

3420. John Dunton; John; Aston Clinton, Bucks; 7.12.1674; [30.11.1674]; 5.12.1681; 7. Dunton was bd for 7 years from 'the last of November'.

3421. Robert Halsey; Robert (d); Edmonton, M'sex; Tn; 9.2.1691; 9.2. 1691; 7.3.1698; 7.

3422. Thomas Hodgkinson; Peter; Somerford=Booths, Ches; Y; 2.11.1696; 2.11.1696 - ; 7.

3423. John Lawrence; Edw; St Gyles Cripplegate, [London]; Cl; 7.9.1674; 7.9.1674; - ; 7.

3424. Darmond Newman; John; Reading, Berks; G; 16.10.1654; 16.10. 1654; 4.11.1661; 7.

3425. James Parkehurst, bookbinder, fd by redemption 5.12.1664, Thomas Parkhurst his brother paying 20 nobles (Court-Book D).

3426. John Parkhurst; James (d); London; C & St; 7.11.1681; 7.11.1681; - ; 7.

3427. Robert Robinson; Thomas (d); Citty of Oxon; Bs; 6.2.1682; 6.2.1682; 6.7.1691; 7. Fd by Brabazon Aylmer and fined 2s. 6d. for not being t.o. at the hall.

3428. Ralph Smith. Fd by Parkhurst 2.8.1697. Bd to George Powell (q.v.) 6.5.1685.

3429. George Swynnock; George; great Kymbell, Bucks; Cl; 2.7.1667; 2.6.1667; 5.10.1674; 8.

3430. Thomas Taylor; Thomas; Burbridge, Wilts; Cl; 21.1.1661; 21.1.1661; 11.2.1668; 7.

PARREY, Leonard

3431. Thomas Burnham; William; Burrough of Southwark; [Surr]; Weaver; 2.9.1661; 2.9.1661; - ; 8.

PARROTT, William

3432. Robert Horsington. Fd by Parrott 1.2.1657. Bd to him (as Horslington) 7.10.1639.

3433. Christopher Reisord. Fd by Parrott 28.6.1641. Bd to him (as Resold) 5.5.1634.

PARSONS, Amos

3434. Daniell Mayo; Wm; Poulshott, Wilts; Y; 17.1.1648; 25.3.1648; - ; 7.

3435. John Shackston; Richard; Lapford, Dev; Y; 1.4.1650; 1.4.1650; - ; 7.

PARSONS, Marmaduke

3436. John Feild. Fd by Parsons 1.2.1641. Mrs Parsons had been fined shortly after 14.7.1640 'for binding John ffeild her apprentice at a Scriveners' (Jackson 489).

PARSONS, William

3437. Robert Linbye; John; parish of St Clements Daines, M'sex; Bu; 7.6. 1686; 7.6.1686; - ; 7.

3438. Charles Osborne; Thomas; London; C & MT; 8.11.1686; 8.11. 1686; 5.2.1694; 7.

3439. Wm Vandenancker; Martin; London; Mch; 2.11.1691; 2.11.1691; - ; 7.

PASHAM, Thomas

3440. William Hull; William (d); London; C & Cooper; 7.8.1682; 7.8. 1682; - ; 7.

3441. Joseph Roberts; Joseph; Patchill, N'hants; Y; 5.7.1675; 5.7.1675; 7.8.1682; 7.

3442. John Solman; John (d); Bromfeild, Essex; Y; 4.11.1672; 4.11.1672; - ; 9.

PASKE, John
3443. Thomas Drant. Fd by Paske 7.3.1683. Apparently never formally bd.

PASKE, Robert
3444. Thomas Wicks; John; London; C & Dy; 2.5.1670; 2.5.1670; - ; 7.

PASSENGER, Sarah, Widow
3445. Ebenezar Tracey. Fd by Mrs Passenger 3.11.1690. Bd to John Wright (q.v.) 1.10.1683.

PASSENGER, Thomas, I
3446. John Back; Thomas; Hints, Kent; - ; 3.5.1675; 3.5.1675; 3.4. 1682; 7.
3447. Josiah Bleare; Tho; Guildford, Surr; Mealman; 2.8.1675; 2.8.1675; 2.10.1682; 7. Fd as Bloare.
3448. James Dennison. Fd by Passenger 1.9.1684. Apparently never formally bd.
3449. Thomas Passinger; John; Gilford, Surr; 1.10.1683; 1.10.1683; 12.6. 1693; 7.
3450. Robert Radford; John; City of Oxford; Sh; 3.3.1669; 3.3.1669; 3.4.1676; 7.
3451. Richard West; Richard; Guilford, Surr; Schoolmaster; 2.5.1670; 2.5.1670; - ; 7.

PASSENGER, Thomas, II
3452. Henry Parsons; Henry; Guilford, Surr; D; 21.6.1693; 21.6.1693; 11.11.1700; 7. Fd by Passenger and Ebenezar Tracey and described as servant to Tracey.

PATE, Benjamin
3453. John Pym; Philip; London; Mch; 12.11.1677; 12.11.1677; - ; 7.

PATTISON, Jane, Widow
3454. Richard Fletcher; Thomas; Blockley, Worcs; Y; 17.4.1648, 17.4. 1648; 9.5.1655; 7. T.o. 3.2.1651 to Henry Evans, his original master's name being given as John Pattison.

PATTISON, John
3455. Richard Barnes; Tho; Citty

of Glocester; Y; 6.5.1644; 21.12.1643; - ; 8.
3456. Robert Browne; Robte; London; Coachman; 4.5.1646; 4.5.1646; 3.7.1654; 8. Rebd to John Orme 7.12. 1646, but fd by Pattison.
3457. Richard Stone. Fd by Pattison 13.1.1641. Bd to him 30.6.1634.

PAVIT, Nathaniel
3458. John Eaton; Thomas (d); London; C & Go; 1.12.1662; 1.12.1662; 7.11.1670; 7.

PAWLETT, Edward
3459. [Edward Pawlett. Fd by redemption 15.4.1692; but see next entry.]

PAWLETT, George
3460. Edward Pawlett; Edward (d); Grantham, Lincs; Bs; 2.11.1691; 2.11. 1691; - ; 7. Possibly fd by redemption 15.4.1692: see preceding entry.

PAWLETT, Robert
3461. Charles Brexton; Cornelius; farnham, Surr; G; 7.12.1663; 7.12.1663; 4.3.1672; 8.
3462. Tracy Parr; Ralph; Furnivalls Inne, - ; G; 26.3.1672; 26.3.1672; - ; 7.
3463. George Pawlett. Fd by patrimony 3.12.1683.
3464. Robert Wells. Fd by Pawlett 2.3.1685. Apparently never formally bd.

PAXTON, Edmond
3465. Francis Kitchin; Henry; Bulsour, Derby; Y; 3.2.1651; 3.2.1651; 1.3.1658; 7.
3466. John Penn. T.o. 3.5.1669 from Henry Chase to Paxton, but there is no record of the original binding.
3467. John Roane; Robte; Greenwich, Kent; G; 24.3.1647; 25.3.1647; 1.6.1657; 7. Originally bd to William Tibbs (q.v.) 1.6.1646. Fd by Paxton.
3468. Thomas Warkhouse; Jno (d); Sherrington, Norf; G; 5.4.1658; 25.3. 1658; 12.6.1666; 8.

PEABODY, Samuel

3469. Edward Harris; William; Hampton, M'sex; - ; 2.4.1677; 2.4. 1677; - ; 7.

3470. John Horiks; John; Much Wenlock, Surr [*sic* for Shrops]; Dy; 3.7.1682; 3.7.1682; - ; 7.

PEABODY, Thomas

3471. John Buncker; John; Groue, Bucks; Grazier; 3.8.1646; 3.8.1646; - ; 7.

3472. John Gibbons; Thomas (d); Longlane, M'sex; Chandler; 6.6.1664; 24.6.1664; - ; 8.

3473. Isaac Herbert. Fd by Peabody 5.10.1646. Bd to him 12.12.1638.

3474. John Leigh; Thomas; London; C & Mr; 2.8.1658; 25.3.1658; - ; 8.

3475. Samuell Peibody. Fd by patrimony 6.12.1669.

3476. Edward Willis; Edward; Citty of New Sarum, Wilts; Y; 7.7.1656; 7.7. 1656; 3.8.1663; 7.

PEACOCK, Daniel

3477. Gerard Denet; Thomas; Elmbridge, Worcs; G; 7.3.1681; 7.3.1681; 7.10.1689; 7.

3478. Bartholomew Ferriman; Bartholomew; London; C & Ha; 1.8.1687; 1.8.1687; - ; 7.

3479. Daniel Peacock; Daniel; [London]; [C & St]; 3.3.1684; 3.3.1684; - ; 7. Bd to his father.

3480. Robert Peacock; Ferdinandoe; Redburn, Herts; Y; 22.2.1675; 22.2. 1675; - ; 7.

3481. Thomas Turnor; Tho; Saffron Walden, Essex; M; 1.6.1674; 1.6. 1674; 1.10.1688; 8.

3482. John Wright; Roger (d); London; C & MT; 3.9.1672; 3.9.1672; 6.10.1679; 7.

PEIRCE, Isaac

3483. [Isaack Peirce. Fd by patrimony 22.12.1675.]

PEIRCE, Timothy

3484. William Peirce; John; New-

berry, Berks; M; 6.11.1671; 6.11.1671; 14.1.1679; 7.

PEIRCE, William

3485. William Monins; - ; - , - ; - ; 2.8.1697; 2.8.1697; - ; 7.

3486. Edward Tayler; Edward; Blechley, Bucks; G; 21.1.1691; 21.1. 1691; - ; 7.

PEIRCEHAY, John

3487. William Fowler; William; Barnes, Surr; Sh; 6.5.1659; 6.5.1659; - ; 7.

PEIRCEHAY, William

3488. John Peircehay. Fd by patrimony 3.5.1658.

3489. William Shury; Wm (d); Battersey, Surr; Y; 3.7.1648; 3.7.1648; - ; 7.

PEIRSON, John

3490. William Budden; Robert; Ringwood, S'hants; Y; 3.8.1674; 3.8. 1674; 7.1.1684; 7.

3491. Willm Perkins; Geo (d); Parrish of St Sepulchers, M'sex, Coachharnessmaker; 7.1.1684; 7.1.1684; 1.2. 1692; 8.

PEIRSON, William

3492. William Johnson; Henry; London; C & Wheelwright; 5.12.1698; 5.12.1698; 3.12.1705; 7.

PENFORD, Thomas

3493. Samuel Brightwell. Fd by Penford 8.5.1693. Bd to Francis Baugh (q.v.) 4.8.1684.

3494. Thomas Budd; James; West Horseley, Surr; Cl; 2.12.1689; 2.12. 1689; - ; 7.

3495. John Delander; Nathaniell (d); London; C & Clockmaker; 5.2.1700; 5.2.1700; - ; 7.

3496. Thomas Elmes; Robert (d); Citty of Gloucester; G; 7.8.1693; 7.8. 1693; - ; 7.

3497. Samuel Petcher; Francis; Somerby, Leics; Grazier; 3.5.1686; 3.5. 1686; - ; 7.

PENN, John

3498. William Barnes; Thomas; London; C & Cu; 4.12.1671; 4.12.1671; 6.8.1683; 7.

3499. Henry Danvers; John (d); North Goley, S'hants; G; 7.1.1684; 7.1.1684; 7.8.1699; 7.

3500. John Ford; Allen (d); London; C & St; 4.12.1699; 4.12.1699; - ; 8.

3501. Richard Greene; Richard (d); Bestford, Worcs; - ; 6.5.1700; 6.5.1700; - ; 7.

3502. Wm Harvey; Joseph (d); London; C & Cu; 12.4.1692; 12.4.1692; 7.8.1699; 7.

3503. Gilbert Howell; John; London; C & Salter; 5.6.1690; 5.6.1690; - ; 7.

3504. William Hull; George; London; C & Ha; 6.12.1675; 6.12.1675; - ; 8.

3505. Edward Jones. Fd by Penn 2.4. 1705. Bd to Benjamin Major (q.v.) 2.3.1685; t.o. 1.8.1687 to Penn.

3506. Owen Lloyd; Owen (d); Towne of Denby, [Den]; G; 6.4.1696; 6.4.1696; 3.5.1703; 7.

3507. Thomas Smith; John; Redford, Notts; Y; 6.10.1690; 6.10.1690; - ; 7.

PENN, William

3508. John Bayliffe; Edward (d); Chippenham, Wilts; G; 2.6.1684; 2.6. 1684; - ; 7.

3509. Robert Penn. Fd by patrimony 3.5.1675.

PENNITHORNE, Ferdinando

3510. George Gradon. Fd by Pennithorne 15.9.1647. Bd to him 1.7.1640.

3511. Wm Hallott; Samuell (d); London; Bu; 15.9.1647; 15.9.1647; - ; 8.

3512. Thomas Hancocke; John; Cleauepepper, Wilts; H; 1.12.1656; 1.12.1656; - ; 7.

3513. William Jones; Walter; Stanton, Glos; H; 2.7.1655; 2.7.1655; - ; 7.

3514. Symon Walcott; Henry (d); Helpringham, Lincs; Y; 7.11.1642; 7.11.1642; 4.5.1657; 7. Fd by Pennithorne and George Gradon.

PERO, John

3515. Benjamin Price. Fd by Pero and John Southby 26.3.1701. Bd to Southby (q.v.) 7.11.1692.

PERRIS, Henry

3516. Phillip Godfrey; Stephen; London; C & Founder; 2.5.1692; 2.5.1692; - ; 7.

3517. James Pendred. Fd by Perris and Henry Lee 3.6.1700. Bd to Lee (q.v.) 8.5.1693.

PERRY, Katherine, Widow

3518. Leonard Sowerby; Peircivall; St Martyns in the feilds, M'sex; Farrier; 10.1.1649; 10.1.1649; - ; 7.

PETTIT, John

3519. Samuell Newam; Jno; Ringsteed, N'hants; Mason; 13.1.1653; 13.1. 1653; - ; 8.

PETTY. Samuel

3520. Roger Ive. Bd to Petty 5.3.1638; t.o. 4.12.1643 to Robert Burrough. Fd by Petty and Burrough 10.3.1645.

PHELPS, Richard

3521. Peter Hooker; George; Strelley; Notts; T; 17.1.1648; 17.1.1648; - ; 7.

3522. George Otway; Ed; Stoneden Massey, Essex; Cl; 9.7.1663; 9.7.1663; 2.10.1676; 7.

PHILLIPS, William

3523. Daniell Brown; John (d); London; C & Salter; 25.6.1662; 25.6.1662; 4.7.1670; 8.

3524. Norton Cambridge; Norton; parish of St Anne in the liberty of Westmr, M'sex; G; 13.3.1693; 13.3. 1693; - ; 7.

3525. Wm Carpenter; Benjn; London; C & D; 5.6.1690; 5.6.1690 - ; 7.

3526. Christopher Conningesby; Richard; London; G; 2.6.1679; 2.6. 1679; 4.10.1686; [7]. The term of binding is not given.

3527. Edward Eaton; Francis Citty; of Westminster; Cook; 4.11.1689; 4.11.1689; - ; 7.

3528. Benjamine Major. Fd by Phillips 7.7.1684. Bd to Daniel Major (q.v.) 18.6.1677.

3529. Daniell Major; Gabriell; Leicester; Cl; 6.12.1669; 6.12.1669; - ; 7.

3530. Richd Mawson; Richard; the Burrough, Leics; G; 3.12.1683; 3.12.1683; 1.10.1694; 7.

PHIPPS, George

3531. Richard Harison. Fd by Phipps 3.10.1642. Bd to him 2.10.1633.

PICKERING, William

3532. Richard Adams; James; - , M'sex; Farrier; 6.5.1644; 6.5.1644; - ; 10.

3533. Nicholas Tomlyn; Gitting (d); Twivill, N'hants; L; 5.4.1641; 25.3.1641; - ; 9.

PIERCY, Thomas

3534. Edmond Aston; John; Gretton, Glos; G; 21.1.1661; 21.1.1661; - ; 7.

3535. Adam Brett; Robert (d); Whitestanton, Som; Knight; 3.12.1667; 3.12.1667; 7.5.1677; 7.

3536. Thomas Davis; George; Treabbott, Flint; G; 4.3.1678; 4.3.1678; - ; 7. The master's name is given as Peacy.

3537. John Ford; Francis (d); Newland, Glos.; Cl; 5.4.1669; 5.4.1669; - ; 7.

3538. George Lutly; Adam; Lawton, Shrops; E; 1.7.1661; 1.7.1661; - ; 7.

3539. Nicholas Tourner; John; East Bourne, Sussex; G; 5.9.1670; 5.9.1670; - ; 7.

3540. Edward Turbervile; Trayolis (d); Nobody, Worcs; G; 20.9.1658; 20.9.1658; - ; 7.

3541. Roger Vaugham; Roger; Salisbury, Wilts; G; 5.5.1668; 15.5.1668; - ; 7.

3542. Edward Willescott; Thomas;

Sutton, Berks; E; 16.12.1656; 16.12.1656; 18.1.1664; 7.

PIERREPOINT, Thomas

3543. Thomas Burrell; Thomas; Horsham, Sussex; G; 3.10.1659; 3.10.1659; 4.7.1670; 7. Fd as Barrell.

3544. Timothy Smart. Fd by Pierrepoint and Humphrey Blunden 1.8.1653. Bd to Blunden (q.v.) 2.7.1646.

3545. Samuell Torbucke; Thomas; London; C & MT; 5.9.1653; 25.3.1653; 1.4.1661; 8.

PIGGOTT, Edward

3546. Thomas Dolling. Fd by Piggott 24.1.1642. Bd to him 19.1.1635.

3547. Christopher Greene. Fd by Piggott 31.3.1656. Bd to him 4.3.1633.

3548. Thomas Wilcox; Richard; St Giles in the Fields, M'sex; T; 7.7.1656; 7.7.1656; - ; 7.

PIKE, John

3549. John Harrison; William (d); London; T; 7.7.1690; 7.7.1690; 8.11.1697; 7.

PISTELL, Richard

3550. Edw Mompesson; Edw; Langton, Isle of Purbeck, Dors; G; 11.4.1665; 11.4.1664; - ; 7. This entry occurs only in the Court Waste Book. Pistell was a Surgeon, though free of the Company.

PITT, Moses

3551. Charles Shortgrave. Fd by Pitt 1.3.1686, but fined 2s. 6d. 'for not being bound at ye Hall'.

PLACE, John

3552. James Blackwell; Peter; Barnett, Herts; V; 4.9.1682; 4.9.1682; 7.10.1689; 7. T.o. 3.10.1687 to Samuel Carr, but fd by Place.

3553. Thomas Cater; Phillip; London; C & B; 4.3.1689; 4.3.1689; 8.6.1696; 7.

3554. John Cox; John; Marston, Oxon; Y; 10.1.1655; 10.1.1655; - ; 7.

3555. Nicholas Cox; Richard; Stanton St John, Oxon; H; 7.8.1666; 7.8.1666; 1.9.1673; 7.

3556. William Jacob; Edmund; Buscot, Berks; Y; 6.4.1657; 6.4.1657; 3.4.1665; 8.

3557. John Place; John; London; C & St; 12.8.1671; 12.8.1671; 26.3.1674; 7. Bd. to his father; fd by patrimony.

3558. William Place. Fd by Place and John Bourman 3.7.1654. Bd to Bourman (q.v.) 6.10.1645.

3559. Richard Sare; Richard; Oare, Berks; Cl; 4.5.1674; 26.3.1674; 4.8.1684; 7.

3560. Charles Smith; Charles (d); Towne of Southampton; G; 5.9.1659; 25.3.1659; 7.5.1667; 8.

PLACE, William

3561. Henry Cox; Richard; Stanton St Johns, Oxon; Y; 11.2.1668; 11.2.1668; - ; 7.

3562. Norman Nelson; Norman; London; C & V; 4.5.1674; 4.5.1674; - ; 7.

3563. Robert Robinson; Robert; Ardington, Berks; H; 2.9.1661; 2.9.1661; 15.7.1668; 7.

PLATT, Edward

3564. Thomas Morrice; Ralph (d); London; C & J; 5.9.1692; 5.9.1692; - ; 7.

PLAYFERE, John

3565. Thomas Morrice; Thomas; London; C & MT; 6.2.1665; 6.2.1665; - ; 8.

PLAYFORD, Henry

3566. John Church; Robt; Citty of Oxford; Y; 3.6.1689; 3.6.1689; - ; 7.

3567. Edward Conduit; William (d); Wells, Som; H; 8.11.1686; 8.11.1686; 2.5.1698; 7.

3568. John Cullin; Thomas; London; C & B; 4.2.1695; 4.2.1695; 2.3.1702; 7.

PLAYFORD, John, I

3569. John Bligh; John; Citty of Norwich; Weaver; 6.4.1663; 6.4.1663; 11.4.1670; 7. Fd as Bleigh.

3570. James Edwards; Wm (d); parish of St Gyles Crypplegate, London; - ; 5.7.1680; 5.7.1680; - ; 7.

3571. John Ford. Bd to Zachariah Watkins (q.v.) 4.4.1664; t.o. 7.5.1666 to Playford. Fd 2.12.1672 by redemption, by order of the Lord Mayor.

3572. Henry Playford; John; London; C & St; 9.2.1674; 9.2.1674; 1.3.1681; 7. Bd to his father; fd by patrimony.

3573. Zachery Watkins; Sam; Frilson, Berks; Cl; 5.3.1655; 25.3.1655; 7.4.1662; 7.

PLAYFORD, John, II

3574. Robert Jenkinson; Thomas; Citty of Oxon; S; 5.12.1681; 5.12.1681; 4.3.1689; 7. Fd by John Leake, Playford being dead, and fined 2s. 6d. 'for being turned over'. Bd to John Playford Junior.

PODMORE, Robert

3575. Andrew Parker; Samuell (d); London; C & MT; 7.6.1697; 7.6.1697; 5.12.1709; 7.

3576. Saml Podmore; Arthur (d); Hexton, Shrops; G; 3.2.1690; 3.2.1690; - ; 7.

PONDER, Nathaniel

3577. Benjamin Alsop; Vincent; Gettingdon, N'hants; G; 27.9.1672; 27.9.1672; 6.10.1679; 7.

3578. William English. Fd by Ponder 3.11.1679. Bd (as Inglish) to George Saville (q.v.) 1.4.1672.

3579. John Harris, John, Southwarke, Surr; Cheesemonger; 4.3.1678; 4.3.1678; 6.4.1685; 7.

3580. Israel Harrison; Israell (d); Cambridge, Cambs; M; 6.6.1664; 6.6.1664; 5.5.1673; 8.

3581. John Hill; Nicholas; London; C & Ha; 1.8.1670; 1.8.1670; 12.11.1677; 7. Fd by George Marriott.

3582. Isaac Justice; Rice (d); London; C & Leatherseller; 26.6.1682; 26.6.1682; - ; 7.

3583. John Mansfeild; John; Rothwell, N'hants; Plumber; 29.10.1696; 29.10.1696; - ; 7.

3584. John Martin; George; London; G; 7.3.1681; 7.3.1681; - ; 9.

3585. Thomas Saddington; Antho; Melchburn, Beds; Y; 22.9.1675; 22.9.1675; - ; 7.

POOLE, Anthony

3586. Benjamine Pate; Thomas; Harrow on the hill, M'sex; Y; 4.10.1669; 4.10.1669; 6.11.1676; 7.

POOLE, Edmund

3587. Richard Sellwood; Will; Broxburn, Herts; Mi; 4.8.1690; 4.8.1690; - ; 7.

POOLE, Edward

3588. Jerman Bowden; Jerman (d); Melton-Mowbray, Leics; G; 6.6.1698; 6.6.1698; - ; 7.

3589. Thomas Minton; Thomas; parish of Fulham, M'sex; Gardener; 3.9.1688; 3.9.1688; 3.2.1696; 7.

POOLE, Gregory

3590. John Bedder; Richard; Saffron hill (near Clerkenwell), M'sex; - ; 4.10.1669; 4.10.1669; 11.10.1680; 7. Fd as Beddes.

3591. Thomas Norton; Thomas; Hill Morton, War; Cl; 2.10.1676; 2.10.1676; - ; 7.

POOLE, John

3592. Giddon Home; James (d); Eaton, in the Kingdome of Scotland; - ; 2.4.1683; 2.4.1683; - ; 7.

POOLE, Joseph

3593. Barbara Hibbard; Robert; Grove, Shrops; Y; 6.2.1682; 6.2.1682; - ; 7.

POOLER, Humphrey

3594. Benjamin Cautrell; Edward; Hasted, Essex; G; 5.8.1672; 5.8.1672; - ; 7.

3595. Robert Elmes; Robert; Citty of Gloucester; Timbermerchant; 1.12.1679; 1.12.1679; 1.2.1692; 7.

3596. Thomas Grove; John; Hallclose, Worcs; G; 3.10.1687; 3.10.1687; 1.2.1697; 7.

3597. Richard Hooke; Richard; City of Worcester; G; 7.6.1697; 1.5.1697; - ; 7.

3598. Robert Paine; John; Farringdon, Berks; Minister; 3.6.1678; 3.6.1678; - ; 8.

3599. Richard Penniston; Robert; Chippen Barnett, Herts; G; 4.12.1682; 4.12.1682; - ; 7.

3600. William Stonhall; - ; - , Worcs; - ; 6.5.1700; 6.5.1700; - ; 7.

3601. Richard Trow; Gilbert; Tam, Oxon; G; 3.12.1684; 3.12.1684; 1.2.1692; 7.

3602. Edward Underhill; Edward (d); Vpthorpe, Worcs; G; 2.12.1672; 2.12.1672; 7.2.1681; 8.

PORTER, John

3603. [John Porter. Fd by patrimony 3.4.1665.]

POWELL, Edward

3604. Edm Berisford. Fd by Powell and Roger Bartlett 7.7.1662. Bd to Bartlett (q.v.) 7.8.1654.

3605. John Chaundler; William; great St Bartholomews, London; Chandler; 8.5.1665; 8.5.1665; - ; 7.

3606. James Fothergay; John (d); London; C & Ca; 9.9.1678; 9.9.1678; 7.2.1687; 7.

3607. John Herridge; Thomas (d); Chelmsford, Essex; Y; 2.3.1657; 2.3.1657; - ; 8.

3608. William Jans; Michael (d); Mainham, Kildeer, Ireland; G; 6.6.1687; 6.6.1687; - ; 7.

3609. Francis Jewster; Richard (d); London; C & Cw; 5.4.1684; 5.4.1684; 6.7.1691; 7. Fd by Francis Blyth and fined 2s. 6d. for not being t.o. at the hall.

3610. Herbert Jones; Ewstace; Clanger, Herefs; Y; 22.12.1670; 22.12.1670; - ; 7.

3611. John Penn; James (d); London; Pw; 2.8.1697; 2.8.1697; 7.8. 1704; 7.

3612. Edward Powell. Fd by patrimony 2.10.1676.

3613. Robt Powell. Fd by patrimony 2.10.1682.

3614. Willm Reynolds; Robert (d); Ludlowe, Shrops; Y; 2.8.1669; 2.8. 1669; - ; 7.

3615. Benjamin Sprint; Samuel; Clatford, S'hants; G; 4.12.1676; 4.12. 1676; - ; 7.

3616. Richard Torshell; Sam (d); London; C & Gr; 6.9.1675; 6.9.1675; 2.10.1682; 7.

3617. James Wiltshire. Fd by Powell and Richard Torshell 4.7.1698. Bd to Torshell (q.v.) 3.7.1686 and t.o. (n.d.) to Powell.

POWELL, George

3618. Robert Clincar; Valentine; Able Hill, M'sex; Victualler; 6.6.1664; 6.6.1664; - ; 7.

3619. William Hurt; Christopher; London; Glazier; 2.4.1694; 2.4.1694; - ; 7.

3620. Jonathan Janaway; Richard; Raustrup, N'hants; H; 2.12.1661; 2.12. 1661; 20.7.1670; 8.

3621. Ralph Smith; Thomas; parish of St Dunstan in the West, [London]; G; 6.5.1685; 6.5.1685; 2.8.1697; 7. Fd by Thomas Parkhurst.

3622. Henry Whittaker; Benjamn; Itchingswell, S'hants; G; 7.6.1686; 7.6.1686 - ; 7.

POWELL, John

3623. [John Powell. Fd by patrimony 2.11.1674.]

POWELL, Nathaniel

3624. [Nath Powell. Fd by patrimony 2.4.1667.]

POWELL, Walter

3625. Wm Boswell; Jervaice; Nuneaton, War; Y; 22.12.1647; 22.12.1647; - ; 7.

3626. Robert Heiron; John; Cambridge, Cambs; Cu; 10.6.1650; 10.6. 1650; - ; 7.

3627. Wm Newman; Edmond; London; C & Lorrimer; 4.8.1645; 4.8. 1645; 6.9.1652; 7.

3628. James Penroy; Rice; Llangamer, Brecknock; G; 6.11.1654; 6.11. 1654; 1.2.1664; 7. Fd by Powell and Joseph Davis.

3629. Andrew Poole; Tho; Newport, Shrops; Sc; 1.3.1652; 1.3.1652; - ; 7.

3630. Humphrey Robins; William; Liegh, Wilts; T; 2.8.1658; 2.8.1658; - ; 7.

3631. Stephen Thornburrough; Edward; Hartnell, Bucks; Y; 6.10.1662; 6.10.1662; 8.11.1669; 7.

POWLE, William

3632. John Moore; John (d); parish of St Paul Covent Garden, M'sex; G; 28.10.1699; 28.10.1699; - ; 7.

3633. Thomas Osborne; Tho; London; C & Tallowchandler; 6.5.1689; 6.5.1689; 5.7.1703; 7.

3634. [William Powle. Fd by patrimony 4.8.1684.]

PRATT, Mathias

3635. Mathew Edmondson; Mathew; Hull; Yorks; G; 1.2.1675; 1.2. 1675; 6.2.1682; 7.

3636. Samuell Hendrey; John (d); Stepney, M'sex; Mariner; 2.7.1667; 2.7.1667; 3.8.1674; 7.

PRESTON, Richard

3637. Stephen Samon; Richard; London; C & Weaver; 1.10.1677; 1.10. 1677; - ; 7.

3638. Thomas Wharton; Abraham; Long Acre, M'sex; G; 10.1.1670; 10.1. 1670; - ; 7.

PRITCHARD, Robert
3639. Stephen Burton; Nehemiah (d); Hammersmith, M'sex; M; 1.9. 1651; 1.9.1651; - ; 8.
3640. William Johnson; William; London; C & St; 14.4.1656; 14.4.1656; 1.8.1664; 9. Fd by Pritchard and Samuel Wright.

PROSSAR, Enoch
3641. Richard Weeckes; George; - , M'sex; - ; 6.9.1680; 6.9.1680; - ; 7.

PROUDLOVE, Thomas
3642. John Holford. Fd by Proudlove 2.4.1677. Apparently never formally bd.

PULLEYN, Octavian, I
3643. Phillip Brigg; Richard (d); Citty of Norwich; G; 7.11.1644; 25.12. 1643; 14.2.1653; 9. Fd as Briggs.
3644. Sam Dancer; Thomas; London; C & Br; 29.6.1653; 24.6.1653; - ; 8.
3645. Thomas Dicus; Thomas; Dodleston, Flint; Y; 15.6.1646; 15.6.1646; 6.11.1655; 9.
3646. Cave Pulleyn. Fd by patrimony 27.6.1664.
3647. Charles Pulleyn. Fd by patrimony 1.2.1675.
3648. Octavian Pulleyn; Robt; Thulson, Leics; Cl; 20.5.1656; 20.5.1656; 1.6.1663; 7.

PULLEYN, Octavian, II
3649. William Dridon; William; Farmedon, N'hants; E; 6.2.1665; 2.2.1665; - ; 7.

PULLYN, Simon
3650. Symon Cook; Willm (d); Newmarkett, Suff; H; 8.7.1668; 8.7.1668; 1.12.1679; 7. Pullyn is described as a Bricklayer.
3651. Thomas Throw; Thomas; Battersea, Surr; Y; 2.4.1666; 5.3.1666; - ; 7. The master's name is given as Pollin.

PURFOOTE, Thomas
3652. Edward Broughton. Fd by Purfoote 28.6.1641. Bd to him 5.5.1634; t.o. 7.5.1638 to Thomas Badger.

PURSLOWE, Anne
3653. John Chadwick; John; parish of Rochdall, Lancs; Y; 3.2.1679; 3.2. 1679; 1.3.1686; 7.
3654. Benjamin Mawson; Edward (d); London; Y; 12.11.1677; 12.11. 1677; 3.12.1684; 7. T.o. on the death of Mrs Purslowe to Thomas Haley 22.9.1680 and fd by him.
3655. John Millet; Caleb; London; C & Ha; 22.2.1675; 22.2.1675; 26.6. 1682; 7.
3656. Richard Smart; William (d); London; Gr; 12.11.1677; 12.11.1677; - ; 7.

PURSLOWE, Elizabeth, Widow
3657. Henry Edwards; Henry; Hardwick, Oxon; H; 8.3.1642; 8.3.1642; 1.4.1650; [8]. The term of binding is not given.
3658. Moses Gane; Edgar; Gore, Dors; Y; 6.8.1649; 6.8.1649; 5.10.1657; 7.

PURSLOWE, George
3659. Richard Bockham. Fd by Purslowe, Thomas Creake and John Hardestie 8.5.1665. Bd to Hardestie (q.v.) 5.4.1658.
3660. Nich Bowyer. Fd by Purslowe and Henry Bell 2.7.1667. Bd to Bell (q.v.) 7.5.1660.
3661. Edward Cranford; Edward (d); Guildford, Surr; Bricklayer; 6.9. 1669; 6.9.1669; - ; 7.
3662. Humphrey Hunter; Joseph (d); London; C & Cw; 5.5.1656; 5.5. 1656; 1.2.1664; 8.
3663. John Nicks; Isack (d); London; C & D; 30.6.1651; 30.6.1651; 6.9.1658; 7. Fd by Purslowe and Thomas Newcomb.
3664. [George Purslow. Fd by patrimony 6.12.1647.]

RADFORD, Robert

3665. William Humphries; William; Oxford; M; 1.5.1676; 1.5.1676; 4.6. 1683; 7.

3666. Elizabeth Palmer; Thomas; London; C & Cooper; 5.10.1696; 5.10. 1696; - ; 7.

3667. William Radford; Robert; [London]; [C & St]; 6.5.1695; 6.5. 1695; - ; 8. Bd to his father.

3668. Robert Stephens; Richard; London; C & Cook; 1.9.1684; 1.9. 1684; 12.4.1692; 7.

3669. Robert Williamson. Fd by Radford and William Barker 8.4.1695. Bd to Barker (q.v.) 6.9.1686; t.o. 7.9. 1691 to Radford.

RAINSFORD, Mathias

3670. Martin Smith; Fd by Rainsford and George Rea 17.10.1653. Bd to Rainsford 22.6.1640.

RAND, Samuel

3671. Wm Curtis; John (d); Vpminster, Essex; Y; 10.1.1650; 10.1. 1650; 1.6.1657; 7. Rebd to Thomas Cooke (q.v.) 7.10.1650 but fd by Rand.

3672. Samuell Rand. Fd by patrimony 24.3.1656.

3673. John Warter; Josua; London; C & Go; 4.11.1644; 4.11.1644; 9.5. 1655; 7.

3674. Thomas Watson. Fd by Rand 1.6.1646. Bd to him 2.12.1633.

RANDALL, Edward

3675. George Grimes; George; parish of Eltham, Kent; E; 4.3.1678; 29.9.1677; - ; 8.

RANDALL, Elizabeth

3676. Thomas Harding. Fd by Elizabeth Randall 3.2.1696. Apparently never formally bd.

RANDALL, Richard

3677. John Story; Robert; Newcastle vpon Tine; Tn; 3.6.1678; 3.6.1678; - ; 7.

RANEW, Nathaniel

3678. John Cobb; John (d); London; C & D; 3.10.1692; 3.10.1692 - ; 7.

3679. Posthumus Fairclough; Nathaniell (d); Stalbridge, Dors; Cl; 4.12.1671; 4.12.1671; - ; 7.

3680. John Taylor; Mansfeild (d); T; Sherborn, Dors; Clothier; 3.4.1676; 3.4.1676; 7.1.1684; 7.

3681. Thomas Wilkes; Edward; Albriston, Shrops; Y; 7.4.1684; 7.4. 1684; - ; 7.

RATCLIFFE, Thomas

3682. Robert Daniell; Willm (d); Snath, Yorks; Y; 2.7.1667; 2.7.1667; - ; 7.

3683. Richard Dickenson; Richard; Kingstrap, N'hants; H; 2.8.1652; 2.8. 1652; 5.9.1659; 7.

3684. Mathew Evans; John; Llaniglos, Mont; Sh; 6.9.1669; 6.9.1669; 1.7.1678; 8. Entry deleted and noted 'Runn away from his Master' (n.d.), but fd by Ratcliffe 1.7.1678.

3685. Henry Floyd; Morris; London; C & MT; 2.11.1646; 25.3.1647; 3.4. 1654; 7. Fd as Lloyd.

3686. Oliuer Holmes; Xpofer; Bentham, Yorks; G; 5.6.1654; 25.3.1654; - ; 8.

3687. John Jones; Richard; Wrexham, Den; Y; 4.12.1671; 4.12.1671; 2.12.1678; 7.

3688. James Rawlyns; Edward (d); Laughton, Leics; Cl; 2.5.1670; 2.5. 1670; 30.7.1677; 8.

3689. John Smith; John (d); Bedworth, Warr; Cl; 6.9.1658; 6.9.1658; 7.8.1666; 8.

3690. Robert Stephens; Willm; Kingston, Oxon; H; 5.4.1658; 5.4. 1658; 12.2.1666; 8.

RAVEN, Joseph

3691. John Briggs; William; Horsham, Sussex; Ca; 6.8.1694; 6.8.1694; - ; 7.

3692. William Bryan. Bd (as Bryan Wilson) to William Canning (q.v.) 6.6.1687; t.o. 2.3.1691 to Raven.

3693. Richard Croskill; Thomas (d); London; C & St; 8.4.1700; 8.4.1700; - ; 7.

3694. Nathanl Hake; Richard; Plimoth, Dev; Sh; 7.10.1689; 7.10.1689; - ; 7.

RAW, Thomas

3695. Robert Alcocke; Nicholas; Brampton, Hunts; Barber; 7.10.1661; 7.10.1661; - ; 7. On 3.10.1664 Alcocke was reported to have been absent from Raw for over a year (Court-Book D).

3696. John Browne; John; London; C & St; 6.9.1647; 6.9.1647; 3.7.1654; 7. Fd by patrimony.

3697. William Huntley; William; St Giles in the Feilds, [M'sex]; Bookbinder; 3.8.1664; 3.8.1664; - ; 7.

3698. John Maldon; John; Machendon, Essex; Y; 3.7.1682; 3.7.1682; - ; 7.

3699. Robte Raineton; Hamond; Hamersmith, M'sex; Schoolmaster; 3.11.1645; 3.11.1645; - ; 7.

3700. Thomas Raw. Fd by patrimony 2.8.1680.

3701. Robte Sillott; Samuell; Bramford, Suff; Y; 3.8.1646; 3.8.1646; - ; 7.

3702. George Smith; George; Burton Latimers, N'hants; Y; 2.10.1682; 2.10.1682; - ; 7.

3703. John Wells; Willm; Amptill, Beds; Cl; 3.3.1673; 3.3.1673; 6.9.1680; 7.

3704. Willm Weston; Ralph; Langar-Daer, Carnarvon [sic for Carms]; - ; 20.7.1670; 20.7.1670; - ; 7.

RAWLINS, James

3705. Foulke Cleaver; Foulke; Ipswich, Suff; G; 2.7.1694; 2.7.1694; - ; 7.

3706. Wm Fowell. Fd by Rawlins 7.12.1691. Bd to John Wallis (q.v.) 5.2.1683.

3707. Henry Gillibrand. Fd by Rawlins 7.12.1691. Bd to William Tuckey (q.v.) 1.9.1684.

3708. Richd Gillman; Richard (d); Burntwood, Essex; G; 7.3.1692; 7.3.1692; - ; 7.

3709. Thomas Hinton; Richard (d); Parrish of St Andrews Holborne, M'sex; Victualler; 3.12.1683; 3.12.1683; 2.11.1702; 8.

3710. John Pickard; John; Willoughby, Leics; Cd; 6.7.1696; 6.7.1696; 2.8.1703; 7.

3711. Daniell Sell; Henry; Haucksworth, Herts; H; 6.2.1699; 6.2.1699; - ; 7.

RAWLINS, William

3712. Daniel Cook; Walter; - , Glos; - ; 3.5.1675; 3.5.1675; 8.5.1682; 7.

3713. Bryon Kitson; Willm (d); Fawley, Bucks; Cl; 2.5.1670; 2.5.1670; - ; 7.

3714. Wm Mosse; Wm; Coventry, War; I; 4.12.1682; 4.12.1682; 27.3.1693; 7.

3715. Francis Perkins; George (d); London; Coach-harnessmaker; 20.10.1699; 20.10.1699; - ; 7.

3716. Nicholas Smith; Thomas; Parish of Stepney, M'sex; Weaver; 5.8.1700; 5.8.1700; 6.10.1707; 7. Fd by Richard Janeway.

3717. Richard Snow; Richard (d); Lackerly, Wilts; H; 6.5.1672; 29.9.1671; 1.12.1679; 8.

3718. John Sutton; William; Stickfeild, Dors; Cl; 5.8.1678; 5.8.1678; 26.3.1688; 7.

RAWLINSON, Thomas

3719. Richard Ballard; Robert; London; C & BSg; 24.9.1649; 24.9.1649; 2.3.1657; 7.

3720. Wm Clement; Geo; Weston Subbidge, Glos; H; 6.12.1652; 6.12.1652; 22.12.1659; 7.

RAWORTH, Ruth, Widow
3721. James Cottrell. Fd by Mrs Raworth 3.8.1646. Bd to John Raworth 6.8.1638.
3722. Edward Hall; Arthur; Leicester, Leics; H; 5.8.1647; 5.8.1647; 4.12.1654; 7.
3723. John Raworth. Fd by patrimony 8.5.1665.
3724. Andrew Sowle; Francis; parish of St Sepulcres, London; Y; 6.7.1646; 6.7.1646; 1.8.1653; 7.

RAWSON, John
3725. Richard Owfall. Fd by Rawson, Ralph Downes and Edward Jelley 3.4.1665. Bd to Jelley (q.v.) 1.3.1658.

RAWSON, Thomas
3726. Wm Dove; William; Appleton Le Street, Yorks; Cl; 5.6.1690; 5.6.1690; - ; 7.

RAYBOLD, William
3727. Charles Raybold; John; Kinver, Staffs; Y; 2.4.1655; 25.3.1655; - ; 8.

RAYMENT, Jane
3728. Thomas Janes; William (d); Tookesbury, Glos; Felmonger; 3.6.1700; 3.6.1700; - 7.
3729. William Tayler; John; Harlow, Essex; Cl; 7.5.1694; 7.5.1694; 1.6.1702; 7.

RAYMENT, William
3730. James Goodwin; James (d); London; C & MT; 7.5.1688; 7.5.1688; 3.2.1696; 7.
3731. [William Rayment. Son of John Rayment; fd by patrimony 2.7.1680.]

REA, Francis
3732. Steven Allen; Josias; Drogtwich, Worcs; G; 6.11.1654; 6.11.1654; - ; 7.

3733. Sampson Evans; Thomas; Welland, Worcs; Cl; 5.12.1659; 5.12.1659; 5.9.1670; 7.
3734. William Rea; Anne; Mordeford, Herefs; Widow; 5.8.1672; 5.8.1672; - ; 7.

REA, George
3735. Martin Smith. Fd by Rea and Mathias Rainsford 17.10.1653. Bd to Rainsford 22.6.1640.

READ, George
3736. Christopher Hardie; Christophr; parish of St James, M'sex; - ; 4.12.1699; 4.12.1699; - ; 7.

REAKINS, Edward
3737. William Bryan; Wm; Mortlack, Surr; Waterman; 2.10.1676; 2.10.1676; - ; 7.
3738. John Lochard; Robert; St Martin in ye feilds, [M'sex]; Watchmaker; 3.7.1676; 3.7.1676; - ; 8.
3739. James Read; James; the Kingdome of Scotland; - ; 6.4.1674; 6.4.1674; - ; 7.

REDMAINE, John, I
3740. James Flory; Thomas; London; C & B; 7.2.1681; 7.2.1681; 3.5.1697; 7. Fd by Elizabeth Redmaine, widow.
3741. Thomas Lello; Thomas (d); London; C & D; 6.9.1658; 6.9.1658; - ; 8.
3742. Daniel Redmain. Fd by patrimony 4.8.1673.
3743. John Redmaine. Fd by patrimony 18.6.1677.
3744. [John Redman. Son of Richard Redmaine; fd by patrimony 21.3.1649.]
3745. William Reyner; William; London; C & St; 5.8.1672; 5.8.1672; 6.9.1680; 7.
3746. Isaiah Ward; William; London; C & J; 11.10.1680; 11.10.1680; 6.8.1688; 7. Fined 2s. 6d. 'for not being turned over at the Hall'.

3747. John Wells; John; City of Lincolne; Milliner; 1.8.1670; 1.8.1670; 5.8.1678; 8.

REDMAINE, John, II

3748. Jonathan Cotton; John; London; C & Leatherseller; 5.12.1681; 5.12.1681; 3.7.1700; 7.

3749. Thomas Orum. Fd by Redmaine 9.2.1691. Bd to Elizabeth Mallett (q.v.) 4.6.1683.

3750. Edward Price; Henry; London; Sh; 3.4.1682; 3.4.1682; 7.10. 1695; 8.

3751. William Redmayne. Fd by patrimony 5.3.1688.

3752. Richard Smith; Richard; Marston, Oxon; Y; 3.10.1681; 3.10.1681; 4.3.1689; 7. Fd by Henry Harefinch and fined 2s. 6d. 'for his being turned over'.

REDMAINE, William

3753. Richard Bassell; Richard (d); Hampstead, M'sex; Y; 3.10.1681; 3.10. 1681; 7.9.1691; 7.

3754. Edward Bird; Edward; London; C & Painterstainer; 20.12.1700; 20.12.1700; - ; 7.

3755. Wm Booker; Francis; St Clemt Danes, [Westminster]; T; 22.2.1675; 22.2.1675; 8.5.1682; 7.

3756. Samuell Copson; John (d); Cleborack, Leics; Ca; 5.6.1699; 5.6. 1699; - ; 8.

3757. Edward Ellis; Richard; London; C & Girdler; 8.6.1668; 24.6.1668; - ; 7.

3758. Thomas Greene; Robt; Cambridge; Mr; 3.3.1684; 3.3.1684; 7.8. 1693; 7.

3759. Job King; John; Tewksbury, Glos; Sc; 3.8.1674; 3.8.1674; 1.10. 1683; 7.

3760. William Nost. Fd by Redmaine and James Orme 2.12.1700. Bd to Orme (q.v.) 3.7.1693.

3761. John Peirson; George; St

Gyles Cripplegate, M'sex; Gl; 1.12. 1662; 1.12.1662; 6.12.1669; 7.

3762. [William Redmaine. Son of Edmund Redmaine; fd by patrimony 9.2.1657.]

3763. Edmund Redmayne; - ; London; C & St; 27.3.1699; 27.3.1699; - ; 8. Probably bd to his father, but his father's christian name is not given.

REISOLD, Christopher

3764. John Syms; Henry; Whitfeild, Oxon; Y; 10.1.1649; 10.1.1649; 16.1. 1656; 7. Fd by Reisold and George Calvert.

3765. Charles Tracey; Edward; London; C & Cw; 19.3.1646; 25.3.1645 [sic]; 5.6.1654; 8. The master's name is given as Reiford, and the starting date for the term of service, namely 'our Lady day last', is probably an error for 'our Lady day next'. Fd by Reisold and Richard Westbrook.

REYNOLDS, Rowland

3766. Thomas Bedford; Henry (d); St Mary Magdalens Bermondsey, [Surr]; Cook; 6.11.1671; 6.11.1671; - ; 7.

3767. Edward Byne; Edw; Pyworthie, Dev; Cl; 5.7.1669; 5.7.1669; - ; 7.

3768. John Pratt; William; Elliston, Staffs; Y; 1.3.1686; 1.3.1686; - ; 7.

3769. Thomas Reynolds; Thomas; Asston, Oxon; Cl; 11.4.1681; 11.4.1681; - ; 7.

RHODES, George

3770. Robert Gerrard; Miles (d); Wiggan, Lancs; Y; 18.11.1651; 18.11. 1651; 6.12.1658; 7.

3771. John Knowles; Willm; Burley, Yorks; Felmonger; 5.7.1669; 5.7.1669; - ; 7.

3772. Anthony Lawson; Wm; Spalford, Yorks; Y; 2.11.1646; 2.11.1646; 5.12.1653; 7.

3773. William Warner; John (d); Knasbrough, Yorks; Dy; 6.6.1664; 25.3.1664; 1.4.1672; 8. Fd as Warren.

RHODES, Henry

3774. Thomas Bever; Robert; Mortimer, Berks; Y; 27.3.1682; 27.3.1682; 2.12.1689; 7. Fd as Beaver.

3775. Benjamin Bragg; George; London; C & Leatherseller; 4.7.1687; 4.7.1687; - ; 7.

3776. Francis Fossett; Christopher; parish of St Martin in the Feilds, M'sex; Victualler; 4.7.1692; 4.7.1692; - ; 7.

3777. [Henry Rhodes. Fd by redemption 26.3.1680.]

3778. William Russell; William (d); London; Mch; 4.9.1699; 4.9.1699; - ; 7.

RHODES, Thomas

3779. Francis Buckston; Hugh; Draitwitch, Worcs; Mason; 7.5.1683; 7.5.1683; - ; 7.

3780. John Capper; Michaell (d); Westerne, Notts; Y; 7.12.1657; 7.12.1657; - ; 7.

3781. John Fenn; John; Hempton, Norf; Kemmer; 7.10.1672; 7.10.1672; 26.3.1680; 7. The father's trade is probably that of woolcomber.

3782. Walter George; George Watkings; Lanhanell, Mon; G; 7.10.1661; 7.10.1661; 6.9.1669; 7.

3783. John Hudson; Willm (d); City of Durham; G; 31.8.1668; 31.8.1668; 6.9.1675; 7.

3784. [Thomas Rhodes. Son of Matthew Rhodes; fd by patrimony 3.9.1655.]

3785. John Smith; Ambrose; Richmond, Surr; 4.10.1669; 4.10.1669; - ; 7.

RICE, Austin

3786. Daniell Griffith; John; Rowwood, Shrops; Y; 3.5.1658; 3.5.1658; - ; 7.

RICHARDS, Godfrey

3787. Thomas Dalton. Fd by Richards 7.5.1683. Apparently never formally bd.

RICHARDS, Richard

3788. [Richard Richards. Fd by redemption 2.12.1689.]

RICHARDSON, Edmund

3789. Wm Lewis; William (d); Twitminster, Som; Cl; 2.3.1691; 2.3.1691; - ; 7.

3790. Robert Smith; Henry; parish of St Bottolph Aldersgate, London; Go; 4.10.1697; 4.10.1697; 5.3.1705; 7.

RICHARDSON, John

3791. Hezekiah Cramphorne; Daniell; Bishops Stortford, Herts; Y; 6.11.1682; 6.11.1682; 13.11.1689; 7.

3792. John Craven. Fd by Richardson and Henry Fletcher 3.12.1660. Bd to Fletcher (q.v.) 7.2.1653.

3793. John Hassell; John; London; MT; 5.7.1680; 5.7.1680; 6.8.1688; 8. Fd as Halsell.

3794. Edward Maddox. Fd by Richardson 8.6.1691. Bd to John Marlow (q.v.) 5.4.1684.

3795. Peter Pike; John; Shaftesbury, Dors; Bs; 3.4.1676; 3.4.1676; 7.5.1683; 7.

3796. William Prickett; Tho; Kendall, W'land; Y; 1.6.1674; 1.6.1674; 5.7.1681; 7.

3797. Francis Pulling; Rowland; - , M'sex; - ; 3.6.1678; 3.6.1678; 6.7.1685; 8.

3798. Daniell Reynolds; Thomas (d); Bishopp Stortford, Essex; Ca; 1.2.1697; 1.2.1697; 7.8.1704; 8.

3799. John Richardson. Fd by patrimony 13.5.1678.

3800. William Richardson. Fd by patrimony 8.11.1680.

3801. Thomas Seamine; John (d); Bromeley, M'sex; G; 1.7.1678; 1.7.1678; - ; 7.

3802. Henry Tyler; Henry; Stanstead Mount Fitchet, Essex; Victualler; 1.7.1689; 1.7.1689; 6.7.1696; 7.

3803. Robert Whiskin; Miles; London; C & Cd; 8.5.1699; 8.5.1699; 3.6. 1706; 7.

3804. Tho Winstanley; Wm; Quenden, Essex; G; 1.2.1692; 1.2.1692; - ; 7.

RICHARDSON, Richard

3805. Gualter Ledsam; Richard; Causham, Wilts; G; 2.3.1657; 2.3.1657; - ; 7.

RICHARDSON, William

3806. William Andrews; William; London; C & F; 18.6.1677; 18.6.1677; 1.8.1687; 7.

3807. John Baily; John (d); London; C & MT; 4.11.1672; 4.11.1672; - ; 7.

3808. Robert Cox. Fd by Richardson and Thomas Newberry 5.9.1664. Bd to Newberry (q.v.) 2.3.1657.

3809. Francis Faram; Robert (d); Tottenham, M'sex; Bl; 1.8.1687; 24.6. 1687; 2.4.1705; 9.

3810. Richard Guning; Richard; Reading, Berks; T; 27.9.1695; 27.9. 1695; - ; 7.

3811. Tho Hanford; Wm; Darby; Mr; 9.2.1680; 9.2.1680; 7.3.1687; 7.

3812. William Hobart; Edward; Somersham, Hunts; H; 2.10.1654; 29.9.1654; 7.12.1663; 9. Fd as Hubbert.

3813. Edmund Richardson. Fd by patrimony 1.8.1687.

3814. Thomas Stocker; Thomas; London; C & St; 2.10.1699; 4.9.1699; - ; 7.

3815. William Walsor; Samuell (d); Citty of Canterbury, [Kent]; Cl; 6.11. 1682; 29.9.1682; - ; 8.

3816. Willm Whitehead; Tho; St Albones, Herts; Mi; 3.10.1670; 3.10. 1670; 4.3.1678; 7.

3817. Thomas Willmiet; Thomas; Wissall, Notts; - ; 2.3.1663; 2.3. 1663; 3.10.1670; 7. Fd as Willamott.

RICHMOND, Peter

3818. William Collyer; William (d); Trubbridge, Wilts; Cd; 8.4.1700; 8.4. 1700; 1.9.1712; 7. Fd by James Wiltshire.

3819. Ann Hill; John; London; C & Ha; 6.6.1687; 6.6.1687; - ; 7.

3820. Samll Staines; Samuell (d); Birchberry, Essex; Y; 3.7.1693; 3.7. 1693; 11.11.1700; 7.

3821. Edward Stiles; Francis (d); Kingston super Thames, Surr; Bu; 2.7.1683; 2.7.1683; 6.10.1690; 7.

3822. Thomas Tebb. Fd by Richmond 11.6.1694. Bd to John Meakins (q.v.) 2.5.1687.

3823. Robert Woolley; Robert; Bishop Stortford, Herts; G; 2.8.1680; 2.8. 1680; - ; 7.

RIDLEY, John

3824. Sol Day; Richard; Eastbatshold, Suff; Clothier; 22.6.1653; 22.6. 1653; - ; 7.

RITHERDEN, William

3825. [William Ritherden. Son of Ambrose Ritherden; fd by patrimony 1.8.1659.]

RIX, John

3826. Richard Hiller; John; - , Wilts; Y; 8.11.1680; 8.11.1680; 7.7. 1690; 7. T.o. (n.d.) to Sampson Chaplaine and fd by him, but fined 2s. 6d. 'for not being turned ouer att the Hall'.

3827. William Jones; Henry; Warley Hall, Essex; Y; 10.9.1677; 10.9. 1677; 6.6.1687; 7.

3828. George Mortimer; George; Marleborough, Wilts; G; 5.7.1675; 5.7.1675; 2.6.1684; 7.

3829. Matthias Tooth; John; St Giles, M'sex; Cooper; 2.6.1679; 2.6. 1679; - ; 7.

ROBERTS, Edwin

3830. William Bowman; Alexander; Swarbey, Lincs; Mason; 2.6.1656; 2.6. 1656; - ; 7.

3831. Richard Wright; John; Ancaster, Lincs; T; 6.3.1648; 6.3.1648; - ; 8.

ROBERTS, Jasper

3832. Francis Pyke; Francis (d); Pewsey, Wilts; Y; 4.9.1699; 4.9.1699; 4.11.1706; 7.

3833. Thomas Welton; Thomas; parish of Christ Church, London; Bl; 5.6.1699; 5.6.1699; - ; 8.

ROBERTS, John

3834. Shipwash Duckett; Henry (d); London; C & Mr; 12.6.1666; 12.6.1666; - ; 8.

3835. Samuel Nash; Lancelott (d); Lambourne, Essex; Y; 5.5.1673; 5.5.1673; 6.3.1682; 7.

ROBERTS, Robert

3836. John Barriffe; Henry; Flitton, N'hants; H; 4.6.1694; 4.6.1694; 2.6.1701; 7.

3837. Samuel Bryan; William; Scalford, Leics; Doctor in Physick; 3.11.1690; 3.11.1690; - ; 7.

3838. Simon Clarke; William; Warwick, War; G; 7.3.1692; 7.3.1692; - ; 7.

3839. Sam Darker; Sam; London; F; 3.11.1679; 3.11.1679; 8.11.1686; 7.

3840. William Johnson; Wm (d); Garnsey, S'hants; Cl; 4.12.1699; 4.12.1699; - ; 7.

3841. Humphrey Martin. Fd by Roberts 5.8.1689, but fined 2s. 6d. 'for being bound by a Forraine Indentr'.

3842. Michael Martin. T.o. from Anne Maxwell to Roberts (n.d.) Bd to Mrs Maxwell (q.v.) 7.4.1679 and fd by her 3.3.1690.

3843. Dorman Newman; Hugh; Reading, Berks; - ; 2.4.1683; 2.4.1683; 7.4.1690; 7.

3844. Samuel Noone. Fd by Roberts 6.5.1689. T.o. to Roberts but the name of Noone's original master is left blank. Fined 2s. 6d. 'For his not

being turned over at this Comys Hall'.

3845. Christopher Norbury; John; Brampton, Hunts; E; 6.2.1699; 6.2.1699; 4.3.1706; 7.

3846. Mathew Reynolds. Fd by Roberts 15.2.1700. Apparently never formally bd.

3847. James Roberts. Fd by patrimony 7.11.1692.

3848. Jasper Roberts. Fd by patrimony 6.5.1695.

3849. Nevill Simonds. Fd by Roberts 15.2.1700. Apparently never formally bd but see entry No. 1804.

3850. Robert Stafford. T.o. from Anne Maxwell to Roberts (n.d.). Bd to Mrs Maxwell (q.v.) 8.5.1682 and fd by her 5.5.1690.

3851. James Stile; John; Dorchester, Dors; Gardener; 7.11.1692; 7.11.1692; 4.12.1688; 7.

3852. John Talbott; John (d); London; C & Plumber; 8.4.1700; 8.4.1700; 9.6.1707; 7.

3853. Joseph Whitehead; Benjamin; Purton, Wilts; Y; 7.8.1699; 7.8.1699; - ; 7.

ROBERTS, William

3854. John Frowde; Cuthbert; Warminster; Wilts; S; 5.8.1650; 5.8.1650; - ; 7.

3855. Gawen Langford; Wm; Gussage St Andrew, Dors; G; 24.11.1645; 24.11.1645; - ; 7.

3856. Wm Semyn; Francis; London; G; 2.4.1649; 25.3.1649; - ; 9.

3857. Thomas Weekes; Thomas (d); London; C & Ha; 11.2.1646; 11.2.1646; - ; 9.

3858. Richard Wood; Hattill; Eydon, N'hants; G; 10.1.1650; 29.9.1649; - ; 8.

ROBINSON, Humphrey

3859. Jherom Farley; Roger; Herreford, Herefs; G; 5.9.1664; 5.9.1664; - ; 8.

3860. Thomas Hacker; Thomas (d); London; C & Gr; 20.5.1656; 24.3.1656; 4.4.1664; 8.

3861. John Martyn. Fd by Robinson 1.3.1643. Bd to him 4.2.1635.

3862. Barnard Robinson; Barnard; Torpenhow, Cumb; Cl; 6.8.1651; 24.6.1651; 18.12.1658; 8.

3863. Francis Robinson; Bernard; Torpenna, Cumb; Cl; 10.12.1653; 10.12.1653; - ; 7.

3864. Titus Robinson; George; Newport, Mon; Cl; 3.3.1668; 3.3.1668; 5.8.1678; 7. T.o. 12.8.1671. to Francis Smith and fd by him.

3865. Thomas Young; William; St Giles=Wimborne, Dors; Cl; 10.5.1641; 1.5.1641; 7.5.1649; 8.

ROBINSON, Jonathan

3866. William Abbinton; Thomas; Beminster, Dors; G; 12.8.1671; 12.8.1671; 6.10.1678; 7. Fd as Abbington.

3867. Thomas Atkinson; Richard (d); London; C & Sk; 6.11.1699; 6.11.1699; - ; 7.

3868. John King; Francis; Hempsted, Herts; - ; 7.12.1691; 7.12.1691; 5.6.1699; 7.

3869. Richard Mayne; John (d); Plymouth, Dev; Mch; 8.5.1682; 8.5.1682; - ; 7.

3870. Robert Maysent; Joseph (d); Hatfeild, Essex; G; 7.7.1679; 7.7.1679; - ; 7.

3871. John Wyatt; Hen; Berrivil alias Parvil, M'sex; - ; 1.10.1683; 1.10.1683; 3.11.1690; 7.

ROBINSON, Josiah

3872. John Alife; John (d); Rochford, Essex; Apothecary; 20.11.1672; 20.11.1672; - ; 7.

3873. John Lawrence; Christopher; Cane, Dors; Cl; 7.2.1670; 7.2.1670; 5.3.1677; 7.

ROBINSON, Thomas

3874. John Spark; Geo; Hulton,

Bishop=Prick of Durham, [Lancs]; - ; 2.7.1677; 2.7.1677; 6.10.1684; 7. Fd as Sparkes.

ROBINSON, Titus

3875. John Merrey; Thomas (d); Citty of Worster; Y; 7.5.1683; 7.5.1683; - ; 8.

ROCKALL, Abel

3876. John Chalfont; John (d); Chippen Wickham, Bucks; G; 3.7.1682; 3.7.1682; - ; 8.

3877. William Gray; John; High Wickcome, Bucks; Bu; 4.12.1693; 4.12.1693; 7.7.1701; 7. Fd by Rockall and Robert Whitledge.

3878. William Rockall; William (d); Parrish of High Wickham, Bucks; G; 1.3.1686; 1.3.1686; 4.9.1693; 7. Fd by William Hawkins.

3879. Robert Whitledge. Fd by Rockall 7.11.1687. Bd to Allen Foord (q.v.) 11.10.1680 and fined 2s. 6d. 'for not being turned over at the Hall'.

ROCKALL, William

3880. Isum Bennett; Charles (d); London; C & Bl; 8.5.1699; 8.5.1699; 1.7.1706; 7.

ROGERS, Michael

3881. John Harvie; John (d); London; C & Cd; 14.10.1641; 14.10.1641; - ; 9.

3882. John Violett; Thomas; London; C & MT; 5.3.1649; 5.3.1649; - ; 7.

ROGERS, Richard

3883. Robert Collis. Fd by Rogers 22.7.1648. Bd to him 28.9.1637.

ROGERS, William

3884. Edmund Herringman; Edmund (d); London; Hosier; 5.3.1694; 5.3.1694; - ; 7.

3885. Thomas Longland; Thomas; Ipsden, Oxon; G; 5.9.1681; 5.9.1681; - ; 7.

3886. John Pemberton; John; Croyden, Surr; Barber; 3.6.1700; 3.6.1700;
7.7.1707; 7.

3887. Benjamen Tooke; Benjamen;
London; C & St; 5.9.1687; 5.9.1687;
4.3.1695; 7.

ROOKES, Thomas

3888. John Barrett; John; Bedlam,
- ; - ; 4.4.1664; 4.4.1664; - ; 7.

3889. John Clark; Thomas; London;
C & Ha; 6.9.1669; 24.6.1669; - ; 8.

3890. John Collis; William (d);
London; C & Ca; 12.7.1658; 12.7.1658;
- ; 7.

3891. Benjamin Monger; John; Tunbridge, Kent; - ; 24.9.1674; 24.9.
1674; - ; 7.

3892. Robert Paske; Clemt; Castle
Hereford, Essex; Mr; 11.2.1661; 11.2.
1661; 7.4.1668; 7.

3893. Samuell Withers; Edward;
London; C & Leatherseller; 7.8.1666;
16.7.1666; - ; 7.

3894. Thomas Wright; Tho; Church
Horniburn, Worcs; Cl; 1.2.1675; 1.2.
1675; 6.3.1682; 7. Fd 'By Order of the
Lord Majors Court of Aldermen dated
the Second of March. 1681 [= 1682]'.

ROPER, Abel

3895. Thomas Dring. Fd by Roper
7.8.1648. Bd to him 5.10.1640.

3896. Christopher Eccleston; Robert;
Landen Grange, Bucks; E; 5.9.1653;
24.8.1653; 4.11.1661; 8.

3897. Henry Herringman; John (d);
Kessalton, Surr; Y; 20.1.1645; 1.8.
1644; 28.6.1652; 8.

3898. John Isted; Samuell; London;
C & Tallowchandler; 7.12.1696; 2.11.
1696; 8.11.1703; 7.

3899. Richard Mendall; Richard
(d); London; Porter; 5.9.1698; 5.9.
1698; 3.12.1705; 7.

3900. Marma Moore; Edward; Bar-
wick vpon Tweed; G; 28.9.1652; 28.9.
1652; - ; 8.

3901. Thomas Orrell; Thomas; Tamworth, Staffs; G; 4.12.1671; 1.11.1671;
- ; 7.

3902. Matthew Peryn; Samuel;
Littleham, Dev; Cl; 4.12.1648; 1.12.
1649 [*sic*]; - ; 8. The starting date
for the term of service, namely 'the
first of Decbr: next', is presumably an
error for 'the first of Decbr: last'.

3903. Abel Roper; Isaack; Ather-
ston, War; - ; 6.10.1679; 6.10.1679;
7.11.1687; 8. Described in the entry of
freedom as servant to Christopher
Wilkinson and fined 2s. 6d. 'for his
being turned over to Mr Wilkinson not
at the Hall'.

3904. Francis Saunders; Francis (d);
London; - ; 4.12.1676; 4.12.1676;
19.12.1683; 7. Fd by Henry Herringman.

3905. John Weaver; Edmund (d);
London; C & St; 5.10.1657; 29.9.1657;
31.1.1666; 8.

ROTHWELL, Andrew

3906. Edward Chase; Jo (d); Cald-
cott, Cambs; G; 7.7.1651; 7.7.1651;
- ; 8.

3907. Thomas Cushey; Thomas;
Marketstreet, Beds; I; 5.6.1654; 5.6.
1654; 10.6.1661; 7.

3908. Willm Elliott; Hugh (d); London; C & Ha; 7.4.1668; 24.6.1668;
- ; 7.

3909. Henry Hougton; Henry; Newbery, Berks; Ha; 2.8.1669; 29.9.1669;
- ; 7.

3910. Timothy Pierce; William (d);
Newberry, Berks; D; 4.6.1660; 4.6.
1660; - ; 7.

3911. John Taylor; John; Geydon,
War; Y; 7.7.1656; 7.7.1656; - ; 8.

3912. Henry Tidd; Rich (d); Wellin,
Herts; Cl; 1.3.1652; 1.3.1652; - ; 8.

ROTHWELL, John, I

3913. Robert Penn; Wm; London;
G; 1.3.1641; 25.12.1640; 4.3.1649; 8.

3914. Andrew Rothwell. Fd by patrimony 4.2.1650.

3915. Michael Shawley. Fd by Rothwell 16.5.1642. Bd to him 1.12.1634.

ROTHWELL, John, II
3916. William Barrett; Wm (d);
Ireland; Cl; 1.8.1642; 24.6.1642; 4.10.
1652; 8.
3917. Richard Erpe; Fran (d); Lynn,
Staffs; G; 3.9.1655; 3.9.1655; - ; 8.
3918. Wm Grantham. Fd by Rothwell 3.2.1645. Bd to him 7.8.1637.
3919. Jeremy Heirons; Michaell;
London; C & MT; 6.12.1647; 24.6.
1647; 3.9.1655; 8.

ROTHWELL, William
3920. John Walmesley; James; London; C & Leatherseller; 9.2.1642; 10.1.
1642; 24.3.1649; 8.
3921. Wm Weekeley. Fd by Rothwell 2.11.1646. Bd to him 3.9.1638.

ROYCROFT, Samuel
3922. John Dighton; Thomas; London; C & S; 2.3.1685; 2.3.1685; - ;
7.
3923. Henry Smith; Henry (d); London; Mariner; 6.6.1681; 6.6.1681;
2.10.1693; 7.
3924. Thomas Tayler; Thomas;
Woollavington, Som; Y; 26.3.1683;
26.3.1683; - ; 7.
3925. Henry Wythins; John; London; C & Ha; 4.11.1678; 4.11.1678;
- ; 7.

ROYCROFT, Thomas
3926. Thomas Austin; Thomas;
Broadway, Worcs; G; 7.2.1676; 7.2.
1676; 26.3.1683; 7.
3927. Thomas Braddyll; Edward;
Bragbourne, Lancs; G; 5.2.1672; 5.2.
1672; 3.3.1679; 7.
3928. Christopher Darby; Christopher (d); Winchester, S'hants; Mch;
7.7.1673; 7.7.1673; - ; 8.
3929. Robert Edwards; - ; - ,
- ; G; 7.12.1674; 7.12.1674; 6.2.
1682; 7.

3930. William Edwards; William;
Wollavington, Som; - ; 12.2.1666;
12.2.1666; 3.3.1673; 7.
3931. James Gregory; James (d);
London; C & Ha; 6.6.1659; 6.6.1659;
- ; 7.
3932. Henry Hyett; Nath; Wins-
comb, Glos; Mr; 2.12.1650; 2.12.1650;
- ; 8.
3933. Thomas Pattenden; John (d);
Nettlested, Kent; Cl; 6.10.1651; 6.10.
1651; 6.12.1658; 7.
3934. William Rider; William (d);
London; G; 27.7.1660; 27.7.1660;
- ; 7.
3935. Samuel Roycroft. Fd by patrimony 10.9.1677.
3936. Nathaniell Serjeant; John (d);
Owld, N'hants; Mr; 3.12.1667; 3.12.
1667; 22.12.1675; 8.
3937. Thomas Taylor; Richard;
Worcester City, Worcs; Cl; 4.10.1669;
4.10.1669; 2.10.1693; 7.

ROYSTON, Richard
3938. Maurice Athens; William;
Citty of Oxon; Bu; 3.11.1662; 3.11.
1662; 8.11.1669; 7. Fd as Atkins.
3939. Robert Clavell; Roger (d);
Isle of Purbeck, Dors; G; 11.3.1650;
11.3.1650; 11.3.1657; 7.
3940. James Collins; Tho; Samford,
Dev; Cl; 3.9.1655; 24.6.1665; 30.6.
1663; 8.
3941. Wm Curteyne; Wm; Kenning-
ton, Berks; Y; 17.1.1648; 25.12.1647;
- ; 8.
3942. Charles Dawson; Thomas (d);
Ardington, Yorks; G; 6.11.1671; 6.11.
1671; - ; 7.
3943. Thomas Flesher; Thomas; Otley, Yorks; Y; 6.9.1669; 6.9.1669; 6.11.
1676; 7.
3944. Anthony Haviland; Thomas
(d); London; C & St; 18.1.1647; 18.1.
1647; 4.8.1656; 7.
3945. William Hensman; William;
parish of St Sepulchers, London; Book-

binder; 7.9.1663; 7.9.1663; 4.7.1670; 7.

3946. William Longmore; Thomas; Kinver, Staffs; Y; 22.8.1648; 25.7.1648; - ; 8.

3947. Luke Meredith. Fd by Royston 13.5.1684. Bd to Jonathan Edwyn (q.v.) 7.5.1677.

3948. Edwd Pepys; Saml; Cliffton, Bucks; Cl; 6.8.1683; 6.8.1683; 3.11.1690; 7. Pepys was t.o. (n.d.) to Henry Mortlock and fd by him but fined 2s. 6d. 'for not being turned over at the Hall'.

3949. Richard Pokins; John; Denton, Oxon; G; 9.2.1674; 9.2.1674; - ; 7.

3950. Charles Selby; James; Wandon, Bucks; - ; 2.6.1679; 2.6.1679; - ; 7.

RUMBALL, Edmund

3951. Stephen Butcher; Stephen; parish of St Paul Covent Garden, M'sex; Victualler; 5.6.1699; 5.6.1699; - ; 7.

3952. Daniell Wells; Stephen; London; C & Bl; 6.2.1682; 6.2.1682; - ; 7.

RYLAND, Thomas

3953. Richard Walker; Thomas (d); Quinton, Glos; H; 2.4.1660; 2.4.1660; - ; 7.

SABIN, John

3954. John Parradine; Geo (d); Bedford, Beds; Linendraper; 1.10.1655; 1.10.1655; - ; 8.

SADLER, Theodore

3955. Mathew Turner; Thomas; Towne of Monmouth; Y; 6.4.1663; 6.4.1663; 5.12.1670; 7.

SALISBURY, John

3956. Samuell Ballard; Samuell (d); Coventry, [War]; Clothier; 4.9.1693; 4.9.1693; 3.3.1701; 7. Fd by Salisbury and John Nicholson.

SALISBURY, Thomas

3957. Wm Turnbull; John (d); Edenburgh, Scotland; G; 5.6.1690; 5.6.1690; - ; 7.

SALSBY, Nicholas

3958. Thomas Graygoose; William (d); Bengoe, Herts; Y; 7.6.1641; 1.3.1641; - ; 8.

3959. John Jenkes; Ambrose; Woodstanway, Glos; Cl; 4.5.1641; 4.5.1641; 3.9.1649; 8.

3960. John Taylor; John; Burford, Oxon; Sh; 6.9.1647; 24.6.1647; - ; 8.

SAMPSON, Jacob

3961. Roch Gary; John; Westminster; Brewer's Clerk; 8.11.1680; 8.11.1680; - ; 7.

SARE, Richard

3962. Thomas Isaac; Philip (d); Carlow, Ireland; Mch; 3.10.1692; 3.10.1692; - ; 7.

3963. Thomas Leving; Francis (d); London; C & D; 1.9.1684; 1.9.1684; - ; 7.

3964. Thomas Stevens. Fd by Sare 2.8.1697. Apparently never formally bd.

3965. Richard Williamson; Thomas (d); Kirkby-Stephen, W'land; Mch; 7.8.1699; 7.8.1699; - ; 7.

SARE, Thomas

3966. Edward Payne; Edward (d); Derby; Cl; 9.1.1671; 9.1.1671; 7.11.1687; 7.

SATTERTHWAITE, Humphrey

3967. William Bancks; William; London; C & Cw; 5.3.1660; 5.3.1660; - ; 7.

3968. Isaac Bowles; Isaac; London; C & Sk; 6.11.1671; 6.11.1671; - ; 7.

3969. John Brenson; John; London; C & MT; 7.11.1664; 7.10.1664; 6.11.1671; 7.

3970. John Burton; John; Fosbrooke, Staffs; Mr; 2.10.1654; 2.10.1654; 7.10.1661; 7.

3971. Thomas Giles; Simon; London; C & Farrier; 7.6.1658; 7.6.1658; - ; 7.

3972. Henry Hodges; Henry (d); London; C & Cw; 4.11.1661; 10.10. 1661; - ; 8.

3973. Thomas Sanden; Thomas; Citty of Chichester, Sussex; Y; 2.8. 1680; 2.8.1680; - ; 7.

3974. Robert Satterthwait; Humphrey; London; C & St; 7.3.1670; 7.3. 1670; - ; 7. Bd to his father.

3975. Andrewe Satterthwaite; Richard (d); London; C & St; 3.5.1669; 3.5.1669; 7.10.1672; 7. Fd by patrimony.

3976. William Stevenson; Willm; Abington, Berks; Mr; 7.10.1672; 7.10. 1672; - ; 7.

SATTERTHWAITE, Richard

3977. Lawrence Alman; Lawrence; London; C & Go; 10.6.1661; 24.6. 1661; - ; 8.

3978. James Barker; Richard; Standish, Lancs; Cl; 1.5.1654; 1.5.1654; - ; 7.

3979. Robert Dicher; Robert; Shawbury, Shrops; I; 5.1.1657; 5.1.1657; - ; 7.

3980. Andrew Nicholson. Fd by Satterthwaite 6.5.1644. Bd to him 26.3.1636.

3981. Humfrey Satterthwaite. Fd by patrimony 1.12.1651.

3982. John Satterthwaite. Fd by patrimony 3.4.1665.

SATTERTHWAITE, Samuel

3983. Roger Bartlett; Roger; Watleton, Oxon; Sh; 18.1.1647; 24.6.1647; 27.6.1654; 7.

3984. Roger Cox; John; Beineham, Suff; G; 14.6.1652; 24.6.1652; - ; 7.

3985. Richard Haynes; Richard; Chinner, Oxon; Mr; 7.7.1645; 7.7. 1645; 2.8.1652; 7.

SAUNDERS, Francis

3986. Bennet Banbury; Cyprian; Knipton, Leics; Cl; 18.8.1692; 18.8. 1692; - ; 7.

3987. Edward North. Bd to Joseph Knight (q.v.) 6.4.1685; t.o. 7.10.1689 to Saunders.

3988. Thomas Whitehand; Tho (d); Little Wilbram, Cambs; G; 25.6.1688; 25.6.1688; - ; 8.

SAVILLE, George

3989. William Inglish; Robert (d); London; C & Mr; 1.4.1672; 1.4.1672; 3.11.1679; 7. Fd as English by Nathaniel Ponder.

3990. Thomas Rogers; Thomas; Hunsden, Herts; Y; 4.11.1668; 4.11. 1668; - ; 7. Entry deleted; m.n. 'Crossed out by Order of Cort of the First of Aprill. 1672.'.

SAWBRIDGE, George

3991. Abraham Ambler; John (d); Ledbury, [Herefs]; Cl; 5.12.1659; 1.5. 1659; 4.6.1667; 8.

3992. Thomas Bickerton; Thomas; Barkby Thorpe, Leics; G; 7.9.1696; 7.9.1696; 6.8.1705; 7.

3993. John Braynt; John; London; Dy; 3.9.1655; 1.6.1655; - ; 8.

3994. Willm Brownwick; John (d); Ilmorton, War; H; 1.1.1668; 1.1.1668; 1.2.1675; 7. Fd as Bromwich.

3995. Awnsham Churchill; William; Dorchester, [Oxon]; Bs; 4.5.1674; 4.5.1674; 6.6.1681; 7.

3996. Augustin Dry; Augustin; London; C & Cw; 1.7.1672; 1.7.1672; - ; 7.

3997. Thomas Sawbridge; William; Helmorton, War; 2.8.1658; 24.6.1658; 16.7.1666; 8.

3998. Thomas Sawbridge. Fd by patrimony 2.11.1685.

3999. Seward Wade; Willm (d); Dorchester, Dors; Mch; 10.1.1670; 10.1.1670; - ; 7.

4000. Richard Wylde; Richard; Abedore, Herefs; G; 26.3.1679; 26.3.1679; 4.4.1687; 8. Fd by the executors of George Sawbridge.

SAWBRIDGE, Hannah, Widow

4001. Thomas Barnard; Thomas; Abbadoore, Herts [*sic* for Herefs]; G; 3.11.1684; 3.11.1684; - ; 7.

4002. John Eves; Edward; Wallsall, Staffs; Ironmonger: 4.9.1682; 4.9.1682; - ; 7. Bd to the widow of George Sawbridge.

SAWBRIDGE, Thomas

4003. Isaack Hughes; Hugh; Bosby, Herefs; Y; 4.8.1679; 4.8.1679; 6.12.1686; 7.

4004. Job Kellington; Richard; Wheldrick, Yorks; Cl; 1.2.1675; 1.2.1675; 6.2.1682; 7.

4005. Robert Parris; William; London; C & D; 5.10.1685; 5.10.1685; 10.9.1694; 7.

4006. George Sawbridge. Fd by patrimony 4.8.1690.

4007. Willm Sawbridge; Willm; Hill Morton, War; H; 1.8.1670; 1.8.1670; 1.10.1677; 7.

SAYWELL, John

4008. Edward Archer. Fd by Saywell and William Hope 3.4.1654. Bd to Hope (q.v.) 6.4.1646.

4009. George Madden; James (d); London; C & Apothecary; 5.6.1654; 5.6.1654; - ; 7. Fd as Middon.

4010. John Starkey; George; Isleywalton, Leics; G; 9.11.1646; 9.11.1646; 6.11.1655; 8. Fd by Saywell and Luke Fawne.

SAYWELL, William

4011. Margrett Hebb; Adrian (d); London; C & Ha; 2.10.1671; 2.10.1671; - ; 7.

SCIENCE, John

4012. John Science; John (d); Tetsworth, Oxon; Y; 19.11.1695; 19.11.1695; 7.12.1702; 7.

SCOTT, Robert

[The following note appears under date 5.12.1687: 'Mr. Scotts man turned over to Adiel Mills'. It probably refers to Charles Hoffman.]

4013. Samuell Carr; Edward; London; C & BSg; 2.8.1669; 2.8.1669; 6.11.1676; 7.

4014. Peter Hills; Henry; London; C & St; 2.11.1674; 2.11.1674; - ; 8.

4015. Charles Hoffman; John (d); parish of Saint Paules Covent Garden, M'sex; G; 3.12.1684; 29.9.1684; - ; 8.

4016. Ben Walford; Ralph; London; C & MT; 7.4.1679; 7.4.1679; 3.5.1686; 7.

SCOTT, Samuel

4017. Leonard Parker; John; London; C & D; 6.11.1693; 6.11.1693; 3.2.1701; 7.

SEALE, Thomas

4018. Charles Seale. Fd by patrimony 9.9.1689.

4019. John Seale. Fd by patrimony 31.1.1679.

4020. Richard Seale. Fd by patrimony 8.6.1691.

4021. William Seale. Fd by patrimony 11.10.1680.

SEALEING, Mary

4022. [Mary Sealeing. Daughter of William Sealeing; fd by patrimony 7.12.1674.]

SEARLE, Samuel

4023. John Angell; John (d); Beare Church, Essex; H; 1.6.1657; 24.6.1657; - ; 8.

4024. Thomas Greene; John (d); Epping, Essex; G; 1.3.1642; 25.12.1641; 23.6.1652; 7. Fd by Francis Searle.

4025. Richard Joad; Richard (d); Westmawlin, Kent; G; 26.3.1651; 26.3.1651; 6.12.1658; 7.

SEDGWICK, John

4026. Philip Langley; Richard; Hackney, M'sex; Cl; 1.10.1677; 1.10.1677; - ; 7.

SEILE, Ruben
4027. [Ruben Seile. Son of Robert Seile; fd by patrimony 6.5.1695.]

SELLER, John
4028. Jeremiah Lathum; Thomas (d); Stifford Hall, Essex; G; 7.2.1687; 7.2.1687; - ; 7.
4029. [John Seller. Fd by patrimony 26.3.1686.]

SEYLE, Henry
4030. Richard Allington; Adrian (d); Burbidge, Leics; G; 3.9.1660; 3.9.1660; - ; 7.
4031. Thomas Gournay; Francis (d); London; C & MT; 6.5.1651; 24.6.1650; - ; 9.
4032. Wm Palmer; Francis, Saddington, Leics; G; 23.6.1652; 23.6.1652; 27.6.1659; 7.
4033. Henry Seile; John; Oslaston, Derby; Y; 2.10.1643; 2.10.1643; 7.10.1650; 7.
4034. Christopher Wilkinson; John; Gorefield, Bucks; Grazier; 5.10.1657; 5.10.1657; 5.12.1664; 7.

SHARLAKER, Richard
4035. Henry Dale. Fd by Sharlaker 1.3.1642. Bd to him 1.12.1634.

SHARPE, Henry
4036. Peter Whaley. Fd by Sharpe 2.7.1645. Apparently never formally bd.

SHAWLER, Edward
4037. Thomas Hanson; Lewis; Harwell, Berks; Mr; 6.4.1657; 6.4.1657; 2.5.1664; 7.

SHEARES, Margaret, Widow
4038. Simon Neale; Robert (d); St Brides, London; Distiller; 6.6.1664; 6.6.1664; 5.8.1672; 8.

SHEARES, William
4039. John Holden. Fd by Sheares 3.3.1651. Apparently never formally bd.
4040. Robert Miller; Robt; Cambridge; I; 11.6.1655; 11.6.1655; - ; 8.

4041. William Sheares. Fd by patrimony 31.3.1656.

SHEELES, William
4042. Thomas Cater; Thomas; Ospringe, Kent; Cl; 2.11.1658; 2.11.1658; - ; 7.

SHELDEN, Joan
4043. William Mason; Tho (d); Beeston, Ches; H; 6.10.1656; 6.10.1656; - ; 7.

SHELDEN, Robert
4044. Robte Spencer; Thomas; Budbrooke, War; Cl; 7.12.1646; 7.12.1646; 10.1.1654; 7.

SHELDENSLOW, Dorothy
4045. [Dorothy Sheldenslow. Fd by redemption 26.3.1688, paying £5.]

SHELL, George
4046. William Pullman; Samuel (d); Parish of St Botolph without Aldgate, London; Ropemaker; 4.7.1687; 4.6.1687; - ; 8.
4047. Robert Smith; Thomas (d); Edmundthorpe, Leics; Y; 3.3.1684; 3.3.1684; 2.12.1700; 7.

SHEPHERD, Henry
4048. Richard Pistell; Wm; Haughton, Dors; Cl; 3.9.1655; 3.9.1655; 3.11.1662; 7.
4049. Leonard Rawson; James; Aron in the Isle of Purbeck; Cl; 3.10.1642; 3.10.1642; - ; 7.

SHEPPARD, John
4050. Walter Afflett; Walter; Heddington, Oxon; Y; 5.6.1671; 5.6.1671; - ; 7.
4051. Elizabeth Hammond; John; London; C & Cw; 3.8.1674; 3.8.1674; - ; 7.

SHEPPARD, Thomas
4052. Symon Burges. Fd by Sheppard 4.3.1689. Bd to George Calvert (q.v.) 6.2.1682.
4053. Christopher Gardyner; William; Croyden, Surr; G; 3.8.1691; 3.8.1691; - ; 7.

4054. Samuell Hodgson; Thomas; London; C & Patternmaker; 10.9.1694; 10.9.1694; 1.9.1701; 7.

4055. Samuel Jones. Bd to John Tottenham, Citizen and Merchantailor of London, for 8 years from 14.10. 1679; t.o. 7.2.1687 to Sheppard and fd by him 4.9.1688.

4056. Edward Sheppard; Richard; - , Derby; Y; 5.2.1683; 5.2.1683; 5.6.1690; 8.

4057. Henry Vernon; Henry (d); London; C & Mr; 6.2.1693; 6.2.1693; - ; 7.

4058. Wm Watson; Francis (d); Graseley, Derby; H; 2.12.1689; 2.12. 1689; - ; 7.

SHERMAN, Thomas

4059 John Rosewell; James; Combhay, Som; Clothier; 1.7.1672; 1.7.1672; - ; 7.

4060. [Thomas Sherman. Son of Luke Sherman; fd by patrimony 6.2. 1671.]

4061. Henry Vynicomb; Thomas; Paultemore, Dev; Y; 4.3.1672; 4.3. 1672; - ; 7.

SHERRINGTON, William

4062. Robert Barber; Thomas; London; C & Carman; 22.2.1675; 22.2. 1675; - ; 7.

4063. Richard Boddington; Nicholas; Churchover, War; H; 5.4.1669; 5.4.1669; 7.6.1676; 7. Fd as Bonnington.

4064. Thomas Burt; John; London; C & Ha; 3.10.1642; 3.10.1642; - ; 8.

4065. George De la Hay; Timothy (d); London; C & MT; 4.10.1675; 4.10.1675; 4.2.1683; 8. Fd as Delannoy.

4066. Robert Smith; Henry; London; C & Ha; 27.4.1646; 27.4.1646; 1.5.1654; 8. Fd by Sherrington and William Bourden.

SHIRLEY, Benjamin

4067. Richard Bassett; Edward;

Brownes Over, War; Y; 7.6.1676; 7.6.1676; - ; 7.

4068. [Benjamin Shirley. Fd by redemption 7.6.1675.]

SHOTWELL, Joseph

4069. William Franklin; William (d); parish of St Andrew Holborne, M'sex; L; 8.5.1693; 8.5.1693; - ; 7.

4070. Roger Graetrake; James (d); Edmonton, M'sex; Ca; 8.5.1693; 8.5. 1693; - ; 7.

SHREWSBURY, William

4071. Stephen Foster; Solomon; Mayfeild, Sussex; Mr; 6.11.1671; 6.11. 1671; 2.12.1678; 7. T.o. 9.2.1674 to George Calvert, but fd by Mrs Taylor.

4072. Charles King; Giles (d); parish of St Margaretts Westminster; G; 3.8.1696; 3.8.1696; - ; 7.

4073. Theodore Shortgrave; William; Halson, N'hants; - ; 16.1. 1665; 16.1.1665; - ; 7.

4074. Thomas Shrewsbury; John (d); Plumpton, N'hants; J; 8.11.1686; 8.11.1686; - ; 7.

4075. James Steward; Rowland; London; C & Pw; 9.9.1700; 9.9.1700; - ; 7.

4076. Henry Tollett; William; Saint Clements Danes, [Westminster]; G; 4.8.1684; 4.8.1684; - ; 7.

SHRIMPTON, John

4077. Jeremiah Bayly; Acquillah; High Wickham, Bucks; Weaver; 8.5. 1682; 8.5.1682; 9.2.1691; 7.

4078. John Phillipps; John (d); London; C & Silkthrowster; 1.10.1694; 1.10.1694; 7.7.1707; 7. Rebd to Edmond Beresford (q.v.) 8.4.1700 and fd by him.

4079. Zachariah Poor; 'Parish Child of the parish of St. Peter le Poor in Broadstreete London'; 8.6.1691; 8.6. 1691; - ; 8.

4080. Edward Wills; Mathew (d); Eovill, Som; Cl; 6.2.1671; 6.2.1671; - ; 7.

SILVESTER, Joshua

4081. George Salter; George; London; C & Gr; 7.3.1698; 7.3.1698; 4.6.1705; 7.

SIMONS, Mary, Widow

4082. Jessey Bruce; Thomas; London; C & Armorer; 7.7.1656; 7.7.1656; 7.9.1663; 7.

4083. Thomas Harvey; William; City of Worcester; Clothier; 1.7.1661; 29.9.1661; - ; 7.

4084. John Hervey; Robert (d); London; C & Glazier; 6.8.1667; 6.8. 1667; - ; 7. Mary Simons is described as the widow of Matthew Simons.

4085. John Round; John (d); London; C & Bricklayer; 3.7.1654; 3.7. 1654; - ; 7.

SIMONS, Matthew

4086. Wm Browne; Alex (d); London; C & D; 27.4.1646; 1.5.1646; - ; 7.

4087. Edward Chapman; Edward (d); London; Sc; 6.12.1647; 6.12.1647; - ; 8.

4088. Christopher Shelton; Thomas; London; C & Tallowchandler; 2.7. 1649; 25.12.1649; 2.3.1657; 7.

4089. Sam Simons. Fd by patrimony 3.3.1662.

4090. Charles Sumptner; George; London; G; 4.11.1641; 4.11.1641; 6.11. 1648; 7.

4091. Nicholas Symmons; John; old Stratford, N'hants; Y; 3.12.1649; 1.1. 1650; 5.1.1657; 7.

SIMONS, Nevill

4092. Samuell Clark; John (d); Kedderminster, Worcs; Cl; 7.10.1661; 7.10.1661; 3.4.1671; 7.

4093. John Freeman; Richard; Newington Greene, M'sex; G; 4.5.1674; 4.5.1674; - ; 7.

4094. John Kidgell; Tho; towne of Cambridge; Y; 2.6.1673; 2.6.1673; 7.7.1680; 7.

4095. Gerrard Langbane; Gerrard; Citty of Oxford; - ; 4.3.1672; 1.2. 1672; - ; 8.

4096. Joseph Milborne; Luke (d); Roxwell, War; Cl; 7.6.1669; 7.6.1669; - ; 7.

4097. Thomas Salisbury; Robert; Heatland, Den; G; 6.12.1675; 6.12. 1675; 3.11.1684; 7.

SIMONS, Samuel

4098. John Ashburne; Alexander; Burton upon Stodder, Lincs; Cl; 9.2. 1674; 9.2.1674; 7.3.1681; 7.

4099. Thomas Collynes; Willm; Gumley, Leics; H; 7.3.1670; 7.3.1670; - ; 7.

4100. William Taylor; William (d); London; C & Ca; 2.10.1676; 2.10.1676; - ; 8.

SIMONS, Thomas

4101. Nevill Symons; Rich; Purton, Wilts; Y; 16.8.1647; 16.8.1647; 5.3. 1655; 7. Fd as Simonds.

SIMPSON, Ralph

4102. William Middleton; Thomas (d); Hampsted, M'sex; G; 4.2.1695; 25.12.1694; 4.10.1703; 7.

4103. Henry Redding; John; Suttoncoldfeild, War; G; 7.6.1686; 7.6.1686; - ; 8.

4104. George Ward; George; Chalbury, Oxon; T; 7.3.1681; 7.3.1681; - ; 7.

SIMPSON, Richard

4105. George Baylis; William; Citty of Worster; Cw; 2.7.1683; 2.7.1683; - ; 8.

4106. Henry Chawkling; Henry (d); Tunbridge, Kent; Sh; 1.10.1688; 1.10. 1688; 7.10.1695; 7.

4107. Edward Gray; John (d); - , - ; - ; 7.2.1681; 7.2.1681; - ; 7.

4108. Joseph Hall. Fd by Simpson 4.10.1676. Bd to Philemon Stephens (q.v.) 4.10.1669.

4109. Henry Hamond; John; the Devizes, Wilts; Bs; 7.8.1682; 7.8.1682; - ; 8.

4110 Benjamin Johnson; Wm (d); Citty of Litchfeild, [Staffs]; G; 6.12.1675; 6.12.1675; 4.6.1683; 7.

4111. Michaell Johnson; Willm (d); Lichfeild, Staffs; Y; 11.4.1673; 11.4.1673; 5.10.1685; 8.

4112. Robert Knaplock; William (d); London; Jeweller; 7.11.1681; 7.11.1681; 2.12.1689; 8.

4113. William Marshall; William (d); Charlebury, Oxon; - ; 7.7.1662; 7.7.1662; 2.8.1669; 7.

4114. Robert Pepper; William (d); parish of Vssick, Lancs; Y; 4.7.1698; 4.7.1698 - ; 7.

4115. Daniel Richards; Daniel; Burrough of Carmarthen, Carmarthen; G; 2.11.1691; 2.11.1691; - ; 7.

4116. Edward Roberts; Edw; Basham, Den; G; 4.12.1676; 4.12.1676; - ; 8.

4117. Benjn Simpson; Richard; [London]; [C & St]; 7.3.1692; 7.3.1692; 3.4.1699; 7. Bd to his father.

4118. Thomas Simpson; Richard; London; C & St; 6.8.1683; 6.8.1683; 6.10.1690; 7. Bd to his father; fd by patrimony.

4119. John Smith; Thomas (d); Moulsey, Surr; H; 3.5.1669; 3.5.1669; 7.5.1677; 8.

4120. John Symson; Thomas; Chalbury, Oxon; Sh; 8.6.1668; 8.6.1668; - ; 7.

4121. Stephen Tickner; William; Waybridge, Surr; Tn; 1.10.1683; 1.10.1683; 6.10.1690; 7.

SIMS, John

4122. William Burch. Fd by Sims and Edward Farnham 11.2.1668. Bd to Farnham (q.v.) 3.9.1660.

4123. John Francklyn; Thomas; Chelsey, M'sex; - ; 7.7.1673; 7.7.1673; - ; 8.

4124. Richard Leonard alius Fisher; Wm; Thorpe, Surr; G; 4.2.1689; 4.2.1689; - ; 7.

4125. John Sanders; Jesper; London; C & MT; 3.3.1656; 3.3.1656; - ; 7.

4126. Samuell Snignell; Thomas; Barnes; Surr; H; 12.6.1666; 12.6.1666; 7.7.1673; 7.

4127. Samuell Tidmarsh; Richard; City of Oxon; Tn; 7.11.1670; 7.11.1670; 2.12.1678; 8.

SKEGNES, Christopher

4128. Robert Bird. Bd to Tobias Wicker (q.v.) 7.2.1687; t.o. 7.10.1689 to Skegnes.

SKELTON, Henry

4129. William Archer; Thomas; Ware, Herts; Bargeman; 6.12.1669; 6.12.1669; - ; 7.

4130. Seth Brooks; Edward (d); Derby, Derby; Maltster; 7.9.1685; 7.9.1685; - ; 7.

4131. Abraham Bull; John; Shore= Ditch, M'sex; G; 7.9.1691; 7.9.1691; - ; 7.

4132. John Collins alius Taunton; Richard; Waymouth, Dors; B; 4.8.1679; 4.8.1679; 4.6.1705; 7.

4133. William Haukinson; Thomas (d); Dawbury Leeze, Derby; Y; 7.12.1674; 7.12.1674; - ; 7.

4134. Thomas Hieron; Joseph; London; C & Whitebaker; 7.3.1659; 7.3.1659; - ; 7.

4135. William Hoare; Anthony (d); London; C & Weaver; 4.10.1658; 4.10.1658; - ; 7.

4136. James Howse; Robert (d); Ware, Herts; I; 12.6.1666; 25.3.1666; - ; 7.

4137. Charles Larkin; William (d); London; C & Cu; 6.4.1663; 6.4.1663; - ; 8.

4138. [Henry Skelton. Fd by patrimony 5.1.1657.]

4139. Robert Spencer; Robert; parish of St John in Wapping, M'sex;

Mealman; 2.12.1695; 2.12.1695; - ; 7.

SLATER, Daniel
4140. Thomas Brockett; Charles (d); London; C & F; 6.6.1670; 6.6.1670; 1.10.1677; 7.
4141. John Harris; Alexandr; parish of St. Margaretts Westmr, M'sex; G; 5.5.1679; 5.5.1679; 7.6.1686; 7.
4142. Edward Newman; Daniel; Seavenock, Kent; G; 6.3.1676; 6.3.1676; 7.5.1683; 7.

SLATER, Sarah, Widow
4143. Thomas Pyke; William; Prescott, Lancs; Y; 30.9.1684; 30.9.1684; - ; 7.

SLATER, Thomas
4144. George Goulborne. Fd by Slater 16.1.1643. Bd to him 7.12.1635.
4145. Henry Harvey. Fd by Slater 6.4.1646. Bd to him 3.9.1638.
4146. Francis Kindon; Nich; Chadsley, Worcs; Y; 5.10.1646; 5.10.1646; 17.10.1653; 7.
4147. Thomas Rawson; Robert; London; Glazier; 6.5.1644; 6.5.1644; - ; 7.

SMART, Israel
4148. George Dawson; Thomas; parish of St Andrews Holborne, M'sex; Surgeon; 2.3.1674; 2.3.1674; - ; 7.

SMART, Timothy
4149. Hugh Albyn. Fd by Smart and Alice Albyn 7.11.1659. Bd to Mrs Albyn (q.v.) 6.10.1651.
4150. William Hickson; Willm; Barraby, Lincs; H; 14.4.1656; 24.6.1656; - ; 7.

SMETHWICKE, Francis
4151. Robte Purden. Bd (as Robert Burden) to Henry Gosson 4.12.1637; t.o. 2.5.1642 to Smethwicke.

SMETHWICKE, John
4152. John Frank. Fd by Smethwicke 26.1.1642. Bd to him 19.1.1635.

SMITH, Abraham
4153. [Abraham Smith. Fd by redemption 3.10.1692. Smith paid 3s. 4d. and 'Two Guineys Poors Box'.]

SMITH, Charles
4154. Edw Child; John (d); New Brandford, M'sex; Felmonger; 1.3.1680; 1.3.1680; - ; 8.
4155. Thomas Hawkins; William; Bruminger, War; - ; 3.6.1672; 3.6.1672; 4.7.1681; 7.

SMITH, Elizabeth, Widow, I
4156. Wm Ridges; Joseph; London; C & Sk; 6.7.1691; 6.7.1691 - ; 7. Elizabeth Smith is described as the widow of John Smith.

SMITH, Elizabeth, Widow, II
4157. Ralph Smith; Ralph (d); London; Bookbinder; 7.7.1690; 7.7.1690; - ; 8. Bd to his mother, Elizabeth Smith.

SMITH, Francis
4158. Edith Colledge; Stephen (d); London; C & J; 6.5.1686; 6.5.1686; - ; 7.
4159. Edward Dent; John; Cherry Willingam, Lincs; H; 4.9.1654; 4.9.1654; - ; 8.
4160. Joseph Doe. Fd by Smith and John Thomas 3.7.1643. Bd to Smith 30.6.1634.
4161. John Gaye; Francis; Edmonton, M'sex; G; 3.2.1673; 3.2.1673; 3.5.1680; 7. Fd by Thomas Burrel.
4162. Abraham Green. Fd by Smith 5.8.1678. Apparently never formally bd.
4163. John Halsey; William; Great Gadston, Herts; Y; 9.5.1655; 9.5.1655; - ; 7.
4164. Richard Mills; Richard (d); Wapping, M'sex; Smith; 6.10.1656; 6.10.1656; 2.11.1663; 7.
4165. Thomas Reyner; John; Manseter, War; G; 14.8.1662; 14.8.1662; - ; 7.
4166. John Rix. Fd by Smith 5.7.1675. Apparently never formally bd.

4167. Titus Robinson. Bd to Humphrey Robinson (q.v.) 3.3.1668; t.o. 12.8.1671 to Smith and fd by him 5.8.1678.

4168. Francis Smith. Fd by patrimony 3.5.1686.

SMITH, George

4169. [George Smith. Fd by patrimony 7.3.1653.]

SMITH, Hannah, Widow

4170. Samuell Babbington; Randolph (d); parish of Banbury, Ches; Y; 5.8.1695; 5.8.1695; - ; 7.

4171. John Burgess; Henry; Chalne, Wilts; Y; 5.9.1687; 5.9.1687; - ; 7.

4172. John Hunt; William; - , Wilts; Y; 7.4.1679; 7.4.1679; - ; 7. Mrs Smith's christian name is not given, but see next entry.

4173. William Hunt. Fd by Hannah Smith 4.7.1687. Apparently never formally bd unless this apprentice is John Hunt, bd to Mrs Smith 7.4.1679: see preceding entry.

4174. Robert Smith; Robert (d); London; C & St; 6.11.1683; 6.11.1683; - ; 8.

SMITH, John, I

[It is improbable that all apprentices listed below were bound to the same master.]

4175. John Bedingfield; Edmond; Kirby, Norf; G; 1.3.1653; 1.3.1653; 2.12.1661; 8. Bd to John Smith. Linendraper of Paul's Alley.

4176. Roger Collingwood; Cuthbert; Darlton, Dur; E; 1.12.1656; 25.12.1656; - ; 8. Bd to John Smith, Linendraper of Paul's Alley.

4177. Wm Dormer; Robte; great Missenden, Bucks; E; 16.3.1648; 19.1.1648; - ; 8. Bd to John Smith, Linendraper of Paul's Alley.

4178. Joseph English; John (d); London; C & Dy; 3.4.1682; 3.4.1682; 2.12.1689; 7.

4179. George Heinsworth; George; Bickerton, Yorks; G; 27.6.1654; 1.5.1654; - ; 8. Bd to John Smith, Linendraper of Paul's Alley.

4180. Robert Hodgson. Fd by Smith 20.4.1653. Bd to him 4.12.1637.

4181. Francis Hubbard. Fd by Smith 7.1.1684. Bd to John Whitlock (q.v.) 4.9.1676.

4182. William Hutchinson; Cuthbert; Studhow, Yorks; G; 1.8.1659; 29.9.1659; - ; 8. Bd to John Smith, Linendraper of Paul's Alley.

4183. Richard Latham; Richard; Allerton, Lancs; - ; 7.9.1663; 7.9.1663; - ; 8.

4184. Francis Nicholls; Francis; St Margaretts Westminster, M'sex; Cook; 3.8.1685; 3.8.1685; - ; 7.

4185. Thomas Piercy. Fd by Smith 18.12.1656. Apparently never formally bd.

4186. Geo Ravenscroft; James; London; G; 3.11.1651; 3.11.1651; - ; 7.

4187. George Rowse; George; London; T; 9.10.1666; 9.10.1666; - ; 7. Bd to John Smith, Linendraper of Paul's Alley.

4188. John Vovsden; William; Petworth, Sussex; G; 2.7.1683; 2.7.1683; 6.7.1691; 7.

4189. Gilbert Whitehall; John (d); Yeldersley, Derby; G; 2.11.1657; 25.3.1657; 2.4.1667; 8. Bd to John Smith, Linendraper of Paul's Alley.

SMITH, John, II

4190. [John Smith. Fd by redemption 24.10.1676.]

SMITH, Margaret, Widow

4191. Simon Hutchinson; Cutbert; Studhowe, Yorks; - ; 4.10.1669; 4.10.1669; - ; 8. Margaret Smith is described as the widow of John Smith.

SMITH, Nicholas

4192. John Roberts; John; London; C & MT; 3.7.1671; 1.1.1671; - ; 8. Smith is described as a Scrivener in Holborn.

SMITH, Ralph

4193. Adoniram Bifeild; Adoniram; Fullham, M'sex; Cl; 7.5.1649; 7.5.1649; 20.5.1656; 7.

4194. Benjamine Billingsley; John (d); London; G; 2.3.1657; 25.12.1656; 6.6.1664; 8. Fd as Billinley.

4195. Ralph Hartley; Ralph (d); London; C & Sc; 10.1.1655; 1.1.1655; - ; 8.

4196. Thomas Mercer; Nathaniell; St Pauls Cray, Kent; Tn; 3.4.1671; 3.4.1671; 7.4.1679; 8.

4197. Richard Parker. Fd by Smith 19.11.1695. Apparently never formally bd.

4198. Ralph Smith. Fd by patrimony 5.12.1670.

4199. Robte Tutchin; Robte; Dorchester, Dors; Cl; 22.3.1642; 22.3.1642; 2.9.1650; 8. Rebd to Luke Fawne 5.12.1642 and fd by him.

4200. Wm Warman; Steven; London; C & Cook; 4.3.1644; 1.3.1644; - ; 8.

SMITH, Richard

4201. Josiah Stedman; Wm (d); London; C & Go; 4.12.1676; 4.12.1676; - ; 8.

SMITH, Robert, I

4202. John Allen; Willm; Tamworth, War; I; 6.5.1661; 6.5.1661; 6.9.1669; 8.

4203. Andrew Bayley; Andrew; Wolverhampton, Staffs; BSg; 3.3.1669; 3.3.1669; - ; 7.

4204. Richard Bragg; Richard; Kinges Norton, Worcs; Y; 8.6.1668; 8.6.1668; - ; 7.

4205. Thomas Micchell; John (d); city of Westmr; G; 7.7.1673; 7.7.1673; 11.10.1680; 8.

SMITH, Robert, II

4206. [Robert Smith, 'a freeman of the Merchantailers Company London', fd by redemption 5.3.1688, paying £10.]

SMITH, Samuel

4207. Stafford Anson; Wm; Shuttbarrow Manner, Staffs; G; 4.12.1682; 4.12.1682; 20.12.1689; 7.

4208. John Bagshaw; Henry (d); Ridghall, Derby; G; 6.6.1687; 6.6.1687; - ; 7.

4209. Samuel Buckley; Samuel; London; C & Ha; 15.2.1688; 11.2.1688; 1.12.1701; 7.

4210. John Compton; John (d); London; Weaver; 4.8.1690; 4.8.1690; - : 7.

4211. Thomas Gifford; Thomas; London; G; 2.8.1647; 24.6.1647; 4.5.1663; 8.

4212. Jeffery Wale; Charles; Saffron-Waldon, Essex; E; 4.7.1698; 4.7.1698; - ; 7.

SMITH, Thomas, I

4213. Nathaniell Eldred; Walter; London; C & MT; 6.11.1643; 29.9.1643; - ; 8.

4214. Thomas Russell; Joseph; London; Ha; 6.7.1646; 24.6.1646; - ; 8.

SMITH, Thomas, II

4215. [Thomas Smith. Fd by translation from the Company of Joiners 24.5.1647.]

SNIGNELL, Samuel

4216. Nathaniel Moody; Sam; City of Coventry, [War]; Woollendraper. 5.10.1674; 5.10.1674; - ; 7.

SNOW, Ralph

4217. John Clarke; Robert (d); parish of Stepney alius Stebunheath, M'sex; Mariner; 3.5.1697; 3.5.1697; 2.4.1705; 7.

4218. John Pigg; John; London; C & MT; 3.6.1695; 3.6.1695; - ; 7.

SNOW, Richard

4219. Thomas Bancroft; John; London; Cd; 7.4.1684; 30.4.1683; - ; 7. The father's name is given as Barncroft, and the apprentice is said to be bound 'to Richard Snow and Ann his wife from the 30th Aprill. last'.

4220. Peter Cokel; Peter (d); parish of St Giles without Cripplegate, London; Weaver; 4.5.1691; 4.5.1691; - ; 7.

4221. Charles Snowe. Fd by patrimony 5.8.1672.

SNOWDEN, Thomas

4222. Wm Anderton; Wm; Wakefeild, Yorks; Cw; 9.2.1680; 9.2.1680; 7.2.1687; 7.

4223. Emanuel Bloome; Benjamin (d); parish of Stepney, M'sex; Parchmentmaker; 5.10.1691; 5.10.1691; - ; 8.

4224. John Cluer; Henry (d); Basingstoke, Hants; Cd; 6.5.1695; 6.5.1695; 4.5.1702; 7. Fd as Cleuer.

4225. John Hinkley; Edward; - , M'sex; Pw; 1.7.1695; 1.7.1695; - ; 7.

4226. Thomas Ilive; Isaack; London; Tobacconist; 3.6.1678; 3.6.1678; 7.10.1689; 8. Fd by Thomas Milbourne and fined 2s. 6d. 'For not being turned over at the Hall'.

4227. William Jacob; William; parish of St Anne Black Fryers, London; Cd; 6.7.1696; 6.7.1696; - ; 7.

4227a. George Lloyd. Bd to Robert Stephens (q.v.) 5.12.1681, pro forma, but served his time with Snowden.

4228. John Rowse; Charles (d); Statton, Leics; - ; 5.7.1680; 5.7.1680; - ; 7.

4229. John Saywell; Christopher (d); London; C & Bl; 6.2 1699; 6.2.1699; 4.3.1706; 7.

4230. John Sharpe. Fd by Snowden and Elizabeth Flesher 7.10.1695. Bd to Mrs Flesher (q.v.) 2.11.1674.

4231. Saml Silvester; Mathew; parish of St James Clerkenwell, M'sex; Cl; 2.12.1689; 2.12.1689; - ; 7.

4232. Thomas Snowden. Fd by patrimony 7.11.1698.

4233. Thomas Wilson; Thomas; Chowden, Dur; G; 3.10.1681; 3.10.1681; - ; 7.

SOLLERS, Robert

4234. Thomas Clarke; Simon; parish of St Mary Alderman Berry, London; Dy; 4.3.1678; 4.3.1678; - ; 8.

4235. Wm Sawkins; Nicholas (d); Egerton, Kent; G; 7.6.1680; 7.6.1680; - ; 7.

SOUTHBY, John

4236. Benjamin Price; Denzell (d); Stippord, Essex; Cl; 7.11.1692; 7.11.1692; 26.3.1701; 8. Fd by Southby and John Pero.

4237. Nathaniel Sackett; Nathaniel (d); Citty of Canterbury, [Kent]; G; 6.12.1686; 6.12.1686; 5.2.1694; 7.

4238. [John Southby. Fd, probably by redemption, 2.6.1684.]

4239. Susanna Southby; Henry; South Sarney, Glos; G; 7.4.1690; 7.4.1690; - ; 7.

SOUTHWARD, Benjamin

4240. John Cleave; Abraham (d); Cambridge; H; 6.2.1671; 6.2.1671; 8.4.1678; 7. Fd as Isaac Cleave.

SOWLE, Andrew

4241. John Bradford. Fd by Sowle 3.12.1684. Apparently never formally bd.

4242. Joseph Ellis; Cadwallader; Balla, Merioneth; Schoolmaster; 13.4.1694; 13.4.1694; - ; 7.

4243. Thomas Martyn. Fd by Sowle and Joseph Carter 5.12.1698. Bd to Carter (q.v.) 6.2.1682 and t.o. (n.d.) to Sowle.

4264. Tace Sowle. Fd by patrimony 7.10.1695.

SOWLE, Francis

4245. Francis Sowle; Francis; London; C & St; 6.10.1656; 6.10.1656; - ; 7. Bd to his father.

4246. John Sowle. Fd by patrimony 11.6.1655.

SOWLE, Tace

4247. George Bond; Elias; parish of St Giles Criplegate, London; Cd; 5.7.1697; 5.7.1697; 2.4.1705; 7.

4248. Phillip Gwillim; Phillipp; parish of Cascobs, Rad; Y; 6.4.1696; 6.4.1696; 7.6.1703; 7.

SPARKES, John

4249. Thomas Boucher; John; Yately, S'hants; G; 3.12.1694; 3.12.1694; - ; 7.

4250. Barnaby Webb; John; London; C & Cook; 7.5.1688; 7.5.1688; - ; 7.

SPARKES, Michael

4251. Richard Collins. Fd by Sparkes 8.11.1641. Bd to Samuel Cartwright 27.10.1634.

4252. Lodwick Floid; Lewis; Lanbanner, Rad; Y; 7.7.1641; 7.7.1641; 3.10.1648; 8.

4253. John Loue; Edward; Ensam, Oxon; B; 4.10.1652; 4.10.1652; 7.7.1662; 8. Bd 'with Caution that ye said Appr bee not bred vp with any Printr'. Fd by Sparkes, Henry Weston and Eleanor Cotes.

4254. Josua Miller. Fd by Sparkes 21.10.1646. Bd to him 3.9.1638.

4255. Michaell Sparkes. Fd by patrimony 1.3.1641.

4256. Edward Thomas; Thomas; Bristoll; Bs; 5.10.1646; 29.9.1646; 10.1.1654; 8.

SPARKES, William

4257. Theophilus Fermer. Fd by Sparkes 2.4.1655. Bd to him 4.6.1638.

4258. Stephen Harwood; Wm; London; C & Cd; 7.4.1662; 29.9.1661; 3.10.1670; 9.

4259. Edward Lewis; John (d); Ashbury, Berks; Cd; 2.5.1698; 2.5.1698; 7.5.1705; 7.

SPEED, Samuel

4260. Hatton Awder; Hatton (d); London; C & MT; 1.3.1658; 1.3.1658; - ; 8.

4261. Samuell Cooke. Fd by Speed and Roger Turner 3.12.1660. Bd to Turner (q.v.) 17.10.1653.

4262. John Sedgwick; Stephen; London; C & Br; 6.9.1669; 24.6.1669; 1.10.1677; 8.

4263. George Woorton; Geo; parish of Christ Church, - ; Leatherseller; 7.9.1663; 7.9.1663; - ; 7.

SPENCER, Thomas

4264. Isack Wilson; John (d); Aynstable, Cumb; Cl; 4.2.1650; 4.2.1650; - ; 7.

SPICER, Charles, alias HELDER

4265. Edward Grubb; Thomas; Towne of Cambridge; H; 5.9.1698; 5.9.1698; - ; 7.

4266. Thomas Hardwick; Tho (d); London; V; 4.2.1684; 2.2.1684; - ; 7.

4267. Robert Norton; William (d); St Martins Le grand, [London]; T; 8.11.1675; 8.11.1675; 4.12.1682; 7.

4268. Peter Richmond. Bd to Martin Berneham (q.v.); t.o. 8.11.1675 to Spicer, but fd by Berneham 3.7.1676.

4269. William Ruck; William; Sellvige, Kent; Y; 12.11.1694; 12.11.1694; 1.6.1702; 7.

SPICER, John

4270. John Wilson; John (d); Isle of Eley, Cambs; Cl; 7.6.1669; 7.6.1669; - ; 7.

SPICER, Thomas, alias HELDER

4271. John Clement; John; Owndle, N'hants; G; 2.5.1670; 2.5.1670; - ; 7.

4272. Edward Golding; Edw (d); London; C & Weaver; 1.6.1674; 1.6.1674; 7.8.1682; 7.

4273. Henry Hallett; Henry (d); Exeter, Dev; - ; 5.6.1671; 5.6.1671; 20.12.1676; 7. Fd by redemption.

4274. Christopher Nobbs; John; Bullwick, N'hants; Cl; 7.5.1683; 7.5.1683; - ; 7.

4275. Charles Spicer alias Helder; Richard; great Stoughton, Hunts; G; 27.6.1666; 27.6.1666; 1.12.1673; 7.

SPORIER, John
4276. [John Sporier. Fd by patrimony 12.11.1649.]

SPRINT, Bartholomew
4277. [Bartholomew Sprint. Fd by redemption 7.7.1680.]

SPRINT, John
4278. Benjamin Sprint; Samuell; London; C & St; 8.4.1700; 8.4.1700; 1.3.1708; 7.

SPRINT, Samuel
4279. Samuell Guy; Samuell; - , Bucks; G; 8.11.1680; 8.11.1680; - ; 7.
4280. Thomas Nicholson; James; Sheffeild, Yorks; Y; 5.8.1678; 5.8.1678; - ; 7.
4281. John Sprinte. Fd by patrimony 4.3.1695.
4282. Thomas Yeate; Edward; Malmsbury, Wilts; Clothier; 10.1.1673; 10.1.1673; 8.11.1680; 7.

STAFFORD, John
4283. Thomas Burroughs; Alexander; parrish of St Brides, London; Y; 1.9.1656; 1.9.1656; - ; 9.
4284. John Garroway; John; Chilton, Wilts; Cl; 1.3.1649; 1.3.1649; 1.3.1658; 8.
4285. Wm Hall. Fd by Stafford 7.9.1646. Bd to him 6.3.1638.
4286. Thomas Warden; William (d); St Catherine Creechurch, London; MT; 7.9.1663; 7.9.1663; - ; 8.

STANLEY, Edward
4287. Wm Gamble; James (d); London; C & Embroiderer; 30.6.1645; 30.6.1645; - ; 8.
4288. Richard Westbrooke. Fd by Stanley and Ralph Hartford 20.12.1645. Bd to Hartford 7.11.1638.

STANSBY, —, Widow
4289. William Moulton. Fd by Mrs

Stansby 4.12.1648. Apparently never formally bd.

STARKEY, John
4290. William Checkley; Edward; London; C & MT; 6.7.1678; 6.7.1678; - ; 7.
4291. John Ford; John; Kinsly, Staffs; G; 6.5.1662; 6.5.1662; 7.6.1669; 7.
4292. Edward Hughes; Richard; Melton Mobray, Leics; Y; 2.3.1657; 25.3.1657; - ; 7.
4293. Robert Kettlewell; John (d); Brunton, Yorks; G; 3.11.1673; 3.11.1673; 8.11. 1680; 7.
4294. John Wickens; John; Shittlehanger, N'hants; Y; 22.9.1670; 22.9.1670; 1.10.1677; 7.

STATE, Thomas
4295. Thomas Pasham; John; Piddington, Glos [sic for Oxon]; H; 5.12.1664; 5.12.1664; 8.1.1672; 7.

STEELE, Robert
4296. Daniel Baker; George; London; C & Turner; 7.11.1687; 7.11.1687; - ; 7.
4297. William Burscod; Ralph; Nantwich, Ches; T; 7.11.1698; 7.11.1698; - ; 8.
4298. Abraham Herbert; Abraham (d); - , - ; - ; 2.7.1677; 2.7.1677; 2.5.1687; 7.
4299. Samuell Illidge; George; Nantwich, Ches; J; 4.6.1694; 4.6.1694; 1.6.1702; 7.
4300. John Pennington. Bd to William Norris (q.v.) 8.11.1680; t.o. 2.5.1687 to Steele, but fd by Norris 7.10.1689.
4301. Phillip Powell; Hen (d); London; C & BSg; 7.10.1689; 7.10.1689; - ; 7. T.o. 4.11.1689 to William Walcroft.

STEPHENS, John
4302. Robert Solers; Robert; Cashalton, Surr; G; 2.8.1669; 2.8.1669; 12.2.1677; 7.

STEPHENS, Philemon

4303. Thomas Cockarell; Thomas; Wotton, N'hants; Y; 7.8.1666; 7.8. 1666; 1.9.1673; 7. T.o. 2.5.1670 to John Overton, but fd by Stephens.

4304. Henry Eversden. Fd by Stephens and John Parker 4.5.1653. Bd to Parker (q.v.) 4.5.1646.

4305. Thomas Greenhill; Samuell; Cuckfeild, Sussex; - ; 6.6.1670; 6.6. 1670; - ; 9. Rebd to Robert Stephens (q.v.) 6.3.1671.

4306. Joseph Hall; Robert; Uxbridge, M'sex; M; 4.10.1669; 4.10. 1669; 4.10.1676; 7. Fd by Richard Simpson.

4307. Nathaniell Harvey; Nathaniell (d); Wells, Som; Y; 9.2.1663; 9.2.1663; 6.3.1671; 8.

4308. Ralph Needham; Jervas; Bishopscastle, Shrops; Cl; 6.11.1655; 6.11.1655; 3.10.1664; 9.

4309. Thomas Perpoint. Fd by Stephens 4.10.1647. Bd to him 5.8.1639.

4310. Austen Rice; John; Tarren-Nevill, Sussex; Cl; 20.12.1647; 29.9. 1647; 6.11.1655; 8.

4311. John Ridley; John; Islington, M'sex; Cl; 6.12.1641; 28.10.1641; 6.11.1648; 8.

4312. Elizabeth Stephens. Fd by patrimony 4.2.1684.

4313. James Stephens; Philemon; [London]; [C & St]; 7.3.1664; 7.3. 1664; - ; 7.

4314. Jeremy Stephens. Fd by patrimony 2.7.1655.

4315. John Stephens; Philemon; London; C & St; 27.6.1660; 24.8.1659; 3.10.1664; 8. Bd to his father.

4316. Philemon Stephens. Fd by patrimony 6.6.1659.

4317. Robert Stephens; Philemon; London; C & St; 1.12.1656; 1.11.1656; 2.3.1663; 8. Bd to his father; fd by patrimony.

STEPHENS, Robert

4318. Charles Barker; John (d); parish of St Clements Danes, [Westminster]; T; 6.9.1675; 6.9.1675; - ; 7.

4319. Thomas Barker. Fd by Stephens 7.12.1685. Bd to George Swinnock (q.v.) 2.8.1675.

4320. John Byne; Magnus; Clayton, Essex; Cl; 3.9.1667; 3.9.1667; 7.9. 1674; 7. Fd as Bine.

4321. Thomas Emery; Samuell; Litefeild, Staffs; T; 4.12.1671; 4.12. 1671; - ; 8.

4322. Daniel Framewell; Wm (d); Hackney, M'sex; Smith; 5.10.1691; 5.10.1691; 7.6.1697; 7.

4323. Samll Framewell; Wm (d); Layton, Essex; Bl; 7.4.1690; 7.4.1690; 2.8.1697; 7.

4324. Willm Framewell; Willm (d); Low Layton, Essex; Y; 3.7.1693; 3.7. 1693; 6.7.1700; 7.

4325. Thomas Greenhill; Samuell; Cuckfeild, Sussex; - ; 6.3.1671; 6.3. 1671; - ; 8. Originally bd to Philemon Stephens (q.v.) 6.6.1670.

4326. George Lloyd; Samuell (d); London; C & St; 5.12.1681; 5.12.1681; - ; 8. Lloyd was bd pro forma to Stephens but served his time with Thomas Snowden (Court-Book E, 5.12.1681).

4327. Edw Masters; Edw; Presson, Glos; G; 4.11.1672; 4.11.1672; - ; 7.

4328. William Stephens; Christopher; Henley vpon Thames, Oxon; Ca; 4.12.1693; 1.12.1693; 1.12.1701; 8.

STEPHENS, William

4329. Edward Alleston. Fd by Stephens 1.3.1647. Bd to him 1.3.1633.

4330. John Barnes; Willm; Wickham, Bucks; Y; 5.5.1673; 5.5.1673; - ; 7.

4331. Humfrey Booth; Thomas (d); Stanton, Glos; G; 6.9.1669; 6.9.1669; - ; 7.

4332. John Harding; John; Wo-
bourne, Bucks; - ; 2.3.1663; 2.3.
1663; 7.3.1670; 7.

4333. Thomas Lewis. Fd by Stephens and Robert Collis 6.6.1664. Bd
to Collis (q.v.) 6.4.1657.

4334. John Stephens. Fd by patrimony 21.2.1700.

4335. William Stevens. Fd by patrimony 8.4.1695.

4336. Tymothy Turner; Tho; Rotheram, Yorks; I; 7.3.1670; 7.3.1670;
- ; 7.

STILES, Edward

4337. Jeremiah Caldwall; Tho (d);
Ludlow, Shrops; Tn; 1.8.1692; 1.8.
1692; - ; 7

STONE, Richard

4338. William Hind; William (d);
Eads Weston, Rut; Physician; 6.3.1671;
6.3.1671; - ; 8.

4339. John Store; John; Ramsbury,
Wilts; Chandler; 6.4.1663; 6.4.1663;
- ; 7.

STORER, Valentine

4340. Daniell Lambert; Roger;
Woodmansterne, Surr; G; 26.4.1652;
26.4.1652; 6.6.1659; 7.

4341. Thomas Maddox; Randall;
Edge, Ches; Y; 6.12.1647; 6.12.1647;
9.5.1655; 7. Fd by Storer and Richard
Westbrook.

4342. Henry Marshall. Fd by Storer
7.6.1641. Bd to him 3.6.1634.

STOYNERTON, Thomas

4343. John Tucker; George (d);
London; G; 3.10.1670; 3.10.1670; - ;
7.

STRANGE, Affable

4344. John Fate; Henry; parrish
of St Clements Danes, M'sex; Porter;
7.3.1681; 7.3.1681; - ; 7.

4345. Thomas Sheppard; Richard;

Milton, Derby; Y; 6.9.1675; 6.9.1675;
2.10.1682; 7.

4346. George Strange. Fd by patrimony 2.7.1688.

STREATER, John

4347. Samuel Bridge; Daniel; London; C & Mr; 6.11.1676; 6.11.1676;
6.11.1683; 7.

4348. Jonathan Bull; James; London; C & V; 20.6.1655; 20.6.1655;
7.7.1662; 7.

4349. Samuell Floyd; James (d);
London; C & Leatherseller; 12.6.1666;
25.3.1666; 6.12.1675; 8. Fd as Loyd.
Streater reported 'That LLoyd his
former Apprentice is Married, and that
he hath Surrendred vp his Indenture
&c.' (Court Book D, 5.4.1669), but he
presumably returned to service and was
able to take up his freedom.

4350. Wm Hall; Llodowick; greate
Chilton, Bishopprick of Durham, [Dur];
G; 5.5.1662; 25.3.1662; 7.6.1676; 8.

4351. Edward Harvey. Fd by Streater 4.9.1676. Apparently never formally
bd.

4352. James Lucking; Thomas; London; C & V; 18.1.1647; 18.1.1647;
- ; 8.

4353. William Rawlins. Bd to John
Legate (q.v.) 3.7.1654; t.o. 4.5.1657
to Streater; fd by Legate and Streater
5.8.1661.

4354. Joseph Streater. Fd by patrimony 2.3.1685.

4355. Thomas Streeter; Wm (d);
Lewis, Sussex; T; 5.8.1644; 5.8.1644;
- ; 7.

4356. Phillip Traherne; Jno; Citty
of Hereford; G; 13.7.1657; 13.7.1657;
- ; 7.

4357. John Wallis; John (d); Southwark, Surr; Bl; 5.4.1669; 5.4.1669; 7.6.
1676; 7.

4358. John Wright. Fd by Streater
6.2.1693, but fined 2s. 6d. for being bd
by a foreign indenture.

STREATER, Joseph

4359. William Carter; William; Beckington, Som; Clothier; 11.5.1685; 11.5.1685; - ; 7.

4360. Robert Tookey. Fd by Streater 5.12.1692. Apparently never formally bd.

STREATER, Susan

4361. James Hall; William; St Giles Cripplegate, London; Ca; 3.12.1677; 3.12.1677; 7.3.1687; 8.

SUMPTNER, Charles

4362. Francis Hough; Tho; Manton, Rut; Y; 3.12.1649; 3.12.1649; - ; 7.

SURBUTT, Joseph, I

4363. George Brett; Lawrence; Southwark, Surr; Cu; 4.11.1641; 29.9.1641; - ; 9.

4364. Wm Clarke; John; Isle of Eley, Cambs; G; 3.6.1647; 25.3.1647; - ; 8.

4365. William Clarke; John; Laiston, Herts; Y; 3.12.1649; 3.12.1649; 6.4.1657; 7.

4366. Thomas Elliott; Thomas (d); Newington, Surr; Y; 29.10.1660; 29.10.1660; 12.11.1667; 7.

4367. John George; John; Akington, Worcs; H; 3.7.1654; 6.6.1654; 7.7.1662; 8. m.n. 'with Caution that hee bee not turned our to any other Trade'.

4368. George Grigman. Fd by Joseph Surbutt Senior and Joseph Surbutt Junior 2.4.1666. Bd to Surbutt Junior (q.v.) 1.2.1658.

4369. James Hughes; Geo; Royston, Cambs; Linendraper; 7.12.1657; 7.12.1657; - ; 7.

4370. Thomas Justice; Thomas; parish of Mary White=chapel; Coachman; 30.6.1645; 1.5.1645; 2.5.1653; 8.

4371. Thomas Mason; John; London; MT; 28.6.1652; 1.6.1652; - ; 8.

4372. Walter Powell. Fd by Surbutt 7.7.1641. Bd to him 3.6.1633.

4373. Joseph Surbutt. Fd by patrimony 6.10.1656.

4374. Enoch Taylor; Enoch; London; C & Leatherseller; 7.12.1657; 7.12.1657; - ; 9.

SURBUTT, Joseph II

4375. George Grigman; John; Epping, Essex; Y; 1.2.1658; 1.2.1658; 2.4.1666; 8. Fd by Joseph Surbutt Senior and Joseph Surbutt Junior.

4376. Joseph Surbut. Fd by patrimony 8.11.1680.

SUSSEX, Giles

4377. Henry Allen; Henry; Baseldon, Berks; - ; 7.10.1668; 7.10.1668; - ; 7

4378. Thomas Arnold; John; Benson, Oxon; Y; 6.8.1694; 6.8.1694; 4.5.1702; 7. Fd by William Sussex.

4379. Peter Cutler; Thomas; Burfeild, Berks; Cu; 6.11.1666; 6.11.1666; 6.4.1674; 7.

4380. George Fuller; Geo; Pangborne, Berks; Sh; 7.9.1691; 7.9.1691; 8.5.1699; 7.

4381. William Gatefield; - ; Basseldon, Berks; Cl; 6.7.1685; 6.7.1685; - ; 7.

4382. John Gatfield; James; Basleton Deane, Berks; Cl; 2.5.1687; 2.5.1687; 7.5.1694; 7.

4383. Richd Jovens; Richard (d); Bewdley, Worcs; Y; 3.10.1681; 3.10.1681; - ; 7.

4384. Henry Keffe; Willm; Ninehead, Som; Hotpresser; 4.12.1671; 4.12.1671; 3.5.1680; 7.

4385. Giles Mathews; Griffin; Goosey, Bucks [*sic* for Berks]; H; 7.11.1670; 7.11.1670; 8.4.1678; 7.

4386. Thomas Robinson; Michael; Kendall, W'land; Y; 4.10.1675; 4.10.1675; - ; 8.

4387. William Sussex; Giles; [London]; [C & St]; 2.11.1685; 2.11.1685; 7.5.1694; 7. Bd to his father.

4388. Ambrose Toftwood; London; C & Ha; 8.4.1678; 8.4.1678; - ; 7.

4389. John Walter; John (d); Aston, Oxon; Y; 3.5.1658; 1.3.1658; 26.3.1666; 8.

SUTTON, John

4390. John Litle; Francis; Rexham, Lincs; Y; 1.3.1647; 1.3.1647; 4.12.1654; 7. Fd as Little.

SWALE, Abel

4391. Henry Balderoe; Daniell; Citty of Yorke; G; 7.9.1696; 7.9.1696; - ; 7.

4392. Timothy Child. Fd by Swale 1.12.1690. Bd to Samuel Carr (q.v.) 4.8.1679.

4393. John Hodgkins; Thomas; Aldermanberry, London; Smith; 7.6.1680; 7.6.1680; - ; 7.

4394. John Swalle; Abraham (d); London; C & Weaver; 6.11.1683; 6.11.1683; - ; 7.

SWEETING, John

4395. Edward Farnham. Fd by Sweeting and Henry Overton 7.1.1656. Bd to Overton (q.v.) 20.12.1647.

4396. John Morgan; Rice; Clen, Mont; G; 6.11.1654; 6.11.1654; - ; 7.

4397. Wm Riston; George (d); litle worley, Essex; Cl; 6.9.1641; 24.6.1641; 2.7.1649; 8.

4398. John Sweeting; Lewis (d); Overstoy, Som; Y; 13.9.1661; 29.9.1661; - ; 8.

SWINNERTON, Thomas

4399. William Garrett; Richard (d); London; C & Bl; 5.7.1675; 5.7.1675; - ; 7.

SWINNOCK, George

4400. Thomas Barker; Robert; London; C & V; 2.8.1675; 2.8.1675; 7.12.1685; 7. Fd by Robert Stephens.

TAGELL, Matthew

4401. Wm Godwyn. Fd by Tagell 2.3.1646. Bd to him 11.2.1635.

TAYLOR, John

4402. Thomas Crafts; Thomas (d); parish of Stepney, M'sex; Mariner; 5.10.1691; 5.10.1691; - ; 7.

4403. William Riddoutt; Wm; Sherbourne, Dors; H; 7.8.1693; 7.8.1693; - ; 7.

4404. William Stephens; Robert (d); London; C & St; 7.12.1685; 7.12.1685; - ; 7.

4405. William Taylor; Phillip; Weymouth, Dors; Mch; 6.6.1698; 6.6.1698; 4.3.1706; 7.

4406. James Warr; John; parish of St Martin Westminster, M'sex; G; 2.3.1696; 1.1.1696; 6.3.1704; 7.

TAYLOR, —, Mrs

4407. Stephen Foster. Fd by Mrs Taylor 2.12.1678. Bd to William Shrewsbury (q.v.) 6.11.1671; t.o. 9.2.1674 to George Calvert.

TAYLOR, Randall

4408. John Aliffe; Nicholas; Oakeington, Berks; Bridlemaker; 7.12.1663; 7.9.1663; 4.9.1671; 8.

4409. George Bale; George; London; C & Waxchandler; 6.10.1656; 6.10.1656; 3.10.1664; 8.

4410. Nathan Brookes; Edw; Onelip, Leics; Y; 1.4.1650; 25.3.1650; 5.10.1657; 8.

4411. Phillip Burton; Richard; Preston, Lancs; Bs; 8.7.1668; 8.7.1668; 2.8.1675; 7.

4412. John Maynard. Fd by Taylor 2.4.1688. Apparently never formally bd.

4413. Richard Sparrow; Thomas; Coventry, Wilts [sic for War.]; Sh; 5.12.1653; 5.12.1653; - ; 8.

4414. James Taylor. Fd by patrimony 4.12.1682.

4415. John Warren; John; City of Norwich; Cd; 2.10.1671; 2.10.1671; - ; 7.

4416. John Windell; John; Standon, Herts; Gardener; 1.7.1678; 1.7.1678; 6.6.1687; 7.

TAYLOR, Thomas

4417. Daniell Harrison; Daniell; Guildford, Surr; - ; 3.3.1673; 3.3. 1673; - ; 7.

4418. Andrew Thorneum. Fd by Taylor 1.10.1683. Apparently never formally bd.

TEBB, Thomas

4419. Thomas Hobbs; Thomas (d); parish of Shoreditch, M'sex; Br; 8.11. 1697; 8.11.1697; 4.12.1704; 7.

TEONGE, Thomas

4420. Joshua Gilbert; Joshua; Ashby Falvie, Leics; Cl; 3.4.1699; 3.4. 1699; 6.5.1706; 7.

TERREY, William

[This is probably the man fd as William Turrey 21.1.1644. Tirrey is another form of the name.]

4421. Thomas Bodwell; Thomas; London; C & Cd; 6.8.1667; 6.8.1667; 7.9.1674; 7.

4422. Herbert Higgins; Herbert (d); London; C & J; 5.9.1681; 5.9.1681; - ; 7.

4423. Arthur Jones; Arthur (d); Worcester; Procter; 4.12.1654; 4.12. 1654; - ; 7.

4424. Wm Millward; Josua; London; C & Amorer; 2.3.1646; 2.3.1646; 7.3.1653; 7. Fd by Terrey and Thomas Blashfield.

4425. Richard Procter; John; Stretton vpon=force, War; Y; 1.3.1647; 1.3.1647; - ; 7.

4426. John Sheers; John; London; C & Pw; 1.7.1678; 1.7.1678; - ; 7.

4427. Theodor Sydney; James; City of Hereford; G; 2.5.1670; 2.5.1670; 7.5.1688; 7.

4428. Robert Terrey. Fd by patrimony 5.3.1694.

4429. John Turnor; John; White Fryers, London; Victualler; 6.3.1676; 6.3.1676; - ; 8.

4430. — Turrey. Son of William

Turrey, Citizen and Stationer; fd by patrimony 4.5.1674. The christian name is blank; probably a son of William Terrey.

4431. Samuell Venor; Timothy; Parish of Hackney, M'sex; - ; 2.11.1685; 24.6.1685; - ; 7.

TEY, John

4432. Robert Blayton; Samuell; London; C & Silkweaver; 5.9.1649; 5.9.1649; - ; 7. Originally bd (as Bleaton) to George Flood (q..v) 10.1. 1649.

THACKERAY, William

4433. Phillip Franck; George; Epsom, Surr; Weaver; 19.12.1683; 19.12. 1683; - ; 7.

4434. Willm Miller; Willm (d); London; C & MT; 12.11.1667; 12.11.1667; 7.12.1674; 7.

4435. Thomas Thackery. Fd by patrimony 6.8.1694.

4436. Edward Vize; John (d); London; C & J; 6.4.1674; 6.4.1674; 7.11. 1681; 7.

THOMAS, Edward

4437. Mathew Jeffery; Tho; Kingston Bowsee, Sussex; Cl; 3.7.1657; 3.7.1657; - ; 8.

4438. Francis Leigh; John; Boxley, Kent; G; 2.8.1675; 2.8.1675; - ; 7.

4439. Samuell Newman; Richard; Sison, Glos; G; 4.11.1672; 29.9.1672; - ; 8.

4440. John Whitlock; Richard; London; C & Painterstainer; 7.8.1666; 14.2.1666; 3.5.1675; 7.

THOMAS, John

4441. Charles Brown; Thomas; Ludlow, Shrops; G; 4.12.1676; 4.12.1676; 3.11.1690; 8. T.o. 'to a Fishmonger' (n.d.) and fined 2s. 6d. 'for not being turned over at the Hall'.

4442. Joseph Doe. Fd by Thomas and Francis Smith 3.7.1643. Bd to Smith 30.6.1634.

4443. Palmes Gates; John (d); Newport Pannel, Bucks; G; 3.12.1683; 3.12.1683; - ; 8.

4444. Paule Griffin. Fd by Thomas 2.4.1688. Bd to John Beddoe (q.v.) 11.10.1680 and fined 2s. 6d. 'for not being turned over at the Hall'.

4445. Jonathan Stringer; John; Farnden, Ches; G; 4.8.1662; 1.5.1662; - ; 8.

4446. Daniell Taylor; John; parish of Dunton, Leics; Bookbinder; 3.6.1678; 3.6.1678; - ; 7.

4447. John Thomas. Fd by patrimony 6.4.1656.

4448. William Thomas. Fd by patrimony 26.3.1683.

THOMAS, Lewis

4449. John Garrett; William; Citty of Oxon; Musician; 1.7.1700; 1.7.1700; - ; 7.

THOMAS, William

4450. Richard Grafton; Richd; parish of St Andrew Holborne, M'sex; Bricklayer; 4.10.1686; 4.10.1686; - ; 7.

THOMASON, George

4451. James Allestree. Fd by Thomason 1.7.1647. Bd to him 12.11.1638.

4452. John Baker; Michaell; London; C & St; 6.9.1647; 29.9.1646; 1.10.1655; 9.

4453. Thomas Bedford; Thomas; parish of Antholius, London; Cl; 27.9.1645; 29.9.1645; - ; 8.

4454. John Durham; Thomas; Willersey, Glos; Y; 5.12.1653; 29.9.1653; 7.10.1661; 8.

4455. William Fletcher; Henry; Abbington, Berks; BSg; 2.2.1662; 25.12.1661; - ; 8. T.o. 12.6.1666 to John Baker.

4456. William Sanders; William; Shallingford, Berks; G; 4.8.1656; 24.6.1656; - ; 8.

4457. Henry Thomason. Fd by patrimony 7.4.1662.

4458. George Trent. Fd by Thomason 4.7.1642. Bd to him 14.1.1633.

THOMPSON, Francis

4459. [Francis Thompson. This name appears in the register under the date 8.4.1695. Neither the master's name nor any other information is given.]

THOMPSON, John

4460. Helkia Bedford; Thomas; Boston, Lincs; G; 3.8.1646; 24.6.1646; 27.6.1654; 9.

4461. Thomas Nuthall. Fd by Thompson 2.8.1641. Bd to him 18.7.1631.

4462. Wm Reading; John; Southampton, S'hants; E; 16.5.1642; 16.5.1642; - ; 8.

4463. John Thompson. Fd by patrimony 21.4.1649.

THOMPSON, Mary

4464. James Bostock; Samuell; parish of St Martin in the Feildes, M'sex; T; 6.8.1694; 6.8.1694; - ; 7.

4465. William Wise; John; parish of Stepney, M'sex; B; 1.8.1698; 1.8.1698; - ; 7.

THOMPSON, Nathaniel

4466. John Mayo; Henry; Stratford Bridge, Herefs; G; 1.2.1675; 1.2.1675; 7.3.1683; 8. Fd as John Mayos.

4467. Wm Newbolt; John (d); Citty of Winchester, [Hants]; Pw; 3.11.1679; 3.11.1679; 7.3.1687; 7. Newbolt ran away from Thompson on 1.9.1684 (*London Gazette* 1–4 Sept. 1684).

4468. Mathew Street; Mathew; Havand, Hants; - ; 11.10.1680; 11.10.1680; 7.10.1689; 8.

THOMPSON, Samuel

4469. Timothy Cromlum. Bd to Thomas Whitaker (q.v.) 17.4.1648; t.o. 4.2.1650 to Thompson on the death of Whitaker, but fd under Whitaker's name 24.4.1655.

4470. Thomas French. Fd by Thompson and Thomas Whitaker 14.2. 1653. Bd to Whitaker (q.v.) 13.12. 1645; t.o. 20.9.1648 to Thompson.

4471. Richard Head; Richard (d); Torrington, Som [*sic* for Dev]; Cl; 5.9.1653; 1.6.1653; 4.6.1660; 8. Fd by Thompson and Thomas Drant.

4472. Walter Kettlebey; Walter; Ribley, Shrops; G; 3.11.1656; 3.11. 1656; 2.4.1666; 9.

THOMPSON, William

4473. William Harris; Simon (d); Milton, Cambs; G; 5.4.1658; 5.4.1658; - ; 8.

4474. Obodiah Smith. Fd by Thompson 1.6.1674. Apparently never formally bd.

4475. Nehemiah Thompson. Fd by patrimony 1.6.1674.

THOMSON, Anthony

4476. Edward Fage; Edward; London; C & Gr; 7.9.1657; 7.9.1657; 7.6. 1669; 8.

4477. Thomas Thomson; Thomas (d); Harford, New England; G; 7.8. 1666; 7.8.1666; - ; 8.

4478. Pattison Vicars; Georg; Castle Ashby, N'hants; H; 6.2.1654; 6.2.1654; 2.3.1663; 7.

THORNICROFT, Thomas

4479. John Dearmer; Oliver (d); London; C & Cu; 8.10.1667; 8.10.1667; 2.11.1674; 7.

THRALE, Richard

4480. Sarah Elmeley; John; St Giles Cripplegate, London; Distiller; 12.11. 1677; 12.11.1677; - ; 7.

4481. Daniell Frances; Thomas; London; C & Go; 6.12.1641; 29.9.1641; - ; 8.

4482. Peter Holway. Fd by Thrale 4.7.1642. Bd to him 30.6.1634.

4483. John Syms; John (d); London; C & V; 6.5.1659; 6.5.1659; 7.5. 1666; 7.

4484. Benjamin Thrale. Fd by patrimony 26.4.1672.

4485. James Thrale. Fd by patrimony 27.6.1660.

4486. Francis Wells; George (d); London; C & Ha; 10.1.1649; 10.1.1649; - ; 8.

THURLBY, John

4487. John Hayward; John; parish of St Andrews Holborne, M'sex; G; 7.12.1691; 7.12.1691; - ; 7.

4488. William Rogers; Edward (d); St Olaves Southwarke, [Surr]; Ha; 1.3.1688; 1.3.1688; - 7.

THURSTON, Mathias

4489. William Aris; William; Blackfriars, [London]; Clothdrawer; 7.8. 1654; 7.8.1654; - ; 7.

4490. Thomas Moore; Thomas; Hamburrough, Leics; G; 1.12.1662; 1.12.1662; - ; 8.

4491. Humphrey Page; Hugh; Middlewich, Ches; - ; 7.10.1672; 7.10.1672; - ; 7.

4492. Richard Paine. Fd by Thurston and Robert Browne 7.4.1662. Bd to Browne (q.v.) 2.4.1655.

TIBBS, William

4493. Benjamine Andrewes; Benjamine; Markyat Streete, Herts; G; 13.12.1671; 21.12.1671; - ; 7.

4494. John Arden; Henry; Chelmsford, Essex; T; 6.8.1667; 6.7.1667; 5.10.1674; 7.

4495. Isaac Babington; John (d); Rumford, Essex; Dr of Physick; 6.9. 1658; 24.6.1658; 16.7.1666; 8.

4496. Henry Beagin; Nicholas; Putney, Surr; B; 6.5.1658; 6.5.1658; - ; 8.

4497. Henry Clarke; Edward; great Gadsden, Herts; Y; 5.10.1646; 5.10. 1646; 13.10.1653; 7.

4498. George Coppin; Osmond; London; Ha; 2.5.1653; 2.5.1653; 7.5. 1660; 7.

4499. Henry Nye; Phillip; London; Cl; 4.8.1662; 24.6.1662; 4.7.1670; 8.

4500. William Paman; Henry; London; C & Ha; 7.8.1654; 7.8.1654; 6.10.1662; 8. Fd by Tibbs and Robert Franklin.

4501. John Roane; Robte; Greenwich, Kent; G; 1.6.1646; 24.6.1646; - ; 8. Rebd to Edmond Paxton (q.v.) 24.3.1647; fd by Paxton 1.6.1657.

4502. James Walley; Henry; London; C & St; 6.5.1650; 6.5.1650; 6.5.1657; 7.

TIDMARSH, Samuel
4503. Rich Carter; Rich; Citty of Oxford; Carrier; 1.3.1680; 1.3.1680; - ; 7.

TILSON, Christopher
4504. [Christopher Tilson. Fd by redemption 26.3.1688, paying £5.]

TIMPERLEY, Christopher
4505. Symon Beamon; Robte; Chipping=Norton, Oxon; H; 18.1.1647; 18.1.1647; - ; 8.

TOMLYN, George
4506. John Ainger; John; London; C & Cd; 2.11.1658; 29.9.1658; - ; 8.

4507. William Brooman. Fd by Tomlyn and Matthew Walbank 5.9.1642. Bd to Tomlyn 3.2.1634.

4508. Thomas Legatt; John (d); Chatham, Kent; G; 2.6.1645; 25.3.1645; 5.12.1653; 8.

4509. Thomas Read; George; St Gyles Cripplegate, M'sex; G; 19.1.1663; 19.1.1663; - ; 8. Entry deleted; m.n. 'Dead'.

4510. Stephen Rich; Stephen (d); Cambridge; Cl; 2.4.1666; 15.12.1665; - ; 8.

4511. Gideon Royar; Jno (d); Couent Garden, M'sex; Go; 6.11.1655; 29.9.1655; - ; 8.

4512. John Tomlyn; George; Newington, Kent; Y; 4.12.1648; 25.12.1648; 28.3.1659; 7.

TOMLYN, John
4513. Robert Walters; Robt; Thame, Oxon; Tallowchandler; 5.12.1659; 5.12.1659; - ; 9.

TOMLYNS, Richard
4514. Daniell Ballard; Daniell; Bisley, Glos; H; 1.6.1646; 1.5.1646; - ; 8.

4515. Robert Bolter; John; Abingdon, Berks; M; 4.5.1657; 4.5.1657; 6.6.1664; 7.

4516. Robert Deeves; Richard (d); London; C & Gr; 18.11.1641; 18.11.1641; 10.1.1649; 7.

4517. John Jones; Arthur (d); - , Glos; G; 3.11.1651; 3.11.1651; - ; 8.

4518. Nicholas Rand; John (d); Redmarshall, Dur; Cl; 18.1.1647; 25.12.1646; - ; 8.

4519. Mathias Thurston. Fd by Tomlyns and John Dallom 5.9.1653. Bd to Dallom (q.v.) 3.8.1646.

4520. Obediah Tomlyns; Richard; London; C & St; 3.4.1665; 3.4.1665; 3.6.1672; 7. Bd to his father; fd by patrimony.

TONSON, Jacob
4521. John Allen; John (d); London; C & Ha; 2.12.1689; 2.12.1689; 3.5.1697; 7.

4522. Wm Dobbs; Ralph; London; C & Farrier; 1.9.1679; 1.9.1679; - ; 8.

4523. James Magnes; James (d); Covent Garden, M'sex; St; 6.9.1686; 6.9.1686; - ; 7.

4524. John Newton; Wm; Kirby Lonsdale, W'land; - ; 1.12.1679; 1.12.1679; 4.4.1687; 7.

TONSON, Mary, Widow
4525. Samuell Mabbatt; Thomas (d); parish of St Andrew Holborne, M'sex; Sc; 6.5.1695; 6.5.1695; - ; 7.

4526. Egbert Sangar; Edward; parish of St Paul Covent Garden, M'sex; T; 6.3.1699; 6.3.1699; 3.3.1707; 7.

4527. Ralph Valentine; John (d); Manchester, Lancs; Mr; 1.8.1692; 1.8.1692; - ; 7.

TONSON, Richard

4528. Owen Griffith; Griffith Roberts; Bachytaint, Carnarvon; G; 7.2.1681; 7.2.1681; - ; 7.

4529. William Horsley; William; London; C & D; 3.11.1684; 3.11.1684; - ; 7.

4530. William Powle; Thomas; London; C & Cw; 13.5.1678; 13.5.1678; - ; 7.

4531. John Wood; John (d); St Andrews Holbourne, M'sex; J; 6.6.1687; 6.6.1687; - ; 7.

TOOKE, Benjamin, I

4532. James Adams; James; Linn Regis, Norf; Mr; 1.10.1677; 1.10.1677; 6.10.1684; 7. Fd as Adamson.

4533. Bartholomew Baker; Bartholomew (d); Worcr; G; 6.6.1698; 6.6.1698; 9.9.1706; 7. Bd to Benjamin Tooke Senior.

4534. Henry Bonwicke; John; Mickleham, Surr; Cl; 13.6.1670; 13.6.1670; 1.10.1677; 7.

4535. Charles Roderick; Peirce; Wem, Shrops; G; 4.8.1684; 4.8.1684; - ; 7.

4536. Richard Simons; Richard; Purton, Wilts; Y; 1.9.1673; 1.9.1673; - ; 8.

4537. Baptist Tutton; Richard; London; C & Glazier; 7.5.1683; 7.5.1683; - ; 7.

4538. John Watts; John (d); Swainscomb, Kent; Rector; 5.5.1684; 5.5.1684; 25.6.1691; 7.

TOOKE, Benjamin, II

4539. William Tooke; Benjamin; London; C & St; 6.7.1696; 6.7.1696; 2.8.1703; 7. Bd to Benjamin Tooke the younger.

TORSHELL, Richard

4540. James Wiltsheire; Ephraim (d); parish of Shafford, Essex; Y; 3.7.1686; 3.7.1686; 4.7.1698; 7. T.o. (n.d.) to Edward Powell and fd by Torshell and Powell.

TOWES, John

4541. Thomas Aylway; John; London; C & MT; 6.2.1671; 6.2.1671; 3.2.1680; 7. Fd as Alway.

4542. Joseph Dell; James; St Albans, Herts; Farmer; 23.12.1663; 23.12.1663; 9.1.1671; 7.

4543. Cleophas Hawkins; Edward (d); London; C & Mr; 3.3.1656; 25.12 1655; - ; 8.

4544. Thomas Wallis; Sam; Marlebrough, Wilts; Gr; 2.4.1655; 2.4.1655; - ; 8.

TOY, Humphrey

4545. Jonathan Spencer; Miles; Wallingworth, Suff; Cl; 4.5.1641; 1.5.1641; - ; 8.

TRACEY, Ebenezar

4546. Henry Parson. Fd by Tracey and Thomas Passenger 11.11.1700. Bd to Passenger (q.v.) 21.6.1693.

TRACEY, Edward

4547. Anne Wood; Edward; London; C & Mr; 4.3.1700; 4.3.1700; - ; 7.

TRACEY, John

4548. [John Tracey. Son of Charles Tracey; fd by patrimony 6.2.1693.]

TREAGLE, John

4549. Wm Beckwith; Lawrence; Richmond, Yorks; Y; 14.10.1641; 18.10.1641; 7.5.1649; 7.

TRIPLETT, Ralph

4550. Richard Bushrod; Richard; Dorchester, Dors; G; 28.7.1645; 28.7.1645; - ; 7.

4551. Lawrence Hales. Fd by Triplett 15.3.1641. Bd to him 12.1.1631.

4552. Thomas Hammersley; William; Wedgwood, Staffs; G; 9.2.1657; 29.9.1656; 2.5.1664; 8.

4553. Thomas Rawlinson; Emanuell; London; C & MT; 1.3.1641; 1.3.1641; 6.3.1648; 7.

4554. Richard Samborne; Fran; London; Go; 1.3.1641; 1.3.1641; - ; 7.

4555. Edward Shawller; Michaell; Riseley, Beds; Y; 22.8.1648; 22.8.1648; 1.9.1656; 8.

4556. John Viner; John; Westmr; Cl; 6.9.1652; 24.6.1652; - ; 8.

TRISTRAM, Robert

4557. Thomas Jennings; Thomas; Sheffeild, Yorks; Cu; 6.6.1692; 6.6.1692; - ; 7.

4558. John Theak; John (d); parish of St Giles Criplegate, M'sex; Chandler; 5.12.1698; 5.12.1698; - ; 8.

TUCKE, Anthony

4559. George Fullwood. Fd by Tucke 16.1.1643. Bd to him 14.1.1636.

TUCKEY, Humphrey

4560. John Bellinger; Wm; London; C & Girdler; 24.8.1642; 24.6.1642; 24.6.1650; 8.

4561. John Bowden; John; London; C & Bl; 6.10.1662; 24.6.1662; - ; 8.

4562. Henry Chase; Thomas; Petersfeild, S'hants; G; 3.5.1647; 25.3.1647; 2.4.1655; 8.

4563. Ellis Hookes; Tho; Citty of Westminster; G; 5.8.1650; 5.8.1650; - ; 8.

4564. Ambros Isted; Richard (d); Lewis, Sussex; G; 3.12.1655; 3.12.1655; 7.3.1664; 8.

4565. St John Litchfeild; Leonard; Citty of Oxon; Printer; 1.2.1664; 29.9.1663; - ; 8.

4566. Thomas Mors; Tho; - , Wilts; Y; 5.2.1655; 5.2.1655; 7.7.1662; 7.

TUCKEY, John

4567. Richard Shawler; Edward (d); London; Distiller; 21.6.1695; 21.6.1695; 1.3.1703; 7.

TUCKEY, William

4568. Henry Gillibrand; Henry (d); Liddenston Lovell, Oxon [sic for Bucks]; Cl; 1.9.1684; 1.9.1684; 7.12.1691; 7. Fd by James Rawlins.

4568. John Tuckey; Willm; London; C & St; 2.10.1682; 2.10.1682; 7.10.1689; 7. The entry of freedom states that Tuckey was turned over, and notes a fine of 2s. 6d. 'for not being turned over at ye Hall', but the new master's name is left blank.

4570. [William Tuckey. Fd by redemption 3.12.1677.]

TUNMAN, John

4571. Math Hart; Math; Hillington, M'sex; Y; 6.5.1648; 6.5.1648; 5.5.1656; 8. Fd by Tunman and William Atkinson.

TURNER, Adam

4572. [Adam Turner. Son of Thomas Turner; fd by patrimony 7.8.1673.]

TURNER, Henry

4573. Paul Turner; Henry; London; C & St; 6.10.1656; 6.10.1656; 26.3.1666; 7. Bd to his father; fd by patrimony.

4574. William Turner. Fd by patrimony 10.1.1655.

TURNER, Matthew

4575. Thomas Mathews; Thomas (d); London; C & MT; 4.5.1674; 4.5.1674; - ; 7.

4576. Thomas Metcalfe; John; Richmond, Yorks; G; 6.9.1686; 6.9.1686; - ; 7.

TURNER, Roger

4577. Charles Bostocke; Robte (d); London; C & St; 26.3.1657; 26.3.1657; - ; 7. Reported gone from his master; indentures cancelled 28.6.1658.

4578. Samuell Cooke; Nicholas; London; C & Cw; 17.10.1653; 25.12.1652; 3.12.1660; 9. Fd by Turner and Samuel Speed.

4579. Benjamine Davis; John (d); London; G; 12.7.1658; 12.7.1658; - ; 8.

4580. Henry Long; Henry; Cookham, Berks; Cw; 15.6.1646; 15.6.1646; 29.6.1653; 7.

TURNER, William, I

4581. Arthur Calcott. Fd by Turner 18.5.1654. Apparently never formally bd.

4582. James Clifford. Fd by Turner 16.3.1648. Apparently never formally bd.

4583. Thomas Seale. Fd by Turner 3.7.1648. Bd to him 3.6.1634.

TURNER, William, II

4584. Joshua Worrall; Joshua; High Highland, Yorks; Y; 5.9.1698; 7.11.1697; 5.3.1711; 7. Fd by Christopher Bateman.

TWYFORD, Henry

4585. Edward Barker; Robert; St Martins Le Grand, [London]; V; 1.5.1676; 1.5.1676; - ; 8.

4586. Thomas Evans; John; London; C & MT; 1.3.1666; 1.3.1666; - ; 8.

4587. Thomas Glew; James (d); Belton, Lincs; H; 6.2.1654; 6.2.1654; 24.1.1662; 8.

4588. Ayres Hunt; Thomas; Wantage, Berks; I; 20.5.1685; 20.5.1685; - ; 7.

4589. John Leigh; John; Shelton, Staffs; G; 26.3.1662; 26.3.1662; 2.5.1669; 7.

4590. Richard Moore. Bd to Nathaniel Butter 4.4.1636; t.o. 4.5.1641 to Twyford.

4591. Beniamin Southwood. Fd by Twyford 1.3.1662. Apparently never formally bd.

4592. Timothy Twiford; Henry; Burton upon the water, Glos; G; 13.8.1649; 13.8.1649; 1.9.1656; 7.

TWYFORD, Timothy

4593. Richard Antrobus; Robert (d); Liegh, Kent; Cl; 2.8.1658; 2.8.1658; - ; 8.

4594. John Butler; John (d); Biglesworth, Beds; Y; 3.3.1668; 3.3.1668; - ; 7.

TWYN, John, I

4595. Wm Balfore; Alexander; London; G; 21.3.1649; 21.3.1649; - ; 9.

4596. Thomas Bramston; Beniamyn; London; C & Cu; 21.3.1649; 21.3.1649; 6.12.1675; 9.

4597. John Twinn. Fd by patrimony 6.10.1679.

4598. Joseph Walker; William; Darnell, Yorks; Cu; 1.10.1660; 1.10.1660; 8.10.1667; 7.

4599. Symon Walton; Edward; Westbury, Wilts; Cw; 1.2.1658; 1.2.1658; - ; 7.

TWYNN. John, II

4600. Richard Bush; John; parrish of St Buttolphs Aldersgate, London; Sawyer; 7.6.1686; 7.6.1686; - ; 7.

TYAS, Charles

4601. Thomas Passinger; Thomas; Guilford, Surr; - ; 7.9.1657; 25.7.1657; 5.2.1666; 8.

4602. John Williamson; John (d); Guildford, Surr; Y; 4.5.1663; 4.5.1663; 6.5.1670; 7.

TYLER, Evan

4603. William Allexander; Edmund; London; C & Go; 5.10.1657; 3.8.1657; - ; 8.

4604. Thomas Ashton; Dan (d); London; C & Armorer; 2.10.1654; 25.3.1655; - ; 8.

4605. Nicholas Browne. Fd by Tyler 6.10.1662. Apparently never formally bd.

4606. Thomas Deauer; Jnc; London; C & St; 23.1.1654; 23.1.1654; 11.2.1661; 7. Entry deleted; m.n. 'this Appr. is gone away wth Consent of his Mr & Father' (n.d.); but fd by patrimony.

4607. Lawrence Gough; Francis; London; C & Mr; 4.10.1669; 4.10. 1669; - ; 8.

4608. Richard Hunt. Fd by Tyler 7.5.1666. Apparently never formally bd.

4609. Richard Jon. Fd by Tyler 7.2.1676. Apparently never formally bd.

4610. Thomas Melvyn; Wm; London; Schoolmaster; 2.8.1641; 29.9. 1641; - ; 8.

4611. Thomas Teonge; Henry; parish of Spernhall, War; Minister; 3.6. 1678; 3.6.1678; 5.8.1695; 7.

4612. Henry Tilley; Robert; London; Sc; 5.8.1678; 5.8.1678; 26.3.1686; 7. Fd by William Miller as executor to Evan Tyler deceased.

4613. George Townsend; William; South Sarney, Glos; 15.1.1673; 15.1. 1673; 4.12.1682; 7.

4614. Benjamine Wailes; George; London; C & Cw; 6.12.1669; 6.12. 1669; 20.12.1677; 8.

TYM, Robert

4615. William Chantrell; William; Peopleton, Surr [sic for Worcs]; Y; 1.8.1648; 1.8.1648; - ; 7.

TYTON, Francis

4616. Willm Bowtell; John; London; C & I; 16.9.1668; 16.9.1668; 6.3.1676; 7.

4617. William Canning. Fd by the executors of Tyton 2.8.1686. Bd to George Marriott (q.v.) 14.1.1679.

4618. Richard Freshwater; Heybridge hall, Essex; G; 12.11.1649; 12.11.1649; - ; 8.

4619. Richard Hall; Richard; Westminster, M'sex; G; 10.1.1654; 10.1. 1654; 11.2.1661; 7.

4620. Nathaniell Hobson; John; Holbeech, Lincs; G; 3.7.1656; 3.7. 1656; - ; 7.

4621. Samuell Hughes; Edward; Parish of St Martins in the Fields, M'-sex; G; 6.8.1660; 6.8.1660; - ; 8.

4622. Arthur Jones; John (d); London; C & St; 4.10.1675; 4.10.1675; 4.12.1682; 7.

4623. Henry Marsh; Mich (d); London; Clockmaker; 1.7.1650; 1.7.1650; 5.10.1657; 7. Fd by Tyton and George Latham.

4624. Richard Taylor; George (d); Hornesey, M'sex; Cl; 3.8.1646; 3.8. 1646; - ; 7.

TYTON, William

4625. Wm Anthony; Marke (d); London; Limner; 17.1.1648; 17.1. 1648; - ; 7.

4626. Edward Best; Richard (d); London; T; 3.8.1646; 3.8.1646; - ; 8.

4627. Andrew Hawkesworth; Thomas; London; Y; 25.4.1650; 1.5.1650; 26.3.1661; 8. Rebd to Richard Burton (q.v.) 5.9.1653 and fd by him.

4628. William Randall; Richard; Oxsted; Surr; Cl; 10.1.1655; 25.12. 1654; - ; 8.

4629. Thomas Stapleton; Edward; St Martins in the Feilds, [M'sex]; G; 19.1.1652; 19.1.1652; - ; 7.

UDALL, Lawrence

4630. Nathaniell Brooke; John; Haddingham, Bucks; Cl; 1.12.1645; 1.12. 1645; - ; 7.

4631. Samuell Cherry; Samuell; East Clandon, Surr; Cl; 3.2.1651; 3.2. 1651; - ; 7.

4632. Richard Dixon; Richard (d); Kevington, Leics; H; 6.4.1657; 6.4. 1657; - ; 7.

4633. John Godman; John; Hemsted, Herts; Y; 4.10.1669; 4.10.1669; 6.11.1676; 7.

4634. Thomas Hawson. Fd by Udall and Thomas Ellis 5.4.1642. Bd to Ellis 6.5.1634.

4635. Wm Mendy; Nicholas; Kingsley, Bucks; Y; 1.3.1644; 1.3.1644; 3.3.1651; 7.

4636. George Thresser. Fd by Udall 3.3.1647. Bd to him 2.4.1638.

4637. Laurence Udall. Fd by patrimony 11.2.1661.

UNDERHILL, John

4638. Walter Dun. Bd to Joseph Milner (q.v.) 9.11.1646; t.o. 1.7.1650 to Underhill and fd by Milner and Underhill 25.6.1657.

4639. Richard Fowkes; Nicholas (d); Caldecott, N'hants; H; 1.10.1660; 1.10.1660; - ; 7.

UNDERHILL, Thomas

4640. Richard Butler; William; Sutton Colfeild, War; H; 6.8.1655; 24.6.1655; 30.6.1663; 8. Fd by Underhill and Abraham Miller.

4641. Edward Chapman; Thomas; Newbold, Leics; Y; 5.5.1656; 5.5.1656; - ; 7.

4642. Beniamyn Cottrell; Thomas; London; C & MT; 22.6.1641; 1.5.1641; 10.1.1648; 9.

4643. Samuell Dunn; Wm; Ormskirke, Ches [sic for Lancs?]; Cl; 2.7.1653; 2.7.1653; - ; 7.

4644. Mathew Keinton; Thomas; Salisbery, Wilts; Clothier; 1.6.1646; Easter Day 1646; 6.2.1654; 8.

4645. William Oldham; John; London; C & Mr; 3.10.1653; 25.12.1642; 5.3.1677; 9.

4646. Thomas Underhill. Fd by patrimony 1.2.1675. Probably the son of Thomas Underhill, although the father's christian name is not given.

UNDERWOOD, Ralph

4647. James Stewart; Dugald; parish of St Margrett Westminster; G; 7.8.1693; 7.8.1693; - ; 7.

UNITT, George

4648. William Parsons; William; Miniard, Som; Y; 6.10.1690; 6.10.1690; - ; 7.

VADE, James

4649. Humfrey Lewis; Humfry; London; G; 1.9.1679; 1.9.1679; - ; 8.

VAVASOR, Nicholas

4650. Affable Strange; Alexander; London; J; 6.12.1647; 6.12.1647; 2.6.1656; 8. Fd by Vavasor and Gabriel Baskerville.

VEASEY, John

4651. Benjn Farnworth; Samuell (d); Town of Nottingham; T; 5.8.1689; 5.8.1689; 2.11.1696; 7.

4652. John Hudson; John (d); Reddriffe, Surr; Mariner; 2.3.1685; 2.3.1685; - ; 7.

4653. John Muston; John (d); Cittie cf Coventrey, War; G; 7.11.1681; 7.11.1681; 4.3.1689; 7.

4654. Edward Terrell; Timothy (d); London; C & Cook; 1.2.1697; 1.2.1697; 7.2.1704; 7.

VERE, Thomas

4655. Richard Burt; John; London; C & Ha; 6.11.1655; 6.11.1655; - ; 8.

4656. Henry Harling; John; Kirbey Lansdale, W'land; Y; 1.4.1650; 1.4.1650; 1.6.1657; 7.

4657. Thomas Jenkins; John; Moreton, Herefs; Y; 17.1.1648; 29.9.1647; 1.10.1655, 8.

4658. John Jourdan, Tho; St Pulchres, London; BSg; 22.2.1675; 22.2.1675; - ; 7. Rebd to Vere 3.5.1675 for 7 years from 3.5.1675.

4659. Edward Oliver; Willm; Billarykey alius Greate Bursted, Essex; G; 2.12.1668; 2.12.1668; - ; 7.

4660. Edward Olliver; Edward; Shoreham, Kent; Cl; 3.12.1667; 3.12.1667; 6.12.1675; 7.

4661. Charles Vere; John; London; C & Gr; 26.3.1666; 21.12.1665; - ; 7.

4662. Nathaniell Wright; Rich; Tedmarsh, Berks; Cl; 3.8.1657; 3.8.1657; 5.2.1666; 8.

VICARIS, Thomas

4663. [Thomas Vicaris. Son of Richard Vicaris; fd by patrimony 2.6.1662.]

VINCENT, Anthony
4664. Henry Huffen. Fd by Vincent 6.3.1648. Bd to him 1.10.1638.

4665. Anthony Vincent. Fd by patrimony 3.9.1655.

4666. John Vincent. Fd by patrimony 6.2.1660.

VINCENT, Robert
4667. Francis Atkins; Francis; London; C & F; 5.5.1690; 5.5.1690; - ; 7.

4668. John Crofts; Richard; London; C & Cd; 5.2.1700; 5.2.1700; 3.3.1707; 7.

4669. Richard Deards; Richard (d); London; C & F; 25.6.1688; 25.6.1688; - ; 7.

4670. Robert Heming; Henry; London; C & Founder; 3.12.1694; 3.12.1694; 4.5.1702; 7.

4671. James Hurst; James (d); Woodman Court, Sussex; G; 5.6.1690; 5.5.1690; - ; 8.

VIZE, Edward
4672. John Tofte; Samuel; London; G; 3.12.1684; 3.12.1684; - ; 7.

WALBANK, Elizabeth, Widow
4673. Richard Tonson; Jacob; London; C & BSg; 7.4.1668; 7.4.1668; 4.9.1676; 7. Bd to the widow of Matthew Walbank.

WALBANK, Gilbert
4674. Tho Awsiter; Thomas (d); Southall, M'sex; G; 3.5.1680; 3.5.1680; - ; 7.

4675. Burnell Chappell; Edward; Southwell, Notts; Cl; 2.8.1669; 2.8.1669; - ; 7.

WALBANK, Matthew
4676. George Andrews; Bartimeus; Magdalen-Lavar, Essex; Cl; 5.4.1642; 25.3.1642; 4.6.1649; 8.

4677. William Brooman. Fd by Walbank and George Tomlyn 5.9.1642. Bd to Tomlyn 3.2.1634.

4678. Beniamyn Crooke; Tho; Hamersmith, M'sex; G; 17.1.1648; 17.1.1648; - ; 7.

4679. Samuell Herricke; Tho; Holborne, [M'sex]; G; 1.3.1655; 1.3.1655; 3.3.1662; 8. The entry of freedom notes Walbank as deceased.

4680. John Nightingall; Mathew; Newport pond, Essex; G; 20.12.1651; 20.12.1651; - ; 7.

4681. Josiah Robinson; Origen; London; C & Weaver; 28.3.1659; 28.3.1659; 20.8.1667; 8.

4682. Gilbert Walbanck; Symon; Egington, Derby; Y; 1.3.1649; 1.3.1649; 19.3.1658; 9.

4683. Mathew Walbanck; Mathew; London; C & St; 1.3.1650; 1.3.1650; 5.1.1657; 7. Bd to his father; fd by patrimony.

WALCROFT, William
4684. Phillipp Powell. Bd to Robert Steele (q.v.) 7.10.1689; t.o. 4.11.1689 to Walcroft.

WALFORD, Benjamin
4685. Richard Squerell; Richard; London; C & MT; 5.9.1692; 5.9.1692; - ; 7.

WALKER, James
4686. Joseph Bedcock; William (d); London; C & Br; 7.6.1697; 7.6.1697; - ; 7.

4687. Abraham Dickson; Joshua; parish of Leeds, Yorks; G; 2.10.1699; 2.10.1699; 7.6.1708; 7.

4688. William Munford; William; Carington, Beds; H; 6.2.1693; 6.2.1693; - ; 7.

WALKER, John
4689. William Stones; John; Chesterfeild, Derby; Y; 4.12.1648; 5.11.1648; - ; 8.

WALKER, Mathias
4690. Joseph Goddard; Hugh (d); Norton, Derby; H; 5.9.1664; 1.5.1664; - ; 7.

WALKER, Richard
4691. John Allen; Richard; Citty of Canterbury, [Kent]; G; 6.12.1675; 6.12.1675; - ; 7.

WALL, Thomas
4692. [Thomas Wall. Fd by redemption 25.8.1675.]

WALLIS, Elisha
4693. Beniamin Clarke. Fd by Wallis and John Orme 7.11.1664. Bd to Orme (q.v.) 5.1.1657.
4694. Thomas Whaley; Richard (d); London; C & Go; 2.10.1654; 2.10.1654; - ; 7.

WALLIS, John
4695. Wm Fowell; William; London; C & Gl; 5.2.1683; 5.2.1683; 7.12.1691; 7. Fd by James Rawlins.

WALMESLEY, Ferdinando
4696. Samuell Briscoe; Thomas (d); Aldnam Wood, Herts; G; 7.5.1666; 7.5.1666; - ; 7.
4697. Willm Hobson; Richard; Sepulchrs parish, M'sex; Br; 4.3.1661; 4.3.1661; 2.4.1677; 7.
4698. Thomas Moore; Geo; Citty of Bristow, [Glos]; Woollendraper; 4.1.1658; 4.1.1658; - ; 7.
4699. Thomas Pates; John; Alston, Glos; G; 5.6.1671; 5.6.1671; - ; 7.

WALTHOE, John
4700. John Deeve; Samuell (d); London; Mch; 8.5.1693; 8.5.1693; - ; 7.
4701. Kingsmill Grove; William (d); parish of St Clement Danes, M'sex; Cheesemonger; 4.9.1699; 4.9.1699; - ; 7.
4702. Marke Parker; Marke (d); Sandwich, Kent; Cl; 1.2.1686; 1.2.1686; - ; 7.
4703. Thomas Taylor; Richd; Parish of St Clements Danes, M'sex; T; 5.8.1700; 5.8.1700; 7.9.1713; 7.

4704. John Waltho; Thomas (d); Stafford, Staffs; Barber; 4.7.1692; 4.7.1692; 6.5.1700; 7.

WALTON, Robert
4705. James Walker. Fd by John Overton (q.v.) 6.7.1691, to whom he was bd 1.9.1679; but said to have been originally bd to Walton, and fined 2s. 6d. for not being t.o. at the hall.

WARD, Benjamin
4706. Mathew Crispe; Mathew (d); Ashborn, Derby; Cw; 3.4.1676; 3.4.1676; - ; 8.
4707. Ben Pullin; John; parish of St Mary Woolnoth, London; Ha; 3.6.1678; 3.6.1678; - ; 7.

WARD, Edward
4708. Saml Crabtree; Abraham; parish of St Giles Criplegate, [London]; Silktwister; 1.3.1686; 1.3.1686; 2.4.1694; 7.
4709. George Dowle; George (d); Citty of Bristoll; - ; 6.3.1676; 6.3.1676; - ; 7.
4710. John Matley; William (d); London; C & Sk; 12.4.1692; 12.4.1692; - ; 8.
4711. John Meacham; Edwd; Parish of St James Clarkenwell, M'sex; L; 4.7.1681; 1.6.1681; 7.2.1698; 8.
4712. Thomas Wicks; Richard; London; C & Ca; 2.4.1683; 25.3.1683; - ; 8.

WARD, Richard
4713. Wm Franck; Wm; Cottingley, Yorks; G; 5.4.1642; 5.4.1642; - ; 7.

WARD, Robert, I
4714. [Robte Ward. Son of Chidwicke Ward; fd by patrimony 2.8.1647.]
4715. John Ward. Fd by patrimony 2.8.1658.

WARD, Robert, II
4716. [Robt Ward. Son of John Ward; fd by patrimony 3.5.1686.]

WARNER, William

4717. Anthony Binnie; Joseph (d); London; Surgeon; 9.2.1674; 9.2.1674; - ; 7.

4718. Henry Hartus; Willm (d); Coxwould, Yorks; H; 15.1.1673; 15.1. 1673; 3.5.1680; 7. Fd by William Warren.

4719. Mich Plumer; John; York; Go; 3.5.1680; 3.5.1680; 4.7.1687; 7.

WARNING, Alice, Widow

4720. William Rookes; William; London; C & Leatherseller; 7.12.1663; 25.3.1663; - ; 7.

WARREN, Thomas, I

4721. John Brent; William; Halford, War; G; 3.12.1655; 25.3.1655; 20.12.1677; 8.

4722. John Bush; Edward; Harford, Herts; G; 17.4.1648; 1.11.1647; 3.12. 1655; 8.

4723. Thomas Griffis; Adam; Wisden, Shrops; Cl; 2.5.1643; 2.5.1643; - ; 7.

4724. Thomas Jackson. Fd by Warren and John Crooke 17.11.1645. Bd to Crooke 12.11.1638.

4725. Richard Knowles. Fd by Warren 'for Mr Jo: Norton' 17.4.1648. Apparently never formally bd.

4726. John Law; Mathew; Allerton, Som; Cl; 5.8.1650; 24.6.1650; 2.8. 1658; 8.

4727. Francis Warren. Fd by patrimony 1.2.1664. Probably the son of Thomas Warren, although the father's christian name is not given.

4728. Thomas Warren. Fd by patrimony 7.8.1666.

4729. Willm Warren. Fd by patrimony 21.12.1667.

WARREN, Thomas, II

4730. Richard Phillipps; Richard; London; C & Tallowchandler; 4.6. 1694; 4.6.1694; 1.7.1706; 7.

4731. Joseph Tough; David (d); St Martins Le=Grand, London; Cd; 8.6. 1696; 8.6.1696; 6.3.1704; 7.

WARREN, William

4732. Christian Fowle; John; Stepney alius Stebinheath, M'sex; Mariner; 27.11.1688; 27.11.1688; - ; 7.

4733. Thomas Gladman; Richard; Lyniall Hemsted, Herts; T; 11.2.1668; 11.2.1668; 1.10.1688; 7.

4734. Henry Hartus. Fd by Warren 3.5.1680. Bd to William Warner (q.v.) 15.1.1673.

4735. Christopher Hopkins; Willm (d); Landockey, Mon; Bl; 6.9.1669; 6.9.1669; - ; 7.

4736. Richard Plumton; Richard (d); Parish of St Olave Southwarke, Surr; J; 5.9.1681; 5.9.1681; - ; 7.

4737. Eliz Reede; Richard; St Martin in ye Feilds, [M'sex]; L; 7.8.1676; 7.8.1676; - ; 7.

WARTER, William

4738. Guy Cole; Guy (d); Ashwell, Rut; G; 4.10.1686; 4.10.1686; - ; 7.

4739. John Evitt; George (d); London; C & Cu; 5.12.1692; 5.12.1692; 15.2.1700; 8.

4740. Thomas Gillett; Thomas; the Devizes, Wilts; Clothier; 7.6.1676; 7.6.1676; - ; 7.

4741. Thomas Herne; Clement; London; C & D; 1.8.1698; 1.8.1698; - ; 7.

4742. John Kingsley; John; London, C & BSg; 7.11.1687; 7.11.1687; 4.2. 1695; 7.

4743. John Lenthall; Thomas (d); parish of Hornchurch, Essex; G; 4.9. 1699; 4.9.1699; 9.9.1706; 7.

4744. Sarah Marshall; Edward; London; C & Cook; 12.11.1694; 12.11. 1694; - ; 7.

4745. Ambrose Newton; Richard; Ipswich, Suff; G; 7.3.1698; 7.3.1698; - ; 7.

4746. William Parsons; Tho; St Giles in ye Feilds, [M'sex]; Distiller; 3.6.1678; 3.6.1678; 22.12.1685; 7.

4747. William Ravenhill; William; the Minories, London; G; 7.6.1675; 7.6.1675; - ; 7.

4748. William Tilley; Thomas; London; G; 12.10.1676; 12.10.1676; - ; 8.

4749. William Warter. Fd by patrimony 4.7.1698.

WATERHOUSE, Joshua

4750. Willm Carter; Samuell; London; C & Woollendraper; 5.12.1670; 5.12.1670; - ; 7.

WATERSON, John

4751. John Colebancke. Bd to Richard Whitaker (q.v.) 2.7.1645; t.o. 5.8.1650 to Waterson.

4752. John Edmonds. Fd by Waterson 4.7.1642. Bd to him 30.6.1634.

4753. Edward Hillary; Anth; new Sarum, - ; Cl; 10.5.1641; 10.5.1641; - ; 9.

4754. Henry Thurman; Edward; London; Cl; 22.2.1647; 22.2.1647; - ; 7.

4755. John Wilcocks. Fd by Waterson 5.4.1647. Bd to him 26.3.1639.

4756. James Wynn; Ellis; Easton, Suff; G; 17.11.1645; 17.11.1645; - ; 7.

WATERSON, Simon

4757. Francis Haley. Fd by Waterson and George Eversden 31.1.1666. Bd to Eversden (q.v.) 4.10.1658.

WATKINS, Zachariah

4758. John Foord; Thomas; Citty of Worc; Mr; 4.4.1664; 25.3.1664; 2.12. 1672; 7. T.o. 7.5.1666 to John Playford, but fd by redemption, by order of the Lord Mayor.

WATSON, Thomas

4759. Richard Watson; John; Stanmore Magna, M'sex; G; 1.3.1647; 1.3.1647; - ; 10.

WATTS, Joseph

4760. Richard Cumberland; William; London; C & F; 1.3.1686; 1.3. 1686; 13.3.1693; 7.

WEAVER, Thomas

4761. Gabriell Beadle. Fd by Weaver 4.10.1641. Bd to him 6.12.1631.

WEBB, Elizabeth

4762. [Elizabeth Webb. Fd by redemption 7.7.1684, paying a fine of £1. 1s. 6d. in addition to the usual fee of 3s. 4d.]

WEBB, John

4763. John Atherton; Will; Amptill, Beds; H; 2.6.1656; 2.6.1656; - ; 7.

4764. Williame Browne; William; London; C & I; 27.9.1650; 27.9.1650; - ; 7.

4765. Freeman Fanne; John (d); Hornsey, M'sex; Farmer; 5.6.1654; 1.5.1654; 5.5.1662; 8.

4766. Samuell Greene; Samuell; Ipswich, Suff; M; 4.3.1661; 4.3.1661; 5.7.1669; 7.

4767. Symon Haddock. Fd by Webb 6.7.1646. Bd to him (as Simon Hiducke) 4.8.1635.

4768. Richard Leeds; Richard; Ware, Herts; H; 6.7.1646; 24.3.1646; 3.4. 1654; 8.

4769. Thomas Tatnell; James (d); London; C & B; 6.11.1660; 28.10.1660; 10.11.1668; 8. Fd by Webb and Steven Cope.

WEBB, Nathaniel

4770. Joseph Andrews; Mathew; London; C & Gr; 29.6.1653; 24.6. 1653; 21.1.1662; 8.

4771. Thomas Burrough; Thomas (d); Pedmarsh, Essex; Cl; 27.6.1660; 24.6.1660; - ; 8.

4772. Henry Mason; Wm; Handley, Worcs; Y; 3.5.1652; 24.6.1652; - ; 7.

4773. Henry Wandisly; John (d); Parbold, Lancs; Y; 7.9.1663; 7.9.1663; - ; 8.

WEBSTER, Benjamin

4774. Andrew Bell. Fd by Webster and Thomas Benskin 4.3.1695. Bd to Benskin (q.v.) 2.4.1683.

4775. Amos Coplestone; Amos; Bockonock, Corn; G; 3.10.1692; 3.10. 1692; 7.10.[1700]; 7. Fd by Webster and Daniel Browne.

4776. William Faulkener; Benjamin; London; G; 2.10.1682; 2.10.1682; 3.2.1690; 7. The entry of freedom describes Faulkener as 'Servt. to Saml. Wester & turned over to George Larkin' (n.d.).

WELCHMAN, Samuel

4777. Edward Moyle; John (d); Winbourne, Dors; Cl; 2.11.1696; 2.11. 1696; - ; 8.

WELD, John

4778. John Malden; Thomas (d); East Hanvill, Essex; Y; 1.8.1687; 1.8.1687; - ; 7.

WELLINGTON, Richard

4779. William Thorne; William (d); London; C & V; 7.10.1700; 7.10.1700; - ; 7.

WELLINS, Jonas

4780. John Francklyn; John (d); Towerhill, London; Ship's Master; 2.12.1644; 25.12.1644; - ; 8.

4781. Richard Snow. Fd by Wellins 4.5.1641. Bd to him 3.3.1634.

WELLS, George

4782. Peter James; Peter; Hogsden, [Bucks]; Ca; 7.6.1675; 7.6.1675; - ; 7.

4783. Thomas Newborough; Richard; parish of Stockemilborough, Shrops; Cl; 5.8.1678; 5.8.1678; 7.12. 1685; 7.

WELLS, William

4784. William Cooper; John (d); - , Leics; - ; 3.12.1655; 29.9.1655; 2.11.1663; 8.

4785. Edward Saintleger; Henry; Sirencester, Glos; G; 1.3.1664; 1.3. 1664; - ; 7.

4786. Robert Scott. Bd to Daniel Frere (q.v.) 10.1.1649; t.o. 7.4.1651 to Wells and fd by him and Frere 31.3. 1656.

4787. George Wells. Fd by patrimony 2.11.1674.

4788. William Wells. Fd by patrimony 6.7.1661.

WEST, Simon

4789. John Brown; John; Stanik, Lancs; Y; 22.2.1675; 22.2.1675; - ; 7.

4790. Richard Glascoe; Ezechiell; Epping, Essex; Y; 4.3.1650; 25.12.1649; - ; 8.

4791. Beniamyn Milborne; Andrew; Totnam high=Crosse, M'sex; T; 7.6. 1641; 25.3.1641; - ; 8.

4792. Daniell Peacocke; Ferdin; Redburne, Herts; Y; 7.9.1657; 1.5. 1657; 2.4.1666; 9.

4793. John Stafford; Gilbert; London; C & BSg; 1.12.1645; 1.11.1645; - ; 10.

4794. Beniamin Warde; Beniamin (d); London; C & Sc; 3.4.1665; 3.4. 1665; 26.4.1672; 7.

WESTBROOK, Richard

4795. Richard Dalton; James; Bassingthwaite, Cumb; Y; 1.8.1653; 1.8. 1653; - ; 7.

4796. Edward Gee; Thomas; Woluey, War; H; 6.11.1655; 6.11.1655; 1.12.1662; 7. Fd by Westbrook and Walter Dame.

4797. Thomas Maddox. Fd by Westbrook and Valentine Storer 9.5.1655. Bd to Storer (q.v.) 6.12.1647.

4798. John Shrimpton; Richard; long Crandon, Bucks; Y; 14.6.1647; 1.6.1647; - ; 8.

4799. Charles Tracey. Fd by Westbrook and Christopher Reisold 5.6. 1654. Bd to Reisold (q.v.) 19.3.1646.

WESTON, Henry
4800. John Love. Fd by Weston, Michael Sparkes and Eleanor Cotes 7.7.1662. Bd to Sparkes (q.v.) 4.10.1652.

WESTON, John
4801. Thomas Wade; George; Witney, Oxon; Brazier; 2.11.1646; 2.11. 1646; - ; 8.

WHALLEY, Peter
4802. Samuell Whalley; Peter; London; C & St; 1.3.1650; 1.4.1647; 3.4. 1654; 7. Bd to his father and 'dated by order of Cort. the first of Aprill 1647'; fd by patrimony.

WHATELY, Samuel
4803. Edward Botler; Jno; Wormley, Herts; G; 3.3.1656; 3.3.1656; - ; 7.

WHITAKER, Richard
4804. John Baker; Thomas; Whitstone, Dev; Cl; 30.6.1641; 25.3.1641; 7.5.1649; 8.
4805. John Colebanck; Richard; London; G; 2.7.1645; 2.7.1645; - ; 8. T.o. 5.8.1650 to John Waterson.
4806. Wm Hull; Richard; London; C & D; 11.3.1644; 11.3.1644; - ; 7.
4807. John Mathewes. Fd by Whitaker and Richard Clutterbooke 17.1. 1642. Bd to Clutterbooke 2.9.1633.
4808. Samuell Tompson. Fd by Whitaker and Joyce Norton 17.1.1642. Bd to Joyce Norton 3.2.1634.
4809. Thomas Whitaker. Fd by patrimony 30.8.1641, but originally bd to Joyce Norton 6.2.1637.
4810. Anth Williamson. Fd by Whitaker 29.10.1649. Bd to him 5.10.1640.

WHITAKER, Thomas
4811. Timothy Cromlum; Richard; Quedgeley, Glos; Cl; 17.4.1648; 17.4. 1648; 24.4.1655; 8. T.o. 4.2.1650 to Samuel Thompson on the death of Whitaker.
4812. Thomas Davies; John; London; C & D; 17.4.1648; 17.4.1648; 24.4.1655; 9. Fd as Davis.

4813. Thomas French; Tho; Cambridge, Cambs; G; 13.12.1645; 13.12. 1645; 14.2.1653; 7. T.o. 20.9.1648 to Samuel Thompson, and fd by Whitaker and Thompson.

WHITE, Barnard
4814. John Gadbury; Willm; City of Oxon; Worsted-comber; 13.6.1670; 13.6.1670; - ; 8.
4815. Abraham Rice; Joseph; Burton vpon Trent, Staffs; Sh; 7.5.1683; 7.5.1683; 3.11.1690; 7.

WHITE, Charles
4816. Samuel Herbert; John; Hoxton, M'sex; Feltmaker; 6.6.1692; 6.6. 1692; - ; 7.

WHITE, Daniel
4817. Peter Parker; Peter; Altringham, Ches; G; 2.8.1658; 2.8.1658; 6.1.1665; 7. Fd by Henry Cripps, after less than 7 years' service (Court-Book D).

WHITE, John
4818. William Bothaw; William; London; L; 14.4.1656; 14.4.1656; - ; 7.
4819. John Brown; Tho (d); London; C & Bricklayer; 3.8.1674; 3.8. 1674; 2.10.1682; 8.
4820. Amos Coles. Fd by White and Richard Hodgkinson 7.12.1646. Bd to Hodgkinson 3.10.1639.
4821. Ralph Ravening; Richard; Southwarke, [Surr]; Bl; 19.7.1650; 19.7.1650; - ; 9.
4822. Henry Stone; Thomas (d); London; BSg; 12.8.1671; 12.8.1671; - ; 7.

WHITE, Margaret
4823. Daniell Keene; Richard; St Albans, M'sex; Y; 5.7.1680; 5.7.1680; 1.8.1687; 7. Fined 2s. 6d. 'For his not being turned over at the Hall', but there is no record of Keene having been improperly bd or having served another master.

4824. William Lapley; James; Wotton Vnderidge, Glos; Y; 2.10.1682; 2.10.1682; 7.10.1689; 7.

WHITE, Mary
4825. Thomas Burditt. Said to have been bd to Mary White; t.o. by her to John Heptinstall (n.d.), and by him to Henry Clarke (n.d.). Fd by Clarke 1.10.1688 and fined 2s. 6d. 'for his not being turned over at this Hall'. There is no formal entry of binding.

WHITE, Robert
4826. Robert Argent. Fd by White 4.2.1656. Apparently never formally bd.
4827. Francis Bateson; Dennis; Drury lane, M'sex; Y; 7.3.1670; 7.3.1670; 9.9.1678; 9. In the entry of freedom White is noted as deceased.
4828. Anthony Bryan; Anthony; London; D; 29.6.1646; 24.6.1646; 27.6.1654; 8.
4829. Nicholas Budd; Richard (d); Witney, Oxon; Clothier; 22.2.1647; [22.2.1647]; - ; 9.
4830. Francis Clarke; Thomas; Witney, Oxon; Clothier; 26.6.1668; 24.6.1668; 3.7.1676; 8.
4831. Henry Clarke; Thomas (d); Witney, Oxon; Clothier; 13.1.1669; 13.1.1669; 7.1.1678; 9.
4832. Wm Cripps; Henry; Citty of Oxford; Bs; 1.7.1650; 1.7.1650; - ; 7.
4833. Leonard Custis alius Cliffe; Wm; Cirencester, Glos; Clothier; 27.6.1654; 24.6.1654; - ; 9.
4834. Samuell Drafgate. Fd by White and George Bishop 4.3.1650. Bd to Bishop (q.v.) 5.12.1642.
4835. Abraham Everard; Thomas; Wotton Underidge, Glos; Cw; 1.10.1660; 24.6.1660; 26.6.1668; 8.
4836. Jacob Johnson; Edw; Redding, Berks; Ha; 7.9.1657; 7.9.1657; - ; 7.

4837. Isaack Lane. Fd by White 10.1.1670. Apparently never formally bd.
4838. James Orme. Fd by White 7.5.1683. Apparently never formally bd.
4839. Wm Salman. Fd by White 3.12.1660. Apparently never formally bd.
4840. Edward Sanny. Fd by White 6.6.1681. Apparently never formally bd.
4841. Gabriel Sedgwick; Robert; Bishopprick of Durham, [Dur]; Y; 1.10.1677; 1.10.1677; 6.10.1684; 7.
4842. John Turvey; John; Dencehanger, N'hants; Y; 6.10.1656; 6.10.1656; - ; 7.
4843. Edward Waythen; Wm; Wootton=vnderidge, Glos; Y; 6.10.1651; 29.9.1651; 3.10.1659; 8.
4844. Bernard White; Thomas; Wotton vnderidge, Glos; Mr; 6.2.1660; 6.2.1660; 20.2.1667; 7.
4845. Willm White alias Marshall; Ambrose Marshall (d); Debtford, Kent; Y; 5.2.1667; 5.2.1667; 22.2.1675; 7.
4846. William Whitwood. Fd by White and William Gilbertson 4.5.1666. Bd to Gilbertson (q.v.) 30.4.1658.
4847. William Winnington. Fd by White 5.6.1665. Apparently never formally bd. White was fined 5.6.1665 for illegally binding an apprentice (Court-Book D).
4848. Thomas Wood; William; Witney, Oxon; Clothier; 4.3.1650; 29.9.1649; - ; 8.

WHITE, William, alias Marshall
4849. [Willm White alias Marshall. Fd by patrimony 5.8.1700.]

WHITEHEAD, William
4850. Humphrey Lewis; Roger; London; C & Cd; 6.11.1682; 6.11.1682, - ; 8.
4851. Edward Savory; Edward (d); parish of St Mary Overs Southwarke, Surr; - ; 5.7.1697; 5.7.1697; - ; 7.

4852. Margarett Woodstock; William; London; Gardener; 1.3.1686; 1.3.1686; - ; 7.

WHITEHURST, Francis
4853. [Francis Whighthurst. Son of Richard Whitehurst; fd by patrimony 6.3.1671.]

WHITLEDGE, Robert
4854. Francis Bennett; James; Norton, Suff; Y; 3.7.1699; 3.7.1699; 3.3.1707; 7. Whitledge is described as a bookbinder.

4855. Will Gray. Fd by Whitledge and Abel Rockall 7.7.1701. Bd to Rockall (q.v.) 4.12.1693.

4856. James Holland. Fd by Whitledge 4.2.1695. Apparently never formally bd.

4857. Daniel Whitlidge; William; Holland, Lancs; Y; 5.12.1687; 5.12.1687; 2.3.1696; 7.

WHITLEDGE, Thomas
4858. William Lucas; William (d); parish of St Mary Le=Savoy, M'sex; Seedsman; 5.8.1695; 5.8.1695; 2.8.1703; 7.

4859. James Smalshaw. Fd by Whitledge 7.2.1699. Apparently never formally bd.

WHITLOCK, John
4860. Henry Bridges; Henry (d); Southwick, Sussex; Y; 6.5.1689; 6.5.1689; - ; 7.

4861. John Charleton; Roger; Lambath, Surr; Waterman; 6.10.1690; 6.10.1690; - ; 7.

4862. Francis Hubard; John; London; C & Cheesemonger; 4.9.1676; 4.9.1676; 7.1.1684; 7. Fd by John Smith.

4863. John Vaughan; Nicholas; Parish of St James Clarkenwell, M'sex; 6.3.1682; 6.3.1682; 11.11.1695; 7.

4864. Daniell Winchester; Daniell; Windsor, Berks; Wheelwright; 5.8.1695; 5.8.1695; - ; 8.

WHITTLESEY, Thomas
4865. Walter Wilkes; Walter; Chidderminster, Worcs; - ; 4.4.1664; 4.4.1664; - ; 7. T.o. 12.3.1667 to Roger Brooke on the death of Whittlesey.

WHITWOOD, William
4866. Jeremy Breres; Edward (d); - , Ireland; - ; 1.9.1679; 1.9.1679; - ; 7.

4867. Robert Haunch; Christopher; London; C & Woolwinder; 7.10.1672; 7.10.1672; 3.11.1679; 7. Fd as Hanch.

4868. John Pike; - ; - , - ; - ; 7.4.1679; 7.4.1679; 3.5.1686; 7.

4869. Robert Proddrer; Lewis (d); parish of St Martin in the Feilds, M'sex; G; 9.2.1691; 9.2.1691; - ; 7.

4870. William Sayes; William; Porchester, S'hants; Cl; 2.10.1693; 7.8.1693; 9.9.1700; 7.

4871. John Smith; John; City of Gloucester; G; 18.12.1666; 18.12.1666; - ; 7.

4872. John Wheatley; John (d); London; C & Br; 11.4.1670; 11.4.1670; - ; 7.

WICKENS, John
4873. George Grafton; Ralph; St Sepulchers, M'sex; - ; 7.6.1680; 7.6.1680; 1.8.1687; 7.

4874. Thomas Minors; William; Inner Temple, London; G; 2.6.1684; 2.6.1684; 7.3.1692; 7.

WICKER, Tobias
4875. Robert Bird; Robert (d); Boston, Lincs; I; 7.2.1687; 7.2.1687; - ; 7. T.o. 7.10.1689 to Christopher Skegnes.

4876. John Davie; Richard (d); Yarmoth, Norf; Mch; 3.5.1669; 24.6.1669; - ; 7.

4877. John Houlter; Randolph; Church parish, Lancs; Y; 2.4.1666; 2.4.1666; - ; 7.

4878. John Midow; Thomas; Leedes, Yorks; - ; 9.9.1678; 9.9.1678; - ; 7.

4879. Thomas Porter, Thomas (d); Stock Prior, Worcs; Y; 4.12.1671; 4.12. 1671; 5.5.1679; 7.

4880. John Simkin; Peter; Nelson, Leics; Tn; 4.6.1683; 4.6.1683; - ; 7.

4881. Joseph Taylor; Henry; London; C & D; 11.10.1680; 11.10.1680; - ; 7.

WIDDOWES, Giles

4882. William Dotchin; Richard; Abington, Berks; D; 3.2.1673; 3.2. 1673; - ; 7.

4883. Edward Evetts; Willm (d); Shipston vppon tower, Worcs; - ; 7.6.1669; 7.6.1669; 12.2.1677; 7.

WILDE, Edward

4884. Henry Lacy; William; Kilmiston, S'hants; G; 2.2.1662; 2.2.1662; - ; 7.

4885. Jasper Langhorne; Willm (d); Stevonege, Herts; - ; 2.7.1667; 2.7. 1667; - ; 7.

4886. Humphrey Puller; John; Hartlebury, Worcs; G; 2.3.1663; 2.3. 1663; 7.11.1670; 7.

4887. Martyn Vrlyn; Willm (d); St Martyn in the Feilds, [M'sex]; Bricklayer; 5.9.1670; 5.9.1670; - ; 7.

4888. Ann Wild. Fd by patrimony 6.2.1682.

WILDE, John

4889. Francis Clare; Francis; London; C & B; 6.5.1700; 6.5.1700; 3.11. 1707; 7.

4890. Robert Clare; Robert; St James Clerkenwell, M'sex; Porter; 7.3.1692; 7.3.1692; - ; 7.

4891. Richard Pole; Francis; parish of St Giles Cripplegate, London; B; 9.5.1694; 9.5.1694; - ; 7.

4892. John Shipthorpe; John (d); London; C & Ha; 8.5.1699; 8.5.1699; 3.6.1706; 7.

WILDE, Margaret

4893. William Davy; William; Bolden, Oxon; Cd; 8.4.1700; 8.4.1700; 3.11.1707; 7.

WILDE, Richard

4894. James Wilde; Richard; Abbeydore, Herefs; G; 3.2.1690; 3.2.1690; - ; 7.

WILDE, William

4895. Benjamin Butler; Robert; London; C & Ha; 7.11.1698; 7.11.1698; - ; 7.

4896. Edward Dykes; Richd (d); London; C & St; 7.10.1689; 7.10.1689; 16.10.1697; 8.

4897. Tho Thompson; William (d); London; C & Plasterer; 12.4.1692; 12.4.1692; 8.5.1699; 7.

4898. [William Wild. 'William Wild with his Sons and Apprentices being translated by the Citty from the Art of Cutlers to the Art or Mistery of the Stationers as appears by Indorsemt on the Coppy of his Freedom made the 14th day of July last was this day [2.8. 1686] sworne and admitted into ye Freedom of this Company . . . iijs=iiijd'. Free of the Cutlers' Company 1.3.1668 (Court-Book F, 18.6.1689).]

4899. Benjamine Wilde; William; London; C & St; 13.4.1698; 13.4.1698; - ; 7. Bd to his father.

4900. John Wilde. Fd by patrimony 6.10.1690.

WILDGOOSE, Anthony

4901. John Wildgoose. Fd by patrimony 1.8.1659.

WILFORD, George

4902. George Gray; Geo; London; C & BSg; 3.8.1646; 3.8.1646; - ; 7.

4903. John Rycroft; Thomas (d); Codington, Ches; Cl; 3.10.1648; 25.12. 1648; - ; 8. The Master's name is given as Wilsford.

WILFORD, John

4904. James Hutchinson; James; Citty of York; Mr; 2.10.1671; 2.10.1671; - ; 7.

WILFORD, Joseph

4905. William Gibbs; William; parrish of Flatbury, Worcs; Y; 1.3.1686; 1.3.1686; - ; 7.

4906. William Gun; Henry (d); Saintbury, Glos; Y; 5.12.1681; 5.12.1681; 7.10.1689; 7.

4907. John Hayler; Thomas; Cobham, Surr; Ca; 3.3.1690; 3.3.1690; - ; 7.

4908. John Martin; John; Byfleet, Surr; Gl; 1.8.1692; 1.8.1692; 3.5.1708; 7.

WILFORD, Richard

4909. William Askwith; Christopher; Malton, Yorks; Y; 2.11.1674; 2.11.1674; - ; 7.

4910. Willm Bellinger; Thomas (d); Lackhampton, Glos; Weaver; 3.5.1669; 3.5.1669; - ; 7.

4911. Richard Deane; Jeremy (d); London; C & Surgeon; 5.7.1669; 5.7.1669; - ; 7.

4912. Wm Fowkes; Wm; Islington, M'sex; G; 4.4.1653; 4.4.1653; - ; 7.

4913. Edward Helmestead; John; Chelmesford, Essex; Y; 7.6.1676; 7.6.1676; - ; 8.

4914. John Touch; John; Llanstuffon, Carmarthen; Y; 2.4.1655; 29.9.1654; - ; 8.

4915. John Wilford; Nobell; Parish St Giles Criplegate, M'sex; Cw; 3.12.1660; 1.11.1660; 4.11.1668; 8.

4916. Joseph Wilford. Fd by patrimony 5.12.1681.

WILKINS, Jeremiah

4917. John Atkins; Richard (d); London; C & Go; 7.2.1698; 7.2.1698; 23.3.1705; 7.

4918. Anne Boddily; Richard; Parish of Shreuinam, Berks; - ; 2.11.

1685; 2.11.1685; 7.4.1701; [7]. Bd to Wilkins and to Christian his wife.

4919. James Read; Robert; parish of St Andrew Holborne, M'sex; L; 7.5.1694; 7.5.1694; 7.7.1701; 7.

WILKINS, Jonathan

4920. Richard Millsopp; John; Reading, Berks; Clothier; 6.9.1680; 6.9.1680; - ; 7.

WILKINSON, Christopher

4921. Peter Buck. Bd to William Churchill (q.v.) 6.10.1684; t.o. 22.12.1685 to Wilkinson, but fd by Churchill 2.11.1691.

4922. George Downes; George (d); London; C & Cw; 6.12.1669; 6.12.1669; 20.12.1676; 7.

4923. Timothy Goodwin. Fd by Wilkinson 7.8.1682.

4924. Abel Roper. Fd by Wilkinson 7.11.1687. Bd to Abel Roper (q.v.) 6.10.1679, but t.o. (n.d.) to Wilkinson and fined 2s. 6d. 'for his being turned over to Mr Wilkinson not at the Hall'.

4925. John Rutter; Richard; Kingsley, Ches; E; 9.2.1691; 9.2.1691; - ; 7.

4926. Christopher Wilkinson; Christopher; [London]; [C & St]; 1.7.1689; 1.7.1689; 6.8.1694; 7. Bd to his father; fd by patrimony.

WILKINSON, Joseph

4927. Edward Carey; James; Munden, Bucks; G; 2.10.1654; 2.10.1654; 5.5.1662; 7.

WILLIAMS, John, I

4928. Thomas Chetwin; Raph; Lichfeild, Staffs; G; 5.3.1655; 5.3.1655; - ; 7.

4929. Richard Freeborne; Richard; Citty of Westminster; V; 1.6.1663; 1.6.1663; 6.6.1670; 8.

4930. Willm Fyndall; Willm; Maston, Oxon; G; 8.6.1668; 8.6.1668; - ; 7.

4931. James Gilbertson; George (d); St Thomas Southwark, Surr; Cd; 2.12. 1672; 2.12.1672; 24.3.1680; 7.

4932. William Hall; Wm; Oxford; Printer; 8.11.1675; 8.11.1675; - ; 7.

4933. Richard Harrison; Samuell; London; C & Apothecary; 27.6.1654; 27.6.1654; - ; 7.

4934. Thomas Hearne; Thomas (d); City of Oxon; T; 1.1.1668; 1.5.1667; - ; 7.

4935. Thomas Keightly; John; Bewley, Worcs; B; 2.11.1658; 2.11.1658; - ; 8.

4936. James Lawton; Tho; Claverley, Shrops; Cl; 8.6.1648; 8.6.1648; 2.7.1655; 7.

4937. Thomas Palmer; John; Citty of Lincolne; Cheesemonger; 2.11.1657; 1.8.1657; - ; 8.

4938. John Preice. Fd by Williams 17.5.1643. Bd to him 4.4.1636.

4939. Ralph Rand; Ralph; Godalming, Surr; Dr of Physick; 26.7.1658; 26.7.1658; - ; 8.

4940. Henry Redmayne; John; London; C & St; 1.7.1678; 1.7.1678; - ; 7. Bd to John Williams Senior.

4941. Charles Slystead; Edward (d); Melton, Suff; G; 5.2.1666; 5.2.1666; - ; 7.

4942. Symon Waterson; John; London; C & St; 1.9.1645; 1.9.1645; 24.8. 1652; 7. Fd by patrimony.

4943. John Williams. Fd by patrimony 1.8.1670.

WILLIAMS, John, II

4944. Thomas Newcombe; John; Southam, War; Y; 2.11.1696; 2.11. 1696; - ; 7.

4945. Stephen Pigram; Stephen; Towne of Cambridge; Y; 8.5.1682; 8.5.1682; - ; 7. Bd to John Williams Junior.

4946. Christopher Charles Skegnes; John; Citty of Lincolne; G; 26.6.1678;

26.6.1678; 6.7.1685; 7. Bd to John Williams Junior.

4947. John Williams. Fd by patrimony 4.9.1699.

WILLIAMS, John, III

4948. Wm Lane; John; Hereford, Herefs; Carrier; 22.12.1691; 22.12. 1691; - ; 7. Bd to Capt. John Williams.

WILLIAMS, Rice

4949. Hugh Cartwright. Fd by Williams 6.6.1642. Bd to him 19.1.1635.

4950. Rice Williams. Fd by patrimony 12.6.1666.

WILLIAMS, Richard

4951. Ben Davye. Fd by Williams 24.3.1647. Bd to him 2.12.1639.

4952. Thomas Leacock; Robert; Bishop Sherford, Herts; M; 12.8.1671; 12.8.1671; - ; 8.

4953. Richard Williams. Fd by patrimony 7.10.1668.

4954. Thomas Williams. Fd by patrimony 15.9.1652.

4955. Ralph Wortley; Geo; Altus, Yorks; G; 6.9.1647; 6.9.1647; - ; 7.

WILLIAMS, Thomas

4956. John Harris; Thomas; Walford, Herefs; Y; 23.1.1654; 25.3.1654; 9.5.1661; 7.

4957. George Plowrett; Richard (d); London; C & Woodmonger; 3.5.1658; 3.5.1658; 6.8.1667; 7.

4958. Edward Powell; Edward; London; G; 5.10.1646; 24.6.1646; 3.10.1653; 8.

4959. Thomas West; Richard; Arundell, Sussex; Y; 17.1.1659; 17.1.1659; - ; 7.

WILLIAMSON, Anthony

4960. Deliuerance Kempe; Will; Sudbury, Glos; Cl; 2.7.1655; 2.7.1655; 3.8.1663; 8.

WILLIAMSON, Robert

4961. William Doleman; John; Royston, Herts; G; 2.10.1699; 2.10.1699; - ; 7.

4962. John Griffin; William; parish of St Sepulchres, London; Victualler; 6.5.1695; 6.5.1695; - ; 7.

WILLIS, William

4963. Thomas Harbing; Thomas (d); Charminster, Dors; Y; 7.11.1670; 7.11.1670; 7.7.1679; 8. Fd as Harbin.

4964. Christopher Willis; John (d); Pedlehenton, Dors; Y; 2.7.1677; 2.7.1677; - ; 7.

4965. Christopher Willis. Fd by patrimony 1.9.1679.

WILLISCOTT, Edward

4966. Joseph Phillips; John (d); Vpcott, Herefs; G; 7.12.1674; 6.12.1674; - ; 7.

4967. Edward Shelley; Richard; Midhurst, Sussex; G; 13.1.1669; 13.1.1669; - ; 7.

WILMOTT, John

4968. Roger Smith. Fd by Wilmott 4.12.1648. Bd to him 4.12.1637.

WILSON, Benjamin

4969. John Scourfeild. Fd by Wilson 1.2.1641. Bd to him 2.9.1633.

WILSON, Robert

4970. Phillip Lane. Fd by Wilson 7.11.1642. Bd to him 4.8.1634.

WILSON, William

4971. Francis Davis; Robert; greate Crymbles in the parish of Cocke, Lancs; - ; 7.12.1663; 1.1.1664; - ; 8.

4972. Richard Dykes; Edward; Towne of Lancaster; H; 24.3.1656; 24.3.1656; 1.6.1663; 7.

4973. John Edgar; Ezechiell (d); Halsted, Suff [sic for Essex]; Cl; 14.3.1650; 14.3.1650; 6.4.1657; 7.

4974. George Harvey. Fd by Wilson and John Wright 1.10.1660. Bd to Wright (q.v.) 5.9.1653.

4975. John Hudson; Anthony; London; Sc; 2.8.1652; 24.6.1652; - ; 8.

4976. John Leicester. Fd by Wilson for John Okes 11.3.1650. Apparently never formally bd.

4977. Wm Leicester. Fd by Wilson and John Okes 1.7.1647. Bd to Okes 22.6.1640.

4978. Richard Rider; Richard; London; C & MT; 7.12.1657; 7.12.1657; - ; 8.

4979. Robte Robinson; Robte (d); London; C & Mr; 4.5.1646; 24.6.1646; - ; 8.

4980. Edward Webb; George (d); Ireland; Bishop of Limerick; 4.10.1647; 29.9.1647; - ; 8. Entry deleted; m.n. 'This Appr. by Consent is gone from his mr'.

WINCH, Adam

4981. Abell Rockall; Edward; Ruskam, Berks; Y; 30.6.1668; 30.6.1668; - ; 8.

WINCKFEILD, John

4982. Edward Bryndley; Edward; Meerelane, Staffs; - ; 6.11.1666; 6.11.1666; 9.2.1674; 7.

WINSLOW, Edward

4983. Samuell Baker; Thomas (d); London; Sh; 6.3.1648; 1.5.1648; - ; 9.

4984. Joseph Godfrey; Edw; Royston, Herts; Gr; 26.4.1652; 26.4.1652; - ; 7.

4985. Thomas Lee; Ralph (d); Lyniell, Shrops; T; 3.5.1647; 15.7.1647; - ; 7.

4986. Josyas Winslow. Fd by patrimony 26.4.1652.

WINTER, Isaac

4987. [Isack Winter. Son of Thomas Winter; fd by patrimony 4.12.1648.]

WINTER, John

4988. Ambrose Dennison; Ambrose (d); Wapping, Essex [sic for M'sex]; Ship's carpenter; 26.10.1670; 1.9.1670; - ; 8.

WOOD, Edward

4989. Wm Cranford; Wm; London; G; 13.1.1642; 13.1.1642; - ; 8.

WOOD, Ralph

4990. John Dykes; Edward; Lancaster; - ; 4.3.1661; 4.3.1661; 4.11.1668; 8.

4991. John Sparree; John; St Martins in the Fields, M'sex; Chandler; 5.10.1657; 5.10.1657; 7.11.1664; 7.

WOOD, Robert

4992. James Arnold; James; Ramsbury, Wilts; H; 3.8.1657; 3.8.1657; 3.10.1664; 7.

4993. Raph Boone. Fd by Wood 4.2.1656. Apparently never formally bd.

WOODHALL, - , Mrs

4994. Nath Palmer; Edmond; Barkin, Essex; D; 1.3.1653; 1.3.1653; - ; 7.

WOODHALL, Abraham

4995. [Abraham Woodhall. Fd by patrimony 6.1.1665. The name of both father and freeman is given as Woodfall, but this is almost certainly an error for Woodhall, the father probably being the man fd by Isaac Jaggard 15.12.1626.]

WOODHALL, Humphrey

4996. Thomas Croxen; Edward; Standon, Herts; Y; 21.4.1645; 21.4.1645; - ; 7.

4997. Mathew Petch; George; Scoulthorpe, Norf; Felmonger; 7.10.1650; 7.10.1650; 5.4.1658; 7.

WOOLFE, Nicholas

4998. John Minshew; John; London; C & MT; 7.6.1676; 7.6.1676; - ; 7.

4999. Thomas Tracelove; Thomas; London; C & Cd; 3.2.1685; 3.1.1685; - ; 8.

WORRALL, Samuel

5000. [Saml Worrall. Fd 2.6.1684 by order of the Mayor.]

WOSOLD, Richard

5001. Thomas Maddocks; John; Shrewesbury, Shrops; Dy; 3.2.1673; 3.2.1673; 4.9.1682; 7.

WOTTON, Edward

5002. Nicholas Crockett; Jno; Sheltonwoodhouse, Staffs; Potter; 1.9.1656; 1.9.1656; - ; 9.

WOTTON, Matthew

5003. Arthur Collins; William; London; C & Br; 7.8.1699; 7.8.1699; 6.10.1707; 7.

5004. Richard Greenaway; Ralph; London; C & Ha; 1.2.1692; 1.2.1692; 3.4.1699; 7.

5005. Thomas Jones; Rhees; Aberhaves, Mont; Cl; 7.12.1685; 7.12.1685; - ; 7.

WRIGHT, Edward

5006. Wm Gilbertson. Bd to John Wright Senior 2.11.1640; t.o. after Wright's death to Edward Wright 6.4.1646 and fd by him 6.12.1647.

WRIGHT, Joan, Widow

5007. Edward Mitchell; Robte; Wickham, Bucks; Bu; 6.5.1650; 6.5.1650; - ; 8.

WRIGHT, John, I

5008. Robte Flesher. Fd by 'John Wright bindr.' 6.9.1641. Bd to him, as Robert Fletcher, 4.8.1634.

5009. Wm Gilbertson. Bd to Wright 2.11.1640; t.o. on Wright's death to Edward Wright 6.4.1646 and fd by him 6.12.1647.

5010. Samuell Wright. Son of John Wright; fd by patrimony 31.5.1650.

WRIGHT, John, II

[It is improbable that all apprentices listed below were bound to the same master.]

5011. Joseph Ball; John; Broughton, Oxon; Fuller; 6.6.1644; 25.3.1644; - ; 8. Bd to John Wright Junior.

5012. Samuell Bolton; Adam; Black-borne, Lancs; Cl; 6.11.1655; 6.11.1655; 21.1.1662; 7. Originally bd to Nathaniel Brooks (q.v.) 23.12.1652; fd by Wright and Brookes.

5013. William Cartwright; John; Couentry, War; Bs; 1.3.1655; 1.3.1655; 2.3.1663; 8.

5014. George Conyers. Bd to James Collins (q.v.) 4.3.1678; and t.o. (n.d.) to John Wright. Fd 1.2.1686, after Wright's death.

5015. Robert Francklin; John; Fryan, M'sex; Y; 2.10.1654; 2.10.1654; - ; 8.

5016. John Greenaway; Robert (d); Criplegate, London; Tallowchandler; 3.4.1671; 3.4.1671; - ; 7.

5017. George Harvey; Francis; Westminster; Cl; 5.9.1653; 5.9.1653; 1.10.1660; 7. Fd by Wright and William Wilson.

5018. Joseph Holloway; - (d); Kislingburg; N'hants; Cl; 12.7.1652; 12.7.1652; - ; 7.

5019. Robte Jennison. Fd by Wright and Richard Oulton 5.4.1647. Bd to Oulton 7.5.1638.

5020. Joseph Nevill. Bd to George Edwards (q.v.) 5.5.1645; t.o. on the death of Edwards to Wright 13.4.1648. Fd by Wright and Edwards 4.5.1653.

5021. Wilfriend Phillips; John; London; Cl; 3.10.1681; 3.10.1681; - ; 7.

5022. Ebennezar Tracey; Charles; London; C & St; 1.10.1683; 1.10.1683; 3.11.1690; 7. T.o. (n.d.) to Mrs Passenger and fd by her, but fined 2s. 6d. 'for not being turned over at the Hall'.

5023. Thomas Vere. Fd by John Wright Junior 3.2.1645. Bd to him 14.1.1636.

5024. Nath Wheatly; James (d); Banbury, Oxon; Mr; 3.6.1678; 3.6.1678; - ; 7.

5025. Samuell Widmore; Michaell; Wickham, Bucks; Chandler; 6.4.1646;

6.4.1646; - ; 7. Originally bd to George Cooke (q.v.) 3.10.1642?

5026. Silvanus Wiggins; Silvanus; Wallingford, Berks; Y; 26.6.1682; 26.6.1682; - ; 7.

5027. John Wright. Fd by patrimony 5.10.1663.

5028. Robert Wright. Fd by patrimony 4.11.1668.

WRIGHT, John, III
5029. [John Wright. Son of Cuthbert Wright; fd by patrimony 26.3.1675.]

WRIGHT, John, IV
5030. John Leonard; John (d); Citty of Westmr; BSg; 4.4.1687; 4.4.1687; - ; 8.

5031. Anthony Wild; Robert (d); parish of St Gyles in the Feilds, M'sex; Painter; 25.6.1688; 25.6.1688; - ; 7.

WRIGHT, Mary, Widow
5032. Jonah Dacon; Jonah; London; C & Basketmaker; 23.6.1662; 23.6.1662; 17.5.1671; 8.

WRIGHT, Robert
5033. Warner Hart; John; Grayes Inn, London; E; 7.6.1669; 7.6.1669; - ; 7.

WRIGHT, Samuel
5034. Dorothie Babham; Richard; Weston Turvill, Bucks; G; 1.5.1671; 1.5.1671; - ; 7.

5035. William Johnson. Fd by Wright and Robert Pritchard 1.8.1664. Bd to Pritchard (q.v.) 14.4.1656.

5036. Gamaliell Miller; Peter; Leicester; Br; 1.10.1655; 1.10.1655; - ; 7.

5037. Dorothi Peake; Thomas (d); Rochester, Kent; Dr in Physick; 5.7.1669; 5.7.1669; - ; 7.

5038. Hugh Watts; James; Wincaulton, Som; I; 3.11.1651; 3.11.1651; - ; 7.

WRIGHT, Thomas

5039. Richard Daffie. Fd by Wright 17.11.1645. Originally bd to Arthur Nicholls 6.4.1635; rebd to Wright 2.4.1638.

5040. Richard Farmbrough; Moses; London; C & Upholder; 7.8.1682; 7.8.1682; - ; 7.

5041. John Goring. Fd by Wright 4.8.1645. Bd to him 1.6.1635.

5042. Thomas Hunt; George; Sunning hill, Berks; Y; 4.8.1645; 4.8.1645; - ; 8.

5043. Richard Lewis. Fd by Alexander Fifield 8.11.1641. Bd to Wright 1.3.1630.

WYATT, John

5044. George Baynam; Walter (d); Muckland, Herefs; H; 9.9.1700; 9.9.1700; - ; 7.

5045. Thomas Clement; Thomas; parish of St James Clarkenwell, M'sex; Ha; 1.7.1695; 1.7.1695; - ; 7.

5046. William Hawkins; John; Basingstoke, S'hants; Linendraper; 7.8.1693; 7.8.1693; - ; 7.

WYMUR, William

5047. Richard Whithart; William (d); parish of Dunstones in the West, [London]; G; 4.2.1656; 4.2.1656; - ; 7.

YATES, Thomas

5048. William Banks; James; Rothersfeild, Yorks; Mason; 4.7.1698; 4.7.1698; - ; 7.

5049. Thomas Bayley; Thomas; Burrough of Southwarke, [Surr]; Armorer; 3.5.1669; 3.5.1669; - ; 7.

5050. John Charity; Edward; London; L; 13.5.1678; 13.5.1678; 5.7.1686; 7.

5051. John Flinstone; Tho (d); Dover, Kent; Ca; 1.10.1688; 1.10.1688; 2.12.1695; 7.

5052. John Frankes; Thomas (d); Weldon, N'hants; Mason; 7.3.1670; 7.3.1670; 1.2.1686; 7.

5053. Edward Platt; Edward; Lingsted, Kent; G; 1.2.1675; 1.2.1675; 7.5.1688; 7.

5054. Issac Spervill; John; Ramsbury, Wilts; Bl; 17.7.1690; 17.7.1690; - ; 7.

5055. Lewis Yates; Thomas; London; C & St; 1.3.1686; 1.3.1686; - ; 7. Bd to his father.

5056. Thomas Yates; Thomas; [London]; [C & St]; 1.8.1692; 1.8.1692; - ; 7. Bd to his father.

YORKE, William

5057. Richard Acornman; Michaell; Stepney, M'sex; H; 4.7.1670; 4.7.1670; - ; 7.

5058. Thomas Biby; Thomas; Waltham Abby, Essex; Y; 4.12.1676; 4.12.1676; - ; 7.

5059. John Hale; John; Citty of Bristoll; Tobacconist; 7.9.1685; 7.9.1685; - ; 7.

5060. Robert Hale; John (d); Citty of Bristoll; Mch; 3.8.1696; 29.9.1695; 3.5.1708; 7.

5061. Richard Haynes; Edward; Ailsbury, Bucks; - ; 1.2.1675; 1.2.1675; - ; 7.

5062. Wm Wells; Richard; Mile End, M'sex; Cd; 2.5.1692; 2.5.1692; - ; 7.

5063. Wm York; Christopher; Citty of Bristoll; Cd; 6.10.1679; 6.10.1679; - ; 8.

5064. William Yorke. Fd by patrimony 6.10.1690.

YOUNG, Elizabeth

5065. Elizabeth Turner. Fd by Elizabeth Young 1.5.1676. Apparently never formally bd.

YOUNG, Henry

5066. William Biggs; William; London; C & Ca; 7.6.1686; 7.6.1686; - ; 7.

YOUNG, James

5067. John Banthwaite; John; London; Ha; 7.10.1644; 7.10.1644; 8.6.

1648; 7. T.o. 8.6.1648 to William Dugard and fd (as Brainthwaite) by Young and Dugard.

5068. James Grouer; James; Bedfont, M'sex; Y; 6.10.1651; 6.10.1651; 7.11.1658; 7.

5069. Mathias Inman; John; Kendall, W'land; Sh; 2.11.1646; 2.11.1646; 6.2.1654; 7. T.o. 8.6.1648 to William Dugard; fd by Young and Dugard.

5070. Edward Parnter; Thomas; Lyth, W'land; Sh; 5.9.1642; 25.12. 1642; - ; 7.

5071. Raph Wood. Bd to Robert Young 2.12.1639; t.o. 12.8.1643 to James Young for the remainder of his term except for the last year which is remitted. Fd by James Young 1.8.1648.

YOUNG, Richard

5072. Wm Lillingston; George; Kingslee, Bucks; G; 4.12.1682; 4.12. 1682; 2.7.1697; 7. Fd by Young but fined 2s. 6d. for not being turned over at the hall. There is no record of Lil-

lingston having served another master.

YOUNG, Robert

5073. Richard Cowper; John; Brendle, Lancs; Sh; 28.6.1641; 1.7. 1641; - ; 7. Bd by Young for the King's printers.

5074. William Hinson; John; London; C & Apothecary; 5.4.1641; 5.4. 1641; 7.8.1648; 7. Bd by Young for the King's printing house.

5075. Thomas Hollingworth; John; Bushberry, Staffs; Y; 8.11.1641; 25.12. 1641; - ; 7.

5076. Thomas Jaggard; John; Ingleton, Yorks; H; 7.6.1641; 25.12.1641; - ; 7.

5077. Raph Wood. Bd to Young 2.12. 1639; t.o. 12.8.1643 to James Young for the remainder of his term except for the last year which is remitted. Fd by James Young 1.8.1648.

5078. James Young. Fd by patrimony 1.8.1642.

INDEX OF APPRENTICES

Axtell, John 3035
Ayers, John 3246
Aylmer, Brabazen 103, 1474; Samuell 104; Whitguift 2871
Aylward, John 178
Aylway, Thomas 4541
Ayres, Adam 3101
Ayrton, Richard 111

Babbington, Samuell 4170
Babham, Dorothie 5034
Babington, Isaac 4495; William 513
Bachelor, William 533
Back, John 3446
Backett, Francis 237
Baddeley, Richard 117
Badeley, Richard 2309
Badger, Richard 122
Bagford, Reynold 2552
Bagshaw, John 4208
Baily, John 3807; Mathias 141; Richard 136; Thomas 1354
Baker, Bartholomew 4533; Daniel 4296; Edward 98; Humphrey 155; John 105, 4452, 4804; Randall 3149; Robert 1546; St John 245; Samuell 1922, 4893; Thomas 846, 2463; William 156, 157, 1394
Baldero, Arthur 285
Balderoe, Henry 4391
Baldry, John 161
Baldwer, James 939
Baldwin, Benjamin 847; James 3214; Richard 1437
Bale, George 4409
Baley, Richard 1046, 1242; Thomas 1691, 2801
Balfore, William 4595
Ball, George 341, 2217; James 433; John 697; Joseph 5011
Ballard, Daniell 4514; John 2678; Richard 3719; Samuell 3956; Thomas 937; William 116
Ballett, John 2504
Banbury, Bennet 3986
Bancks, Allen 2660; William 3967
Bancroft, Thomas 4219
Banebridge, Charles 3296
Bankes, John 1314
Banks, William 5048
Bannister, John 1328; Richard 363
Banthwaite, John 5067
Barber, Daniell 200; John 778, 2570; Joseph 1666; Robert 4062
Barker, Anthony 2962; Charles 3177, 4318; Christopher 127; Edward 4584; James 3978; Mathew 176; Thomas 4319, 4400; William 2492
Barloe, William 1301
Barlow, Francis 181; William 2071
Barlowe, William 607, 2718

Barnard, Henry 1962; John 2721; Thomas 4001
Barncroft, Thomas 4219
Barnes, John 185, 4330; Richard 864, 3455; William 3498
Barney, David 1019
Barrell, Thomas 3543
Barrett, John 1362, 2968, 3888; Phillip 932; Richard 3192; William 3916
Barriffe, John 3836
Barroughes, William 1042
Barrow, Henry 594; Nathaniel 3172
Barsham, John 286
Bartholomew, Benjamin 2858; George 3335; Isaac 990
Bartlett, John 193; Leonard 1325; Roger 3983; Samuel 194, 933; Thomas 158; William 2625
Barton, Noah 2268
Bartram, William 1547
Baskervile, Anthony 2786; Humphrey 1329
Baskervill, John 209
Baskerville, John 3084
Baskett, John 1276
Bassell, Richard 3753
Bassett, Judith 215; Richard 1083, 4067; Roger 1108; Thomas 512
Batchelor, Thomas 1273
Bateman, Christopher 231; Stephen 618
Bates, Charles 1228; Richard 240; Timotheus 3321; William 236
Bateson, Francis 4827
Bathoe, William 837
Batten, Richard 498
Battersby, Robert 247, 1824; William 2563
Baugh, Francis 1341
Bayles, John 2449
Bayley, Andrew 4203; John 858, 3013; Thomas 5049
Bayliffe, John 3508
Baylis, George 4105
Bayly, Jeremiah 4077; Samuell 2362
Baynam, George 5044
Bazen, Thomas 1136
Beacham, Gilbert 3047
Beacroft, George 75
Beadle, Gabriell 4761; John 1796
Beagin, Henry 4496
Beake, James 251
Beale, Edward 1278; John 539; Richard 475; Robert 252; Shadricke 1905; William 2059
Beall, William 1840
Beamish, John 3322
Beamon, Symon 4505
Beard, Cornelius 2336
Beard, Edward 519; Richard 1548; Robert 1675
Beardwell, Benjamine 2219, 3297
Bearsley, Peter 2325
Beathwaite, William 1535
Beauchamp, John 2739
Beaumont, Henry 259; John 3048

Becket, Charles 2734
Beckwith, William 4549
Bedcock, Joseph 4686
Bedder, John 3590
Beddes, John 3590
Beddingfeild, John 538
Bedford, George 483; Helkia 4460; Thomas
    3766, 4453; Timothy 2009
Bedingfield, John 4175
Beech, John 287; William 3298
Beechenoe, James 2024
Beekeman, John 2787
Beesley, Francis 1043
Beeston, William 1936
Beheathland, Elizabeth 2435; Richard 975
Beke, William 1268
Bell, Andrew 316, 4774; Edward 1844; Henry
    273; Richard 232; Roger 317
Bellamy, Thomas 1333
Bellinger, John 4560; William 4910
Bennet, Francis 311; John 2203
Bennett, Francis 4854; Isum 3880; John 299,
    525, 1624; Joseph 3036; William 1625
Benning, William 2527
Bennison, William 318
Bennit, Thomas 3118
Benskin, Thomas 1118
Benson, John 2633; Robert 322; William 3181
Bentley, Richard 2838; Thomas 1921
Benton, William 2713
Beresford, Edmond 196, 326; John 325
Berisford, Edmond 3604; Thomas 2352
Berkly, Francis 3103
Bernard, Samuel 243; Thomas 2969
Berrill, Edward 1521
Berrington, Edward 302
Best, Edward 4626; John 2319
Bettenham, James 464
Bettesworth, Arthur 114
Betts, Thomas 1597
Bevan, William 2258
Bever, Thomas 3774
Beverley, Ellis 195
Biby, Thomas 5058
Bickerton, Thomas 3992
Bifeild, Adoniram 4193
Biggs, William 5066
Billing, Robert 2536
Billinger, Richard 288
Billingsley, Benjamine 4194; John 342
Bing, Swithin 3141
Binnie, Anthony 4717
Birch, George 2405; William 1464
Bird, Edward 3754; Robert 4128, 4875
Birde, John 1400
Birdwistle, John 3057
Birtch, William 1923
Bisbie, Nathaniel 3305
Bishop, Benjamine 2165; John 186, 359; Thomas

    2420; William 838, 1065
Bishopp, John 1582; William 1583
Bissill, James 2970
Blackerby, William 645
Blackmore, Edward 544
Blackwell, George 374; James 687, 3552;
    William 2543
Bladen, William 375
Bladon, John 627, 2892
Blagrave, Obadiah 550
Blague, Daniel 381, 3395; John 627
Bland, Thomas 2406
Blayton, Robert 4432
Bleare, Josiah 3447
Bleaton, Robert 1589
Blechinden, Peirson 1995
Bleigh, John 3569
Bligh, John 3569
Blisse, Joseph 369; Stephen 3264
Bloare, Josiah 3447
Bloome, Emanual 4223; Richard 393
Blount, Charles 1701; Richard 528
Blundell, Edward 1890
Blunke, William 1777
Blyth, Francis 1347
Blyton, Thomas 717
Boate, Isaac 401
Bockham, Richard 1054, 1904, 3659
Boddily, Anne 4918
Boddington, Richard 4063; Thomas 784;
    William 2887
Bodington, George 1208
Bodnam, Robert 1020
Bodnell, Peter 514
Bodwell, Thomas 4421
Bogges, Robert 1629
Boler, James 412
Bolliphant, Edmond 415
Bolt, Charles 2643; John 416
Bolter, Peter 417; Robert 2514, 4515; William
    418
Bolton, Mathew 3284; Samuell 551, 2121, 5012
Bond, Benjamin 1340; Elizabeth 1500; George
    4247; Thomas 382
Bonnington, Richard 4063
Bonwick, James 419
Bonwicke, Henry 4534
Boodle, Richard 3215
Booker, John 1894; William 3755
Boomer, Thomas 1111
Boone, John 2879; Nicholas 425; Ralph 4993
Boorne, Alexander 1125
Boote, William 1676
Booth, Francis 2249; Humfrey 4331; John 1455;
    Thomas 2746
Bosden, William 424
Bostock, James 4464
Bostocke, Charles 4577
Bosvile, Alexander 2472

Charleton, Francis 736; John 4861
Charme, Humphrey 1466
Charnelhouse, Alexander 1906
Charnlee, Thomas 737
Charnock, William 1591
Charrott, John 2112
Chase, Edward 3906; Henry 4562; James 739
Chatfeild, Stephen 893
Chatterton, Lawrence 21
Chatwin, John 3373
Chaundler, John 3605
Chawkling, Henry 4106
Checkley, William 4290
Chedley, William 699
Cheese, Richard 746, 3216, 3384
Cherrett, William 531
Cherry, Samuell 4631
Chessell, Thomas 743
Chetham, William 3347
Chetwin, Thomas 4928
Child, Edward 4154; Thomas 2601; Timothy
    689, 4392
Childe, Ephraim 2081
Chinery, Richard 1611
Chiswell, Richard 752
Cholmley, Phillipp 759
Chowne, Robert 1092
Christmas, Richard 1710
Christopherson, John 2421
Chubb, Joseph 1525
Church, John 3566; William 1438
Churchill, Awnsham 3995; Joseph 2934;
    Joshua 2814; William 3030
Clapp, John 2284
Clare, Francis 4889; Robert 4890
Clark, Elias 132; George 2250; John 787, 806,
    2985, 3889; Samuel 4092; William 647
Clarke, Andrew 991; Benjamine 3357, 4693;
    Daniell 3186; Edward 2507; Francis 4830;
    Henry 4497, 4831; James 1661; John 278,
    799, 878, 1937, 2348, 2502, 3236, 4217;
    Joseph 1655; Jotham 1608; Peter 779;
    Robert 835; Samuell 836, 2010, 2497;
    Simon 3838; Thomas 775, 800, 828, 829,
    4234; William 843, 4364, 4365
Clarkson, John 2755
Clavell, Robert 3939; Roger 855
Clavill, Richard 492
Clayton, William 636
Cleave, Alexander 1907; Edward 69, 1370;
    Isaac 4240; John 4240
Cleavely, Francis 493
Cleaver, Foulke 3705; Henry 865; John 862
Clement, Giles 2980; John 4271; Richard 1303;
    Samuel 1459; Thomas 5045; William 3720
Clerdue, Francis 866; William 1536
Clerk, William 147
Clerke, John 868; Joseph 788; William 871,
    2221

Cleuer, John 4224
Cliffe, Leonard 4833
Clifford, James 4582; John 1551
Clifton, Dominican 3385; Josua 872
Clincar, Robert 3618
Clinton, Ferdinando 347
Cliss, Nathaniell 3418
Clopton, Thomas 1377
Clowes, John 874
Cluer, John 4224
Coates, James 2983; John 72; William 1216
Cobb, John 3678; Oliver 2212
Cobbell, William 2457
Cockarell, Thomas 3374, 4303
Cockatt, Thomas 1426
Cocker, Joseph 1
Cockerill, Thomas 879
Cockett, Thomas 426
Cockrell, Thomas 3374, 4303
Codbid, William 992
Coe, Andrew 886; Thomas 1630
Cogan, Francis 1141
Coggan, Francis 571, 3052
Coke, John 2437
Cokel, Peter 4220
Cole, Edward 2247; Guy 4738; James 628,
    889; Tymothy 1100
Colebancke, John 4751, 4801
Coleman, Thomas 1047
Coles, Amos 2166, 4820; James 1060
Colledge, Edith 4158; Richard 403
Collier, Joseph 3419; Nicholas 1698; Thomas
    3142
Collington, John 1261
Collingwood, Roger 4176
Collins, Arthur 5003; Gabriel 919; Henry 1604;
    James 3940; John 1356, 4132; Lawrence 924;
    Richard 707, 4251; Thomas 16, 319;
    William 453
Collis, John 3890; Robert 3883; William 129
Colls, Thomas 1889
Collyer, John 2389; Tobias 572; William 3818
Collynes, Thomas 4099
Collyns, Freeman 3217
Colson, William 2971
Coltman, William 738, 2709
Combe, William 1603
Combes, Charles 639
Comferford, Nicholas 2098
Comins, John 2353
Compton, John 4210; William 2558
Conduit, Edward 3567
Conniers, George 922; Joshua 1130
Conningesby, Christopher 3526
Constable, Francis 3257; Henry 2490; Richard
    130
Conyers, George 923, 5014; Joshua 940; Marke
    938
Cook, Daniel 3712; Symon 3650

Cooke, John 1126, 2585; Samuell 4261, 4578; Thomas 909, 2025, 2194; William 3102
Cooper, John 965, 2840; Nathan 2354; Richard 1908; William 1909, 4784
Cope, Jonathan 969; Stephen 767, 830; Thomas 2275, 3268; William 2907
Copeland, John 3299
Coplestone, Amos 573, 4775
Coppin, George 4498
Coppleston, Amos 573, 4775
Copson, Samuell 3756
Corant, William 1246
Corbett, Ben 1427; John 2680; Simon 3288; Thomas 654
Corchin, Thomas 2157
Cordell, John 1899
Cordwell, Mathew 1645
Cornish, Gabriell 2337
Corsnett, Francis 2305
Cosgrove, Henry 3014
Cossens, Thomas 2669; Thomas 1868
Cotes, Andrew 984
Cotgrave, Thomas 998, 2190
Cotterell, Thomas 3252
Cotton, Jonathan 3748
Cottrell, Beniamyn 4642; James 3721; Wanderton 2167
Coulston, George 3112; John 2865
Couly, Jane 2438
Coundley, Gilbert 648
Court, Thomas 1066
Courthope, Brian 1014
Cowell, Thomas Smith 1424
Cowley, William 428
Cowper, Richard 5073
Cowse, Benjamin 753; William 3253
Cox, Benjamine 2511; Charles 3312; Gabriell 1572; Henry 3561; John 1024, 3554; Nicholas 574, 3555; Robert 3208, 3808; Roger 3984
Coxall, John 2138
Crabtree, Samuel 4708
Cracherod, Mordant 1926
Crafford, Charles 822, 1872
Crafts, Thomas 4402
Crale, Daniell 3076
Cramphorne, Hezekiah 3791
Crampton, Francis 1160
Crane, Thomas 1966
Cranford, Edward 3661; Joseph 1269, 1776; William 4989
Craven, John 1578, 3792
Crawley, Andrew 1807; Edward 1048
Crayle, Benjamin 848; James 1297
Creak, Robert 1055
Cresbey, William 941
Creswell, Richard 1773
Cripps, Henry 3366; John 3407; William 1057, 4832

Crispe, Mathew 4706; Samuel 989
Crockatt, Thomas 1869
Crockett, Nicholas 5002
Croft, Edward 343
Crofts, Charles 182; Edward 3306; John 2046, 4668; Robert 776, 1305
Croker, Robert 2863
Cromlum, Timothy 4469, 4811
Crooke, Beniamyn 4678; William 1067
Croome, George 1087; John 2710, 3218
Crosbey, Edward 1088
Croskill, Richard 3693; Thomas 2528
Crosland, Cristopher 2251
Crosley, Henry 1089; John 459
Cross, William 2020
Crosse, Phillip 2062
Crouch, Edward 1938; George 1096; John 1097; Nathaniell 727; Samuel 1098, 1104
Crowley, Theodore 110
Croxall, John 2138
Croxen, Thomas 4996
Crumpe, John 2422
Crutch, John 1711
Cruttenden, Henry 2935
Cuffande, John 1927
Cullin, John 3568
Cumberland, Richard 4760
Cunningham, James 2115; Robert 1467
Curteyne, William 3941
Curtis, John 1812, 2936; Langley 2919; William 961, 3671
Cushey, Thomas 3907
Custis, Leonard 4833
Cutler, Peter 4379; Richard 1385; Robert 2279

Dabb, Francis 2450
Dacon, Jonah 5032
Daffie, John 1465, 2012; Richard 5039
Dagnall, Mathias 1137; Stephen 187; William 620
Daintie, Joseph 1142
Dainty, John 1139; Thomas 1143
Dale, Henry 4035; John 1315
Dallow, John 709
Dalloway, John 1693
Dalston, Theodosius 121
Dalton, Gifford 3207; Isaac 2193; Richard 4795; Thomas 3787
Danby, James 1928
Dancaster, John 2741
Dancer, Nathaniell 1119; Samuel 3644
Danchey, Richard 404
Daniell, John 3088; Lyonell 623; Robert 3682; Thomas 748, 2602
Danvers, Henry 3499
Darby, Christopher 3928; Clement 1579; John 1168, 1178, 2102; Samuell 3015
Darker, Samuel 3839
Darley, John 142; Thomas 500

Darnell, John 2491
Darrell, Edward 1184
Dauglas, Jeofferey 2116
Daunsey, Phillip 1144
Davenport, Edward 1169; Ralph 1942
Davie, John 4876
Davies, Joseph 2005; Thomas 2186, 4812
Davill, Joshua 2513
Davis, Benjamin 4579; Edward 1626; Francis 4971; James 780, 1068; John 1502; Lewis 2252; Maurice 2125; Richard 1929; Thomas 3536; William 1191, 2451, 2862
Davison, Bartholomew 1408; John 2843
Davy, William 4893
Davye, Ben 4951
Dawes, George 336
Dawgs, Edward 3324; Thomas 1799
Dawkes, Icabod 1203; Thomas 1204, 1205
Dawlman, Isaiah 1272; Richard 364, 993
Dawson, Charles 3942; George 4148; James 1001; Robert 2390
Day, Robert 3168; Solomon 3824
Deakills, Thomas 629
Deane, Margaret 2439; Richard 4911
Deards, Richard 4669
Deare, Edward 1236
Dearmer, John 4479
Deaver, Thomas 4606
Deellee, John 2090
Deeve, John 4700
Deeves, Jonathan 801; Robert 4516
Delacourt, Anthony 1774
De la Hay, George 4065
Delander, John 3495
Delannoy, George 4065
Delaporte, Nathaniell 1994
Dell, Joseph 4542
Delues, Ralph 1744
Denet, Gerard 3477
Dennis, George 3197; John 568
Dennison, Ambrose 4988; James 3448
Dent, Edward 4159
Denton, Jeremy 1699
Dermer, John 910, 1275
Desborough, Christopher 2519
Desburrough, Thomas 1244
Desermew, Joel 2276
Dew, Richard 1247; William 2038
Dey, Henry 2215
Dicher, Robert 3979
Dickens, Robert 3150
Dickenson, John 1813; Richard 3683
Dickins, William 1260
Dickson, Abraham 4687; Thomas 1480
Dicus, Thomas 3645
Dier, John 637
Diester, Francis 3258
Dighton, John 3922
Dill, Walter 1900

Dingley, Henry 437; Thomas 894
Dixon, Richard 4632
Dobbs, William 4522
Docray, Ephraim 3065
Dod, Edward 1778, 3206; Richard 1943
Dodd, Nathaniell 1967; Robert 1873
Doe, Joseph 4160, 4442
Doewell, William 2168
Doleman, John 217; William 4961
Dolling, Thomas 3546
Dolman, Richard 985
Done, Sachariah 1381
Dormer, John 698; William 4177
Dorrell, Edward 1277
Dorrington, John 1986
Dotchin, William 4882
Doughty, Thomas 2763
Dove, Francis 2011; William 3726
Dover, James 1282; Nathaniel 911, 3095; Symon 895, 1212
Dowce, Thomas 454
Dowell, William 2168
Dowle, George 4709
Dowly, James 1036
Downes, George 4922; Thomas 559
Downham, Thomas 1289
Downing, William 1292, 3016
Dowse, Francis 370
Drafgate, Samuell 357, 4834
Drant, Thomas 1449, 3443
Draper, John 3043
Drewe, Mathias 1302
Dridon, William 3649
Dring, Daniel 1306; Peter 807; Thomas 1307, 3895
Driver, James 227; Samuell 1101
Drury, Anthony 3325; Samuel 950
Dry, Augustin 3996
Duckett, Mathew 2946; Shipwash 3834
Duehurst, Joseph 2576
Duffe, Henry 3005
Dugard, Richard 2888; Thomas 2185; William 1318
Dugdale, Thomas 1610
Duke, Robert 643; William 2623
Duley, John 1025
Duly, Thomas 1324
Dun, Walter 4638
Duncombe, Ellis 2724
Duncon, Charles 1326
Dunkin, Thomas 839
Dunn, Samuell 4643
Dunne, Walter 3071
Dunstan, Thomas 2627
Dunton, John 3420
Durborne, Thomas 2291
Durfy, Francis 440
Durham, John 4454
Durrant, Thomas 1944

Dutton, John 808
Dykes, Edward 4896; John 4990; Richard 4972
Dymensdell, Samuell 2802
Dyos, William 1742

Eales, Thomas 3077
Earnly, William 1409
East, Richard 1224
Eaton, Edward 3527; John 3458; Thomas 1677
Eccleston, Christopher 3896
Eddowes, Samuel 434
Edgar, John 4973
Edlyn, Richard 1357
Edmonds, John 4752; Samuell 1018; Thomas 2103
Edmondson, Mathew, 3635
Edsall, Henry 902
Edwards, David 468; Esra 3017; Henry 3657; James 256, 3570; Latheus 329; Raph 2109; Richard 2407; Robert 3929; Thomas 68, 1779; William 365, 1358, 3930
Edwin, Jonathan 2122; William 270, 2202
Edwyn, Jonathan 536
Egglesfeild, John 1371; Thomas 1209
Eglesfeild, Thomas 1439
Eggleston, Edward 2862
Ekins, Nathaniell 282
Elan, William 2705
Eland, George 42
Elcom, Jonas 2520
Eldred, Nathaniell 4213
Elis, Clement 148
Elliott, Humphry 1488; John 2937; Thomas 4366; William 3908
Ellis, Abraham 1976; Edward 3757; Francis 1380; Joseph 4242; William 1386
Elliston, Oliver 1185
Elmeley, Sarah 4480
Elmes, Robert 3595; Thomas 3496
Elrington, Thomas 2914
Ely, Thomas 1145
Emery, George 1703; Thomas 1396, 4321
Emmerton, Ralph 2069
Enderby, Samuell 1069
Engham, Vincent 1002
England, John 2440; Thomas 2320
English, Joseph 4178; William 3578
Erpe, Richard 3917
Esnead, Charles 1401
Evance, Daniell 976; Robert 3254
Evans, Benjamine 2292; David 2372; Edward 1953; George 2836, 2912; Henry 203, 711; James 3075; John 175, 1417, 2226; Jonathan 2797; Mathew 3684; Morris 2481; Sampson 3733; Thomas 4586; William 1331
Eve, Thomas 3147
Everard, Abraham 4835
Everet, William 2769
Everingham, George 2661; John 763; Robert

1187, 2815; William 1428
Evernden, Simon 1450
Eversden, George 1451; Henry 3401, 4304
Eves, John 4002
Evetts, Edward 4883
Evitt, John 4739
Ewer, Stephen 1170; William 1678
Ewrey, William 1308
Ewstace, Edward 1874
Eyloe, John 1131
Eyre, Anthony 2764
Eyres, William 912
Eyton, Nathaniel 809

Fabian, Thomas 1460
Fage, Edward 4476
Fairclough, Posthumus 3679
Fairfax, William 262
Faithorne, Henry 2901
Falconbarge, John 2662
Fanne, Freeman 4765
Fanshaw, Coppin 3031
Faram, Francis 3809
Farbrew, John 3089
Farley, Jherom 3859; Thomas 443
Farlow, Samuel 913
Farmbrough, Richard 5040
Farmer, Nathaniel 1910
Farneham, Edward 3367, 4395
Farneworth, Joseph 3414
Farnham, Edward 3367, 4395
Farnworth, Benjamin 4651
Farr, Thomas 3230
Farrow, John 2293
Farthing, George 323; Thomas 183
Fassett, Thomas 1642
Fate, John 4344
Fauconberge, John 2662
Faulkener, William 4776
Faulkner, Edward 3309
Fawcett, Richard 1468
Faywell, John 168
Fearbanck, Richard 2521
Feild, Henry 1498; Hester 1503; John 2117, 3436; Simon 2158
Feilder, John 2844
Feilding, Richard 1769, 2674
Fellow, Robert 2379
Felton, Adam 118
Fenn, John 3781; Richard 380
Fenwick, Roger 263
Ferman, Daniel 2113
Fermer, Theophilus 4257
Ferrice, Samuell 662
Ferriman, Bartholomew 3478
Ferris, John 2169
Fetherstone, Cuthbert 1154
Feven, Malcomb 1738
Fifield, Alexander 1510

Haynes, John 2040; Joseph 1200; Richard 3985, 5061
Hayward, John 4487
Hazard, Joseph, 3265
Head, Godfrey 1512; James 1262; Richard 1299, 4471
Hearne, Francis 1359; Thomas 4934
Heath, Samuell 1834
Heathcote, John 1196
Heathcott, William 3019
Heathfield, Jonathan 1115
Heaviside, Richard 219
Hebb, Margrett 4011
Hedges, Gabriel 2973
Heiern, John 555
Heinsworth, George 4179
Heinth, Symon 994, 1877
Heiron, Francis 2049; Robert 3626; Samuel 2242
Heirons, Jeremy 3919
Helder, Charles 4275
Helders, Thomas 3397
Helme, Richard 2057
Helmes, John 2060
Helmstead, Edward 4913
Heming, Robert 4670
Hendrey, Samuell 3636
Henfrey, Richard 143
Henley, John 290
Hensman, William 3945
Heptinstall, John 23; William 2063
Herbert, Abraham 4298; Isaac 3473; Samuel 4816
Herne, Thomas 4741
Herricke, Samuell 4679
Herridge, John 3607
Herringman, Edmund 3884; Henry 3897; John 2076
Herrons, Jeremy 3919
Hervey, John 4084
Hewes, Benjamine 2803
Hewett, Francis 2084; Henry 1237; John 1442; Richard 1865
Hews, John 2569
Hewson, Richard 2089
Heyborne, Robert 2974
Hibbard, Barbara 3593
Hickman, Henry 2987; John 2424; Spencer 33
Hicks, Benjamin 2101; John 3180; Richard 3072
Hickson, William 4150
Hide, Charles 503; Francis 2256
Hiducke, Simon 4767
Hieron, Thomas 4134
Higgins, Christopher 3403; Herbert 4422; Robert 986
Highstreete, Matthew 1686
Hill, Ann 3819; Benjamin 692; John 2868, 3581; Leonard 888, 2328, 2816; Thomas 2759; William 1319, 2105
Hillary, Edward 4753

Hiller, Richard 725, 3826; Samuel 2114
Hilliard, Nathaniell 713
Hillman, Stephen 1192
Hills, Gillam 2126; Henry 2127, 2128; John 2129; Peter 4014
Hillyard, Robert 134
Hinckson, John 2144
Hind, William 4338
Hindly, George 2548
Hindmarsh, Joseph 3408
Hinkley, John 4225
Hinson, William 5074
Hinton, Thomas 3709
Hoare, William 4135
Hobart, William 3812
Hobbs, Charles 2041; Thomas 4419
Hobland, James 339
Hobson, Nathaniell 4620; William 4697
Hodgekinson, Ralph 2171
Hodges, Henry 3972; Joseph 257; Robert 3326; William 1491
Hodgkins, John 4393; Thomas 2172
Hodgkinson, Richard 2173; Thomas 2174, 2672, 3422
Hodgson, Robert 4180; Samuell 4054; Thomas 229, 522
Hoffmann, Charles 4015
Holbrooke, Thomas 2093
Holden, Francis 2702, 3276, 3383; John 4039; Richard 2182
Holding, Thomas 8
Holdrup, James 892
Holford, John 3642; Samuel 2188; William 1421
Holland, James 4856; Richard 891, 2618; William 1015
Hollingworth, Thomas 5075
Hollis, John 1412
Holliwell, George 1526
Holloway, Edmund 1117; Joseph 5018; Richard 174
Holmes, John 338; Oliver 3686
Holmwood, George 3331; Thomas 502
Holt, Michael 2195; Ralph 1940, 1945
Holway, Peter 4482
Home, Giddon 3592
Hooke, John 1133; Nathaniell 271; Richard 3597
Hooker, John 790; Peter 3521
Hookes, Ellis 4563; William 3009
Hooper, Francis 2183; John 733; Nicholas 1830; Thomas 2454
Hope, William 2205
Hopkins, Christopher 4735
Hopper, George 2209, 3290
Hore, John 1930
Horiks, John 3470
Horne, George 2774; Robert 444; Samuel 1458, 1673; Thomas 2021, 2216; William 3266
Hornesby, John 1801

Horsington, Robert 3432
Horsley, John 515; William 4529
Horsman, Thomas 220, 2364
Horton, Edward 1471; George 39; William 2227
Hose, John 904
Hosge, William 1300
Hoskins, Ambros 2130
Hoth, Thomas 2236
Hough, Francis 4362; William 649
Houghton, William 3349
Hougton, Henry 3909
Hoult, Mary 3107
Houlter, John 4877
How, Job 2938; John 840, 1957; Joseph 2663
Howard, Charles 3002; James 869; Jonas 1134
Howell, Gilbert 3503; Nathaniell 896, 2106
Howes, Jeremiah 2243; John 2244; Joseph 2245; Samuell 3369
Howlatt, Thomas 308
Howse, James 4136
Hoyle, Samuell 816
Hubard, Francis 4181, 4862
Hubbard, Francis 4181, 4862
Hubbert, Moses 1472; William 3812
Hucklefoote, Thomas 1352
Huddleston, George 2791
Hudgibutt, John 685
Hudson, John 3783, 4652; Thomas 2725, 3342, 4975
Huffen, Henry 4664
Huggans, John 2804
Huggeford, Henry 1734
Hughes, Edward 4292; Francis 3289; Isaack 4003; James 2210, 4369; Samuell 4621; William 124
Hughs, James 4369; Obediah 2902; Thomas 2750
Hull, William 3440, 3504, 4806
Hume, Allexander 1075
Humfrey, John 1173
Humphrey, Richard 2316
Humphreys, Isaac 191; John 1080
Humphries, William 3665
Humphry, Samuell 1179
Humphryes, Richard 2274
Hunbolt, Gabriel 2277
Hunscott, John 2281
Hunt, Ayres 4588; John 1422, 2085, 2429, 3198, 4172; Joseph 1404; Phillip 2312; Richard 2805, 4608; Samuel 3108; Thomas 3122, 5042; William 693, 2344, 2349, 4173
Hunter, Humphrey 3662
Huntley, William 3697
Hurlock, Beniamine 2306
Hurst, Henry 1952; James 4671; John 2350
Hurt, Christopher 1855, 2881; Thomas 1856; William 3619
Huse, Jacob 755
Hussey, Christopher 665

Hutchens, Thomas 726
Hutchins, Thomas 1504
Hutchinson, James 4904; Simon 4191; William 4182
Huttchinson, Leonard 608
Huttoph, Peregrine 1707
Hyatt, Richard 2189
Hyett, Henry 3932
Hyllary, John 1828

Ibitson, Robert 995; William 1946
Iles, William 3189
Iley, Thomas 2107, 2271
Ilive, Thomas 3020, 4226
Illidge, Samuell 4299
Ingersole, Richard 684
Inglish, William 3989
Inman, Mathias 1320, 5069
Innocent, Richard 2164
Ireland, William 1704
Irvine, Gerrard 2110
Isaac, Thomas 3962
Isburne, Thomas 2343
Islip, Adam 1003
Isted, Ambros 4564; John 3898
Ivatt, Faithfull 486
Ive, Roger 445, 624, 3520
Izard, Anthony 2360, 3143
Izode, Wenman 1920

Jackman, Francis 2817; John 1084; Nathaniell 2302
Jackson, Benjamin 2361; Christopher 3277; Henry 2055; Humphry 2965; John 112; Joseph 1382, 1878; Thomas 1076, 4724; William 3004
Jacob, John 2369; William 3556, 4227
Jaggard, Thomas 5076
James, Andrew 95; Charles 1167; George 3132; John 2375; Peter 4782; Robert 3187; Thomas 61, 744, 2711; William 1633, 2286
Jamett, Thomas 1016
Janaway, Jonathan 3620
Janes, Thomas 3728
Janeway, Isaac 1919
Jannaway, Richard 2391
Jans, William 3608
Jaye, Eliphall 2896
Jeffery, Mathew 4437
Jelley, Edward 1266; William 1573
Jellis, John 446
Jemsone, William 2530
Jenkes, John 3959
Jenkins, Thomas 4657
Jenkinson, Robert 2629, 3574
Jennaway, Richard 360
Jenner, Nathaniell 791
Jennings, Thomas 4556
Jennison, Robte 3364, 5019

[201]

Lawrence, Henry 1771; James 859; John 3423, 3873
Lawson, Anthony 2594, 3772
Lawton, James 4936
Lazenby, John 813
Lea, Charles 2559; John 11
Leaborne, John 2712
Leach, Francis 2611; Thomas 2603; William 2604
Leacock, Thomas 4952
Leadbetter, Jeremiah 1188
Leake, Charles 2636; John 2637; Mathew 1148; Richard 943; William 2638
Ledsam, Gualter 3805
Lee, Charles 2874; Christopher 2842; George 2655; Henry 340, 438, 1287; Humphrey 50; John 683, 2664; Joseph 2651; Ralph 1006; Richard 2654; Stephen 1218, 2657; Thomas 2656, 2665, 4985; William 2666
Leech, Francis 2605; William 556
Leeds, Richard 4768
Leek, John 2818
Lees, David 1821
Leete, John 221, 1310; Thomas 2676
Legatt, Thomas 4508
Le Gay, Benjamin 457
Legg, John 151
Leicester, John 3338, 4976; William 3339, 4977
Leigh, Francis 4438; John 3474, 4589; Thomas 1931
Leighbourne, John 2712
Lello, Thomas 3741
Leming, Thomas 2002
Lennier, Lyonell 2811
Lenthall, John 4743
Leonard, John 5030; Richard 4124
Lett, Ralph 1006
Letts, John 469
Levett, John 1731
Leving, Thomas 3963
Lewcy, Richard 2693
Lewis, Abraham 3247; Edmond 851; Edward 12, 3133, 4259; Humfrey 4649, 4850; John 96, 2696, 2698; Richard 1515, 2154, 2699, 5043; Stephen 2695; Thomas 928, 2703, 4333; William 3789
Ley, Thomas 388
Leyborne, William 2707
Lidgold, Nicholas 146
Lightfoot, William 1267
Lilley, Richard 2692; Samuell 73; Steven 2727; Thomas 1085
Lillicrop, Peter 1564
Lillingston, William 5072
Lilly, Joseph 2726
Limpany, Edward 2737; John 2743; Robert 2735
Linagar, Thomas 1972, 2574
Linbye, Robert 3437

Lincolne, Stephen 1270
Lindsey, William 1978
Linegar, Thomas 1972, 2574
Lingard, Christopher 1740; Thomas 2751
Lintott, Barnaby Bernard 1912, 2756
Lipscomb, John 1190, 1443
Lister, Thomas 3115
Litchfeild, St John 4565
Litgould, Samuell 2760
Litle, John 4390
Litleboy, Robert 1732
Littleboy, Thomas 1732; William 3256
Littlebury, George 3032
Littleton, John 2494
Lloyd, George 4227a, 4326; Henry 470; Humphry 1259; Owen 3506; Samuell 4349
Lochard, John 3738
Lock, Martha 1692
Locke, John 2776; Thomas 100
Locker, John 1601
London, Robert 3109
Long, Christofer 2078; Henry 4580; John 2819; Josias 471; Marcus 1814; William 24
Longland, Thomas 3885
Longmore, William 3946
Lord, Henry 2869
Lorkin, Humphrey 587
Love, John 987, 4253, 4800; Luke 1397
Loveday, Aaron 734; William 2780
Lovekin, John 1482
Lovell, Francis 700; Henry 1802, 2781
Lowden, Robert 1456
Lowdon, John 575
Lowe, John 2099; Richard 348; Robert 2716
Lowen, John 2782; William 1028
Lownds, Robert 2688
Lownes, John 2785; Samuell 9
Lowry, Brampton 2029
Loyd, John 3003; Samuel 4349
Lucas, John 1487; William 2584, 4858
Lucking, James 4352
Ludford, Eustace 2792
Lutly, George 3538
Lutton, John 3237
Luxford, Thomas 413
Lydiate, John 3222
Lympany, Edward 2738
Lynnell, John 2757

Mabb, Thomas 2175
Mabbatt, Samuell 4525
Machen, Benjamine 714
Mackmath, John 2947
Macock, Thomas 2820
Madden, George 4009
Maddison, Charles 304; Henry 205; James 2832
Maddocks, Thomas 5001
Maddox, Edward 2864; Thomas 3794, 4341, 4797

Millert, Roger 3362
Millet, Caleb 1871; John 3655
Millett, John 447
Millner, Jeremiah 2834
Mills, Benjamin 2094; Bryan 88; Francis 576; Richard 4164; Thomas 1290, 1816
Millsopp, Richard 4920
Millward, William 4424
Millyn, Henry 673
Milner, Thomas 3073
Milnes, Thomas 1106
Milward, William 392
Mind, Benjamin 565, 582
Minors, Thomas 4874
Minshall, John 408; Randall 3116; Thomas 3078
Minshew, John 4998
Minton, Thomas 3589
Mitchell, Edward 5007; John 371; Robert 1848; Thomas 3259
Mody, Seth 2196
Mogge, Daniell 3046
Moggs, Daniel 3086
Mohun, Christopher 349
Moirriell, John 448, 1353
Mole, Jervas 1374
Mompesson, Edward 3550
Monckton, Phillip 3000
Money, John 1180; Richard 2613
Monger, Benjamin 3891; Richard 3087
Monins, William 3485
Monke, George 2639; John 451
Montford, Richard 3171
Moodey, John 2752; Nathaniel 4216
Moone, Richard 674
Moore, Edward 1038; George 2920; John 1029, 3090, 3632; Joseph 728, 2459; Marmaduke 3900; Richard 644, 4590; Robert 3094; Thomas 4490, 4698
Morace, Henry 2753
More, Edward 1584; John 1656, 2856; Mercy 1351; Robert 137; Samuell 3375; Thomas 1541
Moreclock, Henry 516, 2246
Moreton, Peter 455
Morey, Edward 764
Morfey, John 3307
Morgan, Edward 3100; John 1861, 4396
Morkitt, Richard 2206
Morphew, John 2455
Morrell, Gunther 1883; Thomas 1473
Morrice, James 557; Mathew 769; Thomas 3564, 3565; William 1165, 1322, 1484
Morris, Mathew 131, 2345
Mors, Thomas 4566
Mortimer, George 3828
Mose, William 2704
Mosse, Thomas 2824; William 3714
Motherby, Richard 633

Mott, Benjamin 988
Mould, Beniamin 3161
Moule, Gregory 675, 2282
Moulson, William 793
Moulton, William 765, 4289
Mount, Richard 1527, 3166; William 3167
Mountague, Henry 2729
Mountford, William 125
Mountfort, John 1419
Mountgomery, Hugh 272
Mowbray, George 1721
Moyce, Thomas 1181
Moyle, Edward 4777
Mudd, Strangeways 331
Muggs, Stephen 2921
Mullins, Thomas 2377
Munford, William 4688
Murden, John 3162
Murfin, William 1996
Muston, John 4653
Myn, Francis 3182
Mynd, Benjamin 565, 582

Nappier, Edward 3183
Nash, Samuel 3835
Nealand, William 3190
Neale, John 1121; Robert 1413; Simon 4038
Nealer, Roger 1414
Needham, Ann 3199; Benjamine 384, 2689; Ralph 4308
Neile, William 3201
Nelme, Henry 3409
Nelson, Austen 1793; Mathew 1947; Norman 3562
Nevill, John 3204; Joseph 1360, 5020
Newall, John 1619
Newam, Samuell 3519
Newbery, Thomas 283
Newbolt, William 4467
Newborough, Thomas 4783
Newby, John 2299
Newcomb, Edward 3223; Richard 85, 3233; Thomas 996, 1258, 3224
Newcombe, Richard 1567, 3134; Thomas 4944; William 2332
Newell, John 3235
Newington, John 1030
Newlin, Thomas 2595
Newman, Darmond 3424; Dorman 3843; Edward 4142; Hugh 3239; Samuell 4439; Thomas 3240; William 3627
Newton, Ambrose 4745; John 716, 4524; Robert 2606; William 3249
Nicholls, Francis 4184; Henry 1866
Nicholson, Andrew 3980; John 1575; Richard 2994; Thomas 4280
Nicks, John 3225, 3663
Nightingall, John 4680
Nobbs, Christopher 4274

Peachell, Edward 2667
Peacock, Daniel 3479; Richard 1202; Robert 3480
Peacocke, Daniell 4792
Peake, Dorothi 5037
Peale, Moreton 762, 1700
Pearse, Francis 1897
Pearson, Jonothan 57
Pease, Henry 1405
Peasely, John 2800
Peast, Edmond 930
Peble, Mathew 954
Peck, Symon 449; William 421
Peckett, Thomas 1507
Pedmore, Robert 3105
Peerse, John 10
Peete, William 2470
Peibody, Samuell 3475
Peirce, Isaack 3483; Thomas 2708; William 3484
Peircehay, John 3488
Peirson, John 3761; William 2067
Pelley, Edward 300
Pemberton, John 3886
Pen, Joseph 1674
Pendred, James 2646, 3517
Penfold, John 3099
Penford, Thomas 249
Penn, John 3466, 3611; Robert 3509, 3913
Penne, Humphrey 3333; John 741, 2535
Pennington, Andrew 702; John 1008, 3270, 4300
Penniston, Richard 3599
Penrey, James 1195, 3628
Pentor, Henry 3125
Pepper, Robert 4114
Pepys, Edward 3117, 3948
Peregrine, Charles 1708, 3135
Perkins, Francis 3715; Henry 1334, 3033; William 3491
Pero, John 2314
Perpoint, Thomas 4309
Perris, Henry 1343
Peryn, Matthew 3902
Perry, Robert 2510
Petch, Mathew 4997
Petcher, Samuel 3497
Petersverhesselt, John 2883
Petit, John 2030
Petre, Francis 350
Pett, Samuell 2404
Pettit, John 1335
Petty, John 2382
Phelpes, Richard 3152
Phillipps, John 4078; Richard 4730
Phillips, John 327, 2966; Joseph 4966; Joshua 1373, 2304; Joy 1219; Noell 313; Wilfriend 5021; William 2690
Phillpott, John 1849
Philpott, James 2329

Pickard, John 3710
Pickering, John 2394
Piddock, Joseph 2022
Pidgeon, Stephen 577
Pierce, Timothy 3910
Piercy, Thomas 4185
Pigg, John 4218
Pigram, Stephen 4945
Pike, John 4868; Joseph 2417; Peter 3795
Pilkington, Steven 3011
Pinder, Richard 655
Pine, John 2982
Pinfold, James 2370
Pinker, William 1766
Pinney, William 2273
Pinnock, Edward 1973
Piper, John 2845
Pistell, Richard 4048
Pittard, Charles 431, 856
Pitts, Thomas 2035
Place, John 3399, 3557; William 442, 3558
Plant, Richard 1879
Platt, Edward 5053
Playfere, John 2079
Playford, Henry 3572; John 320, 1714
Plowrett, George 4957
Plowright, John 2616
Plumer, Michael 4719
Plumpton, John 955
Plumton, Richard 4736
Plyer, John 770
Podmore, Robert 3105; Samuel 3576
Pointing, Henry 3096
Pokins, Richard 3949; Thomas 2941; William 2222
Pole, Richard 4891
Pollard, Samuell 722
Pomfrett, Thomas 1628
Ponder, Nathaniell 1696; Robert 473
Pool, Joseph 2989, 3413
Poole, Andrew 3629; Anthony 1344; Edmund 2095; Edward 2149; Gregory 863; Joseph 2989, 3413; Solomon 1585; Thomas 3387
Poor, Zachariah 4079
Pope, Richard 1569; Samuell 2549; William 1523, 2640
Porter, John 3603; Thomas 4879
Powell, Adam 1094; Edmund 2826, 3136; Edward 3612, 4958; George 1363, 1981, 2052; John 305, 3623; Nathaniel 3624; Phillip 4301, 4684; Robert 2068, 3613; Walter 4372; William 3293
Powle, William 3634, 4530
Poynton, William 1240
Pratt, John 1031, 1161, 2942, 3768; Mathias 2408
Preast, Joseph 166
Preice, John 4938
Preston, Othniell 1519; Richard 2365

Serjeant, Nathaniell 3936
Sewster, George 1751
Shackston, John 3435
Shadd, John 750
Sharpe, John 1531, 4230
Shaw, John 153, 1609; Ralph 2812; Thomas 394
Shawler, Richard 4567
Shawley, Michael 3915
Shawller, Edward 4555
Sheares, John 14; William 4041
Sheers, John 4426
Sheffeild, Sherard 3352; William 2953
Sheilds, William 2310
Shelden, Robert 66
Sheldenslow, Dorothy 4045
Shell, George 1253
Shelley, Edward 4967
Shellmerdine, Thomas 2315
Shelmerdine, John 1446
Shelton, Christopher 4088
Shephard, John 2557; Robert 719
Sheppard, Abraham 2388; Edward 4056;
    Thomas 3328, 4345
Sherborne, Samuell 47
Sherman, Thomas 4060
Sherrington, William 1885
Sherring, Henry 1902
Sherwood, George 4, 1516; John 210; Mathias
    652
Shipthorpe, John 4892
Shirley, Benjamin 4068; Phillip 1617
Shittlewood, John 2652
Short, Edward 2414
Shorter, Solomon 2331
Shortgrave, Charles 3551; Theodore 4073
Shorthazell, John 2288
Shotwell, Joseph 58
Shrewsberry, William 2488
Shrewsbury, Thomas 4074
Shrimpton, John 1992, 4798
Shury, William 3489
Shuter, John 1723, 3060; Richard 561
Shybrough, Edward 1010
Sibley, Edward 211
Sillott, Robert 3701
Silver, Daniell 656
Silverton, Ralph 1206
Silvester, Jesse 1758; Joshua 80; Samuel 4231
Simkin, John 4880
Simmons, Nevill 1804
Simonds, Joseph 1477; Nevill 1804, 3849
Simons, Richard 4536; Samuel 4089
Simpson, Benjamin 4117; Richard 2074;
    Thomas 4118; William 945
Singleton, James 2120; John 1867; Thomas 2685
Sisson, Thomas 294
Skegnes, Christopher Charles 4946
Skelton, Henry 4138; James 2108
Skinner, Charles 1023; Luke 1733

Slade, Joseph 1850
Slape, John 86, 2141
Slaple, John 86, 2141
Slater, Daniell 1747; Robert 2357
Slatter, James 3138
Sledd, Joseph 3210; William 372
Sly, George 414; John 490
Slystead, Charles 4941
Smales, John 963
Smalshaw, James 4859
Smart, Israell 1447; Richard 3656; Timothy
    398, 3544
Smelt, Mathew 2775
Smith, Abraham 4153; Charles 1934, 3560;
    Francis 2037, 4168; George 3702, 4169;
    Henry 1378, 3923; Jo 2839, 3316; John 1182,
    2263, 2409, 2456, 3689, 3785, 4119, 4871;
    Layton 222; Leonard 2561; Martin 3670,
    3735; Nicholas 979, 3716; Obadiah 4474;
    Ralph 3428, 3621, 4157, 4198; Richard 1918,
    3382, 3752; Robert 439, 3790, 4047, 4066,
    4174, 4206; Roger 4968; Samuell 390, 1672;
    Thomas 154, 258, 1111, 1432, 2192, 3507,
    4215; Willliam 87, 695, 1176, 2031
Smythes, William 3025
Snart, Richard 704
Snignell, Samuell 4126
Snodham, Thomas 2323
Snodon, George 1383
Snow, Ralph 2731, 2884; Richard 3717, 4781
Snowden, Thomas 4232
Snowe, Charles 4221
Solers, Robert 4302
Solman, John 3442
Southby, John 4238; Richard 223; Susanna 4239
Southen, John 1586
Southwood, Beniamin 860, 4591
Sowerby, Leonard 3518
Sowle, Andrew 374; Francis 2014, 4245;
    John 4246; Tace 4264
Sowton, John 1337
Spark, John 3874
Sparke, Hugh 1316; Robert 3126; William 1254
Sparkes, Jeremiah 250; Michaell 4255
Sparree, John 4991
Sparrey, Thomas 3226
Sparrow, Richard 4413
Speake, Henry 2340
Speed, Samuell 373; Thomas 3243
Spence, Edward 625
Spencer, Abraham 1528; Jonathan 4545;
    Joseph 1379; Robert 4044, 4139; Thomas
    1602, 2228
Spervill, Issac 5054
Spicer, Charles 4275; John 1255, 3091; Nicholas
    1570; Thomas 3397
Spire, William 1207
Sporier, John 4276
Spragg, Carew 1227

Wattlework, Humphrey 101
Wattleworth, Mathew 548
Watts, Anthony 1494; Hugh 5038; John 1435, 4538; Joseph 3056; William 1051, 1892
Way, Edward 321
Waythen, Edward 4843
Weale, Richard 1544
Weaver, John 3227, 3905
Webb, Barnaby 4250; Charles 3127; Edward 4980; Elizabeth 4762; John 407; Josuah 81; Nathaniell 2998; Theodore 1571; Thomas 225, 1529
Webster, Benjamin 1256; Richard 1843; Thomas 2830; William 1040
Weeckes, Richard 3641
Weedon, Luke 782
Weekeley, William 3921
Weekes, Thomas 3857
Weekly, John 1975
Welchman, Samuel 1162
Weld, John 1285
Wells, Beniamyn 1784; Daniell 3952; Francis 4486; George 4787; John 3703, 3747; Robert 3464; Steven 1050; William 1785, 2500, 4788, 5062
Welton, Thomas 3833
Weme, Sebastian 1730
Wenburne, William 1462
West, Charles 1660; John 1388; Richard 3451; Thomas 4959
Westbrooke, Richard 2000, 4288
Westley, John 3380; Timothy 2083
Weston, William 3704
Westrey, Thomas 1819
Wettenhall, Lewis 3027
Whaley, Peter 4036; Thomas 4694
Whalley, Samuell 4802
Wharton, Humphrey 3051; Thomas 3638
Whateley, John 1221, 2915
Wheatley, John 4872
Wheatly, Nathaniel 5024
Wheeler, John 3120, 3278
Whetton, Joseph 2809
Whighthurst, Francis 4853
Whip, Robert 827
Whiskin, Robert 3803
Whitaker, Thomas 3283, 4809
White, Bernard 4844; Charles 3188; Daniell 679; Henry 479; Humphrey 758; John 277, 395, 578; Matthew 226; Samuell 1059, 1653, 1681; Thomas 1862; William 1499, 4845
Whitehall, Gilbert 4189
Whitehand, Thomas 3988
Whitehead, Joseph 3853; Nathaniell 1222; William 3816
Whitfeild, Thomas 2762
Whithart, Richard 5047
Whiting, Benjamin 2367
Whitledge, Robert 3879

Whitley, James 2810
Whitlidge, Daniel 4857; Robert 1590; Thomas 2143, 2387
Whitlock, John 4440
Whittaker, Henry 3622
Whittington, George 450
Whittle, Michael 2831
Whittlesea, Thomas 2717
Whitwood, William 1706, 4846
Wickens, John 4294
Wickers, Tobias 1102
Wicks, Thomas 3444, 4712
Widmer, Samuell 947, 5025
Widmore, Samuell 947, 5025
Wiggins, Silvanus 5026; Thomas 2918
Wigmore, George 482; Thomas 1013
Wilcocks, Benjamin 797; John 4755
Wilcox, Thomas 3548
Wild, Ann 4888; Anthony 5031; Edward 1153; John 2044; Seth 2886; Thomas 1448, 1454; William 4898
Wilde, Benjamine 4899; James 4894; John 4900; Joseph 1079
Wildgoose, John 4901
Wilfeild, John 981
Wilford, George 1017, 3093; John 4915; Joseph 4916; Richard 3350; Roger 2211
Wilkes, Richard 3295; Thomas 3681; Walter 546, 4865
Wilkins, Jeremiah 2198; Jonothan 3244; Richard 4501; William 109, 1041
Wilkinson, Christopher 4034, 4926; Joseph 948; William 1665
Willamott, Thomas 3817
Willescott, Edward 3542
Williams, Clement 593, 2945; Edward 1836; John 188, 680, 1767, 2428, 2649, 4943, 4947; Rice 4950; Richard 4953; Thomas 494, 2483, 4954; William 3228
Williamson, Anthony 4810; John 1235, 4602; Richard 3965; Robert 180, 3669
Willington, Richard 423
Willis, Christopher 4964, 4965; Edward 3476; John 520; William 2979, 3081
Willmiet, Thomas 3817
Willmott, John 1135; Richard 2229
Willoughby, Robert 265, 2018
Willowes, James 3360
Wills, Edward 4080
Wilmot, William 3001
Wilson, Bryan 681, 3692; Edward 2262; Isack 4264; James 315; John 1313, 4270; Robert 2754; Thomas 4233
Wiltsheire, James 3617, 4540
Wiltshire, James 3617, 4540; William 3156
Winch, Adam 2991
Winchcomb, Benedict 1576
Winchester, Daniell 4864
Wind, John 1837

INDEX OF PLACE NAMES

This Index of Place-names has been put in one alphabetical sequence, unlike the volume for 1605–1640 which adopted a county arrangement. Entries have been made both for the forms written in the Register, and for the modern versions as far as possible; changes of county boundaries since the seventeenth century have been ignored, and places are credited to the counties to which they belonged at the date of binding.

The editor and the Society are grateful to Mrs. R. H. Morgan for compiling this Index, and to Professor Melville Richards, Dr. B. G. Charles, Mr. R. J. Thomas and Mr. Gwyn Walters for identifying the Welsh place-names.